"This is an extraordinary volume and one that thoroughly illuminates the process of writing and the condition of the writer. It is a necessity for anyone who would make the writer's art his study. It is also wonderful reading." —ROBERT STONE

Excerpts from *Our Private Lives*

"The *New York Times* did not include *Mr. Bedford* in its most notable books...I thought: well,...I will exist in spite of them. I may even outlive the *New York Times*." —GAIL GODWIN (*1983*)

"[Philip] Roth a man who wears his heart on his sleeve, thus rather vulnerable to injury; part of his exceptional generosity. Tells story of man bleeding in front of God but trying to hide blood from His sight apologetically." —EDWARD HOAGLAND

"Parties are killing. The thing I hate most in women is their picking curiosity, dying to know who one's lover is and even more dying to dump on one highlights of their sexual romps." —EDNA O'BRIEN

"Jesus, I'd rather be a genius than a saint (but in my mind the sentence keeps coming out reversed—I'd rather be a saint than a genius). The psychopath, I'm afraid reluctantly, I must relinquish—at least temporarily." —NORMAN MAILER (*1955*)

"...What is the fear of the journal but a quite reasonable fear of the future self glancing back; this 'future' self very possibly ill, unhappy, bereft, frightened, lonely. So that my happiness Now is cast in an ironic light Then. So that, addressing a future self, I feel moved to pity." —JOYCE CAROL OATES (*1987*)

OUR PRIVATE LIVES

Journals, Notebooks and Diaries

OUR PRIVATE LIVES

Journals, Notebooks and Diaries

EDITED BY DANIEL HALPERN

VINTAGE BOOKS · A DIVISION OF RANDOM HOUSE, INC. · NEW YORK

First Vintage Books Edition, January 1990

Copyright © 1988 by Antaeus, New York, N.Y.
Preface copyright © 1989 by Daniel Halpern

All rights reserved under International and Pan-American Copyright
Conventions. Published in the United States by Vintage Books, a divi-
sion of Random House, Inc., New York. Originally published as
Journals, Notebooks, and Diaries by The Ecco Press, New York, in 1988.
Published by arrangement with The Ecco Press.

Library of Congress Cataloging-in-Publication Data
Our private lives : journals, notebooks, and diaries / edited by Daniel
  Halpern.—1st Vintage Books ed.
      p. cm.
    ISBN 0-679-72532-6 : $10.95
    1. Authors—Diaries. 2. Prose literature—20th century.
  I. Halpern, Daniel, 1945–
  PN453.O97   1990
  808.88'3'0904—dc20   89-40065
                                                          CIP

Manufactured in the United States of America
10 9 8 7 6 5 4 3 2 1

CONTENTS

◆ ──────────────── ◆

PREFACE

◆ ————————————————————————————— ◆

What follows these short prefatory remarks is a group of thirty-nine surprisingly individual and illuminating journal excerpts. Upon embarking on this project, my primary concern was that these excerpts would
sound monotonously alike in a "Dear Diary" sort of way. Because the
contributors are all accomplished writers of prose and/or poetry—
although not all "creative" writers—this turned out to be an unnecessary worry. Many of the contributions were copied from
notebooks—typed and tidied up some; others were written specially for
this assignment—by writers who had not, or not consistently, been keepers of journals. My letter of request made it clear that it was unimportant
whether or not the writer had in fact kept a journal—both existing journals and journals written on assignment would be welcome. What was
not discussed in my letter or at any later time, nor addressed by any one
of the contributors, was to what extent those sometimes crude, everyday
notations were rethought, revised, polished, and shaped beyond simple
tidying—we will never know which of these come to us as they were written, in the heat of the daily moment; which appeared here after some
sprucing up; and which were written *as if* they had been part of a pre-
existing journal.

Many of the writers, upon receiving my query, responded with
heightened spirit at the prospect of turning this form of privacy into
something public; at the same time, a number of contributors asked with
no small degree of nervousness if I had been looking over their shoulder
and had somehow caught them in the secret act of journal keeping. As it
turned out, the notion of secrecy—but perhaps "privacy" would better
serve here—was not left behind at the writer's desk, but instead became a
part of assembling and editing this collection of notebooks, journals, and
diaries. As the texts arrived, having left their previously solitary exis-
tences for the general viewing, I was asked with peculiar consistency
whether or not an entry was too personal, whether it was too self-
involved or too revealing, perhaps even sophomoric, and so on.
Although some editorial cutting took place in consideration of space and
proportion, nothing was taken out because of its "personal" nature.

On bad days and good days alike, writers of journals ask themselves
questions about *this life* in *and* out of their occupations, be they artists,
doctors, anthropologists, oilmen, or politicians. In these pages you will

be party and witness to some of those private dialogues and negotiations. The subjects are as various as the voices that emerge from the writing: working as an oilman on the Gulf, a firefighter in the Grand Canyon, or an anthropologist on an Apache reservation—"Anthropological fieldwork rests on the premise that it is perfectly acceptable for strangers to intrude uninvited on the thoughts and activities of other people" (Keith Basso). For the writers of poetry and fiction represented here, these journals illustrate in what ways there is life after art. As a genre, the journal provides an arena in which to address aspects of the *created* fictional world, and welcomed simultaneously is the *lived* world: the *exterior* of daily event and occasion, and the *interior* of thought, rumination, and response—"Perhaps it is easier to write a novel than survive it" (Jim Harrison).

Depicted in the journals are a weekend with the Rainiers in Monaco, a trip to the Cambodian border, a boat trip on the Congo River—"Monkey looks, when smoked, like smoked fish, which can also look like smoked snake" (V. S. Naipaul)—and riding with truckers in the American South—"Had *I* ever been in a gun fight? he enquired. No. Well, he'd been in more than he could remember, both as a policeman and a trucker. I'd find his 'trucker's friend' right under the seat, if I cared to look" (Oliver Sacks). Norman Mailer gives us a quick portrait of another writer—"Hemingway's peculiar weakness is that he's a Taker, his heroes are all Takers. His idea of courage is that you can take it. It never seems to have occured to him once that courage might also consist of giving."

Journals provide a format and the opportunity to observe for and to oneself, to organize and document the footage as it reels out before us. For keepers of journals, a significant aspect of the experience is to *re-experience* through this private re-telling, both at the time of the writing and at some later time, when the evidence is returned to, whether in tranquility or otherwise. To observe and note with care the unrolling of one's life is also to provide insurance against the gradual and possibly inevitable collapse of our human memory. As Kafka noted with keen accuracy on November 7, 1921, "This inescapable duty to observe oneself: if someone else is observing me, naturally I have to observe myself too; if none observes me, I have to observe myself all the closer."

—DANIEL HALPERN
Princeton, 1989

OUR PRIVATE LIVES

Journals, Notebooks and Diaries

GAIL GODWIN

◆ ——————————————————————————— ◆

A Diarist on Diarists

*This inescapable duty to observe oneself: if someone else
is observing me, naturally I have to observe myself too;
if none observes me, I have to observe myself all the
closer.*

—KAFKA, *November 7, 1921*

*I fall back on this journal just as some other poor devil
takes to drink.*

—BARBELLION

I am enamoured of my journal.

—SIR WALTER SCOTT

Diarists: that shrewdly innocent breed, those secret exhibitionists and
incomparable purveyors of sequential, self-conscious life: how they fasci-
nate me and endear themselves to me by what they say and do not say.
If my friends kept diaries, and if I read them, would I know them as well
as I know Kafka, standing in front of his mirror, playing with his hair?
And Virginia Woolf, languishing because of a snide remark made about
her novels by an undergraduate. And poor Dorothy Wordsworth, trying
valiantly to stick to descriptions of sunsets while losing all her teeth. And
Pepys, giving a colorful account of his latest fight with his wife. And
Camus, coolly observing, "Whatever does not kill me strengthens me."
Or plantation owner William Byrd, "dancing his dances" and "rogering
his wife" (code words for bowel movements and sexual intercourse). Or
the anonymous Irish scribe driven to confide into the margin of a medieval text: "I am very cold without fire or covering . . . the robin is singing
gloriously, but though its red breast is beautiful I am all alone. Oh God
be gracious to my soul and grant me a better handwriting."

/ 9

In the old days everybody kept diaries. That's how we know that "Carlyle wandered down to tea looking dusky and aggrieved at having to live in such a generation": from Caroline Fox's diary; and that Henry James "kept up a perpetual vocal search for words even when he wasn't saying anything": from his nineteen-year-old nephew's diary; and that when Liszt played, he compressed his lips, dilated his nostrils and, when the music expressed quiet rapture, "a sweet smile flitted over his features": from George Eliot's diary. People came home from their dinners and visits and wrote down what others said and how the great men looked and who wore what and who made an ass or a pig of himself ("A little swinish at dinner," the diligent Dr. Rutty wrote of himself in his eighteenth-century diary). Those who stayed home alone also documented their evenings. ("I dined by myself and read an execrably stupid novel called 'Tylney Hall.' Why do I read such stuff?" wrote Macaulay.) Even a literate body snatcher gave an account of himself before he turned in at night: "March 16, 1812, Went to Harps got 3 Large and 1 Large Small, 1 Small & 1 Foetus, took 2 Large to St. Thomas's, 1 Large to Guy's."

Are there fewer diarists now? It seems so, to me, but perhaps I'm unusual in that I have not one friend who keeps a diary—or at least who admits to it. Sometimes I'll happen upon a diarist and we greet each other like lonely explorers. Last spring I discovered a fellow diarist over lunch, and what a time we had discussing the intricacies of our venture-in-common, our avocation . . . specialty . . . compulsion? We confessed eccentricities (he has a pseudonymn for the self that gambles; I often reread old journals and make notes to my former selves in the margin). We examined our motives: why keep these records, year after year? What would happen if we stopped? *Could* we stop? We indulged in shoptalk: hardbound or softcover? lined or unlined? about how many pages a night? proportion of external events to internal? Did one write more on bad days than on good? More or less on quiet days? (More, we both decided.) Did we feel honor-bound to report in at night, even when exhausted—or intoxicated? Ah, it was a good lunch we had.

"I should live no more than I can record, as one should not have more corn growing than one can get at. There is a waste of good if it be not preserved." This, from Boswell, expresses the aspect of duty that many diarists typically feel. Queen Victoria continued her diary strictly as a duty from the age of thirteen to eighty-two. Unfortunately, much of it reads like it. Many diaries, left by long-forgotten owners in attic trunks, describe neither affairs of state nor the table talk of great geniuses nor the growing pains of profound souls. But a sense of *accountability* emanates from these old books. ("Went with Maud to Chok's for a soda. J.L. lost two heifers from shipping disease . . . nothing of interest to record today.") Man and woman was beholden to the *recording* of God's hours, be they interesting or not.

> No mighty deeds, just common things,
> The tasks and pleasures each day brings.
> And yet I hope that when I look
> Over the pages of this book,
> Twill be (and, if so, I'm content)
> The record of five years well spent.

This, from the title page of my mother's college diary, offers captured memory as incentive to daily diligence. *Nulla dies sine linea*, it orders, and my mother obeyed, detailing in tiny handwriting, in a variety of inks, the social and mental highlights of 1932–36. People seemed to go to the movies every day, sometimes twice in one day. They ate a lot of spaghetti—but, of course, there was a Depression. No longer a diarist, my mother offered the little blue and gold book to me (we had to pick the lock—she had no idea it was even hers until we opened it). Her parents had given her the five-year diary as a going-away present for college, and she felt she owed it to them to write in it. I'm glad she did. How many daughters can read—in purple ink—about the night they were conceived?

Now I'm the only practicing diarist in my family. Not one of my friends keeps a diary, as I've mentioned. "To tell the truth, I've never thought I was that interesting," says one. "I'm not a *writer*," says another. A third writes letters, sometimes three or four every evening, and says this serves the purpose of a diary. Another person who is a very prolific writer has advised me to "put all that material into stories rather than hide it in your journals. When you feel haunted or sad, write a story about a person, not necessarily yourself, who feels haunted or sad. Because, you see, it's the feelings that are universal, not the person."

Art, fiction, if it is to be public, must tap the universal. A diary by its very nature is the unfolding of the private, personal story—whether that story be told from a distance (the "I" in a political diary, observing affairs of state; the "I" in the captain's log, marking latitude, longitude, and the moods of the sea) or with the subjectivity of a person whose politics and moods and sea-changes exist inside his own head. I need to write a diary, just as I need to write fiction, but the two needs come from very different sources. I write fiction because I need to organize the clutter of too many details into some meaning, because I enjoy turning something promising into something marvelous; I keep a diary because it keeps my mind fresh and open. Once the details of being me are safely stored away every night, I can get on with what isn't just me. So, as I explained to my friend, the fictional and the diary-making processes are not interchangeable. I had to keep a diary for many years before I could begin writing fiction.

Like Victoria, I, too, began keeping track of my days at the age of thirteen. But it was not because I felt the young queen, whose comings and goings would one day be read by the world. Nor did anyone make me a present of a sumptuous diary with a lock and key that cried out to be made the repository of secrets. I made my first diary, with half-sheets of notebook paper, cardboard, and yarn, and I wrote in it passionately, because I felt there was nobody else like me and I had to know why—or why not. "I don't believe people exist whose inner plight resembles mine; still, it is possible for me to imagine such people—but that the secret raven forever flaps about their head as it does about mine, even to imagine that is impossible." That is Kafka at thirty-eight, speaking for me at thirteen—and for diarists not yet born.

There are many books about diarists, and some of them make fascinating reading. What is odd, however, is that many of the authors do not seem to be diarists themselves: they write with the air of scientists, observing this peculiar organism called a "diarist" from the other side of a polished lens. F. A. Spalding states in *Self-Harvest, a Study of Diaries and Diarists* that we seldom if ever find development within the individual diary, either in what is recorded or in the manner of recording it. Also that "diarists who hope to aid memory continue to the end to complain of the lack of it." Also that diaries do not seem to teach diarists "how the better to spend my time for the future," even if they read over their diaries, "and few do so." Spalding also says that, except for Scott and Byron, "there is hardly an example of a diary written out of a first-class creative mind." "We cannot imagine a Shakespeare keeping a diary," he says. In fairness to Mr. Spalding, he wrote his book before access to the Kafka diaries was possible—or Virginia Woolf's; though maybe he wouldn't have considered these writers first-class creative minds. As for Shakespeare, that enigma, who can say with certainty whether he did not jot down his moods and plots for plays into a little book that lies crumbling in the earth or awaiting its finder in some forgotten cranny?

Every true diarist knows that having a relationship with a diary is like having a relationship with anyone or anything else: the longer it lasts, the more it is bound to change. When I began my diary, at age thirteen, I traversed that naked space between my mind and my little book's pages as hesitantly as a virgin approaching a man who may or may not prove trustworthy. Now, two-and-a-half decades later, my diary and I have an old marriage. The space between us is gone. I hardly *see* my diary anymore. And yet, there is a confident sense that we are working together. We have been down many roads together, my diary and I (I use the singular, but what I call "my diary" resides in many separate books—some of them lost, others maimed or destroyed [more on this later]), and I have been neglectful and insincere and offhand and have not always shown consideration for this fellow traveler of mine. In adolescence, I weighed him down with feelings of gloom and doom; in late teens, I wasted his pages cataloguing the boys who fell into, or eluded, my snare; in my twenties, I drove him to near death-from-boredom with my lists of resolutions, budgets, and abortive plans for "the future." Sometimes I shunned the sight of him, and I wrote my secrets on sheets of loose paper—not wanting to be bound by him—and, of course, those pages are now lost. In my thirties, as my craft of fiction was consolidated and I felt I had "something of my own," I returned to him with new respect. I told him when good things happened, and shared ideas for future work. As I became less trapped in my universe of moods and recognized my likeness to other people and other things in the universe-at-large, my entries began to include more space. Now there are animals and flowers and sunsets in my diary, as well as other people's problems. As a rule, I complain less and describe more; even my complaints I try to lace with memorable description, because . . . yes, Mr. Spalding, diarists do reread their diaries, and how many times I have exclaimed aloud with rage when I looked up a year or a day, hoping to catch the fever or the flavor of the past, and found only a meager, grudging, "I feel awful today." So now I write for my future self, as well as my present mood. And sometimes, to set the record straight, I jot down a word or two in old diaries to my former self—to encourage, to scold, to correct, or to set things in perspective.

As for memory, I don't complain of the lack of it or use my diary to improve it, as Mr. S. would have me do. It is rather that I know one of us has it—my diary or me—and so, if I can't remember something, I look it up. (Though, as I've said, sometimes nothing's there except a mood nobody wants anymore.) Yet, though I frequently look things up, or sometimes browse through a year, I have never read my diaries straight through, and possibly never will. I have tried, a couple of times, but there are simply too many of them, and, after a while, I get the peculiar dizziness that comes from watching a moving train while on another moving train. One cannot live two lives at once, for long periods of time.

Early or late, there comes a time in every diarist's life when he asks himself: "What if someone should read this?" If he truly recoils at the thought, he might take measures to prevent it, writing in cipher, like Pepys, or in mirror-writing (da Vinci's notebooks) or in a mixture of foreign languages. One seventeenth-century schoolmaster wrote his diary in a notebook so small as to be illegible without a magnifying glass, the whole in abbreviated Latin. (The diary was four inches by two and a half inches; and there were seventy lines to the page!)

But far, far more prevalent, I think, is the breed of diarist who writes for *some* form of audience. This audience may be God, it may be a friendly (or unfriendly) spirit (witness the way some diarists must justify their self-contradictions and shortcomings); or it may be one's future self (at thirty-eight, Virginia Woolf wrote in her journal that she was hoping to entertain herself at fifty) or . . . in many cases, more often than we may care to admit . . . we write for some form of posterity. How many diarists can honestly say they have never once imagined their diaries being "discovered," either before or after their deaths? Many of us hope we will make good reading. (I occasionally catch myself "explaining," in my diary: putting in that extra bit of information that I know quite well but cannot expect a stranger to know.)

In *The Golden Notebook* Doris Lessing writes about a pair of lovers, each of whom keeps two diaries. It is understood tacitly between them that one diary may be "secretly read" but the second diary, the really private one, may not. Of course, one of the partners cheats and the couple is sundered forever because of this unpardonable breach. I know perfectly well that if I had a partner who kept a diary (or two diaries) I would probably cheat. Several times over my diary-keeping years, people have read my journals. Some sneaked and were caught (perhaps others sneaked and were not); a few let me know about it, in a variety of ways. One left a cheerful note: "Enjoy the halcyon days!" Another tore out a handful of pages. Another tossed the whole book into the Atlantic Ocean. On several occasions I have actually read parts of my diary aloud to someone. But too much "publicity" is destructive to a diary, because the diarist begins, unconsciously perhaps, to leave out, to tone down, to pep up, to falsify experience, and the reason for the undertaking becomes buried beneath posings.

The prospect of people reading my diaries after I am dead does not disturb me in the least. I like to think of pooling myself with other introspective hearts: madmen (and women), prudes, profligates, celebrities, outcasts, heroes, artists, saints, the lovelorn and the lucky, the foolish and the proud. I have found so many sides of myself in the diaries of others. I would like it if I someday reflect future readers to themselves, provide them with examples, warnings, courage, and amusement. In these unedited glimpses of the self in others, of others in the self, is another of the covenants posterity makes with the day-to-day.

RICK BASS

◆ ──────────────────────────── ◆

An Oilman's Notebook:
Oil Notes

In the fall of 1985, my twenty-seventh year, I read indirectly from the poet-novelist Jim Harrison a quote from Kafka, about "freeing the frozen sea within us."

I know how to find oil, but I'm a horrible speaker: I couldn't sell men's magazines on a troop ship. And I don't know if I can even write well enough to explain how oil is in some places, and not in others. I get frustrated. It seems sometimes that the best way to communicate the presence of oil—or perhaps of anything—is to revert to gutteral *ugs* and growls, and just go out and by damn sink a hole in the ground, shove the pipe down there deep enough, until oil begins to flow up out of it, bubbling, with its rich smell of hiddenness, and the energy of discovery. And then to point to it: to say, There it is. Always, I want to do that. I want biceps to sheen; I want tractor-trailers to groan, bringing materials in and taking oil out, and drilling breaks to squeal. (You're drilling through a hard formation: bearing down—then the drill bit pierces a softer formation, one that is more capable of storing oil—the pipe shifts, sinking down into this softer formation, going faster, and it makes a barking, torquing, squealing sound—it sounds exactly like beagles. . . .)

I want by stamping on the ground hard enough to make that oil come out. I want to skip legalities, permits, red tape, and other obstacles.

Sometimes I feel almost out of control, and that what is down there is between the oil and me. I want to go immediately and straight to what matters: getting that oil.

My father calls me "animal." I was a fencepost in the third-grade play. I bump into things often, and run over others, frequently.

But I know where oil is, and I want to try to explain to you what it feels like, how it is, to know this.

I just do not know how to do it—show you—because it is three-dimensional, or even beyond: it is future, undrilled, and I am present,

knowing. I don't know yet, without drilling, how to bridge that gap.
It is the frozen sea within me.

I know how to find oil.

Barrels—that's the standard term in the oil industry for measuring fluid.
Barrels of oil, barrels of water . . . one barrel equals forty-two gallons. As
far as oil wells go, I generally like to think of anything that makes more
than 100 barrels a day as a good well, and anything less than that, a
smaller well. People do produce oil wells sometimes, from shallow
depths, at very low rates—three, four, five barrels a day, if the prices are
high enough—but you must always be aware of your operating costs. If
you have the well "on pump"—hooked up to a rod pump that draws
the oil up the casing, by suction—that'll be a cost, for the electricity and
maintenance of the pump—and then you've got the actual physical costs
of transporting the oil. And taxes, and lease burdens. And water: sometimes you'll make water, with your oil, and have to separate the two.
You can't sell water, not the old ocean water you sometimes produce
from your formation, water from millions of years ago, salty, the ocean
then.

You can't just dump that water on the ground, either, not with the
little oil drops and filminess in it, and expect it to just dry out, and not
damage anything or make a mess. So you've got to haul it off by truck,
or pump it down into what they call a salt-water disposal well—usually
an old abandoned oil well—and into some formation, deep down there,
that does not and never will contain drinking water. You put the water
back into the earth.

You put the oil back in, too, but that is a different story, and
happens when you die, when the hydrogens and carbons which you and
your customers burn go up into the sky, out into the atmosphere as
energy dissipated, and come back down, in different forms, for a while,
anyway. . . .

Nothing can truly disappear. It can only be rearranged, so that it
gives that appearance.

The hydrogen and carbon atoms are not smashed; they are not
destroyed. Their form is merely altered.

Corn, oak trees, sea kelp, bryozoans, rotifers, algae, rabbits, two-by-
fours. . . . The carbon goes around the earth, the hydrogen does too,
temporary, everywhere it goes. Maybe they are one thing for only a few
years, a few hundred million years. Sometimes the two link up, the

hydrogens to a carbon, and sit down low in the earth and hide, as oil. But again: only for a while.

I hate coal. I won't spend much time here because my being a petroleum geologist seems to cast an overwhelming bias on the whole thing. But if I weren't dependent on finding and marketing oil and gas, I'd still despise energy generated from coal. I've seen the way it's mined, out west, the things it does to the wildest and most beautiful country. It cuts down the miners in Appalachia, the residents, even. I've seen the lakes up in Vermont and New York, turned to sterile pools, like trays in a lab, from its acidity: dead timbers of trees standing in and all around the shores, not even rotting, just dry and dead, acidified, like a graveyard: acid rain.

Coal is filthy, it comes out of buried swamps, which are oxygen-reducing environments, and these swamps, and their coal, contain much sulphur. When the coal is burned, it releases the sulphur into the atmosphere (the air we breathe), which combines with moisture, H_2O, to form sulphuric acid: H_2SO_4. It falls down on our heads, our properties, lives, and earth.

There are methods of safely "scrubbing" the sulphur from the coal as it is burned, at the power plants (smokestacks rising high into the air: launching pads for the poison: the word is *spew:* trying to get it up into the winds aloft so that it, the sulphur emission, will leave the plant's vicinity: there [dusting of hands]: [innocent]), but our country doesn't enforce this scrubbing process requirement of its coal-fired power plants, so, I hate coal.

Fireplaces, and the burning of wood—our forests, things cut and killed for no reason beyond romance, before their prime—are 90 percent inefficient in the heat they deliver. It all rises: up the chimney, pure waste, of life and clean air. Walk through the neighborhood on a cold night. Yes it smells good. Enjoy it if you can.

Nuclear, solar, hydroelectric and wind power are the only sources cleaner than gas. Nuclear's the only power more volatile than gas. What I am saying is that gas can get the job done, and is a friend, and safe. Good.

This isn't a commercial. This is how it really is. You haven't seen bad until you've seen coal.

The man who owns my company: Mr. H. He is sixty, slightly balding, getting heavyset, like an ex-athlete, is terribly shy, terribly successful, has every material thing that ever was. He owns castles in Scotland, he owns jets, he owns electric garage-door openers, and when he wants wine he does not have to go to the store to shop for it. He's really gotten his success, as they say, only in the last twenty years. There's no one in town, or in the South, in the oil business, who doesn't remember him, when.

I work all the areas for Mr. H., all the ones he is interested or active in. Texas, Oklahoma, Kansas, north and south Louisiana (two entirely different worlds), Mississippi, Florida, south Alabama . . . north Alabama . . . did you know that oil and gas have never been found in Georgia? I am told that the state is offering a million dollar reward to the first person who can find some. It may be a tough chore.

I have fallen in love with the underground geology of north Alabama (and the area extending on over into the siltier portions of north Mississippi)! The area up there that I work, where I spend all my spare time, learning and theorizing, studying and mapping, musing, is shaped like a triangle, with the V pointing south, straddling the Mississippi–Alabama state lines, and at the basin's north end, the sands that hold the oil and gas—old buried beaches—Mississippian (Paleozoic) in age— two hundred and fifty million years ago—are only about 1,000 feet deep—you feel that you can almost reach down with your hands, reach in up to your elbow, and find the old histories, without the formality and expense of a drilling rig—and then, down at the bottom of that triangle, the V, as the old sea (what was then and still is now the Gulf of Mexico) retreated, two hundred and fifty million years ago—in that deeper, narrower part of the basin, the sands lie five and six thousand feet deep. And for now, that's the end of the basin; the deep southern part. Beyond that, it seems that the gulf ended, and Ocean, without sand, began.

There don't seem to be any more of the rolled-around sand grains lumped together with sufficient porosity to hold the thing I am looking for: decayed organisms, dead life, usually leaking out of tightly packed mudstones and into the clean, porous sands.

The pressure of the world sitting above these shales and mudstones and decayed organisms pushes down, and there is heat, and the hydrogens and carbons in the old organisms reassemble into oil and gas. The oil and gas starts to flow, to move again, to move forward if it can, and upward.

It always tries to climb higher than it is: moving, like a miner, through and between pin-head spots of porosity, trying to get up to the area of least pressure—back to the earth's surface, where it used to be—and like some video game, up it will continue to move, slowly, picking its way, until the past earth—younger, higher rocks, but rock formations also buried—can trap it, and prevent the mutiny: blocking its upward progress with a fault, a blanket of impermeable shale, through which nothing can travel . . . not until time and ice and earthquakes and rains and rivers erode the mountains above this trap back down to the trap itself, can the oil and gas begin to move again. Or if a geologist can sense, as in a child's game, that there is something hiding, trapped, unseen, beneath that shale, and can find the pocket where it is, and poke an eight-inch-diameter hole into the trap, however shallow or deep it might be, then the oil—always seeking the lesser pressure, the surface—is just about obliged to come out. It is as daring a rescue as ever there was.

This north Alabama area is called the Black Warrior Basin. There were a few wells drilled in it along obvious faults in the 1900s—1907, for example—where oil and gas was actually coming up the planes of faults, all the way up to the surface, home-free. They'd use that fuel for ridiculous purposes: snake oil, pitch and tar for boats, bathing cuts on livestock with it. And then there was another handful of wells drilled during both of the World Wars, a few very shallow gas wells that were stumbled into—this great triangular buried sea, gulf, that they knew nothing about. They just cranked up and started drilling, *hoping*—true pioneers—and then in the sixties and early seventies, gas began to be worth something, oil too, and the basin has since become one of the ten hottest exploration areas in the country. It doesn't have the reserves of basins in Venezuela or the USSR, or if it does, they haven't been found yet, but it is American oil and gas, and it is shallow, and people who want to work for themselves rather than another person are especially able to work in this basin since the wells are not as expensive to drill. Independents, these people are called. They account for a tremendous amount of the oil and gas found in the country. Not depending on anyone other than themselves. It's good that our country knows how and where to drill for a thing we need.

Some of the newer geologists call it "the Warrior Basin." I always call it "the Black Warrior Basin." That's its full name and not using it is like writing Xmas for Christmas or USA for United States, or calling the Black Forest in Germany "the Forest," and I don't like it. Perhaps I am not compromising enough, true. But Black Warrior describes it better than Warrior, makes it darker and more buried and mysterious, and it's only the new people, trying to shortcut in, playing catch-up, that try to cut off even the name. Most of the old guys who were around before it got hot, who helped make it hot, who knew about it then and were trying to keep it a secret, still call it by its full and right name. If something's bigger than you, then you have to show it respect, no matter how immobile it may seem to be, I think.

All I can come up with are the words lust, passion, gluttony. If you spend your life being hungry, missing more often than hitting (even the best geologists do this) then wants are sharpened in you. It seems that perhaps when you make your occupation out of such a life, spend your livelihood in the *pursuit* of such a thing, looking for something for a living that is very hard to find, it puts a little additional stir in the other want-tos. Chemistry; biology? I don't know.

I think it is chemical. Spending all my time *hunting* for a thing gets other tastes and hungers alerted and receptive, too, so that they, like the suspicion of where oil is, are felt keenly, sharply. Sometimes I want everything. Or want to look for it, anyway.

I put air into the truck tires, in the small town of Terry, on a bright day. It seemed like a major accomplishment: the sort of thing that could shift the pendulum, the momentum of the day, into the good; nothing bad could happen, after that.

But more: Elizabeth—my girlfriend—and I washed cars; her old dependable Chevrolet and my wickedly unreliable truck. If life, and living, is not like oil, then I do not know what is. I know that it will not last forever—I spray the hose over the hood of her car in the warm sun, making her laugh. I'm determined not to devalue life on days such as this one, even years such as this, when there appears to be an excess.

An excess, in the tanks, yes. In the jerry cans. But underground? How could anyone be fooled, when stopping to consider it?

We fall asleep hard, tired, holding each other. We may have twenty years left, or three months, or forty years, or more: but it is a finite unit, like the quantity of anything in the world, and I do not take it for granted, but rather, try to be surprised at its continued presence, and thankful that, at the surface, anyway, its waning is not apparent.

We go to New Orleans. I order her a steak that could be used for an anchor on a battleship. The back of my hand on her cheek, touching it, that smoothness; nothing lasts. Old seas are buried. A species of dinosaur may go extinct after only six million years. We will live to be eighty, with health failing after sixty: a fact. We drove to Arkansas one weekend and ate fried fish in a lakeside restaurant at night. Moths batted at the screens, and at the lights.

I used to have a company car, but too many things kept happening to it (them). The insurance company that covers all of Mr. H.'s businesses said that they had to cut me out of their coverage, like the soft part of an apple (they didn't say that), or the entire company's holdings would have to be released from the policy. I told Mr. H. that I guessed I understood. I was distressed, but also for some reason proud, in a sophomoric way. What Tom McGuane, as well as the Catholic Mass, calls the hidden fun of "fomenting discord."

Once I sank one of my company cars in a swamp near the Red River. I had to swim out. It was frightening. Nasty, muddy water. I was driving out from the rig's location, having finished logging, going back out on the board road, which had flooded during the night: about half a foot of water stood above the boards. I had to go slowly and guess where the road was and wasn't by looking up at the lane cut through the woods, and hoping the boards stayed beneath me. A few of them were floating, loose, pointing in all directions. What I didn't know was that there was a very deep drainage ditch on either side of the board road.

It all looked the same, with six inches of water covering it: like a broad, shallow, muddy swamp. I drove slowly. I got off the board road and didn't know it. I was creeping along, water lapping just below the headlights. Suddenly there was a down-elevator feeling and brown water came rushing up over the hood, and up onto my windshield. I didn't even turn the key off: I scrambled out through the window and swam two strokes back to the board road while the muddy waters closed in around the roof of my, Mr. H.'s, car. It came to rest on the bottom so that you could only vaguely see the opaqueness of the roof. The lights looked very dim down there, and then they faded entirely. Many bubbles.

I stood on the board road in water only slightly above my ankles and waited for someone from the rig to drive by, who could pick me up and take me back in to have a little chat with the bulldozer operator. I was to learn much about bulldozers, while out on wells for Mr. H., the things they could and could not do. For Christmas that year, Mr. H. gave me a twenty-foot length of chain. I think that sometimes I daydream, driving, going out to wells, or coming back, but I can't remember. If I do, this is not a good thing, but how can you help but think, and muse, while you are driving? I had to rent a car to drive home in, and I paid for it with muddy money and in wet jeans, wet tennis shoes, a wet shirt. When you're going to or from a well, you can't dally. You can't let anything stop you. The earth and the well are bigger than you are but you have got to try to hold your own against them anyway. My clothes were bad-smelling and swampy and when I got back out onto the dark of the interstate I took them all off and drove seventy miles an hour with the windows down and it felt good and fortunately for Mr. H. I was not stopped. I stopped by my apartment, got dry clothes, and took the logs on in to his château. We spread them out on the table in the kitchen and discussed the different formations, and decided to run pipe on it, and attempt to make a well. I forgot to tell him about the car. Everything is so much smaller than the act of finding oil, that it must be like belonging to a cult, I would think. But it takes over you. It gets in you. You feel as if it is you, and not the oil or gas, that is trapped down there, and being pressured down upon. You want to find it, and have it come rushing up toward the surface. Like a diver, deep below, looking up at the bright of sky: rising.

Terms I will try not to sling around without telling you what they are. Toolpusher—more often just called "pusher." He doesn't push anything. He is in charge of the drilling crew: roughnecks and roustabouts. The driller is in charge of the pusher. The driller has got to be a mean sunuvabitch. The pusher has to be the second meanest. The crews are called tours, in their aggregate, pronounced "towers," and I don't know why. There is an evening tour (twelve hours) and a morning tour (twelve hours), on most inland drilling operations.

Everyone's got to wear helmets, hard hats.
Whenever there's lightning, you stop.
No smoking.
Sometimes the pipe will get stuck. You can't go any deeper but also you can't come back out. When this happens it is the driller's responsibility, even though it might have been the pusher's fault or inattention. It can be a million-dollar problem, and it is the chief thing that makes drillers so mean: fear of getting stuck. Of having to abandon the hole: junk it, and walk off. Of not allowing the geologist to even find out whether anything was down there or not. Never knowing. Having to second-guess, forever.

You don't have to drill straight down either. You can drill directional holes—also called crooked holes, slant holes—and they are remarkable displays of technology. Say you suspect there's oil under One Shell Plaza (at a depth of ten thousand feet). You can back up to the nearest vacant lot, move your rig in, tell the engineers where your target is, and they'll put a directional bit on the end of the pipe, the drill string: they'll drill at an angle, taking surveys as they go and correcting accordingly, until they drift across the target, and then they'll drop straight down. It is like magic.

Anything can be done in the oil field. If you think there's oil somewhere, and have the dollars and desire to find out, it will be done. There is no such thing as I-Can't. It is wonderful.

Finding oil is sometimes like the feeling you get driving a little over the recommended speed limit on that sharp turn on the interstate outside Baton Rouge en route to Lafayette, when you come around that climbing corner pulling Gs and truck blast a little too fast and then after that whip of a turn find yourself looking up at that space-age takeoff ramp they call a bridge that spans, after the vertical climb, the Mississippi River. You've been driving along all morning on this pretty but bland interstate, humming along into predictability and all of a sudden there are all these surprise marks on the landscape: intense abruptions, challenges to the spirit. You find yourself almost racing up that bridge even before you've fully acknowledged its existence. You look down and see water. It makes the backs of your hamstrings, and a wide zone across your chest, tingle. That is what finding oil is like.

This is a thing oilmen (masc. and fem.) do: they put oil in sample jars, little solid glass cups with screw-on caps, and then they can hold the oil. You can unscrew the cap and smell it. You can set it on your desk. If it is a high-grade condensate it will look like Orange Nehi and smell like unleaded. If it is low-grade 20° asphaltic, it will smell like tar, and be sludge black. Of course if there is H_2S in it there will be a sulphur smell, rotten eggs, and sour gas is lethal at even modest concentrations. It must be treated first.

It's wonderful to hold the oil that you have found in the field. The sample bottles are the same ones used for bottling the sidewall cores before sending them to the lab for analysis (the screw-on lid prevents any gasses from seeping out). The bottles are frosted on one side. You can write your sentimental, dizzy thoughts on this frosted surface with a fine fancy pen, though just as many do it in the field, at the first well test, with nubby pencil, black Marksalot, whatever's handy. The field's name (or wildcat), state, county, date, formation, and depth. I've got a bottle from Atascosa County, Texas, a wildcat, the first well my father ever drilled by himself, 5,300 feet down. It smells good. It's blackish-green, and I've had it almost twenty years now.

I don't know if I'm really communicating it to you—the strength and importance of these little bottles when they have oil in them.

You can have a medal from the Olympics; suppose the 1,500 meters was your event. Or you could have a photo of yourself hitting a home run in the World Series. But you can't hold those things and you can't put them in a bottle and see them after they are gone. Immortal as those other things may sound, capturing energy is really the most magnificent thing.

The bottles all seem to be alive, empowered. Bigger than you, in a two-ounce jar.

Hold it up to the light. Tilt it slightly. Lower it and unscrew the cap. Smell it. Touch it with your finger.

When no one else is in the office, put the cap back on and hold it up to your ear. Picture an ancient seashore. A world so different from the one we are in now it is frightening.

There are people in my industry who like the picture they make doing something, rather than the thing itself, or who make Ds and Fs in college and then marry the boss's daughter and become insufferable (learning to aim other people's work in their direction, leaping atop it as it hurdles past); they are people who cannot do their job, cannot quite understand it, and are bitter and resentful because of this, and spend their hours plotting, whining, doing everything but the thing they should be doing, finding oil. Strong words, but oh some days the office is a den of snakes and reptiles and ghouls. On those days, the best thing to do is to just duck your head, and drill the oil, get the oil. Eat peaches, strawberry waffles for breakfast. Kiss your girlfriend, kiss your lover. Get the oil.

This goes for any profession.

KEITH H. BASSO

◆ ————————————————————————— ◆

Strong Songs: Excerpts from an Ethnographer's Journal

Almost thirty years ago, in the spring of 1959, I borrowed an old Ford station wagon from my parents and drove across the country to the village of Cibecue, an isolated community of 900 people located near the center of the Fort Apache Indian Reservation in east-central Arizona. My main purpose in going to Cibecue was to determine if linguistic and ethnographic fieldwork might be possible there, and, if it was, whether or not I would find it to my liking. As things turned out, I spent most of the summer away from the village, working with a crew of six Apache men who were building a cattle trap and stringing barbed wire fence in high country to the north. Moved by the beauty of the Arizona landscape and fascinated by what little I saw of Western Apache life, I resolved to return to Cibecue in 1960 and use all of my time learning about the community. The notes and jottings presented here, some of which have been lightly edited, are taken from a journal I kept between June 25 and August 26 of that year. It was, as the saying goes, a very good year. I was twenty years old—naive, earnest, and roundly inexperienced. I was also keenly excited. As I drove onto the Fort Apache Reservation, I sensed that I was embarking on an adventure of large proportions, and that my experience at Cibecue would prove fruitful and rewarding in unexpected ways. I was not disappointed.

June 23

A splendid drive to Cibecue. You turn off the highway, rattle across an ancient cattle guard, and proceed on a narrow dirt track which curves around the base of a conical red-rock butte. Badly pitted and covered with layers of dust, the road passes through a shallow canyon and then rises abruptly as it twists up the broken flank of a low mountain. This is Western Apache country—red cliffs, red rocks, red soil, red dust. Dark-green juniper trees and shaggy-bark cedars. Clumps of blue-green piñon trees and an occasional ponderosa pine. Blooming cholla cacti—small, delicate, waxy blossoms—white, yellow, orange, pink, some a vivid purple. A vast blue sky.

The country opens up on the far side of Cibecue Mountain. There are barbed wire fences now and I saw several cows with newborn calves. Then a motley quartet of horses—short, thin, scraggly, wary. After a few more miles, the road drops gently into a handsome valley partitioned down the middle by a winding stream lined with towering cottonwood trees. The Apache live here, on both sides of the stream, their camps separated by cornfields, vegetable gardens, horse corrals, and large ceremonial dance grounds. I continued on until I reached the center of Cibecue, a dispersed cluster of sun-baked buildings made up of two trading posts, two churches (Lutheran and Catholic), and a schoolhouse made of stone. In front of Apache Traders, the largest trading post and local post office, I saw two Indian children—a boy and a girl—and a pregnant Indian woman. The boy was studying an insect on his foot while the girl blew vehemently on a plastic harmonica. The woman was talking through an open window to someone inside. I walked toward the door and smiled at the little girl. She turned away immediately—and kept on blowing.

The trading post was dark and cool inside. Wide wooden counters. An antiquated cash register. Tall wooden shelves stocked with canned goods, denim shirts and jeans, boxes of boots and shoes, bolts of brightly colored fabric from which Apache women make their full-length dresses. A glass display case filled with candy and chewing gum. A refrigerated cooler filled with cuts of meat. Saddles and saddle blankets, bridles and reins, horseshoes, cowboy hats, axes, pick-axes, a broken juke box in the corner. The smell of leather, kerosene, and freshly butchered beef.

There were perhaps a dozen customers, all of them Apaches. They stood calmly in different places around the store, waiting to be served. Some were conversing quietly. The language they speak is entirely their own, although occasionally a borrowed English word—"shuggy" (sugar) "cheezh" (cheese), "canny" (candy)—creeps into their talk. Western Apache is a tone language, like Chinese, and when it is spoken well, especially by women with high-pitched voices, it takes on a distinctly musical quality, rising and falling in precise cadences which are striking to the ear. Conversations in Apache sometimes resemble spoken fugues.

I was greeted warmly by Don Cooley, owner of Apache Traders and part Apache himself. A tall man who walks with a limp, he has a lean face, calm eyes, and a cautious, gentle smile. He runs his store with widely acclaimed largesse, dispensing easy credit ("Give her an extra ten"), small cash loans ("Pay me whenever"), and ample gifts of food and clothing to persons in dire straits ("It gets bad in the winter"). There are tight-fisted traders on the Fort Apache Indian Reservation, but Don Cooley, whose good will is legendary, is surely not among them. I will be living this summer in a house belonging to Don's younger brother. The house is located less than 500 yards from the trading post, and since the trading post is the hub of daily life in Cibecue, I could hardly be better situated to learn something—anything!—of what that life involves. Don's advice on how to begin: "Hell, I don't know. Just hang around."

June 26
Time in Cibecue is a seamless affair, open and unfettered, which proceeds without benefit of minutes, hours, "lunchtimes," "bedtimes," jangling bells and buzzers. All that matters is the rising and setting of the sun, and this is an ancillary sort of way. Day and night glide smoothly into each other, and many Apache activities—working, cooking, sleeping, socializing—seem lightly affected by the transition.

I am learning people's names and some of them are quite spectacular: Wooster Kataagi, Bland Tessay, Percy Peaches, Benedict Shadow, Romeo Dazen, Shawnee Pina, Hoke Josay, Armer Lavender, Sladen Machuse, Clay Lupe, Harry Tony, and Minor Moody.

Everyone in Cibecue has an Apache name as well. These names are typically bestowed during early childhood, frequently in response to some memorable or humorous event. A good example is provided by Dan Tessay, a distinguished-looking man in his early sixties, whose Apache name means "Bushy Anus." As a toddler, Dan was playing near his mother while she plucked feathers from a wild turkey. He stumbled, sat down hard on the feathers, and stood up with several of them clinging to his bare bottom. His grandfather, who observed the incident, was much amused and created Dan's name on the spot. Other Apaches, like Ernest Murphy, acquire names when they reach adulthood. A soldier in World War II, Ernest was wounded by shrapnel in Belgium. His left leg required a skin graft and the skin he received was taken from a non-Indian. The operation was a success and when Ernest returned to Cibecue he was given the name "Whiteman's Leg."

This evening I visited Teddy Peaches, an elderly acquaintance from last year. He was drinking from a bottle of wine and seemed happy to talk.

His English is good and I could follow most of what he said. He told me that he had worked for many years as a carpenter on the Santa Fe Railroad, repairing depots and trestles from Oregon to Boston. Once, when he was greasing bolts on the underside of a trestle, he lost his grip and fell to the bottom of a canyon. As he was falling, he cried out, "Let me live!" He was unconscious for two days. During that time he rose up into the clouds and talked to God and Jesus. They looked like twins, both had blond hair and blue eyes. They asked him if he wanted to go back to earth. He said, "Yes, I am still young yet." Then they decided to give him a test—if he could determine which of the two was God he would be allowed to return to this world. He suddenly recalled that "Jesus sits on the right hand of God," so he was able to give the right answer. This is how Teddy held onto his life.

I have spent the last two days trying to pronounce the Apache term for "black." No success. Discouraging.

June 28
Dudley Patterson, a cheerful man with whom I worked last summer, showed up this morning with two horses—a chestnut mare and a bay gelding. Both were available for rent and both looked sound. I chose the mare when Dudley announced that the gelding was "pretty good at bucking."

There is to be considerable ritual activity in Cibecue this summer. Already, I know of plans for three curing ceremonies and two girls' puberty dances. I have learned also that several "medicine men" (the term is used by English-speaking Apaches) have been singing to keep lightning at a safe distance from people's camps. What, in God's name, do the local missionaries make of this?

Roy Quay, a clerk in the trading post, told me that he was struck by lightning fourteen years ago. This happened close to the school. When the lightning came down it looked like a "red arrow." Roy was knocked off his feet. The earth around him smelled like gunpowder. He staggered home and lay down. For a while he was so dizzy he couldn't stand up. Then he went to find a medicine man who would sing for him. A ceremony was performed four days later. I asked Roy what would happen if someone hit by lightning didn't get sung over? He said: "It will kill him pretty quick—or maybe he get real sick each time a storm comes."

Last week I had an amiable conversation with Roy Nickerson, an older man who is related by clan to Don Cooley. Today, in the store, Roy passed by me without so much as a glance. I must have offended him—but how?

An Apache man with gray hair rode up to the trading post on a white horse. He was riding double with his wife. He was wearing a tall black hat and she was wearing a dress the color of red wine. They made a striking couple.

I saw a lovely Apache girl—black hair, almond-shaped eyes, luminous skin the color of *café au lait*. She was wearing shoes without socks.

These things are not a part of life in Cibecue: electricity, television, indoor plumbing, cooking stoves, adequate medical services. These things are: kerosene lamps, storytelling, water from the creek, outdoor cooking fires, too much sickness.

July 2

I saddled the mare at dawn and rode to the cowboy camp at Lonely Pine. Small hawks were hunting over the grassy flats north of the village, and a pair of ravens picked busily at the corpse of a jackrabbit. A coyote appeared out of nowhere, paused for a moment, and vanished behind some bushes. Deep quiet upon the land.

When I arrived at Lonely Pine the cowboys were branding calves. I drank a cup of well-boiled coffee with Norbert Josay, the roundup cook and another acquaintance from last year. Then I joined the others in a large corral where about forty head of cattle were bunched together in a corner. George Enfield, an experienced brand-reader, was matching cows with calves, identifying each pair for his ropers, Francis DeHose and Hickerson Pina.

Hickerson Pina ropes calves with consummate grace marked by absolute economy of movement. Mounted on a small gray horse, he approaches the herd and slowly maneuvers for position. Then, rising in his stirrups and leaning slightly forward, he takes two quick turns over his head, releases, and watches without expression as his loop settles softly over the neck of a calf thirty feet away. A single complex motion—perfectly calculated, perfectly controlled, perfectly executed. After drawing in slack, Hickerson drags the calf to a point near the branding fire. Here, two men wrestle it down, cut a notch in its ear, and apply the hot irons. The work is done quickly, efficiently, and soon the calf is back on its feet. Hickerson turns his horse, measures out a new loop, and moves back to the herd to make another throw. An artist with a lariat, he is seventeen years old.

July 4
Together with Nashley Tessay and two of Roy Quay's sons—Lansford (age ten) and Alvin (age five)—I drove to the Fourth of July Rodeo at Show Low, a small Mormon settlement about forty-five miles from Cibecue. In the parade beforehand there was a simple float, sponsored by the local hospital, which featured a "doctor" and "nurse" standing beside a "patient" lying in bed. As the float approached us, Lansford whispered to Alvin that the doctor was coming to give him an injection. Alvin darted into the car and hid behind a seat. He refused to come out until we reached the rodeo grounds. Lansford and Nashley found this hilarious.

Trouble at Cibecue. A teenage boy was badly beaten up after an all-night beer party. His mother, fighting mad and intoxicated herself, has been searching for his assailants most of the day. She is said to be carrying a loaded .22 revolver.

Teddy Peaches ripped his hand open on some barbed wire. I fixed him up as best I could and walked him home. He offered to sell me some of his land, saying he needed the money to buy a house in New York City. The joke fell flat. I think there are times when Teddy is a very lonely man.

July 5
Tragedy! Late this morning, on the highway south of Show Low, a car driven by a man from Cibecue collided with a tractor owned by the Arizona Highway Department. The operator of the tractor was killed instantly, as were two of the driver's children. A third child is in critical condition at the Indian Hospital at Whiteriver. The Cibecue man, who had been drinking, escaped with minor injuries. Estimated speed at time of impact: 80 mph. Everyone is stunned.

July 9
The two children who died in the auto accident four days ago were buried this morning at a cemetery northeast of Cibecue. It is still not known if the other child will survive. Sadness and searing grief.

There was heavy rain this afternoon accompanied by tremendous bolts of lightning. The storm lasted less than twenty minutes. Afterward, the air smelled clean and sweet and the red soil of Cibecue looked almost black. One lightning bolt killed two horses in a pasture across the creek.

July 11
Dudley Patterson and Ernest Murphy came by the house while I was washing clothes. They were at loose ends and stayed for over an hour. We drank a pot of coffee and talked of unusual things.

Dudley reported that a ceremony will be held next Saturday night for a young man named Warren Gregg. According to Dudley, Warren's mind has been "upside down" since he returned to Cibecue a year ago from a boarding school in Utah. Normally gentle and soft-spoken, Warren became aggressive toward his sister early in May and shortly thereafter agreed to enter a hospital at Phoenix. Now his mother is anxious to have him home, and to this end has hired Leon Beatty, a local medicine man of singular skills, to diagnose the cause of his illness. But Warren himself will not be present for the occasion. Leon Beatty will sing over a set of Warren's clothes. After a diagnosis has been made, Warren will come back from Phoenix to participate in a curing ceremony, a different kind of ritual, more costly and elaborate, which should alleviate his sickness by attacking and neutralizing its cause. I expressed surprise that Leon Beatty would sing for someone so far away. Dudley looked at me with a faintly puzzled expression. "Strong songs," he said. "His songs can go across the world."

Reaching inside his hat, Ernest Murphy produced a small eagle feather with a turquoise bead tied to its shaft. "We pray with this one," he said. "We pray for long life, stay safe, keep trouble away from camp." Ernest went on to observe that only certain medicine men may take feathers from eagles. If you kill an eagle, you must hide it immediately. Then you must find a medicine man and bring him to where the bird is concealed. After blessing the eagle with "holy yellow powder" (a mixture of corn pollen and cattail pollen), the medicine man sings four songs, removing one breast feather at the end of each song. You must pay the medicine man for his services by giving him thirty-two feathers. "If you don't do like this, if you try to pull them out yourself, something bad will happen." I asked Ernest which of the medicine men in Cibecue were regularly called upon to take eagle feathers. He answered quickly. "There's only one left—Leon Beatty."

I spent most of the afternoon practicing my meager Apache vocabulary. It has grown a bit during the last two weeks but my confidence to use it has not. This morning, while Dudley and Ernest were here, a grasshopper crawled across the floor. I pointed to it and spoke the word for "insect." Dudley burst into laughter. What I had said, he informed me, was "vagina." He went on to point out that the difference between grasshoppers and vaginas was quite considerable, an astute observation which prompted a broadly grinning Ernest to ask me if I were a virgin.

July 12

Approximately 60 percent of the families in Cibecue live in traditional dome-shaped wickiups. Constructed of cedar posts and plaits of beargrass, some of these circular structures stand fifteen feet high and measure up to twenty-five feet in diameter. In summer, wickiups are used mainly for sleeping and changing clothes. All other domestic activities take place outside, usually under brush-covered ramadas—commonly called "shades"—which provide welcome protection from the sun and driving blasts of rain. Inside a shade, one is likely to see a few pieces of homemade furniture, cooking utensils beside a smoldering fire, and a wide assortment of objects suspended from nails which have been driven into the shade's supporting posts—shirts, hats, calendars, framed photographs of children, ropes, spurs, cradleboards for babies, flashlights, ears of corn hung from their husks, strips of drying meat, and numerous little bundles, tidy and mysterious, fashioned from paper and pieces of cloth. Filled to brimming with signs of their users, Western Apache shades—cool, relaxed, intimate in an off-hand sort of way—are "occupied" in the richest sense of the term. It seems to me that they are also full of love.

July 14

I walked to the trading post and saw Leon Beatty sitting on the porch. The eminent medicine man did not cut an impressive figure. A small man, stooped and heavyset, he has a fleshy face and peers at the world through very thick glasses. He was wearing a battered old hat and a pair of delapidated sneakers. An eagle feather was attached to his shirt with a safety pin. He was eating an orange Popsicle. As he sat in the morning sun, a thin black puppy approached him and lay down inches from his feet. He spoke to the dog and it moved away. Then he called it back and gave it half the Popsicle.

Don Cooley told me that Leon Beatty is fifty-six years old. His first wife died three years ago. His new wife, whom he married several months ago, is just eighteen.

More shocking news—another Apache child has died. According to Roy Quay, the little girl (age three or four) was alive and well this morning. She was found dead at her camp shortly before noon. Her body was blue. Roy interprets this as a sure sign of witchcraft. "When a dead person show blue like that some poison man done it, no question. If they want to get you, they say words—that's all." Roy then related a story about two Apache men who were working together in a field. One was plowing with a team of mules while the other followed behind him, planting corn. The man who was planting suddenly dropped dead. His face and tongue were blue.

July 15
Bland Tessay, the oldest Apache living at Cibecue, came to the store today with one of his grandchildren. He is nearly blind and totally deaf. Nashley Tessay, who addresses him as "uncle," believes he is ninety-six years old. If this estimate is correct, Bland Tessay would have been a boy of eight when the the Fort Apache Reservation was established in 1872. The past is so imminent here it is palpable.

Bothered by a cold for the last three days, I sought help from Teddy Peaches' sister-in-law, Annie Peaches, who arranged for me to "breathe roots." She put a three-inch piece of manzanita root into a pot of boiling water and let it steep for about ten minutes. Then she instructed me to put a blanket over my head, lean over the pot, and inhale the steam. After taking three or four deep breaths, my nose began to run. Now, some five hours later, my sinuses are completely clear.

July 16
Leon Beatty sings tonight. I will attend the ceremony with Dudley Patterson and Ernest Murphy. Although I am eager to see what happens, I know I will feel conspicuous and self-conscious. When I asked Dudley how I should conduct myself, a quizzical expression crossed his face. "Show respect," he said. Then he grinned. "And don't talk to nobody about grasshoppers."

We arrived at the camp of Warren Gregg's mother just as the sun was setting. Three wickiups, two shades, a tar-papered shack. There was considerable activity. A knot of women, seated on blankets beneath an apple tree, prepared stacks of white tortillas, while four men, sweating hard, chopped firewood nearby. Small children raced about happily—playing tag, chasing after dogs, laughing, kicking up clouds of dust. Other people waited quietly beside their horses. A flock of crows clattered by overhead.

As the sky began to darken, two men carrying drums emerged from a wickiup and walked toward one of the shades. This was where the ceremony would take place. The interior of the shade had been cleared of all personal belongings, and a fire was burning in a shallow pit near the main entrance. A few feet from the fire, Warren Gregg's clothes hung on a coat hanger suspended from a beam, and directly beneath them, resting on top of a broken wooden cupboard, was a pair of his shoes. Next to the cupboard, neatly arranged on the seat of a chair, I saw the tail of a Mule deer, a ceramic butter dish filled with holy yellow powder, and four sprigs of some leafy plant. Beside the chair, attached to the tip of a five-foot stake, an eagle's wingfeather extended parallel to the ground. The feather was pointed south, toward Phoenix.

More and more people entered the shade. They stood in total silence and all I could hear was the crackling of the fire and a dog barking outside. Presently, Leon Beatty came in, accompanied by two assistants. He went straight to the chair in the front of the shade. Speaking softly in Apache, he picked up the deer's tail, dipped it into the dish of yellow powder, and brushed it over Warren Gregg's clothes and shoes. He repeated this blessing four times. Then he walked to a bench about six feet away and sat down between the two men with drums. Moments later, the drummers had established their beat and the medicine man began to sing. His voice sounded thin and reedy, as if strained from overuse, and it was difficult to hear over the thumping of the drums. He sang for a couple of minutes and stopped abruptly. He cleared his lungs and spat. Then, cupping his hand around his mouth, he began to sing again. This time his voice was strong. In flawless unison with the drums his song came pouring forth—an ancient song, compelling in the architecture of its unfamiliar sound, a modern song, squarely addressed to the needs of a fellow man in trouble. His voice rose and fell, rose and fell, and the song gathered force. He was singing louder now, well beyond the reach of the drums, and the power of his words—his work—his prayer—filled the shade completely. On the wingfeather of an eagle, his song was headed for Phoenix.

July 17

I awoke this morning to the sound of church bells. First call to Mass at the Catholic church. With the drums of last night's ceremony still pounding in my ears, it seemed decidedly strange that two such different sounds—two such different symbols—should be found together in the same community. Which one, drums or bells, will be heard most often at Cibecue in the future?

Today, I produced my first comprehensible sentence in Western Apache. Sitting outside with Alvin Quay, I pointed to my horse and said, "That horse eats grass." Alvin, who turned six last week, glanced at the animal, fixed me with a disbelieving stare, and responded in his own language. "Horses always eat grass." Although my observation failed to impress Alvin, I thought the fact of its delivery—and of his responding to it in Apache—was nothing short of astonishing. Perhaps there is hope for me after all.

Anthropological fieldwork rests on the premise that it is perfectly acceptable for strangers to intrude uninvited on the thoughts and activities of other people. This is a dubious premise, and recognizing it as such has helped me to appreciate how very polite and roundly accomodating most Apaches are. Their generosity in this regard—the sheer graciousness with which they tolerate my inquisitiveness and the silly disturbances I inject into their days—has been truly extraordinary.

July 22

Warren Gregg has returned to Cibecue. He is happy to be home and everyone at his mother's camp is glad to see him. Dudley Patterson, who spoke with him this afternoon, says he looks thin and pale. Warren didn't much like being at the hospital in Phoenix—it was "too lonely," he said—but the white people there were friendly and attentive. When Dudley inquired if he had "noticed something" the night Leon Beatty sang over his clothes, Warren reported that he had developed a throbbing headache. It went away early in the morning but for the next two days he felt "tired and kind of dizzy." I asked Dudley if that was good or bad. My friend smiled broadly. "It's good," Dudley said. "It's pretty good all right!"

EPILOGUE

Following my stay at Cibecue in the summer of 1960, I decided to become a serious student of Western Apache culture. As a result of that decision, plus a growing number of more personal reasons, I returned to the village every summer for the next twenty-eight years. I plan to return again. Most of the Apache people named in these pages are gone now, and most of them went before they should have. There are times, especially during the lightning season, when their absence washes over me like a cool rain. There are other times when I shake my fist at the sky.

THOMAS BERGER

◆ ———————————————————————— ◆

Touring Western Europe, 1956:
Excerpts from a Journal

During World War II, I served with a U.S. Army medical unit in Britain, France, and Germany, ending up in the summer of 1945 with the first American Occupation forces in Berlin. After some weeks as a hospital patient in Paris I returned to the States in the autumn of the same year and did not go back to Europe until this trip, eleven years later, taken in the company of my wife, whose quixotic idea it was thereby to spend every cent we had in the world, save a hundred dollars on which to exist when we got home (neither of us had a job). If money is a preoccupation throughout the journal, it's because mine was rapidly dwindling. It might be worth mentioning here that in two months we spent about $1500, a figure that includes the round-trip fare on Holland–America steamships. As it turned out, Jeanne was right: seeing Germany again made it emotionally possible for me to discard the manuscript in which I had been hopelessly enmired since early '54 and, in the ensuing year and a half, write my first novel, *Crazy in Berlin.* Finally, I should note that the postcard purchased at the Baths of Diocletian, showing the skeleton-on-spikes above the legend "Know Thyself," is today, and has been throughout the decades, mounted on the wall above my desk.

Paris / April 17, 1956

In September 1945, on an afternoon pass from the army hospital at Beaujon, walking on a blood-poisoned foot, and diverted for a time by a Parisian who naturally assumed that an American soldier seeking the Louvre wanted the department store of that name, I got to the museum just in time to see Milo's Venus and the Winged Victory before the place closed for the day. Now I determine that both of these works are sturdily in place—which means that at least some of Western civilization remains intact—and then go on to linger before Mantegna's *St. Sebastian,* to which I am probably drawn by my fantasies of maintaining a stiff upper lip when under attack by enemies numerically superior but morally base—and aren't they all?

Paris to Nice / April 19
When the train stopped at Aix-en-Provence a young woman entered the compartment and, hearing J. and me converse in English, introduced herself as a keen student of our tongue. Marguerite teaches primary school in Nice and on her day off secretly studies for a graduate degree in English. She hopes subsequently to come to America as an exchange teacher, but fears her coworkers would enviously obstruct this project were they privy to it. When the train arrived at Nice she led us to a pension owned by a friend of hers. This man, whose English is very faulty but whose pronunciation is excellent (precisely my situation in French), gave us a special rate, the equivalent of $1.50 per night for bed and breakfast, because (1) it is out of season and (2) Marguerite represented us as being her American cousins.

Nice / April 20
We called in at Marguerite's school, not long before closing time: she wanted us to see the children in action. The headmistress, a heavyset woman who was not so severe as quietly authoritative, carrying on her robust shoulders the prestige of the school, is, according to Marguerite, the wife of a Communist and therefore ritualistically dislikes Americans. Our friend, violently pro-Yankee, has had many arguments with her. Indeed, Marguerite's true purpose in inviting us there was to display the decency of Americans as exemplified by J. and me. It was apparently a success, which of course proved little about Americans in general but *was* the kind of proof appropriate to that sort of bias.

The children were remarkable. Even the smallest, three- or four-year-olds, were doing precise needlework, decorating china, and cutting out, very finely, clothing for dolls.

Rome / April 22
After dinner at the pension we repaired to the sitting room, wherein sat: a middle-aged couple who spoke English with a British accent overlaying a German accent that occasionally protruded, the woman maternal and amiable, the man a great heavy bulk with thick-lidded eyes embedded in a face as fat and corrupt-looking as that of a Renaissance Pope (he proved to be delightfully otherwise, but told of an Italian girl who seeing him that day in an antique church made the sign of the evil eye); an impeccably dressed Italian young man whose expression, uncharacteristically, was blank; and an animated chap who wore an enormous handlebar mustache and spoke an antiquated En-

glish in which the expression "my goodness gracious" figured prominently. The middle-aged couple had fled to England from Hitler's Germany. The bland-visaged young man had studied at Harvard on an exchange fellowship, and My Goodness Gracious hailed from Italian Switzerland and was an ardent Catholic. Thus most of the dominant points of view were represented and the political discussion was spirited though genial.

Rome / April 23
From the Capitoline, a vista of the Forum and behind it the loveliest incline in Christendom, the purple and green slopes of the Palatine. A dais of marble in the Forum is said to be Antony's platform for the oration of the death of Caesar. The area is one of diverse heights and expanses, of sundered columns and incomplete arches, and grass and weeds in profusion, amongst which wild cats prowl as they do in the park above Nice, beyond the Berlioz château, and here as there people leave picnic leftovers for the animals.

Rome / April 24
Amongst the memories I carry away from the Vatican's museums are: the high polish on the Laocoön, for which Lessing had not prepared me; a mummy with yellow hair and what seemed to be fingernail coloring; a porphyry bowl large enough to swim in, allegedly used by Nero (but for what?).

In the evening, My Goodness Gracious sensibly abandoned the arid political discussion to make sheep's eyes at a new member of the after-dinner group, a full-blown young lady from Milano, in a dress with a very low-cut neckline.

Rome to Florence / April 25
At the Baths of Diocletian I acquired a postcard reproducing a wall mosaic: a skeleton lying on a bed of spikes, under which is the Delphic injunction: ΓΝΩΘΙ ΣΕΑΥΤΟΝ. And therewith I resolved henceforth to regard myself as more than a passing acquaintance.

Opposite us on the train to Florence sat an Italian woman in her late forties, her face one of those expressive organs perhaps peculiar to this part of the world, capable of instantly producing any expression throughout the human range. She had brought along a large leather valise which when opened revealed enough food for a regiment, along with an equal supply of medicines: the latter she displayed to the compartment while providing an account of her illnesses that was received sympathetically by all present.

We soon became friends with Italia (for such indeed was her name) and when we arrived in Florence she forbade us to take a taxi to the pension I had chosen, as usual, from *Europe on Five Dollars a Day:* her husband, who was calling for her in his car, would suggest better lodgings at a lower cost. This man was waiting on the platform. Tall, handsome, and with a natural grace of the kind that has charmed the world in so many Italian movies, Gino received us as though it were an everyday occurrence to deal with strangers picked up by his wife. As it turned out, he too was a visitor in Florence, playing piano in a night-club orchestra. He insisted on taking us to the hotel where the band stayed. Once there, he demanded for his American cousins the same discounted rate paid by the orchestra: this came to about $3.50.

Time before dinner to visit the Uffizi, where I was especially impressed by the huge (4.48 × 3.90 meters) Cimabue crucifix, mounted at a diagonal between floor and ceiling, some distance from any wall, "representing," as the guidebook so finely puts it, "a moment of more solemn and less intense dramatic feeling" than another at Arezzo. (The official guidebooks to the museums of Italy are superb and written with a candor that permits the disparaging of works that deserve it, e.g., the "worn-out rhetoric" of Bernini's *Truth*, in the Borghese at Rome.) Passing through the Piazza della Signoria, I check out Cellini's claim, in the autobiography, that he insured a front-place rank for his *Perseus* in the Loggia dei Lanzi, that open-air warehouse of sculpture, by soldering it to the pedestal. Today loudspeakers hang from the loggia's ceiling, presumably to carry the harangues of the forthcoming city election campaigns.

Dinner with Italia and Gino at a small restaurant near the Palazzo Pitti. This place too is frequented by the orchestra, and they were there when we entered and rose as one from a corner table to cry, "Signora!" at Italia. Pasta con burro (the spaghetti so delicious of itself that anything but butter would have spoiled it), salad, a steak of the celebrated beef of Firenze, gorgonzola, fruit—the best meal we have yet eaten in Europe, costing about a dollar apiece. Afterward Gino drove us to the heights above the city, for a nighttime vista from the Piazzale Michelangelo ("Michelange'" to the locals, as the Scrovegni chapel in Padua is *la cappella di Giott'*). But then he had to leave for work at the club, which he said was too expensive for rational people; thus never were we to hear the orchestra perform though sharing their hotel and restaurant.

Venice / April 28

After the incessant motion in Florence, prowling the Uffizi and Pitti and a side trip to Fiesole, then hopping off the Venezia-bound train to visit Giotto's chapel in Padova, catching another train to the city of canals, then the express *vaporetto* to the Rialto bridge, from which, toting our luggage, we wandered the narrow passages in search of the hotel recommended by the leader of Gino's band, we were in a state of exhaustion when we finally found it—and were set upon by the desk clerk as though we were a bone and he a ravenous dog. "You will want a gondola ride: ask me for a reliable boatman and a special price. You must see the islands of Murano and Burano: I'll arrange it. Then you *have* to visit Torcello, where Hemingway goes. And you shall eat all your meals in a famous restaurant, to which I shall send you." Deaf to his importunities, in a back alley (which, owing to the canals, every street seems to be), J., who has a knack for such discoveries, found an anonymous eating place frequented by Italian sailors and other impecunious types, and for the equivalent of thirty-five cents we ate a creditable four-course meal. The proprietress lent me an empty liter bottle, which I took to the wine shop next door and had filled from a barrel of coarse red for a nickel.

Venice / April 29

The weather has been rotten, the Palazzo Ducale is gloomy and damp, the Piazza is filled with pimps for the glass factories, and in this weather even the Byzantine splendors of San Marco are muted, but the *vaporetti* are a joy and cost next to nothing to ride. The Lido was cold and bleak today, but worth seeing if only to examine the sand, of which the grains are alleged to be smaller than most and thus more powdery. (I am not much of a swimmer, but I collect beaches, e.g., Chappaquiddick, Cuba's Varadero, and others.) To put a toe in the water today would be unthinkable.

Kitzbühel / May 1

We're staying with J.'s expatriate sister, Ollie, in a Tyrolean chalet. The locals actually live and work in quaint shops and houses and really wear fuzzy green hats with little brushes in the band and short leather pants held up by crossbar suspenders. The looming Alps are oppressive. I join Dostoyevski, D. H. Lawrence, and Gide in disliking mountains.

Kitzbühel / May 2
After several years here, our small nephew is fluent in German but speaks broken English. We play badminton (*Federball*) on the lawn, to reach which he sometimes eschews the door, to "go the window out."

Vienna / May 4
Ollie's Viennese friends, Hermann & Jutta, conveyed us to a modest hotel in a northwestern district of the city. In the concierge's window a heavy, tough old woman wearing a cloth dust cap. Her voice is deep as a man's. She was much taken with the smallest member of the party, whom she called *der Daniel in der Löwengrube*, nevertheless and notwithstanding our manifest respectability—mother & child, man & wife— demanded the room rent in advance. Perhaps because, as the evening proved, the place was largely an *hôtel de passe*.

Vienna / May 5
The Doctors Haas, husband and wife, relatives of J.'s friends in New York, gave us the grand tour in their tiny Czech car. Herr Doktor, a Jew, was concealed in their apartment for four years during the Nazi time, while his wife continued her medical practice in adjoining rooms. They are tireless and generous hosts. The Kunsthistorisches Museum is a great storehouse of the Hapsburg collections, with incomparable Brueghels and countless examples of Velasquez at his most glowing (his color struck me much more forcibly than did that of the celebrated Venetians), and Veronese's *Judith with the Head of Holofernes*, a personal favorite of mine, though my taste in this regard might be predominantly literary. Then on to Schönbrunn, which I prefer to Versailles, especially in its vistas and its adjoining zoo.

Vienna / May 7
Taken by the male Dr. Haas to find Freud's house. He was not sure of the number and stopped at one point on the Berggasse to ask a woman who is sweeping the sidewalk, "Could you please tell us which of these houses was Freud's?" She had no idea. "*Doctor* Freud?" No, sorry. She went on sweeping. "I'm sure it's along here somewhere," Dr. Haas told me. We were about to return to the car when he had a bright idea. "Actually," he said to the woman, "it was *Professor* Freud." "*Ja!*" said she. "Professor Freud lived just there," pointing.

Nürnberg / May 15

Our quarters are on an upper floor of a building of which the ground floor is a bar and under the same management: one registers for a room with the barkeeper. An enormous mastiff maintains order throughout the establishment. In the breakfast room this morning, the animal was about to help himself to our rolls, without opposition from us, when the proprietor appeared and shouted, *"Pfui!,"* that magical command used throughout the German-speaking countries to make a dog desist from whatever it's currently doing. As always, this worked. The beast made a docile retreat.

We visited the castle, much of which was destroyed in the wartime bombings. J. spots, just beyond the wall, a door and mailbox without an accompanying house. Like the Dürerhaus, also damaged in the air raids but now mostly restored, much of the castle is unfurnished and therefore unusually remote in spirit.

Berlin / May 6

The rubble of eleven years ago has been cleared away or at least organized: there are great open spaces, with the bricks stacked neatly by. One sees new buildings everywhere. When I tell the taxi driver I haven't been here since September '45, he speaks ebulliently of the reconstruction. Our pension is in Charlottenburg and is presided over by one Frau Reimers, a jolly Berlin sort who dogs us everywhere, including the W.C., talking through the door that has been closed in her face.

Berlin / May 7

An editor friend helped us get a room in a handsome pension in Dahlem, one of the residential districts, quite a distance from the Kurfürstendamm, but very near Zehlendorf, where I was quartered in 1945. We told Frau Reimers, who was prepared to be hurt by the news, that we were moving in with our German cousins.

Berlin / May 20

We had visited the Russian Sector on a tour bus, but this was the first time on foot. Turning down one bleak street, which was utterly deserted except for clusters of Russian and East German uniforms, both of us felt uneasy. I regretted not having brought along the snapshots portraying me and other Yanks in the early Occupation forces fraternizing with our Soviet allies. I asked a husky member of the Volkspolizei whether it was permissible to walk there. "Why not?" he cried, and he and his comrades chortled so heartily that I almost expected him to add, "What do you think this is, a police state?"

Berlin / May 22
We went to look at the apartment complex in Zehlendorf where my unit was billeted. These low buildings are built around a verdant garden. When my buddies and I arrived in '45, the latter was filled with the furniture of the civilian tenants who had been dispossessed: the Army wanted us to camp out in empty flats. Our colonel took it a step further. In Wannsee, where we had previously been quartered, he had had us sweep the grounds and burn the resulting refuse, which (for this area had been used by the Nazis for a last stand against the Red Army) included live ammunition and grenades hitherto unexploded. Here he made another of his pyres and incinerated the furniture. Perhaps the justification for this was that the Nazis had burned books and later done far worse with fire. In any event, I now stood looking up at the window of the apartment I had lived in as a conqueror—until I saw an apprehensive face behind the curtains, returning my stare. Berlin is not a place where surveillance can be assumed innocent until proven otherwise, so I went back where I came from.

ROY BLOUNT, JR.

◆ ——————————————————— ◆

Don't Anybody Steal These:
From My Notebooks Over the
Last Few Years

So many things that you would think would go without saying, don't.

"Don't miss Shirley Caesar as she do her tribute to Mother as no one else can."

Vereen speculates that the reason for men's generalized consternation about women is that women are the only people men get to know that well.

"He sure is enthused about you."
  "I met him on the highway."

If Ronald Reagan is President, then I don't exist.
  Possibility?
  Reagan accession shocks man into realization life is not real. He stops keeping up with the news. Hence diminished role of government in his life. Paradoxically life becomes more real.
  Then one Sunday evening he comes home from carefree weekend trip with family, hears funny noises out back, finds Ed Meese in his "If You Can't Stand the Heat" apron, cooking steaks on his grill.

subtitles/subtleties

Sometimes I'm afraid I'm just too sweet-natured to write a novel. I don't like to get people in trouble. Why not a novel that manages to keep its characters out of conflict? That would be a trick. That would be doing something.

After a day in the bush, white ex-Kenyan to liberal white South African: "How do you stay so *clean?*"

LWSA: "People have asked me that since I was a boy."

July 27, 1987
Letter from *Antaeus*, they are doing a special issue devoted to "extracts from journals written by various 'types' of writers." (Which type do they think I am?) And so to Albany, Georgia, to make a speech. Eat alligator croquettes and hear of boy so fat, when he stood in the sun grease came out of the corners of his mouth. Stay in home of couple who got rich selling pecans by mail order. Wife grills me about my marital status (checkered), doesn't approve of it.

Too busy traveling to write travel column, which is twenty-eight days late and haven't started it yet. So how in hell keep a journal?

"Until you hit the ball hard a couple of times, you lose the feeling of what it's like. You keep feeling for what the feeling is" —Reggie Jackson.

"You can speak as a prophetess to impress men, but that's not doing the work of God."

"I've dreamed that I was three people twice."

wrapper/reappear

"You can sweeten flour and I'd like it."

> The boys who go to church, they all seem homely,
> The boys who get me going all seem wild.
> Oh, which is better? Me being lonely
> Or running the risk that I'll have Satan's child?

"He hasn't plateaued off. He gets better all the time."

"It's pronounced *Ang*," I told him. "Got more of an *r* sound in it but basically it's I-N-G-R-E-S pronounced *Ang*." That so impressed him that he awarded me a chair in the local university there and I married his daughter Janalee and together we escaped to Baton Rouge, where we now make our home. Means Red Stick. I will be working the Dogbite, S.C., High School Bobcats halftime show; the Fruit Cocktail Festival of Hula, Mississippi; and Blake Thigpen's boy's eleventh birthday party; and on November 19 of this year I'll begin doing three shows a month in conjunction with the National Chemical Spreads Council Jamboree.

Iowan/loan

The only writing worth writing is writing that calls into question not just whether this ought to be written, and not just whether this writer ought to be writing it or anything else, but whether anything ought to be written by anybody, when you get right down to it.

Albemarle/ramble

Kid re another kid at school: "He accidentally writes on himself a lot."

> The way some people are drawn to gay bars
> Or gambling dens, I'm drawn to Zabar's.

"About by a factor of two of the energy consumed in that city."

Her first day in New York, a man offered her $25 to stand on his chest.

chairlift/hairlipped

"Stay just as you are."
    "Well it's the only way I can stay I guess."

veracity/intra-city

Mr. Blair Peach

"What?"
    "Nothing. Oh, nothing."
    "And another thing —"

shoulda/shoulder
    pewter/twerp
    toolshed/sloshed

"He called up and said, 'Linda?' I said yes, and we had a nice talk, he said he'd met me in one of the clubs and we had a nice talk then too. I said which club did he meet me in and he said the Roundelay, and I said I never went in there, and he said, 'Oh shit.' I wasn't the right Linda. It was the wrong number. But he said we ought to meet and I said well we'll see. Now he calls when he gets blue, you know."

> There aint nothing more ridic-
> Lous than a country music critic
> Who never raised chicken corn or hogs.
>   All I got to go on
>   Is acuity and so on
> And two not-even-coonhunting dogs.

"We are reviewing the situation here in terms of providing better defensive provisions in the situation where we are."

HOGS LOOSED AFTER COLLISION
CREATE HAVOC ON A HIGHWAY

"It was just hogs flying through the air and people hitting hogs," said Sgt. George L. Norwood.

"We've had more of that this year I believe, Lurine, than we ever have."

"I just don't understand it."

"But that's just part of the nature of life. And you won't be able to do anything about it."

> All you are now is just dust in a coffin
> Beneath what was once our front lawn.
> If I didn't say "You just fuck off" so often
> I'd swear that it seems you are gone.

singalong/signaling

Three little kids driving—one doing the brake, one the accelerator, one the steering wheel.

> To chase and smoke and bet and swill's
> No substitute for moral will.

Old Indian Bottom Church.

"My Home Is Clean Enough to Be Healthy and Dirty Enough to Be Happy."

Joe Begley of Blackey, Ky.: "I know this is the tail end of the damn world, but sometimes the tail end'll backlash." "When I wake up in the morning I look out the window and see if I'm still here. And if I am I'm the happiest man in the world."

"You talk about *touch*. He had *touch*. Completed a thirty-five-yard pass to a sixty-five-year-old man."

> Saw through my own eyes before I was four,
> Six years later sawed through my floor.
>
> — *The No Illusions Blues*

> Flem Snopes, of Yoknapatawpha,
> Has turned down a Hollywood awpha.
>   "I'm made out of ink,"
> He says, "and I think

Jacket copy on forties paperback novel, the author "was born in the Chicago he brought so violently to life."

George III "went to bed willingly but sillily at nine."

From unpub. John Fergus Ryan novel, *March Beans:* "Persons oddly done up, whose mental illnesses shone through."

Any given generation gives the next generation advice that the given generation should have been given by the previous one but now it's too late.

knowledge/windowledge

Emory McQuorquadale

mildewed/wildeyed

"I better run go fix supper."

"You have no room to talk," said the dentist, a wag.

"You know the society can't keep up with the individual. The individual is a lot crazier than the society. There is no telling *what* the individual will do. Say you're the society. Put yourself in the place of the society. The society is just trying to get along. And all these individuals are going off in all directions! In *all* directions. I mean *all*. Do you have any *idea* how many directions there are? The individual. The fucking individual. What is so great about the fucking *individual*.

"Oh I know. I know I am one. If anybody is. You don't have to tell me. But I'm just saying."

"We got some girls that don't speak English. That's one of them, there. Oh, they can say 'Thank you.' Or 'Ouch.' "

elbow/wobble

"Let's go, let's run some redlights."

"It's only Svengali, talking to himself again."

People give that guy a funny look because his mouth is held that way: slightly open, fake-casual air of somebody afraid somebody is going to give him a funny look. He must have done something at a formative age to attract a funny look and acquired that expression, and ever since then people have been giving him funny looks not because he does anything to warrant them but because he has that expression.

The cat made a little smacking noise and said "ow," complainingly.

Bio of a Bayou Boyo

> Since I lost you sweet darling little honey babe, I'm
> Unable to think of a word or make things rhyme.

"To discuss one's spiritual life journalistically is impossible"—John Cheever in *N.Y. Times* mag. profile of him. Also, one might add, one's journalistic life spiritually.

"I belong to a very small and elite group, most of who, when I started out in it, I couldn't tie their shoes."

All your gargling thoughts come together and flow down over your shoulders like goldilocks. Moment things come right, there! then, just, pluhhhhh.

"We watched Joe and Edie's honeymoon films, and Christ, that had to be, by far, one classic set of Ektachrome. *Ho*-ly . . ."

lacy pants/participants

racehorses/resources

People looking about them not realizing what they look like. People who if they looked just a little more happy would be beautiful, and if just a little more beautiful would be happy.

You can sort of drag things along with it but they don't really drag. Like somebody pouring something good. Like a bird.

Labor contract negotiations: "The two sides are primarily talking language at the moment."

"At the top of the many beautiful facets of the man was his loyalty."

"They hold each other in mutual contempt, which speaks well of both."

"What is going on? It was not so much a question of thinking it was time to go, rather I was thinking like an end to something; of me, an era, of something" —the Shah of Iran.

"I went in to see a man about some relish and came out with fifty dollars worth of T-shirts."

baseline/vaseline
    miseries/miniseries

"It was the scariest thing I ever saw. It had a heel like a shoe and toes like a foot."

Driver of Avis courtesy van at Dallas–Fort Worth airport said she had vegetable garden. Grew some nice squash. Ate some of it, saved rest for little later. "And I found a little cucumber. And I've got two little green peppers." Lives alone, out in country. Snakes. Puts ring of poison around house every night, finds dead snakes all around ring, headed toward house, every morning.

"I'd love to see your squash some time."

"I'm afraid my Valentine wouldn't like it."

"It's nothing I can take credit for. It's just something in my jeans."

"If you have to spray your apple trees forty times a year to get any apples, how did anybody get any apples before they had sprays?"

"Oh, they didn't have all the bugs then."

"In fact I can remember when people tried to raise bugs, and couldn't, to save their life."

"What bugs they did have, they'd spray *them* with something to keep the fish and birds off."

"It's a different day, today."

"Funny as a rubber crutch. You catch yourself just wobbly with it."

Graffito in Tuscaloosa: "I think I won't put this here because I am the only person who really appreciates it and it will be defaced but I don't care because I really know. M."

"Will the passenger leaving an item in the front coat closet please come forward."

Why don't I ever write anything in which I could say, "You could feel the mountains catch their breath"?

Man was writing his dreams down in a book for seven months for therapy, his wife got rid of the book. "She threw away seven months of my dreams!"

The pleasure of writing, in practice, is that of eating a nice juicy steak with loose teeth.

"They in the same bag. I don't know which would jump out first."

She had her raising, had her fears;
Her body had its own idears.

Man lying flat, near-quivering, on street in some kind of pain. He doesn't want to kick, he doesn't want to stiffen, he doesn't want to stand, he doesn't want to lie, he doesn't want to be questioned, he doesn't want to be abandoned, he doesn't want to be still or to move, he doesn't want to be silent or to cry. He doesn't want to clench against the pain, that's too painful, and he doesn't want to ease into it for the same reason. He is so frustrated he can't even scream in frustration. There is nothing he can want except unconsciousness and he doesn't dare relax enough for that or explode into it. He can't stand even to tremble.

scaly ears/fiscal years
    Oslo/also

What is it, do you think?
I am no more vulgar surely
Than Erica Jong,
Though my name is less wonderful;
Why do I assume I will never win
The Alice Faye di Castagnola
Award of the Poetry Society of America?
Why do I think, "I would settle
For the Phil Harris di Castagnola
Award of the Poetry Society of America"?
Here's a clean breast of it:
I think I am not fine enough
For the Beloit Poetry Journal.
Which I've never even seen an issue of!
Where the fuck is Beloit? I
Had a poem in *The New Yorker*!
"Light verse," demurmurs the Muse.
"Rhymes." Why is it that some people's Muses
Bear them aloft and mine is always
Clearing her throat?
I wouldn't mind a Muse that eluded me;
Mine can be had but has
A faraway look in her eye.

"I really believe in the Muse,
By the way," writes Jong.
By the way!
Listen I used to buy
My suits from Muse's menswear
In Atlanta. When I was at *Sports
Illustrated* one of my coworkers
Was Gloria Muuse,
A two-*u* Muse. None of which
May seem either here or there, but
Then that is the way with my
Muse, isn't it? I don't know
Whether there's something
Limited about my Muse herself
Or I let her down; I assume
The latter. I tend
To blame myself in these things,
Until it's too late.

To maximize is to besiege with maxims.

"Quit trying to kiss that chicken. That chicken has been pecking at
horse manure all afternoon."
    "Don't kiss a chicken anyway. It's silly."
    "It don't mean anything to the chicken."

"Do you feel comfortable verbalizing what you have written?"
    "Sometimes."
    "Well, do many people tell you they see a little bit of themself in
what you've written?"

kinkiness/kinesis

DeLeverette "Do It Up" Brown

"I could never love anyone named 'Uwe.' "

It was all knots and bulbs and slime and veins and it was squirming in
the undergrowth making a nose like *k-k-k*, like telling a horse to go only
harder.

"I believe in the Golden Rule, assume he does. Means when he shot at me, must want me to shoot at him."

"That hacked-off lumps of human and animal flesh were offered to the niche-held fetish idols we know." (Notice in Boscastle witchcraft museum.)

Melville in a letter to Hawthorne, after finishing *Moby-Dick:* "Am I not now at peace? Is not my supper good?"

"Oh that my words were now written! Oh that they were printed in a book!" —*Job* xix, 23.

PAUL BOWLES

◆ ———————————— ◆

Journal, Tangier 1987–1988

August 19
Clear. Walked to Merkala. The cherqi was violent, and raised mountains
of dust along the way. On the beach hundreds of small children, hardly
any adults. The boys were beating each other with long strips of seaweed.
Constant smell of the sewage coming out of the conduit at the east end
of the beach. Lalla Fatima Zohra was right to forbid the public to use
the place a few years ago. But that was during the cholera epidemic. A
letter from Paris saying that Quai Voltaire will not agree to letting me
inspect the galleys of any book they may publish. I never asked to see
galleys. I wanted to see typescript before it was set up in type. They
called my request *"légalisme excessif."* Buffie found her two thousand
dollars and passport, hidden somewhere in the flat.

August 20
Paid my last visit to the consulate, and was given the copy of my will,
which they'd been keeping for me. Moving vans in front of the Rési-
dence. Afternoon brought a M. Jebari, doing a thesis at the Sorbonne.
His first suggestion, *La vie et l'oeuvre de Paul Bowles*, turned down. When
he called it *L'horreur et la violence dans l'oeuvre de Paul Bowles*, they
accepted it. Ridiculous. Claude Thomas came by, resentful of the new
contracts Quai Voltaire have sent her to sign. I hope she doesn't eventually lose patience with them and refuse to translate any further works.
I count heavily on her for *Up Above the World*. Bourgois writes that he
expects her to take on the volume of Jane's letters.

August 25
Curious how difficult it is to sustain anger, once the initial flush of it is
over. For three days L. has been coming here to spend the entire afternoon. Twice or three times a year he arrives from Boston, where he's busy
writing that biography which I rejected before he started. Weidenfeld is
aware that it's unauthorized, and I've repeatedly told L. that I won't
help him in any way. At least he asks no questions. Conversation with

him is like talking with the doctor immediately after he tells you: "Yes, you have cancer," and then goes on: "But let's speak about something else." I wonder if he knows how deeply I resent his flouting my wishes. Probably not, since I say nothing, show nothing, and after all this time, even feel nothing.

August 29
L. said goodbye this afternoon; he leaves tomorrow, certainly no more advanced in the preparations for his project than when he came. During the six afternoons he spent here Mrabet did almost all the talking. I think L. must be better equipped now to write on Mohammed Mrabet than on anyone else.

September 1
Jane's agent in New York tells me that the French Society of Authors refuses to pay me any royalties on works by Jane unless I can furnish documents proving that I am her legitimate heir. It's *In the Summer House* which has precipitated the trouble. *Plaisirs Paisibles*, being only a book, went off without a murmur. But the play was broadcast. The society apparently considers radio and TV as needing stricter controls: more money involved.

September 11
Finally saw Mrabet's villa-cum-stable at Mraierh. (Jerez calls the place Charchumbo.) I was startled to see that he'd combined the two in one edifice. Jean-Bernard, who was with us, thought it natural, said it was a common arrangement in France. Of course it is here, too, in the more distant regions. But animals bellow and bleat and smell and draw flies. I can't believe it will be inhabitable. However much enthusiasm Jerez may feel, she won't live in it long.

September 14
I looked through *Libération*'s questionnaire of two years ago: *Pourquoi écrivez-vous?*—this time to see what was the most usual answer. Very few writers claimed financial necessity as a reason for exercising their profession. Many admitted that they had no idea why they wrote. But the majority responded by implying that they were impelled to write by some inner force which could not be denied. The more scrupulous of these did not hesitate to admit that their principal satisfaction was in feeling that they were leaving a part of themselves behind—in other

words, writing was felt to confer a certain minimal immortality. This would have been understandable earlier in the century when it was assumed that life on the planet would continue indefinitely. Now that the prognosis is doubtful, the desire to leave a trace behind seems absurd. Even if the human species manages to survive for another hundred years, it's unlikely that a book written in 1990 will mean much to anyone happening to open it in 2090, if indeed he is capable of reading at all.

October 3
Yesterday two men from the Wafa Bank called on me, handing me a letter from Casa, asking that I lend them two small drawings by Yacoubi for an exhibit they intend to hold there later this month. I said I had no Yacoubi drawings—only paintings—and they answered that drawings had been specified. Instead of shrugging and saying: "*Je regrette beaucoup*," I added that I had had drawings, but that they had fallen behind the bookcases in one room or another, and I didn't know which room or which bookcases, and that I had no intention of moving those heavily laden objects in order to search. A bad idea, since they both volunteered to empty the shelves. Several thousand books. They're coming back this afternoon to do that work. In the meantime I've spoken with Abdelouahaid and Mrabet, both of whom advised me not to let them start. It would take several hours in any case. But A. and M. were in agreement that if the drawings were found and borrowed, I'd never see them again. So now I must face the two Wafa men and say the thing is impossible.

An even more unpleasant prospect is having the British TV crew and *animateurs* arrive week after next to do that interview. This I dread more than anything because of my disappearing voice. (Buffie insists I have cancer of the larynx, and has no patience with me because I won't go for X rays.)

October 13
"When a Jew is dead, he's dead," said Gertrude Stein. Yet both she and Alice Toklas were bad Jews. Stein was a secret Christian Scientist; Toklas openly embraced the Roman Catholic faith in her later years. Is this regression?

October 16
Three and a half decades ago Saïd Kouch, Jane's Arabic professor, said to her: "*Tous les agréments de Tanger ont disparu.*" It was true then, and

meaningless now. Whatever charms the town once had have long since been forgotten. Bulldozers have run wild over the countryside, vegetation has been hacked away and trees everywhere chopped down. Nothing surprising about that. Suburbs have to be put somewhere. But the housewives of the fancy new villas in these suburbs scatter their refuse from the windows, and send their servants to the empty lot next door, to add to the mounds of garbage already there. Buffie has gone back to New York.

October 28
Last night the television crew returned to London, after eleven days in a Morocco without sun. They didn't mind the clouds and rain in Tangier because this made a good accompaniment to *Let It Come Down*, but they had hoped for sun in Fez, and above all in the Tafilelt, where they meant to film landscapes of sand dunes. But the desert was wet and gray. (Today the sky is cloudless.)

October 31
Twenty or more women and girls, apparently on their way to a wedding, walk along the street pounding on drums. Behind them a dozen boys follow, pitching stones at them. Hostility between the sexes begins early.

(They were not on their way to a wedding; they are all seated now on the ground at the top of the hill opposite my bedroom window.)

November 10
Smihi has been shooting *The Big Mirror* for four weeks. Last night he came to remind me that he wanted Mrabet and me to be in a bar scene, not as extras, he was careful to add; he wanted us to converse. I reminded him that such a dialogue would have to be in Spanish. I suggested that Jerez de la Frontera should replace Mrabet, who could be sitting with other Moroccans. Smihi agreed, and said he'd call her hotel when he left here. He told me to be at the Palace today at 2:00 P.M. I went. Jerez was there, in evening dress. The Palace was locked. It was cold in the street. We waited until 3:30. Mrabet drove us back here. At 4:00 Jerez and I returned (on foot) to find the night club still shut, and no actors or crew in evidence. At 5:30 Gavin drove us home. Some time after 6:00 Smihi arrived, apologetic. Just the same, he tried to get me to go back with him to the Palace. I refused, he left, and Jerez and I ate dinner.

The men from the Wafa Bank came and carted away a large

Yacoubi painting for their exhibit in Casablanca. "That's the end of that picture," said Mrabet.

November 11
Mrabet says he had only to look inside the Palace (which he did at some point in the evening) to know that he would never have agreed to be in such a scene. The Moroccans sitting there were all of the kind that drink alcohol and consort with prostitutes, and he could not afford to have himself photographed in their company.

November 15
Rodrigo and I were in the Fez Market yesterday. He drew my attention to a tray of mushrooms at a vegetable stall. "These look exactly like what we call San Isidros," he said. San Isidros are psilocybin mushrooms, he went on, in case I didn't know, which I didn't. He was excited to think they grew in Morocco. I thought that if such a drug existed here, people would know about it, and they very clearly don't. But he bought a dirham's worth and went home, saying he was going to brew them in a tea. Today he came in triumphant. "They're the same hongos. The same thing as in Guatemala." The brew, which he said had a disgusting flavor, kept him awake all night, writing rather than hallucinating. It's hard to believe that psilocybin is sold here in the market and that no one is aware of it. This is probably because mushrooms are not a part of the diet of Moroccans. Still, the Europeans who buy them must have had some strange and unexplained experiences.

December 9
A relatively quiet period after the protracted frustration of last week, when it took six days of running between the postal authorities, the customs, and the censors to get the galleys of *Call at Corazon* into my hands. Owen is publishing a new volume of stories using that title.

December 26
The most ridiculous gadget of the year, in the show window of an Indian shop on the Boulevard Pasteur: a deodorant stick with a built-in compass.

January 16
I have a document from the Société des Auteurs et Compositeurs Dramatiques telling me that I have been admitted *"comme membre succession."*

Presumably I may now receive those royalties, although who knows? The French are still French; like the Moroccans, they part with money only under duress.

January 17
Buffie writes that she was questioned by the police in connection with the murder of Donald Windham. She suggested that the aggressor perhaps had taken exception to something he had written.

January 20
Every morning, weather permitting, I set out on a long walk. It's supposed to help my leg. It makes no difference whether it does or not; I go anyway. Each day I walk to the inaudible accompaniment of a different popular song. It's not necessary to look for them; they pop up from my unconscious. It was some time last summer when I realized that all these old songs from the 1920s were there. I can never remember what song it was that preoccupied me on the preceding day, so now I write them down. Today it was "Red Hot Mama."

January 22
Today's song: "I Gave You Up Just Before You Threw Me Down." I seem to be weak on my legs, or so Abdelouahaid tells me, holding me up. But the weather has been colder than I remember its ever being in Tangier, and that is inclined to keep one's muscles from responding immediately.

January 24
"Sleepy Time Gal." Rodrigo returned yesterday, having had to go twice to Panama on his way to and from Guatemala.

January 26
"Sueños de Opio." Each time I read an article about what the journalists call "the tragedy of Sri Lanka" I wait for the finger of blame to be pointed at the English. Incredibly, it never is. Instead, race, religion, and cultural tradition are combed over until the final impression the reader comes away with is that the conflict was inevitable. Everyone knows that the Tamils did not emigrate to Ceylon on their own initiative. Why did the British want them there? Because they needed an impoverished, helpless group of agricultural workers who could be forced to work for minimal wages. The Sinhalese could not be forced; the Tamils, being in alien territory, were at the mercy of the British.

January 27
"The Alcoholic Blues." The report of Donald Windham's murder proves to have been a hoax carried out by someone who had a grudge against Buffie Johnson. She blames it on a student who lives on the West Coast. He must be the one, she says, because he has AIDS and "can't wait to make trouble" for others.

February 4
Three Japanese called on me today: a Mr. and Mrs. Inuhiko and Riki Suzuki, the editor of the literary monthly *Shincho*, published in Tokyo. Subject of discussion: their plan to translate and publish certain texts of mine. They want me to agree to furnish a preface "for the Japanese public." I told them how *The Delicate Prey* had been pirated twenty-five years ago in Tokyo and published under the title *Kayowaki Ejiki*. This may have been impolitic. Mr. Suzuki said he did not want to deal with an agent. So we'll be working without a contract.

February 6
Rodrigo has bought a falcon. When Mrabet heard this, he decided that he was going to get it away from him, and began to announce his plans for teaching it to hunt.

February 7
The weather is so bitterly cold that I've abandoned my walks. Mrabet arrives early and makes a big fire in the fireplace. I get up to find it roaring. Wonderful these mornings when the temperature in my bedroom is 38° F. Rodrigo has the bird in a cage. He says it's gentle and seems to have no fear of him. It eats fresh raw beef.

February 10
Three Italian journalists all afternoon.

February 12
Brazilian journalist with intriguing first name of Leda. Rodrigo brought the falcon here. A beautiful bird. R. wants to take it to the top of the mountain and set it free. "So it can eat people's chickens," says Mrabet.

February 13
Abdelouahaid and I drove with Rodrigo and the cage to the high point above Mediouna. There was a hard climb over sharp rocks to get up there. Abdelouahaid helped me. When the cage had been opened and

the falcon had been persuaded to come out, Rodrigo threw it upward into the air, and we stood watching it as it flew. There was a strong cherqi blowing which seemed to keep it from rising very far. It flew straight toward the northwest over the pine forest, as though it knew where it was going. Little by little it went up. By that time the cold had got to my bones. I came home and got into bed.

February 20
Incapacitated with a cold since the day we took the falcon up to the mountain. L., my persevering biographer, has arranged a concert of my music as part of the Manca Music Festival in Nice for the third of April. Hard to be properly annoyed with him when he goes to such lengths to be agreeable. He even offered to come from Boston to Tangier and fetch me, if I'd go. I shan't go. I'm too old to put up with being stared at.

March 2
Went to the Wafa Bank to inquire about the Yacoubi painting. It's in Casablanca; the exposition won't be held until April or May. Abdelouahaid and Mrabet believe that the exposition is fictional and that the painting has been sold. This seems unlikely.

March 11
The house which Mrabet was supposed to be building for Jerez is finished, he says, but he is not going to let her have it. The eighty thousand dirhams she gave him a year ago before she returned to New York he used, irresponsibly and one might say criminally, to build the stables he wanted for his animals. The house itself, over the stables, cost three or four times as much, money which I unenthusiastically supplied after the big scene with Jerez. When she came back he expected her to bring more cash, but she didn't, so that he felt obliged to feign great anger. (Attack, before you can be accused.) The house is not yours, he told her. He then proceeded to furnish it, saying he was going to live there himself. There's not a chance of that, since the house has no water, electricity, or drainage. Neither he nor Jerez could live there. As soon as fair weather sets in I'll go out to see the place. Now that it's finished I'm curious.

March 15
A disappointing version of *The Sheltering Sky* arrived today from Madrid. Alfaguara used the same title as the Buenos Aires edition of 1954: *El Cielo*

Protector. A careless translation marred by omissions and errors. Too bad.

April 19

No one was certain whether today or tomorrow would be the first day of Ramadan. We knew only last night when the sirens sounded that today would begin the fast. (This is the second Ramadan with sirens instead of cannon. *Allez demander pourquoi*.) One shot, and you were over the boundary in the land where all is forbidden. They tell you that with today's traffic the cannon would not be heard. This may be true at sunset, but at half past four in the morning the city is silent. Strange that no Muslim has spoken of the ludicrousness of using an air-raid siren to herald a holy day of fasting.

Every year I have to remember to warn people who come for tea that they must leave well before sunset. The hour directly after that is the time to be inside, out of the street. It's the favorite hour for attacking foreigners. The streets are absolutely empty. Not a car, not a pedestrian, not a policeman in view, everywhere in the city. One of my guests, an elderly American woman, was knocked down, kicked, and robbed in the street in front of the apartment house. I felt vaguely guilty of living in a place where such things are taken more or less for granted. But the real guilt is that which I feel in the presence of Muslims. They are suffering and I am not. Here at home I'm obliged to eat and drink in front of them. They always claim that it doesn't affect them to see someone eating. If I want to eat, I can eat, they say. There's no one telling me I can't eat. This is true, but the social pressure is such that anyone seen to be eating in public is arrested and jailed.

Thirst is more painful than hunger, they say. Smokers are irascible for the first few days. As the month wears on, skirmishes between individuals increase in number. But no one will admit that he is short-tempered because of Ramadan. Says Abdelouahaid: "If you're going to be in a bad humor because it's Ramadan, your Ramadan has no value, and it would be better not to fast at all." Nevertheless they *are* likely to be fractious, and I take care not to contradict or criticize them.

April 24

I have a spider whose behavior mystifies me. It's the kind of spider with tiny body and very long legs, and it spins no web. It spends its days hanging by one filament from the bottom of a marble shelf behind the door. For the past three weeks it has been going every night to hang four feet away, near the wash basin. When morning comes it returns to its corner. There are no insects for it to catch at either location, but it never misses a night. If I let anyone know of its existence it's sure to be killed. Spiders are not encouraged to live in the house. Rahma is such a poor housekeeper that the spider probably can count on months of privacy. If Mrabet or Abdelouahaid should catch sight of it, they would unthinkingly crush it. I don't know why I assume that it's entirely harmless, except that it looks nothing like the spiders that attack. These have heavier bodies and thicker legs, and are intensely, militantly black.

April 25
Went last Friday to Mraierh. The climb was painful then, but now after three days the pain is worse, and in the upper leg. This with the usual fire in the *mollet* makes it very hard to walk. I have to assume that eventually it will be better.

April 27
After a week or so of springlike weather, we've now gone back to January, with covered sky and cherqi, and showers from time to time. I've noticed that it's next to impossible for Tangier to reach a warm temperature without the arrival of that cursed east wind, which immediately makes everything feel twenty degrees colder. This is why July often seems more glacial than a calm day in midwinter. I've gone back to having a fire in the fireplace. Pain still strong in my leg, but less so than yesterday, most of which I spent in bed. I'm using a combination of Adalgur and Alpha-Kadol. My mistrust of "patent medicines" dates from early childhood, when I heard only denunciations of pharmaceutical products bearing trade names. They were all reputed to be poisonous. Now it seems that pharmacies (in this third-world country, at least, and probably in most other places as well) sell nothing but such products. It is impossible to get a druggist to go into the back room and prepare a medicine with his hands. Here this may be a blessing; God knows what fatal errors are thus avoided.

May 3
Typical tale of Ramadan violence at the market of Casabarata. A man who prepared chibaqia was sitting on the ground, hoping to attract buyers. (Chibaqia used to be made with honey; now, there being no more honey, it's made with sugar syrup, and isn't very good.) Another man carrying a little portable counter of combs, pocket mirrors, tooth-

paste, and similar objects, sat down near the first, who immediately ordered him to go somewhere else. The second man said he was going to sit there only for a minute, because he was tired. Then he would go on. The chibaqia seller roared: "Safi!", whipped out a long knife and slashed the other with a downward motion, severing his jugular. The wounded man rose, took a few steps, and collapsed. His four-year-old son stood watching while he bled to death. This was the second killing at Casabarata since Ramadan began two weeks ago. There have been others, in other parts of the town, but I didn't get eyewitness reports of them as I did of this one.

May 4

Jerez off to New York today. Unfortunately she came yesterday, bringing a big bunch of roses and lilies. Friday Mrabet had bought an armful of white roses from Kif Kunti, and had arranged them in a large vase. It was Jerez's fatal idea to put Mrabet's roses into a smaller receptacle in order to make room for her own more spectacular array. I didn't think Mrabet would be pleased to see this, but I wasn't prepared for his exaggerated reaction. The insults came fast and thick. Each time she tried to speak, he shouted louder. Anyone used to living here during Ramadan would have backed down and given up trying to reason with the adversary, but Jerez seemed to think conditions were normal, and continued to ask if she had ever done anything to harm him. His shouting grew louder; the insults came in Arabic, Spanish, and English. Then he began to hurl cushions at her, and finally hauled off and gave her a resounding crack in the face. Jerez was bending over him, so she did not fall. But Mrabet jumped up, seized a log from the fireplace, and swung at her, to hit her on top of the head. My shouting at him to sit down and shut up had no effect, but Abdelwahab, who was here as well as Abdelouahaid, came between them and calmed Mrabet for a moment. (Abdelwahab is a Riffian, so that Mrabet was more inclined to listen.) But then Mrabet must have felt that he had been bought too easily, and began to bellow that he was in a room full of Jews who should be killed and not allowed to pollute the air breathed by a Muslim. With this he left the room and we heard him continuing his insults and obscenities as he banged around the kitchen. Jerez by this time was sobbing, and Abdelwahab decided to leave, which he did so quickly that he left his umbrella behind. Abdelouahaid merely sat, shaking his head. He whispered to me: "A horrible man. Heart of tar." I think he was shocked by Mrabet's behavior. I was not shocked, having seen other instances of his insensate fury, but I was ashamed that all this should have happened in my flat, and to a guest of mine. When Jerez went out, still weeping, he shouted: "If you come back from New York I'm going to kill you!" Five minutes earlier she had whispered to me: "Do you think he'll kill me?" and I had smiled and said: "Of course not." So his parting shot was not calculated to comfort her. It's some consolation to know that when she returns it will no longer be Ramadan.

Before Mrabet went home he excused himself to me for his outburst, saying: "She wants to drive me crazy. She kept saying I was a thief. Can she prove it? Does she have a witness?" It's pretty absurd to consider that all this was ostensibly about a bunch of roses that got put into the wrong receptacle, or so it would have seemed to an onlooker. In reality Mrabet has a bad conscience, and when a Moroccan feels guilty, he attacks.

May 5

The spider, after having been absent for the better part of a week, has suddenly decided to return to its regular nocturnal haunt, where it stays the whole time, day and night. It seems to me there's something suspect about this. The identical spot where it used to spend its nights, yet I'm not convinced that it's the same insect. It looks smaller and feebler than before. If it's a different individual, what has happened to the original, and why does this one hang exactly in the place where that one hung? An entomologist could probably give a completely unexpected and satisfying explanation.

May 6

Rodrigo left last night for a week's trip through the south. Since he's never been to Tinerhir I suggested he go there from Marrakech and continue eastward to Er Rachidia and then north to Midelt. He seemed determined to go over the Tizi N'Test to Taroudant, which he already knows. If he does that, he'll probably not go to Tinerhir.

The cassette of the concert in Nice last month, which I thought was lost because it had been removed from the envelope, turned out to have merely been confiscated by the censors because it was not declared. Abdelouahaid brought it to me this afternoon. The two-piano works were execrable—worse than I'd expected. Some of the songs not bad. The solo pianist managed, by dint of rushing like a cyclone through everything, to hit more wrong notes than right ones. Why won't pianists look at tempo markings? My suspicion is that they imagine they make more of an impression by playing as fast as they can, regardless of the metronome indication, like typists eager to show how many words per minute they can turn out.

May 7

From time to time when we're driving in the country, Abdelouahaid recounts something that happened or is said to have happened in a village we're passing through. Some of the stories are of the sort that it would never occur to me to invent. Others are banal, like this one. A couple facing increasingly hard times in their tchar. Last few chickens die of an epidemic. If we want to go on living we'd better leave now while we can still walk. With the girl enceinte, they start walking along the trails, and come to Bab Taza at night. A man sees them and realizes they are from the country, asks them if he can help them. The girl says: "We're looking for a place." "A house?" "Yes." "Come. I'll show you a good house." Takes them to a house he has just bought with the intention of selling it. Before they go in the husband asks the price. (He is entirely without a guirch.) The house is completely empty. After they have been shown around, they ask if they may spend the night in it, and give the owner the reply in the morning. He agrees. They bid one another goodnight, and the owner leaves them there. The husband goes to the well to draw water for washing and taking supper. Sees a small wooden box floating in the shadows down there. When he brings it up, it is locked. He and his wife decide that the owner knows nothing about it. They open it. Full of banknotes. In the morning when the owner comes, they agree to buy the house, which they do with half the amount in the box. Abdelouahaid loves stories about hidden treasure, which are invariably without interest.

◆ ——————————————————————— ◆

Notebook: Speeches

January 13, 1987
This is a day for decision. Our problems are clear: the collapse of agriculture; high rural unemployment except in areas immune to international pressures (we have worked to overcome the loss of factory jobs to overseas competition); increasing numbers of poor children with uncertain futures; too many unskilled workers.

What may not be so clear is our opportunity, indeed our obligation, to continue to prepare our people for and move our state toward the twenty-first century.

We have put off progress in favor of survival.

Survival *requires* progress.

May 16, 1987
When John Kennedy was running for president in 1960, we all divided up and fought our own campaign at my junior high school. Kennedy made a deep impression on me with his call for an Alliance for Progress with Latin America. The message I got, as I remember it today, is that there were millions of poor people down there suffering. Their kids have a right to a future. We're a big, rich, strong country, and this is something that we ought to do because it's the right thing to do. The message we should be preaching today is that we need to do something about this Latin American debt crisis, and the growth rate of the Latin American economy, not just for all those people, the people who nearly three decades ago tacked little pictures of John Kennedy up on the mud walls of their houses, but for ourselves too.

June 21, 1987
I think what you should insist on from every politician in this country, without regard to party, is that you want hardheaded problem-solving which recognizes the legitimacy of the needs of the cities.

July 15, 1987

For thirteen years the people of this state have made it possible for me to be in the public life, but they have not made it *easy* for me to be in the public life. I have been in fifteen separate election contests—as far as I know, more than any other state officeholder in the United States—subject to more rigorous scrutiny and tougher campaigns, more brutal battles than anyone else that I can think of.

The only thing I or any other candidate has to offer in running for President is what's inside. That's what sets people on fire and gets their confidence and their votes, whether they live in Arkansas or Wisconsin or Montana or New York. That part of my life needs renewal.

The other, even more important reason for my decision is the certain impact that this campaign would have had on our daughter. If I had been gone six or seven days a week, think of the impact on an only child. I made a promise to myself that if I was ever lucky enough to have a child, she would never grow up wondering who her father was. And to be perfectly selfish, the thought of missing all those softball games, soccer games, plays at the school, and consultations with teachers mortified me.

When I came home from New Hampshire I was happy, flying like a kite, because of the reception I'd gotten. I really believed that if I could have entered the race right then, within three or four weeks I could have been in second place in New Hampshire. But I could not bring myself to make those phone calls. I made more calls yesterday to tell people I wasn't going to run for President than I had made on any single day since I had been looking at this. I couldn't bring myself to close the deal.

August 19, 1987

One of the reasons I lost in 1980 was that I was responsible for a highway-improvement program which was very controversial. We built a lot of good roads and then people drove over those roads to find the polling places to vote against me. I became the youngest former governor in the history of the republic!

I was driving down one of those improved roads and I stopped at a little country gas station. I walked in and saw an old fellow in overalls.

He looked at me and said, "Aren't you Bill Clinton?"

I said, "Yes, sir."

"Do you know, fellow," he said, "I got eleven folks to vote against you in the last election, and I just loved it."

I asked him why.

He said, "I had to, Governor. You raised my car license fee."

"Now listen," I explained, "this county you live in had the worst roads in the state. We had to send emergency vehicles down here to pull cars out the mud! We had to fix those roads."

He told me he didn't care—that he didn't want to pay for it.

I decided to try a positive approach: "Well that's water under the bridge. Let me ask you this: would you ever consider voting for me again?"

He looked at me and grinned, "You know I would, because we're even now."

I was so excited that I found a pay phone, called my wife, and said, "We're running!"

Near the end of the election about a year later, I walked into a little country store in north Arkansas where the owner had a reputation of knowing what was going on. There was one man in the store drinking coffee, and he said, "Well, son, I voted against you last time, but I'm going to vote for you this time."

I was pleased and told him so, and I asked him why he voted against me last time.

He looked at me matter-of-factly and said, "I had to. You raised my car license fee."

"Well, why are you going to vote for me this time?" I asked.

He said, "Because you raised my car license fee."

I said, "Sir, I certainly don't want to insult you, but it doesn't make any sense to me for you to vote for me this time for the very reason you voted against me before."

He patiently explained, "Oh, son, it makes all the sense in the world. You may be a lot of things, Bill, but you aren't stupid. You're the very least likely one to ever raise that car license fee again. So I'm for you."

October 16, 1987

To me it's clear what's at stake in this presidential election. We are all going to the polls conscious for the first time as a country of the fact that the post–World War II era is over. A majority of us know that America does not dominate the world and will not dominate the world again, at least in the lifetime of anyone in this room.

People complain about the Japanese all the time, but every study that's been done—three in the last two years—on the Japanese system of trade says that if we tore down all of their trade barriers, last year's trade deficit would have been reduced by about 5 percent.

If growth rates in Latin America in 1986 had been what they were in 1978, our trade deficit would have been reduced by 20 percent—four times as much. By permitting Latin America to grow again, we ourselves can grow.

Everybody complains about the Japanese because we had a $60 billion trade deficit with them last year. That's true. We did, but do you know how much money the Japanese invested in this country last year? $100 billion. Without outside money, we are going to have to lower our standard of living today and tomorrow. We'll have to shift spending from consumption and investment to debt service.

I am not pessimistic about the future but I'm telling you we have run out this present string about as long as we can run it. This old dog won't hunt anymore.

I had a course in western civilization with a remarkable man, the late Carroll Quigley. Half the people at Georgetown thought he was a bit crazy and the other half thought he was a genius. They were both right. He said something I'll never forget. He said, "You've got to understand the essence of western civilization. The thing that got you all to this classroom today is the belief in the future. The belief that the future can be better than the present and that people will and should sacrifice in the present to get to that better future. That has taken man out of the chaos and deprivation that has been the condition of most human beings for most of human history. The one thing which will kill our civilization and our way of life is when people no longer have the will to undergo the pain required to prefer the future to the present. That's what got your parents to pay the expensive tuition to get you into this class. That's what got your country through two world wars in this century and a depression in between. That's what produced such unparalleled prosperity. That's what got you here today." Future preference. He said don't you ever forget that.

November 17, 1987

We have been experimenting with a program I'm very excited about, called HIPPY, which is an acronym for Home Instruction Program for Preschool Youngsters. The program was developed in Israel to help immigrant families, most of them poor, uneducated people coming into a highly educated society. Almost twenty years ago now, the Israelis developed a way to teach the mothers of three- and four-year-old kids to teach their children how to speak, think, and reason, to prepare them for kindergarten. They taught even illiterate mothers to do it.

Last February, 49 out of the 50 governors voted for a welfare reform policy which calls for changing the whole system of welfare from an income maintenance system to an education, training, and independence system. Welfare, as it exists today, was developed over fifty years ago for a society that no longer exists. Unfortunately, the problems which bring the parents to welfare are not addressed at all by the system which provides the check.

The real disincentive to work is not benefits, which have gone down 20 percent in real terms since 1973, but instead is the cost of child care and the loss of medical coverage for children if the job taken is a minimum wage job without health insurance.

This proposed package offers mothers a chance to become contributing citizens without being bad mothers. It offers them a chance to break the cycle of dependency.

January 19, 1988
Internationally, the governor's role is more important. Not long ago, you would be criticized at home if you went to Japan. Now you are criticized if you don't go.

In the only partisan fight we have had in years, the Democratic governors got mad because the President had sent out a fundraising letter on behalf of the Republican governors, while the Republicans were all anti-tax like Reagan. In fact, a higher percentage of Republican governors had raised taxes than Democratic governors! Our bipartisan fight arose because the President's letter ignored the decline in partisanship among the governors on the tax issue.

January 29, 1988
The longer I stay in this business, the more I think we should evaluate ourselves not in terms of what others are doing, but in terms of whether we're really making progress on the problems we have.

You read all the estimates on the number of adult illiterates. We need to know who these people are and where they are. Where do they live and how old are they? Are they in the work force or are they idle? Are they people who could do better if they learned to read? Are they people who could get a job for the first time if they learned to read?

February 9, 1988
I was asked last Sunday to go by and talk to a singles Sunday school class in my church. Most of the members are between twenty-three and thirty-eight, most of them business or professional people. The Sunday school lesson I gave them was about the conflict between the idea of progress and the certainty of death. Now, I don't want to get into the theological implications of it, but the basic point is that sometimes it's hard to keep going when you know that the sand's running out of the hourglass. Yet you still have a moral obligation to try to make tomorrow better than today. For a politician the equivalent of that dilemma arises as your term runs out.

GUY DAVENPORT

◆ —————————————— ◆

Journal

Protagoras sold firewood. Demokritos liked the way he bundled it for carrying, and hired him to be his secretary. Mind is evident in the patterns it makes. Inner, outer. To discern these patterns is to be a philosopher.

The caterpillar of the coddling moth feeds on the kernels of apples and pears.

Greek time is in the eye, anxious about transitions (beard, loss of boyish beauty). Hebrew time is in the ear (Hear, O Israel!). What the Greek gods say does not make a body of quotations; they give no laws, no wisdom. But what they look like is of great and constant importance. Yahweh, invisible, is utterly different.

The American's automobile is his body.

Camillus had asked for pure youths and the adjutant without a blink about-faced, looking wildly for a warrant officer. Pure youths, said the warrant officer. Clean, said the adjutant, scrubbed. Young means they won't have had time to sin with any volume. Say recruits who aren't up to their eyes in debt, fresh of face, calf's eyes, good stock. Washed hair. Take them to the flamen, who'll get white tunics on them, and clarify their minds for going into the *fanum* to bring the figure out, proper.

To sit in the sun and read Columella on how to plant a thorn hedge is a pleasure I had to teach myself. No, I was teaching myself something else, and the thorn hedge came, wisely, to take its place. They're longer-lasting than stone walls, and have an ecology all their own. Birds nest in them, and snails use them for a world. Hedgehogs, rabbits, snakes, spiders. Brier-rose, dog-thorn. There are some in England still standing from Roman times.

Being ought to have a ground (the earth under our feet) and a source. It seems to have neither. The Big Bang theory is science fiction. It may be that the expanding universe is an illusion born in physics labs in Paris, Copenhagen, and Berkeley. It is also too eerily like Genesis (being in a millisecond) and other creation myths. It is partly mediaeval, partly Jules Verne. From a human point of view, it has no philosophical or ethical content. It is, as a vision, a devastation, an apocalypse at the wrong end of time. It is a drama in which matter and energy usurp roles that once belonged to gods and angels. It is without life: brutally mechanical. It is without even the seeds of life, or the likelihood.

Store Valby: earliest record of agriculture in Denmark: naked barley, club wheat, einkorn, emmer wheat, and a seed of Galium.

Gibbon turns an idea in his fingers.

French regularity is kept alive as a spirit by turbulence and variation. Only a felt classicism knows novelty. Novelty in the USA is a wheel spinning in futility: it has no tangential ground to touch down and roll upon.

Je ne veux pas mourir idiot. French student demanding that Greek be put back in the curriculum.

The circumcision of gentiles in the USA is a cruel and useless mutilation. Michael Tournier in *Le Vent paraclète* likens it to removing the eyelids. It is an ironic turn of events. The circumcision of the Old Testament was a slicing away of the merest tip of the foreskin, the *akroposthion* as the Greeks called it. In the Hellenizing period of the first century CE (see Maccabees) the rabbinate changed over to total removal of the prepuce, to make a more decisive symbol. Gentiles began to circumcise fairly recently: a Victorian attempt, one among many, to prevent masturbation. (A. E. Housman was circumcised at thirteen.) It is done nowadays by parents so ignorant that they don't know it doesn't need to be done, and doctors, always ready for another buck, recommend it on hygienic principles. It is difficult to think of another such institutionalized gratuitous meanness, the brutal insensitivity of which enjoys universal indifference. A Tireisian conundrum: a male who has never known the sensuality of a foreskin, both for masturbation and for making love, cannot know what he has been so criminally bereft of.

If the Jews returned to cutting away the wedding ring's worth of flesh (as with Michelangelo's David, who has almost all of a foreskin, and as with Abraham, Isaac, and Jacob)—a nicely revolutionary recovery of archaic truth—perhaps American parents would quit agreeing to the mutilation of their children's bodies. But as long as Ann Landers et Cie. continue to idiotize the populace with a rancid puritanism, maiming boys will continue.

It is the saurian mind that has prevailed in our time. Apollo has been asleep for most of the century.

Klee's *Twittering Machine* is a parody of Goya's people out along a limb.

What is the difference between learning as a child and as an adult? There's such a thing as *re*learning. Nietzsche says that philosophy might take as its task the reconciliation of what a child has to learn and knowledge acquired, for whatever reason, in maturity. What's happening when children watch TV? Consciousness is an *ad hoc* response to a webwork of stimuli: intrusions, attractions, claims on one's attention, hurts, disappointments, insults, fears. The critical mind tries to keep its balance in stoic indifference. But turbulence aerates, renews a sense of balance.

The impotence of Andrew Wyeth is that he asks us to see with his eyes subjects about which he has made a decision, and, with the gratuitous meanness of his generation, isn't going to tell us what it is. There is no drama of seeing, as in Picasso and John Sloan. Wyeth makes us into an adventitious onlooker at something he, and only he, was privileged to see.

What got Kipling a bad name among Liberals is his intelligence, humor, and affection. These they cannot tolerate in anybody.

Sartre's idea of literature, the opposite of Pound's, is still within the category that includes Pound. The word "political" has a wholly different meaning in the USA than in France. Our politicians have no interest whatever in changing society, or of making life more liberal. How can they, with a people who have to be sat on, and with criminal exploitation ready to corrupt any liberal exploration of liberty? There is no reversal possible of American mediocrity, which will worsen until we have total depravity of the idea of freedom. There is no American business: only diddling the consumer. The Congress is as incompetent and irresponsible a squanderer of our money as the most loutish tyrant in history.

History is a matter of attention. Parkman was interested in the awful waste of energy in the (wholly unsuccessful) conversion of the Indian. Because he was so appalled by Catholic fanaticism in Canada, what he wrote is a history of reason in the New World.

Denmark begins at the SAS ticket counter, JFK, behind a contingent from Lake Wobegon whose problem is made more complex by a computer that's down. Waiting, I solve a problem of my own. The second floor of SAS is, as its sign in Danish says, the *other* floor. For years I've wondered why in the English ordinals there's the Latin *secundus* between *first* and *third*, the only Mediterranean intrusion into a sequence that's otherwise archaically North Atlantic. But the Danes count *first another third fourth*. Our *another* is *one other*, and the repetition of the *one* must have crowded so useful a word out of the ordinals, to be replaced with monkish, or military Latin.

English is a Romance language the way a porpoise is a fish and a bat a bird. English is the second, or other, language of Denmark, used among themselves with a fluency that is well along toward making it a dialect. A little babu: "fried chickens" on a menu. We do not (thank goodness) have the first hotel we called in Copenhagen, because "the booking have gone to Easter."

Danish, like Dutch, is English unmarried to French.

On Swedish TV, a children's program with a robot who has a spigot for a penis. Another sign that the Danes are a highly moral people who are unembarrassed by the facts of life. Also some comic books and posters you'd go to jail for owning in Kentucky.

Just as Denmark looks familiar, though we've not been here before, the Restaurant Cassiopeia on Nyhavn is wholly unthreatening, cozy, strangely familiar. I have the feeling that I've been trying all my life to get here. We have a table by an old-fashioned window of many small panes looking out on masts, rain, sixteenth-century buildings. We see that Danish cozy is our sense of cozy. Waitress very young, beautiful, friendly. Fish soup, terrine, veal, kidney. A pear and almond ice drenched in a liqueur. Bonnie Jean, the whizz at arithmetic, notes that our meal costs $80.

I buy a blue denim cap, very Danish student of the last century, and call it my Nietzsche cap, remembering that he ordered a Danish student's uniform when he learned that Georg Brandes was lecturing on him at the university here. Bonnie Jean counters by buying a Lutheran housewife's dress, demure, practical, and quite becoming.

The restaurants on Nyhavn are run by children. The cook at The Mary Rose, Ejnar, looks twelve, and the waiters are teenagers.

A profoundly *northern* feel to the graveyard where Kierkegaard and Hans Christian Andersen lie. Pale sunlight, wet conifers.

Sign in a barber shop: *Er taget til Spanien for at bekaempe Fascismen. Kommer straks.* Gone for the day to Spain to fight fascism. Back soon.

At the zoo, which Joyce and Nora once visited in the thirties, a little boy hugging a goat, said to me (I was photographing him), "I am cute, am I not?"

"Of course all young Danes are beautiful," Bonnie Jean says, "they drown the plain ones." It is apparently against the law to be plain, ill-natured, or sober.

The water birds we find in every pond are perhaps grebes. I name them "Bonnie's coot." They can run along the surface of water.

Along the pedestrian street, a young man seated on a four-wheeled contrivance which several friends are pushing. His virile member is out through his fly (silly and bemused look on his face) and erect. One of the friends carrying a sign: *Ja, jeg skal gifte!* Oh boy, do I ever need a wife! They're all gloriously drunk. B.J. is a bit disturbed by so much drunkenness: I point out that they're not drivers. They're wonderfully on foot. Earlier, two twelve-year-old boys so drunk that they have to walk hugging to keep from falling down.

Music everywhere. Children playing Mozart and Telemann on the pedestrian streets. B.J. gives all the change she has to a four-year-old tot who was making a hash of something Baroque on her Suzuki fiddle.

The Sweet Pan Steel Drum Band.

Lunch at the train station in Roskilde, far superior to the best food and service to be had in Lexington. Roast pork, red cabbage, wine, potatoes, banana split.

Bonnie Jean, of fellow Americans in Elsinore: "Travel is very narrowing."

B.J. insists that I buy a Danish Scout manual, and a pair of important-looking straps, blue, lettered *Spejdersport*.

B.J. does not keep a journal, but asks that I put in this one:
   Honesty is the best deceiver.
   Questions are a way of avoiding information.

Rietveld's chair at the Louisiana Museet. It is much smaller than I'd thought, and looks comfortable.

Years ago I wrote in *Tatlin!* that the Baltic is pewter and silver in its lakes of glare. It is.

Helsingør. Coffee and pastry shop, center of local social life. Suddenly all very Bergman: an accurately scaled midget across from me, nattily dressed, and with a woman who seems to be made up for a Strindberg role, dress about 1880, but obviously not all there. Housewives talk about her behind their hands. Eventually a rough sailor type, red-bearded and in a pea-jacket, comes and takes her away. She rolls her hips and eyes as she leaves. The midget continues his coffee. No sign of a circus in town.

A long walk through the deerpark at Klampenborg, sharing Granny Smith apples, children orienteering in all directions (a little boy greets us with "Oh, yes! Oh yes!"). The landscape is a Constable. Immense sense of peace, love, togetherness.

Boy, with mother, rich dark hair, pink scarf, nautical jacket, gray canvas trousers, big sneakers. Relation with mother wholly un-American: more like kids falling in love on a first date.

Bonnie invents "Holstein cat" for the bishops's Webster and Thorvaldsen, whom we speak to every day. The bishop of Copenhagen is also bishop of Greenland: part of his parish.

The statue of Kierkegaard in the garden of the National Library is Lincolnesque, noble, grandiose (seated, with a Bible propped against his chair), writing. The newer, triumphant statue in the circle of theologians around the palace church, is of Kierkegaard the dandy, in tight britches, foppish.

Little Jack Horner, who sat in a corner. (The *Horner* is the Danish *hjornet*, corner.)

Where it was, there must you begin to be. There are no depths, only distances. Memory shuffles, scans, forages. Freud's geological model implies that last year is deeper in memory than last week, which we all know to be untrue. The memories we value are those we have given the qualities of dream and narrative, and which we may have invented.

An American evangelist on Swedish TV reminds me that kinship is one of the most primitive of tyrannies. Our real kin are those we have chosen.

Desire is attention, not gratification of the self. The ego is the enemy of love. Happiness is always a return. It must have been out of itself to be anything at all.

If timespace, then how does time move and space stand still? Time moves through us; we move through space.

County as the satiric unit: Coconino, Bloom, Yoknapatawpha, Raintree, Tolkien's shire, "the provinces."
    Tragedy: house, castle, room. Romance: sea and open country. City: comedy.

The hope of philosophy was to create a tranquillity so stable that the world could not assail it. This stability will always turn out to be a madness or obsession or brutal indifference to the world. Philosophy is rather the self-mastery that frees one enough of laziness, selfishness, rage, jealousy, and such failures of spirit, to help others, write for others, draw for others, be friends.

Athens (which could not tolerate Socrates) and Jerusalem (which could not tolerate Jesus) come down in history as the poles of the ancient world (for Proust, Arnold, Joyce, Zukofsky). If these two long traditions have fused, they have no genetic line. Judaism is closed, is itself exclusively; Athens is diffused and lost.

This paradox: that where exact truth must be found the only guide thereto is intuition, the soul moving like the animal it is by a sixth sense, which Heracleitus called smell, thinking of the exquisite nose of his dog. All the senses must be opened and trained, exercised, clarified.

Psychology is the policeman of the bourgeoisie, enforcing middle-class values with as bogus a science as alchemy or palm-reading. Foucault was right on this point.

In Kafka other people are too close and God is too far off.

ANNIE DILLARD

◆———————————————————◆

Notebook

CAVU: pilot acronym: ceiling and visibility unlimited.

"Let us not pretend to doubt in philosophy what we do not doubt in our hearts." —C. S. Pierce.

Penguins have very long legs. Their skin hangs low. "The birds normally keep their knees folded up under their wings"—to conserve heat. They also have square pupils. —Paul Siple, *90° South*.

Nine of diamonds: the curse of Scotland. On the back of a nine of diamonds, an English Duke wrote the orders for the killing of Scottish wounded.

"Our standard image of a human being is that of a person about ten feet away." —F. N. Spindler, *The Sense of Sight*.

"Following the Custer battle, the paper money found on the soldiers was turned over to the youngsters, who made play tipis out of it." —R. and G. Laubin, *The Indian Tipi*.

serein: "a very fine rain falling after sunset from a sky in which no clouds are visible."

"In Mundugumor, people copulated in gardens belonging to someone else, just to spoil their yams." —M. Meade, *Blackberry Winter*.

"It is beautifully cool and, above all, quiet in the novitiate conference room. One of the novices, Frater B—, laughed and laughed more and more week after week until he finally laughed all day long and had to go home. I am told that once, before one of the singing classes, he laughed so much he rolled on the floor. Life here is funnier than we think. And now it is, once again, quiet." —Merton, *Conjectures of a Guilty Bystander*.

inventio: "a day when something significant connected with a saint, perhaps his tomb, is discovered." St. Stephen's day is Dec. 26; his *inventio* is Aug. 3.

glabella: the space between the eyebrows.

"This Mr. Harte died on 15th May, 1745, and missed many events of interest by doing so." —Andrew Lang.

"One of the dominant wasps here was Anoplius apiculatus, a pretty little red-and-black sprite covered with glaucous pubescence." —Howard Ensign Evans, *Wasp Farm*.

"Though the soul is born clean, man gradually learns to convert it into a chalice in which he mixes his own brand of poison." —Heschel, *A Passion for Truth*.

the umbo at the apex of an orange—a boss or protuberance, as on the scales of pine cones.

"The time of geometry has come to an end, the time of art is over, the time of philosophy has come to an end. The snow of my misery has thawed. The time of growing has ended. Summer is here and I do not know whence it came. It is here. Now is the time to write of many things on which I have ruminated for years, namely of blessed life . . ." —Paracelsus, quoted in Evan S. Connell.

"Spring tells me I have not had enough." —John Hay.

"Cyrus McCormack invented the raper, thus putting hundreds of men out of work." —student paper.

"Poe argued that a poem's excitement can last half an hour 'at the utmost.'" —H. Rosenberg, *The Anxious Object*.

A stone of contention: Pliny, in *Natural History*, said that if a dog had once held in his mouth a particular stone, that stone would always cause contention, wherever it might be.

"A true method . . . tells its own story, makes its own feet, creates its own form. It is its own apology." —Emerson.

Emerson thought he wrote best in sentences; he called his paragraphs collections of "infinitely repellent particles."

"Hear what the morning says and believe that." —Emerson, quoted in Matthiessen, *American Renaissance*.

"The only real infidelity is for a live man to vote himself dead." —Melville, quoted in Matthiessen.

"As Nietzsche knew, all claims to copy nature must lead to the demand of representing the infinite." —Gombrich, *Art and Illusion*.

"All that has been said but multiplies the avenues to all that remains to be said." —Melville, from Matthiessen.

goldbeater's skin: ox intestines.

"Nonhuman primates learn, but they do not teach." —John Pfeiffer, *The Emergence of Man*.

"A hunting-gathering society probably provides more free time for all its members than any other type of society yet evolved." —Pfeiffer.

"One cannot be too scrupulous, too sincere, too submissive before nature . . . but one ought to be more or less master of one's model." —Cézanne, *The World of Cézanne*.

"If all this be not post-Homeric, what is?" —Andrew Lang, *The World of Homer*.

"The limelight . . . which to gaze into is to go blind." —Frederich Buechner.

"Properties we don't notice are like ideas we have not had. They leave no gap in the world; it takes information to specify gaps." —Ulric Neisser, *Cognition and Reality*.

"Let us assemble facts in order to obtain ideas." —Buffon, quoted in Augustin Fabre, *The Life of J. Henri Fabre*.

"Lucidity is the sovereign politeness of the writer. I do my best to achieve it." —Fabre, *Souvenirs Entomologiques*.

Ipse fecit nos et non ipsi nos: It is he that hath made us, and not we ourselves.

chrissoms: infants who die before baptism.

"Would that our writing had been as fine as our lunches!" —Ben Hecht, *A Child of the Century*.

"What I want is the income that really comes in of itself, while all you have to do is just to blossom and exist and sit on chairs." —Robert Louis Stevenson, letter to Henry James, in *Henry James and Robert Louis Stevenson*.

"The ruthlessness of all aesthetes has always impressed me more than their sensitivity." —Laurens van der Post, *The Night of the New Moon*.

"Augustine said of Varro, 'that he read so much that it was a marvel he ever had time to write anything, and wrote so much that it was difficult to see how he found time to read.' " —Robert D. Richardson, Jr., *Henry Thoreau: A Life of the Mind*.

LAWRENCE DURRELL

◆ ——————————————————————— ◆

Endpapers and Inklings

Words falling out of my
vocabulary like teeth out of a head—Proper names escaping,
falling leaves a memory papering the parks.

Invited once to pronounce upon
the nature of poetry to a university audience he was suddenly
overcome with despair at so many babyish *tête de curé* and found
himself beginning, "Hands up all of you who have ever helped wash
and lay out a corpse?" Nobody. Complete silence. He went on:
"Hands up all of you who have watched babies being born?" Again
nobody. "Now don't you see how society protects us against these
two great basic experiences which are the workshop of poetry. It
should be the basis of all our education psychically speaking.
But they put screens round the dying to prevent us from sharing
their triumph. Yet death is the workshop, the foundry where poems
are hammered out, full of the compassion engendered by a hopeless
truthfulness—impermanence is the key!

She had an unrepentant defiant look. It made one
wonder what she had been doing.

She did nothing with such felicity that she
provoked senseless and frantic activity in
those around her.

Advice to his friend Epfs:
"First paint the rose in its physical form as
a pure flower. Next forget the physical form
and paint the perfume. Next forget everything
and paint the idea of the rose—any rose.
Remember that the rose was not created by

nature but by man—a compilation of
tensions like a wine or a water-color. Once
you become a painter you realize that everything
about it is imaginary except the thorns.

Her first glimpse of the French
gave her a strange impression: — café in Le Havre. Kept receiving
glass after glass of Armanac from a silent gentleman in the
corner. How generous the French are, so she thought, but the
waiter explained that the old man has just successfully got
rid of a tape-worm. *"Ce matin la tête a passé—Ça se fête,
quoi!"* It was drinks all round.

Whose was the fanged smile
the love capsules of glittering teeth.

To think in French and write in English
Gives prose grain and poetry sheen.
To do the opposite gives poetry pith
And prose transcendence—every word
Should be drenched in heavenly bias.

Freud
"Vertretung"
Trancendence so deeply
suspect to the scientific
determinist.
Reader, be patient a moment
the incoherence is only
Apparent. The floating
Fragments will all slot
Into each other and cohere.

Our missionaries carried the plague to the
Orient where abundant nature evolved it.

To be dismembered by pixies or defenestrated
by ancient earls—the Duke of Compos Mentis

perhaps? In the Paris of his youth Foucaulet,
Barthes, Sartre, Leiris were regarded with
reverence as *sages*. He could never understand
it. As for Lacan—what a frenzy of ignoble
parody, rhetoric of self-aggrandizement!
All these were, compared to an artist, what a
promising post-office official is to a love letter
he unwittingly sends. Rapidly cooling corpses
of reason.

A young whore smoking a pipe in Raspail with
speed and venom. Violet eyes.

"Do you remember when you paid me
before making love? It was wildly exciting.
In Avignon. At heart every girl wants to be
paid." Simone.

I would like to be called "Your beatitude,
Stalk about in a crimson-lined hood
With rich people addicted to food,
and my back hair done up in a snood,
By the lowest of morals insist.

The orgasm is the point where poetry and
mathematics marry to create whole
futures. The poet is overwhelmingly normal.

The trifling immortality of a posh gravestone
With a cracker motto aloft.

We sit around like thumbless wonders
listening to the sages chuckle.
The philosopher's pig quite unaware of
approaching death.
If life is served art is served and love is
content
Abandon Poke all ye who enter here!
The one Placebo which really does
the trick—love, i.e. surrender.

The two ugly witches Combustion
and Traction rule our world. (Crossing himself he muttered
"Heat over mass equals light. Amen!") and so saying climbed on
to her body praying that the sutra would work. Later on during
the summer he felt himself becoming at last incapable of any
more grief! He started residing as appropriately as the fruit
of a poem in this new griefless state. For so long he had
unconsciously thought that getting old and dying were things
that happened to others! The shock was so great he burst out
laughing, then grew rueful.

Just to complicate matters woman is
born awake and man asleep. After she has woken him with her
kiss he puts her to sleep in another dimension—the fifth: which
opens into futurity. History is born when the couple's love is
in phase, their orgasms simultaneous and wired to sound in
synchomesh. Woman loves the personality of the man—in it she
"reads" the infant she will create and awaken. He loves the
nature of woman, she is his mother. She decodes his flesh, he her
heart. The bazaars of the affect unite. The orgasm is the heart's
pacemaker, the blood's timepiece. Our knowledge of a chronicity
derives from the womb-imprinted rhythms.

Modern poetry written on a
pinball machine. For subject the great gorgonzola
of sex, what else?

Love's bargain basement has men and
to spare, she thought with all the ingenuity
of remorse.

Christianity is a Jewish dilemma involving freedom.
Unrecycled thinking is what is new.

I left Paris in order to hear myself think.
*Il n'y a plus de femmes—ils sont tous
des chariots de fromage.*

Frost in January minus 20 for a week. Dead birds
frozen on the branch—they fall with the first

thaw like ripe fruit—death-ripened. We shall all
end like them—just a stain in the snow.

An ant can envisage a sugar lump as a
whole but can only carry it away grain
by grain. Thought.

Perfumed chequebooks for millionaires.

How to stop the terrible sobbing in the night?
I have looked through every room in the house.

One good thing: there's lots of room in death
No overcrowding that I can see
And no interminable queue
It's but a step, fall into nothingness
Soft as the wool of the Lamb
To discover who I am.

Entered the new griefless state
Coming at last to terms with fate.

Plenty leads to abstinence—Inside every
ogre there is an ascetic eager to fast.

Entering old Provence by the winding roads, the only ones,
down the long corridors of cool planes—diving from
penumbra to penumbra of shade, as if from pool to dark pool,
stark icy in comparison with the outer sunshine and hard-
metaled blue sky. Then at Valence the olives and the
mulberry and the tragic splash of unique Judas. Then as
you advance, coming to meet you, like a signature at the
end of a seive, the steady orchestral drizzle of cicadas
—such strange sybilline music and such a wonderful biography,
too scanty of time, so long underground in the dark east.

                              He was a wholly spontaneous
man, or so he liked to think, and he often laughed

so hard that his false teeth flew out into his lap—
a special form of wit you might say. Gilpin was the
name. Haberdasher of East Dulwich.

Good and evil?
Oh they exist but not in those terms with their
heavy self-righteous attitude. Say rather
the fruitful the enriching against the
counterproductive.
What is that?
The counterproductive is all that refuses
to evolve, to flow, to realize itself by
its transfer into compost for the future.

The novel was invented for the ladies to kill time,
And time was invented to kill the novelist.

How to define the XX century? We are living
out the abjectness of Jesus reincarnated
in Chaplin.

A jaw full of porcelain fangs. The Marseille smile.

He walked about with a mesmerized air,
an air of surprise as if he had just
ejaculated accidentally.

India outstares you—but when you see the
third eye and it winks back you know
you have reached a norm. You are overwhelmed by
                the obvious.
The poetic stance enables one to depict
rogue nature in the plenitude of its
ambiguity—loaves and fishes really
feeding—placebos really healing—the
whole tapestry of the contingent reality.

In my sleep (Oct. 15, 1985) heard the
shrieks of Egyptian pleureuses in a Cairo

street and the wonderful warm bulbous
voice of Dylan reciting from Milk Wood!

The function of religion is to increase our
impatience with our minds.

Poetry—the electricity of distress runs through
the language, invades the syntax.

A poet specializing in the obvious I find nature
full of good sense because it could not be otherwise
than it is: this is the difference between it and
man. Choice.

Greeks found Roman games with sacrifices abhorrent
Their plays were therapies of group identity.
The Romans' were plays of morality and situation.
Greeks' subject were humans in their godly aspect
as destinies.
Romans' were about people and right and wrong.

On Jack the Ripper's tee-shirt the legend: I
am a double agent.

Surprised to see that while his hands made
preparation for suicide his brain had
started to formulate a poem of praise
and fulfillment and bliss toward the universe.
Renunciation and repletion, rejection and
fulfillment—both beckoning him! Nero.

The poetic flashpoint comes where the
meaningless meets the sublime.

Women as gun-bearers of the midnight safari.

The function of art is to enthrall and in
doing so to change, to instruct, to

encourage a new deal of the old cards
which will influence in the direction
of freedom from distress, encouragement of
happiness, well-being.

Jesus had to wait for Freud before he could
realize the gorilla in himself.

Reading the sad biography of TSE in London yesterday
I reflected on the fact that what united us instantly was
when I mentioned my esteem for Laforgue and said that in
him I recognized myself as an artist for whom the whole of
life was a steady daylong nightlong battle against suicide.
Battle against those overwhelming waves of meaningless of
which S. spoke, and then V. who said, "*Il faut se laisser
mourir, il me semble. Pendant des mois et des mois on
tourne autour du pôt! Puis on opte!*"

Suicide the only unforgettable experience.

Whenever I count my blessings I begin with you,
The love bite of whisky shared
In a blue tumbler with a girl in a saffron dressing gown.

Was overheard to say in a low
decided tone "I believe in asparagus."

"I knew she loved me by her attitude to
artists—she woke me at six with a
phone call, arriving almost at once
in a taxi with a bottle of champagne
to tell me 'Borges is dead—I didn't
want you to hear the news from anyone
else but me.' "

The novel, hanging about
waiting to be cinemized.

GERALD EARLY

◆ ———————————————————— ◆

Digressions

Everything's allowed inside oneself.

—LOUIS-FERDINAND CÉLINE

March 28, 1988

And so Jesse Jackson has won the Michigan primary and all the political pundits and pollsters are left aghast, faced with a horror they cannot comprehend and which they did not believe possible: a black man may receive the Democratic nomination for the presidency, a black man has to be taken seriously as a national political figure. It is a sign, this failure of the pundits to assess Jackson correctly, of how expertise and professionalism in this country is nothing more than a mask for an ignorant or, worse yet, a half-ignorant opinion stated with the glib guile of authority. The gestalt of knowledge in our society is a white man sitting in a plush book-lined office, computer terminal on his desk, holding forth for reporters from television and the newspapers, the uniquely contrived hybrid of scholar and mountebank. How can we now predict that Jesse Jackson cannot be nominated and that he cannot become president? We have never had a black mount a serious campaign of such magnitude before. What is the precedent to guide the experts here? The fact that it is virtually impossible for a black to become a third base coach in baseball or a head coach in professional football? But politics is not a game of skill, despite the wins and losses, but the virtuosic rendition of a set of overly familiar images. If the pundits and pollsters, if the party officials had been more knowledgeable of American social and cultural history, Jackson's success would not have come as a surprise, indeed, it would and should have been foreseen and confidently predicted. It should be realized that Jackson's force is his enactment of the myth of the American Joseph, prince in an alien land.

It was to be expected after 1984 that blacks, for two reasons, would back Jackson more heavily in 1988. First, blacks felt that they gained nothing for their loyalty at the 1984 Democratic convention, a loyalty that does indeed date back as far as FDR. When the massacres of the McGovern candidacy in 1972, the Carter candidacy of 1980, and the Mondale candidacy of 1984 occurred and the traditional white Democratic coalitions left the party to vote Republican, blacks stood by the losers. Whites could be romanced away by an appealing conservative Republican, so blacks argued, but we have remained through thick and thin; a steadfastness which has been a two-edged sword for the white Democratic leaders, for they fear that it has been loyalty from black voters which has driven whites away. If that has been the case, it is not the fault of black voters, nor is it their burden to assuage whites that they will vote as a dependable bloc but not act as a special interest. Second, Jackson was much more appealing to blacks than any white who might decide to run with the possible exception of Ted Kennedy, as black attachment to that name rivals their attachment to the names Lincoln and King. The groundswell message was clear to black politicians and ward leaders well before the primary season: blacks generally wished to empower their vote and voice by voting for Jackson. And there were to be no more sellouts as there were in 1984. (Many blacks I talked to thought Jackson should not have capitulated in 1984 to Mondale which, in hindsight, would appear to anyone to have been an horrendous move guaranteed to shut him out of the party forever and to set back the possibility of a black seriously running for president for maybe another twenty years.) The sudden death of Chicago's black mayor, Harold Washington, which resulted in an entire issue of *Jet* magazine being devoted to him, (although no comparable honor was given James Baldwin, a much more important historical and cultural figure; but one has to expect that kind of Philistinism from Johnson Publications), simply galvanized the national black masses to Jackson even more. The bourgeois sensibility, symbolized by Bill Cosby and *Ebony* magazine, was solidly behind Jackson. There was no split this time in the black community over the issue of whether he could be elected. So, we have the nationalist dream of blacks being realized in Jackson's run: all classes of blacks united on the Black Star Line to the White House; for blacks have always wished for some strong leader to unite them. Of course, such unity means that ethnicity, at last, becomes the political and social, psychological and metaphysical refuge that blacks desperately wish it to be. And it is so hard to have ethnicity mean anything anymore in this country which absorbs the novelty of difference like a sponge. No serious criticism was ever presented about a Jackson candidacy, for to criticize him was tantamount to being an enemy of the race or, put in a bourgeois way, an enemy to the advancement of the race. And Jackson is, above all else, a preacher, and black Americans are among those people in this country who still believe that ministers have something to say that is actually worth listening to. It is their historical and cultural legacy: the church and ministers have led them to freedom and to an uneasy, often tragic, if profound, citizenship.

But what of Jackson's ability to attract whites? He could not do so in 1984 because he seemed too much a black candidate, hanging around Louis Farrakan and all that. Now he runs as a liberal and a Populist. And that change accounts for a good deal. It is obvious that what the experts and party bigwigs really fear is not that Jackson is "unelectable"; they do not fear him losing. How could they as a loss gets him out of the way. They fear the possibility that he may win in November and that he could attract whites' votes, that a black politician may be able to speak to and for whites. But there is, undeniably, a decidedly distasteful aspect to this. The liberals and blue-collar workers who voted for Jackson and who will deny that race is the reason are actually supporting him for no other reason than race. Suppose Jackson were white with the same credentials, the same ministerial garb, the same message of, as *The New Republic*, which is now not too far removed for *The National Review* and can be taken just as seriously which means not seriously at all, labeled it, "negative Populism." To be sure, by this point of the springtime in Michigan, this candidate would certainly not be around. Such a candidate would have been hooted out, really, distrusted because of his being a minister, because he smacked too much of being a true demagogue. In other words, the only type of politician who can seriously espouse liberalism in this country is now black. Everyone can believe the sincerity of his message because he is, after all, black and the burden of blackness in this country has been that it is tied to the liberalization of the franchise, to the growth and enlargement of our understanding of the citizen, to the expansion of our conception of humanity. Jackson has this cultural weight which he can use to his advantage. Moreover, he is a civil rights leader, which more deeply authenticates his liberalism than anything else: liberalism and civil rights having become synonymous. So the white who votes for Jackson wishes to express freedom from race consciousness while actually acting inevitably and predictably from the cultural compulsions of race consciousness. We have had eight years of a president whom we would not criticize for fear of facing a truth about why he was elected that we could not bear. Can we afford another such president whom we are reluctant to criticize even as a candidate? Or worse, can we afford a president whom we would wish to destroy for fear of facing a truth about why he was elected that we could not bear? Moreover, how much more of this simplistic Populism can we stand? Are Jackson's facile answers any more serviceable than Reagan's, or do liberals condemn senseless political chatter only from dumb white conservatives? In 1972 George Wallace won the Michigan democratic primary and I wouldn't be surprised if some of the whites who voted for him then voted for Jackson this time around. I suspect at times that Populism is a blind behind which the oligarchy can operate as well as any other.

Jackson reminds one so much of the narrator in Ellison's *Invisible Man*, the southern kid who wanted only to be a black leader and to make rousing speeches which he did, much, ultimately, to his regret. And it is that truculent opportunism and obsessive self-mythmaking that makes Jackson so typically the American confidence man, so seductive as a politician, and so intriguingly ambiguous, if somewhat fraudulent, as a true leader. And so blacks respond that the whites who are running for the Democratic nomination have nothing better to offer and so it is the case. But mediocrity in a black man is not excused simply because we have been for years drowning in white mediocrity passing itself off as merit. But one has to admire Jackson endlessly, the striking mixture of delirium and endurance which mark his tireless campaigning, the brazen egotism and courage to run for such an office and know that he will be the target of more right-wing racist nuts than all the white candidates in history put together; the wiliness that can give credence to such a slogan as "economic violence"—and politics in America has come down to nothing but a series of slogans and gestures of leadership and abilities, not rhetoric, which would be acceptable, but the utter negation of discourse, an admission, a deep confession of futility on the part of those running: they have no answers to problems. They are all like the Invisible Man: they simply wish to give speeches and become leaders, give orders, act important, boss some underlings around. Economic violence is a completely meaningless phrase: what could it truly mean? and one can scrutinize: more jobs, more social programs, more legislation to protect the public from the onslaught of corporations, the redistribution of wealth in America. Who can say? But it sounds so much more forceful than anything anyone else is saying. And it does sound humane, a freshness which is compelling, since we have heard nothing humane from Reagan for eight years. In the end, Jackson's candidacy and our response to it is a signal that America is at the crossroads. The old regime, the old value system based on white male supremacy is breaking up and now, what will be the new cultural consensus? That is the hope, the only real attraction, of a Jackson presidency: that he can help us achieve a new consensus simply on the strength of who he is and not for what he says because Populism as a political message is dead. (Populism is just another form of the strange death of a romanticized America: the family farm died in 1900 or thereabouts; there has never been a chicken in every pot.) And the choice will be clear if he is nominated: more of the old way of the grotesque with the Republicans or something new, possibly a politics freed from the grotesque, with Jackson. Jackson symbolizes our ambivalence. Whites would love to see a black president, the symbolic leader, to end the old race bit once and for all. (And if a black is president it would seem to solve the race problem from a distance; one would still not have to have a black in one's home, one can still hate busing. Indeed, one can still hate blacks with an even greater justification because one can point to the black man in the White House and say, "I voted for him.") But whites are also afraid of what that united symbolism means: the black, symbolic of everything the white has wished to suppress while being everything that he has wished to reach, the paradoxical emblem of both his humanity and inhumanity; and the presidency, that seat of power from which the image of all other power extends. It is easy to say that a white who does not vote for Jackson on racial grounds is simply mirroring the confusion and terror that has become his cultural legacy, but those who wish to flee that heart of darkness by voting for him may, in the end, be spellbound by a greater confusion, entangled in a greater terror, spun by an even more wild frenzy.

March 25, 1988

> *There's a small hotel with a wishing well.*
>
> —RODGERS AND HART

We have passed still another piece of Civil Rights legislation and one wonders how long this ritual will continue. It seems as if we have adopted the position that if we cannot give the dispossessed money or something really useful, then we will shower them with rights that cannot possibly make a real difference in their lives. We ought to be disturbed by the fact that in our attempt to transcend categorizing human beings, we allow our government for humane purposes to categorize them so that in the effort to escape it all one is trapped, Kafkaesque, forever in a perfect labyrinth of nonsense that will not stop people from discriminating but only force them fill out more forms to justify it in their reportage to the government. And the madness of categorizing eventually hypnotizes those who have been victims of it. The deaf students at Gallaudet College rightly demand a deaf president at the cost of wrongly condemning a woman who had been chosen for the job simply because she was not. Is this the only way the oppressed can free themselves in the end, by expanding themselves in symbolic, token oppression? Moreover, ought we to understand human beings in some way other than as part of a category? Could we not make proper use of discrimination, approaching people because we know they are different, instead of insisting that they are the same? Or am I more sinning than sinned against because I can hear Beethoven and a deaf person cannot? It is a loss that cannot be taken lightly and my pity surely will not help but pretending it is not a loss does not help either. I personally am sick of being a "minority," sick of seeing meaningless statistics lumping me with Asians, Native Americans, Hispanics, and other folk on the idiotic basis of not being white (why not lump us together on the basis of not being birds or reptiles?), sick of seeing ads in *The Chronicle of Higher Education* where colleges request vita for their minority vita banks when they have no intention of hiring any blacks—the minority we're really talking about here—at all, which is why they want your vita instead of you; thus I hereby sign off and break off all pledges that I have in that line. I cannot even recall God naming me man. If He or She did, I have forgotten because it happened so long ago. In returning to the subject of expansion, what about the terrific expansion of government powers under the new Civil Rights bill? Are liberals no longer wary of that? I, like Thoreau and Jefferson, have a tremendous distrust of giving the government more powers when it has yet to prove it can handle the ones that it has. Do we really want to expand government intrusion in the field of education, which this bill does, when the government has made such a mess of public and private education that one can only dream of the day when it will get out once and for all? It is a bad business to expand government powers even with the best and most humane intentions unless the government is going to protect us from excessive and unfair taxes, from having to pay for our own health care, from saddling our young with staggering student loans while attempting to get an education that by right ought to be free, from the savage disregard and contempt of corporations. Of course, this new bill will do none of these things; therefore, I cannot possibly see what good it is. It must be admitted that all this Civil Rights business is pure mystification, failing to get at the heart of the problem which is not the attempt to reshape the humanity of people, to get some people to be less racist, sexist, etc.; it is to reshape economic and political realities in this society so that racism and sexism and all the rest become impossible. But it is alas easier to shower people with rights than with money. To continue to pass bills is to admit that not only do these social ills exist but they are practically thriving out of control. In that sense, to pass the bills is to confess the uselessness of them. To get a government to do good is an enormous and largely wasted undertaking, but to try to make the leap from that to making a government be good is impossible. And that is what all this Civil Rights legislation is all about.

January 23, 1988

The talk in Stimage's barbershop this morning was the Mike Tyson–Larry Holmes fight of the night before which everyone in these crowded quarters either saw or heard.

"Holmes was just a shot fighter. Shouldn'ta fought that young boy. That boy just too strong to be messing with."

"Holmes shoulda been sticking and moving like he did them first three rounds. Holmes coulda beat that boy. You just gotta be slick to beat somebody like Tyson."

"Hell, that why Holmes got beat. You can't box Tyson. Holmes just shoulda traded with him from jump street. Just go on out there and say, 'Ok, mother jumper, you think you bad? Well, I'm bad too. Can't be two bad dudes here, so let see who gonna to the hospital.' "

"Man, Holmes just woulda got his butt kicked sooner is all."

"Hey, all I know is Tyson ain't gonna beat on Mike Spinks the way he beat on Holmes."

"Yeah, I'm for that. I'm all for the homeboy. Spinks gonna do better than a lot of folk think."

"You got that right. Especially a lot of white folk. Cause you know it's them white folk that's playing up Tyson big. All that old 'Iron Mike' stuff."

"He's the white folk's fighter. And you hear that sucker's voice?! Sound like Michael Jackson or somebody."

"Emile Griffith used to sound like that, real high. That's why Benny Paret called him a faggot and got killed in the ring."

"Voice sound higher than his old lady's, Robin Givens."

"What you think she marry that cat for, ugly as he is?"

"What you think? She marry him for that money. Cause now she is Mrs. Heavyweight Champion."

"All I know is that Mike Spinks gonna do a number on Tyson. He gonna whip old Iron Mike. Have to call him scrap iron when it's over."

When my barber said that, blowing cigarette smoke whose menthol fragrance reminded me of the comforts of home, a sweetness and longing, because my mother smokes, and that odor of her cigarettes when I was a boy was the pleasure of her company, I thought of an old fighter named Scrap Iron Johnson who once fought Joe Frazier. Indeed, I began to think about my days watching fights in Philadelphia at places called the Blue Horizon and the Arena. Whatever happened to Stanley "Kitten" Hayward who once beat Emile Griffith and gave the welterweight champ two tough fights? He was my favorite local fighter when I was making the transitions from boyhood to puberty to young manhood. I had heard that after his boxing career ended he spent some time in New York and Europe making pornographic films. That was just a rumor. Perhaps he is back in Philly. I always promise myself on my infrequent returns there that I will look him up. But it is never really good to see boyhood heroes in their afterlife. I remember what a favorite he was in Philadelphia, a town which could boast a number of good fighters during the Kitten's heyday, and how often he fought there. I would read every column in the papers about him by sportswriter Stan Hochman. He was never a very good fighter, only competent, sometimes good but never consistently so. He had some good nights and some bad ones. One of his best was when he fought Griffith at the Arena in Philadelphia on October 29, 1968. Gil Clancy, Griffith's manager, screamed that referee Zack Clayton did everything but hold Griffith's hands. As a loyal Kitten fan, I didn't see it that way and agreed wholeheartedly with the judges giving Kitten the win. He did not fare so well the following spring when he lost to Griffith in New York where, I suppose, (I don't remember), the referee was not Zack Clayton. The Kitten had other good nights such as when he beat Bad Bad Bennie Briscoe, another popular local fighter, in 1965 by decision. (Briscoe in 1966 put the finishing touches on middleweight George Benton's career by knocking him out in ten. The loss for us Philadelphia fight fans seemed like the end of one love affair and the beginning of another.) But Hayward had his bad nights as well: he lost to popular, one-eyed local favorite Gypsy Joe Harris in seven in 1966, to welterweight champ Curtis Cokes of Dallas in four in 1964 and he ended his career by being kayoed in one round by Eugene "Cyclone" Hart, a hot local prospect at the time, in 1971. He was not in condition for that fight, as I remember. He was, in fact, completely shot as a fighter by then. Of course, all the fellows in the shop preferred Spinks over Tyson because Spinks was the local fighter, although he no longer lives in St. Louis. Some began to recall the Spinks brothers' local amateur fights and the brutish, sad, absurd professional life of the older Leon. (Alas poor Leon, who brings to mind no one as much as Tommy "Hurricane" Jackson, whose one moment in the sun was the merciless beating he took at the hands of Floyd Patterson during a heavyweight title fight in 1957. He was knocked out in the tenth round. After his fight career, he wound up driving a gypsy cab. In January 1982, Jackson was hit by a car while trying to get into the cab. He seemed on the road to recovery in the hospital but suddenly in February took a turn for the worse and died after developing a blood clot on the brain. Patterson visited him while Jackson was in the hospital. I remember the papers getting a bit of mileage out of that. I keep thinking that Leon will wind up like that, bloody and bowed.) Naturally, for black locals, the "other" fighter, the "enemy" fighter is always white or someone who represents white interests. It is the only way they can symbolize the psychological stakes of the prizefight, capture the design of its adversity. Besides, Tyson is a fighter who always makes his opponents look very bad; they never fight their best fights against him. Muhammad Ali, on the other hand, to make a noteworthy comparison, was someone who brought out the best in his opponents, who seemed gracious and egotistical enough to say: I can beat you even if you fight your best fight. Fighters who bring out the worst in their opponents are not liked so well. Alas, one always waxes sentimental over the local fighter no matter how far from home he is or you are. It is the way of establishing a sense of place and time. And, inevitably, it is a way of saying goodbye to that same place, to that same time over and over again in a kind of homesick craze of wishing always that, as the line goes, you were here.

August 12, 1987

> *What a lovely world this world will be*
> *With a world of love in store.*
>
> —THE GERSHWIN BROTHERS

My father-in-law owns one of those big-screen televisions, the sort that looks like a small movie screen, and he owns one of those satellite dishes that were quite the vogue a few years for people who wanted to beat the high cost of cable until the cable stations fought back by scrambling their signals. The picture on the big television is kind of soft and blurry, not as sharp as a smaller television, and the color is not as true. In other words, my father-in-law now has a virtually useless dish and a television that has mediocre focus. Not a good deal, take it all around. One of the few unscrambled channels still available is the Playboy channel and I once spent the better part of a late night watching some of the programs. I can only recall something entitled *Electric Blue*, which seemed to consist of nothing more than the less outrageous portions of pornographic movies, thrown together in a messy, certainly plotless montage. But I suppose the original movies were plotless enough since one goes to see those sorts of things for the genitals in action and nothing else. And so it was here: pederasty, cunnilingus, group sex, huge breasts that wanted nothing more than to be free of clothing, thighs that wanted nothing more than to be open and receptive to other thighs or to someone's mouth. Of course, now and then, while watching, one wishes one too could be making love to the willing women on the screen or to any woman. But ultimately there seems a huge loneliness that surrounds pornography, the gestures, the bad acting, the dexterity of sex in these films where people are always maddeningly aroused and so easily fulfilled by an act which is paradoxical because it seems so fulfilling and we are so maddeningly aroused yet it does not fulfill and arousal is simply the inveterate flight from the abyss of boredom. Sometimes one is aroused because one is bored. Pornography reminds us that we live in a culture of seduction which, like the film that is misadvertised in Toni Cade Bambara's short story, "Gorilla, My Love," is simply the corruption of genuine allurement, or which finally denigrates our fantasies by making them boring, or, worse still, the obsessively fearful and self-conscious alternative to boredom. What makes pornography bad is not that it graphically shows sexual gyrating. How can someone truly be offended by that? What harm is there in people making love with abandon? Is it bad because they are male fantasies being rendered? But would the actual acts of lovemaking, would the pederasty, group sex and all the rest be any different if they were women's fantasies, would the men be any less objectified than they are in their own fantasies? No, what makes pornography bad is that gyrations are all it *can* render, all it wishes to render and so we have reduced the greatest intimacy, the power of that intimacy, to simply the seduction of taboo-breaking. To watch pornography in the end is simply to watch bad filmmaking and to be made to feel like the little girl in Bambara's story: that you have been cheated, that you are watching the wrong movie.

November 24, 1987

> *. . . and the blues has got my heart.*
>
> —LOUIS ARMSTRONG

Few activities can be as boring as attending academic conferences, listening to papers that you cannot understand, that are not worth the effort of trying to understand, that seem dutiful and unimaginative and filled with the current "hip" lingo of the business, terms like "megafiction" and "postmodern" and such. (As an uneducated friend once said to me, "Folks never know when they talking shit until somebody honest get an urge to wanna open some windows.") For in this too as in everything else in our culture one must be "current," even in the expressions of one's nostalgia. It is too much to listen to papers from people like yourself, unknowns who wish to be known, who are writing for job promotions, or to listen to the pomposity of the bigwigs, the stars, who have nothing to say that you did not already know and who do nothing but repeat the ideas of their latest book, which would not be so bad except the book has nothing much to offer. I know one thing: hardly any of these people would be here if they did not have to be; few would be writing if they could find another job which would pay them as poorly, give them as much fake prestige and free time, and that did not require "publications." It is unfortunate that people in this business are forced to talk endlessly when they have nothing to say and no way to say it, to borrow an old black saying.

I skipped most of the afternoon sessions to go to Harlem, just as I had skipped most of the morning sessions to walk in Central Park. I had been at the conference two days and had only heard one-half of one paper. I went to Harlem to do a spot of reading at the Schomburg, a place I had never set foot in before, despite being an Easterner, despite having gone to New York several times before, despite having been to Harlem.

Harlem looked worse than ever. I thought I was on a street somewhere in Bombay. So many unemployed people milling around, so many junkies milling around. A black woman, Jackie, who I believe is from Oregon, also attending the conference, accompanied me or rather

I accompanied her as she approached me about the idea of going there. We were both well-dressed and this made us the target of panhandlers and beggars. One man was particularly insistent: "Aren't you a Christian?" he asked, but it was too late in the day to make an appeal based on religious guilt or the pious fake duty of doing good for people who, if truth were told, you really would not care were dead or alive. "You are black people too, you know," he shouted at us finally. And so he was right. But race guilt was not enough anymore either. At that moment my race was not enough, not nearly enough to make me one of these. I was torn between feeling: who are these black people? They are none of mine, not my black people, not my poor. Begone from me! But I felt as well the utter squalor, despair, dirt, lonesomeness, loathesomeness of the place was what I could bear because I had grown up black and I had grown up poor. But I could not bear it, not this much, not to this extreme. I only wished to turn my head in shame: To stop feeling a pounding dishonor that hammered in my head like a migraine because I had money, because I was well-dressed, because I was staying downtown at an expensive hotel that was really so close to this as to seem just outside my room window. I wanted to shout: "But I cannot afford to stay in such a hotel; someone else supports me here." I knew it would have made no difference for I had patrons who were willing to support me and they had none; I had access to money and they had none. Finally, I did not have to be there, in bright sunlight, watching in a kind of dreadful fascination, the voyeurism of the removed bourgeoisie, as a line of the dirtiest, most bedraggled people I have ever seen snaked its way through the street and into a store front building on Lennox Avenue. What was it? Why were they lined up there? At last, I discovered that someone, some agency, was giving away food. So this is autumn in New York; it *is* good to *live* it again.

I thought of Warner Sombart's *Why There Is No Socialism in the United States* and Oscar Wilde's "The Soul of Man Under Socialism" and thought that in a crude way the poor here do live under a kind of socialism. They deal with the state and only the state through its numerous agencies which are designed solely to keep the poor alive and to keep them miserable and contained. And they are, the poor, certainly all equal in the measurement of dispossession that has been allotted them. To look about the streets of Harlem is to see the soul of man under America's socialism, is to know that there is too much of a type of socialism in the United States. It is the socialism of the bourgeoisie who refuse to leave the poor alone and whose meddling does the poor little good. And it is all self-serving in the end. Give them food, give them drugs so they won't organize and turn the country upside down. Here we have people with so much leisure that they could cultivate themselves by using museums, libraries, and the parks; but we have so corrupted them with nonsense, made the parks, the libraries, and the museums the provinces of the bourgeoisie to use to cultivate their "precious" children, the playgrounds of the educated, that we scarcely permit the poor to enter these hallowed grounds of culture. That is the double tragedy: that we waste the poor by not putting them to useful work or useful leisure.

I stayed at the Schomberg for a few hours and then left to find a cab back to the hotel which soon became a matter of desperation as few cabs rumble up this way, I discovered, either by day or by night. I was not desperate to leave Harlem from fear. I felt no fear during the entire time I was there and indeed I have never felt fear strolling in any poor black neighborhood and I have walked in more than my share. I had to return to the hotel on time to deliver my paper. I was on. It was showtime in academe.

GRETEL EHRLICH

◆ —————————————————— ◆

From the Journals

Spring, 1985

All these pent-up lusts, passions, sorrows, rages at political corruption, corrosion of the spirit, unnecessary deaths, discriminations, impossible loves . . . what are these? Why do I collapse across my writing table, the sun full on me, the day spectacular, and cry? Why do I feel, not bored, but unused (in the best sense) by a society enslaved? Against mediocrity, against a society that refuses to find solutions to real problems, but only tinkers, whose ingenuity is restricted to the perpetuation of the frivolous . . . against this and against the living dead, the brain-dead, the dead-beats, the heartbeats that make no noise—what sharpness and number of swords could prick holes into the dogmas of greed?

March 31

Dream of the long, twisted branch of a eucalyptus tree with a huge bowl-like nest at the very end and a scarlet tananger flying to and from the nest with a single piece of straw in its beak which she had brought all the way from another part of California.

From Ionesco: "Nothing is true except what happens in dreams within the imaginary world. Realism is an odious fraud. Someone who is a realist is someone who only sees part of reality, who uses this to prop up dogma, an ideology that will pass. . . ."

Then the day really does go, sallow light washes the room like something spit out. Motionless I watch the windows go black and the hayfields bend away in green silence.

April 1

What Flaubert refers to as the *"mélancholies du voyage"* is like the sadness I feel as one season departs and another arrives.

The only restaurant and bar in Shell, the only place for us to gather, was burned down last night, the result of a feud.

June 19

Watched Ray Hunt work with young colts today. He says: "You have to find the life in the body of the horse. It's a force that either tries to escape or gets redirected in circular shapes. Everything goes in a circle, the world ain't flat, and a wheel moves smoothly. When the horse is smooth you can feel the life going through from the hind end, through the feet, into the mind. When the horse's mind gets congested, when his thoughts get wadded up, when he's acting out of control with no thought for the person—there can be a lot of anguish in this. Watch him. When he begins letting his energy go all the way through, when he begins doing the right thing, the easy thing, then he's at peace with the world and with himself."

June 26

Irrigating the lower place, I smell something sweet and look up to see irises blooming. Planted fifty years ago by the homesteader, they still bloom, untended, with no house or gardener nearby. Amazing, in this harsh place where almost nothing grows, where flowers are stunted by deer, elk, cattle, horses, or by miserable heat or cold. Dream that the lights in a tall Manhattan building going on and off all night are really flowers.

July 1

A wild wind comes up. Rain begins and stops. Now it's just blowing and no rain comes out of it; it's blowing the dryness around, mocking our desert needs, blowing the water out of the creeks, blowing the cows down. My colt bucks in place as if the wind had lifted his hind quarters. The sudden lightness we feel is gravity bucking in a wild wind.

July 2

Flaubert: "What a heavy oar the pen is and what a strong current ideas are to row in."

July 4

Cowcamp. Go to bed in the back of my pickup because the bunkhouses were full. The stars above a lone pine tree look like a Ukiyoe print. A string of clouds passes, shaped like carpenter's tools shaken out across the sky. I feel happy and forlorn.

July 15
> Then the days stretch out like single rods
> the color of rust, nicked and scored by the various
> sexual heats, limbic vines twist and travel, bunching
> out in grapes, their green antennae vining my arms,
> and all that we know, which, twisted against who
> we are, climbs the trellis of the day.

July 17
98° in the shade. A whirling leaf catching the light falls like a cinder.

August 2
"Phillip looked away, as he sometimes looked away from the great pictures where visible forms suddenly become inadequate for the things they have shown to us." —E. M. Forster.

August 5
Rain finally. And then, still unbound, the clatter of cicadas clacking high up in every tree, over the wide square of the lake. The mind dappled by sound. Everything resembles the mind, big and small, or, the mind resembles everything in nature, the diffident, resounding chaos. Feel sick, then hungry, then a fast trip to the outhouse. Lie naked in the sun, then sit up with shirt on. Shoes on, then off, all the while, the green that came as suddenly as a blaze because of the rains, loses its tint as if drought blanched and bleached everything it touched, blades of grass are brown fingers of death pointing. A conference of sedimentologists crawls up and down the dry hills on this once-upon-a-time ocean: David Love, Mary Kraus, David Uhlir all say: each rock, each stratum of soil tells such a deep, unfolding story of how the continent was made. Sitting on the lawn outside the banker's house, Tom Brown says, "Knowledge is an upside-down pyramid, starting at a narrow point and forever expanding . . ." Go home and watch the moon rise through binoculars. It is more spectacular for its not being quite full, for its imperfection, and Jupiter's tiny moons are like earrings. From this night on, there will be geologists in my life.

Morning. I walk. I don't cry *about* my life, but cry because of its fullness. The road is dry, kiln-dried with the glaze cracked or is it porcelain without a sheen? The birds' flight grows effortless as the drought continues, pulls the drawstring of moisture. In the colorless sky—what is there?—the geologists visit again and I turn groundward from shifting shadows and heats, changing breezes, wafting sounds of another drainage; choke-cherries ripening and the grass dying and the squash growing obscenely large in soil that cradled shallow seas and submitted to ash that fell continuously for ten thousand years. . . .

August 14

Why is my heart racing? I open the window. Have I been holding my breath all my life? Rocks dance. Their jetés are violent upthrusts, unlimbed blunt percussions. I skitter on subduction faults, detachment faults—like Heart Mountain, which moved twice; and down its rock face, red streaks—like the Buddhist's red threads of passion. Night. The back legs of running horses emit sparks; the moonless sky gathers them.

I lie in bed. The day is motionless, or so I think. But the tectonic plates are at odds. In my California home, they crash against each other, the continent moving west and the Pacific plates moving east. Here, granite pushes against sedimentary rock, producing undulations—synclines and anticlines result and rock, big as a mountain, is thrust up, upended.

August 27

Imagined poverty, real asceticism, the need, always to feel the rockiness of life, and in places where there are berries, the thorns. In ordinary life, in sex, in writing, I laugh at how stiffness and softness trade places. After lovemaking, a softness pervades all parts of the body. One surrenders further, gives up the idea of surrendering, the pretense of acceptance, real fear and self-delusion. Gradually, you harden again and I laugh because it's not just desire but the flip side of what has just come before: it is a gesture of protection, self-defense, an instinct to move against death.

At every moment, we're fractured this way, going toward death, then life, so there is, everywhere, a constant movement, a swelling and deflating, an urge to accommodate opposites. Life magnetizes death and death magnetizes life; we grapple at the edge of things, save ourselves though we don't know it, thrash in the current, hold out compasses that do not give us true north, and leave behind only the beautiful, dunelike, evanescent ripples of each foray, fossilized in rock.

August 28

Dream. I entered a bookstore that became a foodstore. There were booths, as at a county fair. I stopped at one where two naked men with long ponytails were making vinegar. They asked me to taste some and I did. "It's Chinese," I said and they laughed, retorting, "But we're Italian." The vinegar tasted like bean paste mixed with something acrid. I said I'd buy a bottle. Before capping it, they cut off the tentacles of an octopus and dropped them in.

September 1

Woke up cold. Slept with a shotgun on my bed because there's a horse rustler loose, the sheriff said. He made me put the phone by my bed with his home phone number emblazoned on the receiver—"Call if you hear or see anything strange in the night," he said. But there was nothing. Stayed in bed and reread the opening portions of *A Farewell to Arms*. It's like jumping into a symphony. I was swept up at once, then it was music all the way through.

"A holy man named Shinkai was so aware of the impermanence of the world that he never even sat down and relaxed, but always remained crouching." —The Tsurezuregusa of Kenko.

September 17

Annie Dillard talks about how the narrative line has been devalued by modern physics. The narrative line to me is like a Mexican mural: flattened in perspective so all is present; cramped by detail, erotic, various, the flat depth held up in the imagination, its transience, and impermanence nakedly apparent. The narrative does not lead from one place to another, from the past to the future, but more deeply into the present, always the present and its sense of time is in tune with the human heart rather than the chessman's calculating mind; present moves are a means to the future. The narrative line, then, is at rest and jostling at the same time. Like a sonogram of a pregnant woman's belly: the fetus' tiny heartbeat jostled by gas.

September 19

Rain tonight, a slow steady drizzle. I cook a pork roast and drink wine. How delightful after a summer of garden vegetables. Wang Fan-Chih writes:

> All of us receive an empty body
> All of us take the universe's breath
> We die and still must live again
> come back to earth all recollection lost.

Ai! no more than this?
Think hard about it
All things turn stale and flat on the tongue
It comforts people? No
Better now and again
to get blind drunk on the floor
alone.

September 21

Now when I look out across the Basin I see not just ocean (mirage) but
shallow seas, geological twists of fate, ancient depositions like thoughts
stacked up, rotting ash, and overhead, the tail of a comet. Recently, they
sent a satellite through its tail, its "plasma," which is the primal matter
of the universe, its particulars. How delighted W. C. Williams would
have been. I think about newness, about primacies of all sorts, about the
earth's crust and mantle, how water that is new—"juvenile water"—
comes up through the ocean floor and mixes with water that has received
the earth's salts. . . . During an intense earthquake, the earth liquifies.

I drink and drink to sleep so I won't dream of emeralds or be
dropped in cactus or watch the elk, carved by anazazi into rock, jump
into the universe where they will be shot down by men. Is this fall storm
a form of sadness that originates in comet tails, a sadness that has been
here from the moment of the big bang?

Italo Calvino died Thursday of a stroke in Siena.

October 7

Get up at 3:30 A.M., drive to the mountain for first day of roundup and,
holding my saddle on my arm, am sent home by Stan because of my bad
cold. "You've already had pneumonia this year and you ain't gettin' it
again on my outfit," he said. Vitality zapped. Laundry hanging on the
line goes stiff with ice. I've been working on my novel for five months
and am still rewriting the first twenty-five pages. I'm suffering from
seasonal violence: no fall this year. We went from heat and drought to
winter with only one brief interlude of rain. I want to sit quietly and be
warm.

October 11

I want to feel snow come down in me; to know its precise quality; to
give it words.

"Ontological neurosis—an hysteria of being."

October 19
I go east. At a friend's house I'm fed, loved, kept warm. We listen to opera in the middle of the night and I find myself sobbing. The scars of last winter's serious illness dissolve. I relax for the first time in two years.

October 22
At a party, someone talks about adolescent sex: "The first time I beat off, I did it on a rock. The rock was covered with lichen. I can't remember what color it was. The forest was wet and dark."

October 25
Dinner in Chinatown with Dan Halpern, Carolyn Forché, Harry Mattison, Grace Schulman, Bill Matthews, Russell Banks, etc. In the middle of dinner, Harry gets up and rubs Dan's shoulders. "You look tired," he says. He has to have his hands on things always and I love the intense way he looks at each of us. "When I went to visit Carolyn's writing class at Columbia, I told the students they were underprivileged. 'You haven't had the privilege of poverty, of war, or suffering . . .' " That, because they've just returned from years in Central America, the Middle East, and next, South Africa. But I wonder—to keep ourselves honed, must we always sit in the charnel ground, must we always go to the battlefields of the world, isn't all of that here and everywhere, if we'd only see it, sense it, extend our sympathies sufficiently to know the sorrows of plants, earth, watersheds, animals, ourselves?

October 26
Dinner at Carla Maxwell's. It's her fortieth birthday. Among the guests are Pina Bausch's company from Germany. While they converse in German, Carla and I drink champagne from martini glasses, shove our chairs back, and dance to the music of Sophie Tucker singing, "Life Begins at Forty."

October 28
In Vermont, I see a weeping willow whose soft branches, blowing in the wind, look like shoulders heaving—breathlessness or tears?

Halloween
I walk in the Village Halloween parade with Ted Hoagland. He's dressed like a fox and we stop midavenue and howl. The streets are packed, blocked completely from traffic and everywhere I look I see

smiling faces—a glorious moment for New York. The parade is made up of undulating dragons, twenty-foot-high puppets, dancing skeletons, African drummers, a single Puerto Rican dandy, coyote-women and wolf-men, all of us carrying tall corn stalks, our flags, our pledge of allegiance to maize. After the parade breaks up at Washington Square, we drift west, through carless streets. One 6'8" transvestite dressed in a girl's cheerleading suit twirls a baton and, holding a ghetto blaster under the other arm, strides to a Sousa march. On Bleecker Street, a man with a raincoat leans back against stairs. As we pass, he flashes: a huge fabric penis springs out toward us—ten feet long, to much laughter.

Thanksgiving
In Jackson's Hole. Give Mardy Murie "Solace." The next day she said she stayed up half the night reading it, then hugs me, and speaks in a gentle voice about it. We talk wolves, mountain lions, and about why coyotes howl.

November 30
Six below zero. What is beyond Desire, but Desire?

December 3
Saw Steve Canady in the post office. Asked him how he liked my book. He said, "Well, hell, I haven't finished it yet . . . where'd you get all them eight-cylinder words?"

December 10
Dream: I was leading horses across a dam bank to a pasture in the trees. Halfway across, the horses became "horse-men"—human faces, animal bodies. They had gathered at a monastery in the trees. A long white carpet had been laid down as an aisle through the middle of these "disciples." A priest or lama held a huge silver chalice filled with red wine. As everyone turned toward him, he hurled the chalice and the wine spilled across the white rug. I led the horse-men away.

December 18
My friend, my pal, the one most like a younger brother, the one his father wanted me to marry, the best cowboy I've ridden with, the most moral, dignified, wild of them all, the wisest, the oldest for his age as if he were his father—an exact replica in a young man's body, died today. This place, this Wyoming, these days of cowboying will never

be the same without him. Can I even write his name? Joel, Joey, Little Smoke . . .

January 4, 1986
Robert Graves died last week. I read his poem aloud to Joel's friends:

> Take delight in
> momentariness,
> Walk between dark and dark—
> A shining space
> With the grave's narrowness,
> though not its peace.

January 5
Desolation after desolation rolls through me. When Joel's father—Smokey—was rolled into the church in a wheelchair (he'd taken ill after Joel's death), he shook the coffin and cried out, "Why have you done this to me? Everything I did in my life was for you."

As for the verity of rural constancy, of sameness, there is no such thing. I know that of course. If I know anything, it is to expect impermanence . . . and yet . . .

January 14
Last night, saw Comet Halley, gauzy-tailed, moving from left to right, from southwest to northeast, with a beautiful, constrained sense of falling, as if flung against a resistent cloth, but coming anyway, the way people newly in love sometimes do. It was a movement so large, so cosmically grandiose, that its course could not be perceived, yet the overpowering feeling on sighting it in amongst the other glass eyes, was precisely that—of a surging descent, an elegant, unstoppable fall as if the comet were very heavy and the air dense.

Becuase it's warm, the dogs lie out in the snow.

February
Snow on snow on snow and bright hot cobalt days. After eight hours at the typewriter, the dogs get me, and I ski off the veranda until dark.

March
"A poet's morality is the morality of the right sensation." —Wallace Stevens.

Meanwhile, a tongue-shaped cloud dominates the entire sky.

Dantean hell—an historical darkness as well as a momentary one; visionary signs, not just descriptions; the residue of phenomenal shimmerings, of lost heats, natural irridescence; erotic intensities without any specific mention of it.

"Matter gets its 'moving orders' directly from space itself, so that rather than regarding gravity as a force, it should be viewed as a geometry." —John Wheeler.

June 14
Eyes itch, grass going to seed, the strange cry of a bird by the lake we can't see or identify. Shot a rattlesnake with my .410 yesterday. It was coiled only six inches from my leg.

    At the rodeo Chrissy Fitch came into the grandstands holding a bird's nest. She walked through the stands yelling at everyone to look at it!

    Thinking of the word "crush"—denoting St. Augustine's "weight of love." What if love (infatuation, a crush on somebody) were viewed like matter, not as a force, but as a geometry . . .

June 16
Talked with someone I've loved this morning, in person. His physical presence—and the charged air between our two bodies—heavy, saturated, Mahleresque, a complex music with rocking, emotional swells, a flashflood of red creekwater drenching us suddenly, then gone dry, to bone.

June 18
To make a book of essays, a book of questions.

June 19
My colt ran away with me two days ago and I baled off on my ass. No injuries, just bruises.

June 26

       The balm of the body—
       What of that?
       Against consciousness' hurling and the
       clock's eventful diatribe. Sweat

links us uncoupled. Mind
hurts like a fist
through glass. White brain, knob
of indecency.

July 17
Bucked off on my head. Hung in there, checked the cows, though I have
no idea what I was looking at, rode home, helped Press trailer a horse
to the neighbors, as he's leaving today. Face cut and swollen.

July 18
I'm having trouble seeing. Blotches of black behind my eyes. I feel dizzy,
nauseous, disoriented. My eyes don't move in my head. Press gone. I feel
like a blind person, troubling surfaces with tentative hands because my
head doesn't work. Drive to Shell—so hard to see, have to stop and look
for the road, then continue slowly on. A friend takes me to the hospital.
The doctor tells me he hates horses. Nice bedside manner. I'm having
a little hemorrhage, that's all, and they may have to med-vac me to
Billings to drill holes in my skull. How will I find Press, get him out of
the mountains?

Cat scan. They tape my head and chin down, then I have to pee.
Strapped down a second time, I move backward. This is like a tunnel
of love, I think, only a tunnel of light and eerie, spacey silence, the kind
of white noise a distant waterfall makes, hushed . . .

I'm sent home with my hulk of a nurse. He carries me from the
pickup and lays me on the couch where I will stay for the rest of the
summer, unable to read, think, laugh, feel the gaiety of anything. I feel
betrayed by my colt; or else, out of stupidity, I betrayed him. After he
got me off his back, he ran up a hill and back to me again, then turned
and kicked me. The more afraid I am of him, the more afraid he is of
me, but I'm down for the count now and know I must get rid of him.

July 24
The black behind my eyes has gone and I can see but don't want to.
Head pressure, as if the brain tissue were jellyfish, not muscle with nerves;
I have no nerve; nothing connects. People come and go. I can't see,
truly, who they are. No memory loss, but eyes water, and it's sometimes
hard to talk. Then there are glitches, or is that just age? Ursula comes
and goes. She looks like a moon, a mermaid—big, graceful, quiet,
bright—lovely. A letter: Dear Puffy, I was so afraid I would die and join

David and Joel in a limbo that looked like intestines and smelled of human gas. Anyway, because of the face cuts and swelling, my smile isn't right.

July 25

I remember one moment—airborne—hunched over the colt's withers and right shoulder, but I don't remember how I must have rolled to my right, legs splayed, stomach skidding the ground.

Birds. That's all I look at. Today a scarlet tanager makes me happy, then a belted kingfisher during a forbidden drive to the mailbox, and at home, two baby swallows learning to fly.

July 26

Rain. Wake with the same headache, the same lack of desire, the same deadness inside. Nothing stirs me. The twenty-five roosters we raised from chicks spar under the parked pickup truck as if the shaded space between the four wheels was a ring.

July 28

Despair that rambles. This injury is a form of psychic isolation. It plucks my head out of the stream and holds it dry and dark and motionless on a rock where no one can see me. No one who comes around can feel the bruise-heat or the coolness of no desire. My head feels as if it might topple from a frail stem.

August 10

And after the piquant verdancy, all the grasses are rolled up, and the wind funnels them and they drop as something black behind my eyes. Some days to touch you would be everything, would be a single lifetime smoking under a magnifying glass, a single flame. All the clichéd words of ardor make sense to me: flame, crush, sweetheart. Last night, the crescent moon fell down west of my body. A thin cloud pierced it, making a black stitch. Hips jut up from cool sheets—architectural, continental—I opened my eyes and saw where the Milky Way ended, where its white heat tapered off in indigo and in the north, where it began again.

August 25

Tenderness, self-mockery, depression, carefree jocularity, sadness, isolation.

September
A correspondence between the body and the natural world. An equality—between everything and everything. Oceanic cadences.

As he/she drives away, the loins, then the heart actually cramp.

October
Hunting Camp (thankfully, without hunters). The top of Little Baldy—bright silver—pink sky, then steam rising from snow. Air is mist and clouds are snowfalls going elsewhere.

October 10
Hot sun on snow. A howling wind before I woke made me dream about surf—the correlations between water movement, midsea currents, and currents of air. The winds are tides; tides are moons; moons are drops of water. . . . The horses lie down in midday sun.

October 22
"I remember at the Albany airport how you called me sweetie by mistake and how you held me and it made me miss the way you would have been if you had loved me years before. I'm out of my mind here, the wind howls, the green leeches into a white sky. I don't know, maybe it's the time of year or the time of life. I've loved you for twenty years—first, with a childish, shut-mouthed, suicidal passion, and now, with a voluble longing that does not have as its end, any thought of possession . . ."

October 25
Soseki's (the Japanese novelist) wife was so suicidal, he tied himself to her at night so she couldn't get out of bed while he was asleep.

October 27
Hunting in full swing here. Gunshots volley at Hudson Falls—as if bullets were being fired into a woman's vagina. That's how hunting makes me feel. Every sacred place here sullied. These men gun down bulls and bucks who are in rut, as if abridging sexuality, subsuming virility, making the animals' power their own. And only the ornament of big horns and antlers will satisfy them—not the palatability of the meat. To hunt for meat is one thing, to kill for sport is unconscionable.

November
Miami Book Fair. Hot nights, hot days, swinging palms, jet-powered speedboats, a drawbridge that opens at my feet, Richard Ford's sweet

volubility—where his stories are hard and spare, his presence is tender and talkative.

Key West
I go straight to Hemingway's house and where I thought it would be on a high hill with a winding driveway and coral walls and a grand, breezy view of the sea, it is on the same flat that all of Key West is on, shrouded by trees, cheaply furnished, and all the rooms stink with cat-piss. Fly north across the Keys at dawn.

I meet, by chance, a childhood friend who's been a close aide to Reagan in the White House. Despite moral and political differences so huge as to be ridiculous, the old closeness, the childhood affinity built on horseback and beaches remains innocently there. How is this possible?

Richard Ford's pale, ice eyes, the sadness in his hands as he reads from his work, and afterward, his amiable chatter.

I find Stephen Spender wandering around the lobby looking for the door. It's a confusing place. I guide him to the exit. The next night, come in from dinner to find the lobby and three of the floors filled with black families there for a reunion of a black sorority. A wonderful liveliness fills the place—laughter, talking, drinking, singing everywhere. We get out of the elevator, all heads turn to us. Are we on the right floor? C. asks, and everyone laughs. Drinks are offered.

Dialogue:

Why are we doing this?
Because we're getting old. We want to find out what we missed as children.
My dear. May I call you that? You won't be mad?
Stop teasing.
I'm not. (Then he teases.)
But you are.
No, that's different.
I can never tell if you're serious.

(Their legs float out behind them like bait for the past that lies submerged under hot, green water.)

Sunday
Dreamed that I was in small room with a huge north window and one of the characters from my novel, Carol Lyman, took a picture of me.

November 19

Home. A gray day and colder than it looks, than it could possibly be. Winter is a betrayal. I ski on it, imperially, but I am the one who is conquered.

A child's prescience—for which he/she gets no credit—i.e., the way we pick people to love who, years after, are still loved by us. But in between, a Dantean journey—hellish years swaying between childhood and maturity. We know everything about who we are, what we need to survive, to be human; then it's forgotten, confused with other things and, like misguided missiles fired from Vandeberg at dawn, we shoot out over the horizonless sea . . . and only if we're lucky, do we ever come back. By age six, I knew everything I know now. By age twelve, I had loved seriously, two men whom I still love now.

December 18

The anniversary of Joel's death. Get up at 3:00 A.M. A glowing, red and yellow star falls, exploding across the sky. At dawn, go for a walk. A coyote runs across lake ice up Grouse Hill. At lunch I cut an artery with a knife by mistake and think of the priest on the Reservation whose throat was cut. He bled to death because no one had the sense to pinch the bleeding artery closed. I stop the flow of my own blood with a butterfly bandage. Touching it is like touching my pumping heart, like putting my hand deep inside my own body.

December 20

Seeing way back into his eyes: the jolt of the handshake—lightning.

December 21

Winter Solstice.

> A grasping buffeting wind brings clouds
> back—the blue above us
> shrunken as if soured. Up steep
> stairs your ghost-hands
> tremble me
> against blue horseblankets. We strike down
> where the lightning is woven through
> and the cloudbank, the
> white deep, stretches. Treebark slips

and drops all-of-a-piece
and you gather my breasts to your hunger.

June 3, 1987
Rain stopped. Now the sky has stretch marks: clouds thin as scar tissue. High water scours out a hidden room in rock and rolls its silt into our pastures, mounding them with red sand. When Chernobyl burned, one of the radioactive clouds blew over Wyoming. It rained that day and as I was irrigating, pulling and setting dams, the diamonds of water in new grass looked poisoned and I hated the green that came. Everything conspires to do the planet in—perhaps it hurts more to see it happen in this pristine-seeming landscape where water mixes with farmer's chemicals, where birds and coyotes are poisoned, where the air has, for the first time, taken on a dull, smokey look, so that each tiny affront to life, even the killing of a fly, is torture to me. I look away.

June 9
Driving home from Cody, an antelope runs with her two tiny twins behind her. They're so small—but perfectly shaped and colored. They run with their mouths open, drinking air . . . beautiful miniatures.

Dream: he and I were in a Japanese shopping arcade, like the ones in Kyoto, buying silk kimonos and bamboo fishing rods. We were sent to a waiting room, but it was a train platform. We stood, as at the edge of a planet, no sound of a train, only wind. I said, "This is the kind of wind that brings black rain. They have that here." The way we stood, our bodies touched, so bonded and linked, he said, "Listen. Our bodies read our minds."

More rain. Flash floods. Summer tries to come but fails.

June 13
Bluebird is dead. My horse who has been with me since I came to Wyoming, who has herded sheep, followed me from town to town, tracked cattle . . . who, clownishly, shared pans of dogfood with Rusty, clambered up stairs to the veranda and looked in the house, who often stuck his head in the kitchen door on summer days to beg for cookies, who would not be caught the first six months I owned him just to show who had the upper hand, who never bucked, who hated most men, who was so ugly, big-headed, hairy-legged that some ranchers refused to haul him in their trailers, who was the butt of many jokes, who laughed silently at all of us, who knew things but wouldn't tell me except when

I wasn't asking, who gave me a look one day that told me something about the pain of not having language, of the longing to have a communication that was not muddled (on my part), that said, "Animals know things and want things too," who comforted me because we shared hard winters and harrowing lonely years.

Press found him, standing in the corner of the pasture, eating, with his back leg broken in three places, hanging off. To think of that moment of betrayal, of aiming a gun at him and he knew what it was for and why but a betrayal is a betrayal . . . that is and always will be unimaginable. It stops me. It is untouchable.

June 24

Alone in the house, husbandless, horseless, for the first time since November. Now I have the longed-for solitude but I have to wonder which is the greater vanity—solitude in the midst of physical beauty, or the agitated effect of people who stir my heart. The clean pages of this notebook console me. A new beginning after the mire of a long work. Though I know better than to think there are ever new beginnings. Like the walk I took this afternoon—I followed the creek downhill through a field of lilies, blooming cactus. I stared hard at a small waterfall. Ravens tumbled in the dark blue air. But the stench of my dead horse's decaying body permeated the valley. It is the last thing I will know about him.

I pick up a rock. It breaks open in my hand. Inside, its red and blue-gray agate looks like a legbone surrounded by flesh. Like Blue's back leg, broken, dangling. Later, one lazuli bunting comes again and again to the birdfeeder to eat seed, its neck feathers irridescent, turquoise.

July

He sleeps with his mouth open, head back, legs wobbling from side to side, the animal beard stiff in sunlight. He sleeps on his back, one leg hiked up, arms out, wrists loose, fingers spread, like a crane landing. "I feel like a lizard crawling over you, over the sun of you, over the smooth, sweet beauty of your body."

Tesuque, N.M. Arrived at Charlie and Michele's to find them bent over the radio. Three convicts are loose and believed to be in their area. We go out for dinner. The house is at the bottom of a narrow dirt road that winds through arroyos and barrancas and there are no locks on the doors or screens on the windows. "Let them hide here," Charlie says. Coming home, we see the light of a helicopter swinging over piñon trees and bare ground. There are roadblocks on every highway. Cops come and go. "Who are you?" they ask, shining a light into my face. I feel like saying, "I don't know." Three days later, the escapees are discovered in California.

Home and I'm reeling. The sky is black with swallows. It snowed on Bastille Day; a baby bird fell out of its nest and broke its neck; a rabbit is eating its way out of my garden. During my absence, the lake filled so much my blue canoe came unmoored and floats empty. I like talking to you; I'm reeling from that also, my brainstem-bodystem—carbonated. I feel giddy thinking of having you in my life in the human "forever," or in your Franciscan heaven, or if not in the afterlife, then now, no?

God, it's beautiful here . . . lazuli buntings follow the cattle flying up creekbeds and the stiff purple heads of timothy grass teetering on the windy brink of fruition. But there's no one to talk to—no one of like mind, though now I feel as if we were talking all the time, even when you have other women in your arms and you're not listening and I'm laughing at you.

Today I cowboyed. Someone opened the gates on the lower pasture and the cows scattered. I gathered them and trailed them to the pasture by the house. Later, I drank late enough with friends that the Milky Way was hard over our heads like the rib of a whale and your voice came into the noise of my sleep waking me to laughter.

August

Desire. In the midst of people—relatives, children, spouses, he took my hand and said, Let's go to Lake Tahoe (where I've never been). I said yes. We went to a whorehouse built out over the water. The view of the lake was astonishing—black water like lacquer and a huge silhouette of a heron looming close. X told the madame that we wanted a room for a few hours. She laughed at us, our desperation and innocence, and showed us to a tiny space: a mattress fit into a glass cube cantelevered way out over the water—fifty feet or so. When she left we crawled under the comforters and made love over and over and over. There was no stopping it. But once I looked down at the water and asked why it was so black.

Albuquerque again. At the airport, rented a car. When they saw that I was working for *Time* magazine they said, "Oh, are you covering the Harmonic Convergence?" I laughed and said no. Airport chock full of all sorts—latter-day hippies, women with painted fingernails clutching crystals, long-hairs with guitars and bedrolls, a group of garrulous girls from New Jersey. Drove to Tesuque. Charlie and I make drinks and sit on the patio. We can see Los Alamos from there—a direct shot west from his house. The air smells of mineral. We laugh about the "Convergence," we two childhood friends whose lives converge and reconverge in odd, persistent ways. His beeper goes off. He's the medic and fire chief and is always on call. There's a woman at the Bingo Parlor hyperventilating. "She probably lost all her money," Charlie says, as we take off, siren on, red light flashing on top of his car. Bingo parlors are big on Indian Reservations. We run into a tiny room off the enormous, cavernous "parlor"—as big as a K-mart with rows and rows of tables and metal folding chairs, neon lights, and a fish-faced man on a perch in front of a transparent globe bursting with numbered Ping-Pong balls, and women, often siting in pairs, smoking and drinking RC Cola and cherry Coke, bent over their cards.

The woman in question is middle-aged, obese, and hysterical. We put a paper bag over her nose and mouth—high tech, no? and tell her to breathe calmly. She doesn't know "calm." She pants distractedly. Charlie takes her pulse, and tries to soothe her. Nothing works. He listens to her heart and gives her oxygen. She keeps taking the little mask away to talk and he puts it back over her nose. "I'm dying, I'm dying . . ." she keeps crying in a loud voice. "No you're not," he says. Finally, the ambulance comes and we go to dinner. Later, we lie out on the lawn. Are we converging? I ask. A weather satellite draws a straight line through erupting meteor showers and I feel what I can only call a molecular lushness close to my face: the deep powder of friendship. I breathe in. We sleep and roam the hills at dawn.

August 21
I walk along the high road by the lake, muttering to myself. Dreamed I lay across a topographical map of California. The wrinkled top sheet on my feet was a mountain range and a valley. I moved my toes across it, feeling each feature of the landscape. He lay diagonally across the central part of the state. He stared at me and, finally, smiled. "Welcome home," he said, extending his arms, and flying across a vast distance, I let him embrace me. Now, walking, I feel as if my ankles are tied and I'm stretched over the edge of a dark universe. Yet I see things. But what are they to me or I to them? What is my geographical destiny?

November 16
Nothing matters but this. It demolishes the days and happily turns them into passageways. All has become a gangplank to you. I walk the turnabouts, the hesitancies and all goes like smoke, twisting into air. We meet in the eye of our own storm and grope over the rich debris of impossible love. The calm is the false calm of loss and union commingling, of simultaneous hopelessness and fruition. (novel notes)

January 21, 1988
After a morning snowfall—hours of melting quiet—a wind, high in the timbered mountains, issues a steady, hushed roar. If the bicameral mind is two very different things, then the heart is also—like the towering split rock through which a creek patiently drives. The waterfall of my imagination and the real one whose cataracts I climb like a vine, lifts out of my life and goes into my novel, then comes free again. Walking there today, on my birthday, I see that a huge chunk of ice has dropped out of the middle of the frozen cascade, leaving black, wet rock exposed. And so it is with me . . .

M. F. K. FISHER

◆ —————————————————————— ◆

Swiss Journal

*B*ern / *August 1, 1938*

One thing about writing is that it takes time. This last month I have
thought of perhaps a thousand things, to estimate conservatively, that
for some perverse reason I should like to write about; sights or smells or
sounds, or occasionally ideas. This last month —

It is 9:14 at night, a queerly noisy night, with at least two radios
blaring from somewhere over the Kornhaus Bridge, and many people
walking past the hospital, and trains racketing with extra fervor from the
stop by the theater across the Aar to the Kursaal. I can look out and see
the lights slide along the wet black bridge, and the dull shapes of two
floodlighted towers push up into the sky.

I finish a glass of brandy, and want to write about this month, and
know that I am too sleepy. And then I wonder why I do want to write
about it, because I despise talk, and the people who talk, who tell others
about themselves, and the dreadful necessity that pushes them to such
confessions. They must talk. They must expose themselves. It helps
them, and more horribly, it helps others.

That is what bothers me. I hate this need. I've never done much
of it, and I despise it in others. But I know that I am more articulate
than some, and I think well. . . . My God in Heaven! If what I've
learned about pain or food or the excreta of the seasnail can help even
one poor human, I am a rat not to write. Then I know I am wrong.

And now, at 9:23, I am writing, for the first time in more than this
last month. My eyes are sanded with sleep, and my back is numb against
the two limp Swiss pillows.

I look up to see in the mirror above my washstand if there is light
reflected from Dillwyn's room. We tried two pills tonight, that did no
good, and then gave the old faithful shot of Analgeticum at 8:00. He is
asleep, heavily, with his mouth dropped askew. I am fairly sure that by
12:00 he will call me. Then it will be Pantapon.

I can't understand so much noise from town, but of course people
are still celebrating that there's no war. It would have been today.

Yesterday Switzerland would have had general mobilization. Of course we are all glad. I am, and so is Dillwyn. I don't like the idea of those bombs the Germans tried on Barcelona, that are made of aluminum filled with liquid air. I wouldn't mind being killed outright by one, but I am sure that the people who were ¼ mile away but were stunned by them had dreadful headaches.

I hear the Cathedral clock strike 9:30. It always rings first. I have tried to listen to one certain hour, to see if all the clocks ever make the same pattern, but even at 3:00 in the morning they never strike the same way twice. Sometimes they make a beautiful sound. I heard that Shastokovich regretted using so many themes in his first symphony, because he had so few left. He should come here, to the Victoria Spital—the night bells, across the dark Aar, would tell him many new ones.

October 2, 1938

After three days of rain it is really hot in the sun. I sit on Dillwyn's balcony, in a green skirt, a white sweater, and his gray coat which I'll soon take off. Through the crooked glass I see him, distorted as one of his own drawings of pain, being bathed by Sister Irma.

Yes, I must take off the coat. As I wriggle out of it I smell a faint musky hot smell that almost reminds me of something about something we once did together. Was it walking up a hill? Or was it something about a sea pool, with us bending over? No, I cannot say. I feel as if some sound or smell had almost recalled a dream. There for a second was the dream. But what dream? It is too late. Perhaps again some time it will almost be clear again.

I smell rather rummy, too. I am sure that I've read of people who put wine in their well pipes, to burn out the varnish or some such thing. So with the awful looking pipe I bought yesterday, because Dillwyn has decided that now is a good time to learn to smoke one, Sister Irma and I have been playing for the last half-hour. It wouldn't light at all at first, and the nasty pinkish rum kept dropping out of the mouthpiece, and finally it sputtered a few times. Now I stink worse than the pipe well, I know, in spite of its being a cheap shiny one, I wish I could remember how Al liked his—he did it so well and lovingly.

Anne left this book, which is hard to write in. It's the one she meant to keep a journal in. She told me that this was the first summer for twenty-five years that had passed without her filling several notebooks with diary. A good thing, I think. This time last Sunday, or perhaps a little later, she and Dillwyn and I were listening, by his open door, to the earnest singing of ten Swiss. They came, dressed in their church clothes, to sing to a member of their club who is ill here. Their voices were strong and sweet, and a yodel came up like bells through the hideous hospital corridors. We were truly thrilled, and Dillwyn's face looked quiet. So I put twenty francs in an envelope, and wrote on it that someone wished the singers to drink to the word's health. Irma took it down, protesting that such a thing had never been done, and beaming with excitement. And then there was a great scuffling and stamping of thick shoes, and a whispering, and there was the Sängerbund outside the door. They sang and sang, with that rather forced lugubrious hymning that creeps into all Swiss songs, but with a yodel that never missed the tone, like a true bell. We were pleased by that, and I at last was bored by the chapelish verses, and then to our surprise all the singers shuffled in and shook hands with Dillwyn, Anne, Irma, and me. They got in a great tangle of crossed arms and embarrassment, and I too felt quite self-conscious, saying *"Merci, Danke-schön! Merci bien,"* to ten stiff young men. After they had at last filed out, as solemnly as from a funeral, one rushed back in again with a singularly repulsive child in his arms, a Mongol-like four-year-old in a sailor suit, who also shook hands with all of us. We felt tired, and I got some sherry before the door was well-closed behind the paternal pride and the thunder of all their feet. But they had sung nicely.

I was sorry David and Noni weren't here to listen—they'd have been excited and amused, and Dave jealous of the yodeling. It was my fault that they had not come early. When they left, the night before, for Die Pension Schmultz, Noni had said, "When shall we see you—9:00, 10:00, 10:30?" And I'd said "Oh, tomorrow's Sunday—let's all sleep." They had looked a little disappointed, I thought. And then how sorry I was, in the morning, that I'd said that!

But still I dreaded to see them. At 8:00 in the morning Dr. Nigst came in while I was drinking tea, and when I asked him how things were going with Hitler, he lifted his arms and let them flop against his sides, and said, "I really don't know. I cannot feel war near, but— Yes, it looks bad." That was the first time he had said that. And then in about ten minutes came a cable. . . . "Arrange children sailing have written Edith." I read it to Dillwyn, and for a minute almost cried, thinking of their disappointment, and how much more excited Noni was about the accordion lessons than the German ones. But I knew Edith and Rex wouldn't ask them to change all their plans for a hasty thoughtless reason. So I began to gird myself to tell the children they must leave

Europe and us, and go back to American schools again. I watched for them to come across the bridge, and rehearsed how I'd tell them. When I saw them striding along, with the rather shambling deliberate steps of all tall people, I felt sad and nervous.

They were quiet of course. Noni cried a little, not with sobs but with silent tears that ran down her cheeks and made her blow her nose. Then I told them to . . .

October 3, 1938
A cold hard night, the first really cold one. It is only 8:30, but I am tired and in bed. Dillwyn sleeps motionless as a tiger. These nightly bouts of pain are dreadful. I don't know how many more of them either of us can stand. He had Analgeticum at 8:00. Last night Nigst tried a mixture of Pantapon and Scopalanim that made him cry out and weep and babble in the few hours of sleep it gave him. His nerve is finally breaking. He shakes and cries when he feels one of these bouts coming. I am weary and so often frightened. And what must he be?

There is a fair in one of the squares across the Aar. It's melodium annoys me, faintly like a gnat. It reminds me of the fair in Vevey.

But I'll write about that another time. My brain teems with memory, but my eyes are heavy. They always are, now. I know things will change soon. They *must*. Almost five weeks of ceaseless agony —

October 5, 1938
This morning the handsome tall postulante came to make my bed, and I went into Tim's room. In a minute there was a small crash. I wondered what—perhaps a vase, or the blown-glass chicken filled with curaao that Anne and the children had brought me. In a minute more I went in to get a handkerchief. The postulante was whiter than ever, and the brown circles under her eyes were almost black, but it wasn't until tonight that I noticed that the bedside lamp with its glass shade was gone. Now I have an unbelievably old-fashioned thing in a discreet wired skirt of faded cretonne, that throbs with misdirected electricity when I come within two inches of it, and gives, with the mellow generosity of a drunken miser, not quite enough light to write by. It was so silly, like a Rube Goldberg invention, that Dillwyn had to stop his strange yelps of pain to laugh at it, when I took it into his room.

I am drinking what is left of a bottle of bad champagne, now slightly warm, from a toothbrush tumbler. I like it.

When I opened the windows tonight, Bern looked like the more than beautiful backdrop in a heavenly Orpheum Music Hall, with bogus lights on all the towers—Cathedral, Clock Tower, Market, Parliament—and lights pricked fakily all along the Aar and then up the funicular beyond the town to the high hotel.

I can think of a lot of things to write about. Almost any sentence starts a long string of—not thoughts—of reminiscences, impressions. For instance: today an enormous box of really exquisite pale powdery gold chrysanthemums, on long stems, with intense dark leaves, came from those inane pale stupid people the Beutlers. Immediately we thought of how she had been so ill and we had not even asked what hospital she was in. Of course we hardly knew them then—but still— And then I remembered her truly warm sincere note, after Tim came here—the schoolgirl language, so banal, and how nicely and thoughtfully and dully they had entertained us in their new house. I remembered the good bad paintings and the 3rd Symphony that nobody really heard but was still played from a something-or-other kind of cabinet that had been copied from one in the Palace at Avignon by Freddie's cabinet-maker. And then the queer people—the pudgy misunderstood genius of a bank clerk who dribbled his way egotistically from Chopin through Brahms and on to Grieg, with none of us daring to break the rapturous spell of Real Music, and the dry old young man who was the scion of Standard Oil or Pond's Cold Cream or something and had to live with his mother who was living with her mistress, and Léni the vital daughter of Mme. Beutler, who tried to be romantic with him to no avail and then was accused by our guest Mary Powell of being a nymphomaniac in love with her brother Buddy. And then Buddy, the most natural person there, a fourteen-year-old boy who had bought ninety francs' worth of fireworks in honor of the 1st of August, and then went down the elevator to the street far below the breathless balcony where we sat, to set them off and called up to us in his sweet, breaking voice. Buddy was a dark, tall, rather pudgy child—and while he set off pinwheels and called up to us, his pretty mother told us in a flat voice, the voice I'd use for ordering three pounds of peas and an eggplant, how he'd been a cretin until five years ago, when she'd brought him to Territet and Dr. Something-or-other had grafted part of the testicles of a bull onto him. He'd learned to talk and walk and write—in fact he was almost human—since then, and was only one year behind his schoolmates. "Of course, something may slip at any moment," she said bluntly. From far below, Buddy sent up a rocket. "Gee!" he called, and his voice cracked endearingly. "Didja see that?"

Later he and his stepfather Freddie suddenly began to wrestle on the Persian rug in the hall. Sibelius' 2nd ground out starkly, ominously. Freddie was very nice at first, and then began to pull and grow mad. In a few minutes we came in from the balcony, and everybody was peering around under period what-nots and the edges of things. "Gosh, Ma— Freddie's lost a diamond!" Buddy said. "One of those diamond cuff links!"

Mme. Beutler flattened her stomach—she's grown a little fat since her operation, but still looks barely thirty-five—and said, "Oh, Freddy's diamonds!" Then she laughed softly, and looked at us with her black beautiful eyes.

The little fair across the river bellows out its silly gramophone records. It makes the sight of Bern at night even more theatrical—and sometimes I can hear the measured racket of a coaster machine, and the occasional scream of an excited girl, or a man's hoarse shout.

I had tea yesterday at the Nigsts'. It's a queer apartment, with a dressing table all laid out with siver-backed toilet things in the hall, so that the patients can tidy themselves before or after they see the doctor. A shy little maid stood by helplessly while I wrestled with my rubber boots. Then I went into the salon, which has very bad very modern paintings on mulberry damask wallpaper, and an elaborate, shiny-as-only-Swiss-furniture-can-be-shiny set of furniture upholstered in "rich" blue damask, and a table with some flowers on it and the kind of Japanese china tiger—scarlet—that could only be won in a shooting gallery at home.

Tea was strong enough to trot a mouse on, served from the kitchen already poured, in after-dinner coffee cups, and a huge basket of delicious hot stuffed croissants (we each took one), and then a huge tray of rich cakes (we each—three of us—took one), and then dry vermouth for the doctor and me, and cigarettes for us all.

Coming home the doctor got around for the third time to his vacation and how he'd be alone and dining out, and finally said (I felt like the innocent girl being asked to come up to see some etchings), "But do you never go out anymore for meals, now that your brother and sisters are gone?" Hell, I thought to myself. "No," I said sadly. "But why not, Miss Parrish?" We swerved wildly down the street. Well, he's asked for it, I thought. "Because I really don't like to eat alone," I said with a brave sad resigned look—I think. "But"—and we swerved a double swerve—"may I ask you to dine once with us? We have—we eat—I mean to say —" "Oh—but how nice of you, Dr. Nigst! Of course, as you know, if my husband does not go well —" "Oh, but Miss Parrish, I *promise* you that all will be most successful and content!"

I have a half-inch of flat mock champagne still to finish. The mock music grinds flatly on. I think with sharp poignancy of my poor Rex, Edith, torn by the first doubts of old age and their own impotence, of Anne ground between the wheels of self-knowledge and self-dramatization, of David and Norah all too quiet and too knowing. I think of Dillwyn lying rocked in the dark opiate arms of Analgeticum, lulled by the weariness of a shot of Pantapon. I think, vaguely and not too close, for safety's sake, of myself here, there, drugged or alive or dreaming or hysterical —

Schwester Irma left a vase for the Beutlers' chrysanthemums in front of a pot of small white garden blossoms. From my bed I cannot see that the flowers are not springing, cut off and lovely, from water in the vase. But I know that it is empty and that they are growing in the earth, behind it.

October 8, 1938
It is reluctantly that I write, and truly I don't know why I bother. Shall I write in that book tonight, I have asked myself several times today, or shall I have a whole day without a duty letter or a letter home or even a scrap of bread cast upon my own literary waters, even a note thrown to my own future?

Now it is 20:20, and I am in bed, and I have a more than moderately amusing detective story, in a green and white paper cover, called *Obelist at Sea*, and a brandy-and-soda. And Dillwyn seems quiet, with the *piqures* earlier so that Irma could go have her heels straightened before the shoemaker closed shop.

But I am tired—and dull. Last night I slept a long, disturbed, wretched sleep, filled with half-waking dreams of puzzlement and stress. Dillwyn only called three times, and I slept until eight this morning— but God I am tired. I look well. I *am* well. But sometimes I feel weary, weary, weary.

This morning I woke stuffily, heavily, to realize that the winds of the night had probably blown too for Anne and the children, a few hours out of Liverpool. I thought of them with love and pain, pain for them all but especially for Noni. And I was thankful they were gone, at least by distance, from my immediate life.

I hurried to wash and put on a little lipstick, vaseline on my eyelids, two faint lines of brown eyebrow pencil, two swipes of blue eyeshadow to match the blue stars on my scarf and my blue flannel bathrobe, and then a little powder. I brushed my hair and put a ribbon around my head—a blue ribbon, of course.

Then I fixed Dillwyn's coffee. He was dreamily cheerful, after the best and the longest (six hours) sleep for over five weeks. (It's five weeks today that he had the second operation, and I lay here wishing he would die.)

Then I came back to bed, and drank my pale tea and ate an unusually tasteless bun, with butter and synthetic apricot jam. I had a faint nagging ache in my belly.

For a change, I got up before Dillwyn's bath, and dressed, and then held him by his beautiful blue-white hair while he bobbed helplessly about the tub of salt water. Sometimes he is really very funny. I cackle— I can't help it—and so does Irma—and then we sound so funny that he laughs too, even in great pain, I couldn't possibly say what is funny, but I find myself really *cackling*—and then when he begins his careful, high, cautious half-laugh I am helpless. I know he has to do it, so he won't budge his side—but it is funny still.

Then there were massages and so on, with Nigst coming in in the middle, moving very carefully with what I suspect was a hangover from his wife's leaving last night, and then Irma and Schwester Agnes Ina almost driving Dillwyn crazy trying to clean his leg with benzine. They dabbed balsam-juice of some kind on the two places in his leg that look bad.

Then he had a raw egg, and we each drank a little brandy highball while I read a story by G. B. Stern, an obvious, facile, and very entertaining one in a book called *Pelican Walking*, I think.

Dillwyn dressed for lunch, and we ate in my room—always his wretched bouillon with a bromide tablet in it, sweet breads with aubergine (not enough), a roasted pigeon with rice, a glass of St. Emilion 1929, some strange vetetable-marrowish-looking vegetable we didn't taste, a bite of the watery Bernois salad, and some surprisingly good plum tart.

Afterward we put on a few more scarves (the hospital is still far from well-heated), and walked across the Kornhaus Bridge. We stopped at the Bodega, the Café Zu Den Pyramäeau, and drank a sherry. It was a bad sherry, but it is a sympathetic little bodega, and the waiter and the pudgy proprietor are nice—so quietly thoughtful, without drawing attention to us.

We hopped on down the cold street, with people looking nicely at us or not at all, and Dillwyn doing things with his usual meticulous grace. I have a horror of his putting one crutch into a grating, but I don't think he ever will. He is so well-balanced that the vision of his ever crashing over fills me with a nightmare terror. But he won't.

We went to the Café du Théatre, where the chasseur and the waitress were nice, and brought us English journals full of diagrams of how to build a bombproof shelter or where to run in Hyde Park, and two café-cognacs—with free cookies! We wondered if anybody but us remembered the fine meal that Timmy ordered there, a few minutes before he felt the strange cramp in his leg more than five weeks ago. We'd often cogitated about going to the Théatre, and then when we finally decided to, Timmy couldn't until today.

We walked to the taxi stand by the Casino, and a kind, ratlike man drove us slowly to the Viktoria. Dillwyn managed the getting in and out beautifully.

For almost half an hour after he got into bed again, it looked as if he'd fool them this time. But then, after one swallow of hot tea, he was almost out of his head, with the teacup rattling on his chest, and his eyes wild. It was a bad siege. He whispered craftily to me, for the hundredth, the thousandth time, that *now* was the time to help him die. Then he yelped and chittered, like a hyena.

Irma, her eyes red—that too for the hundredth time, gave him two Pyramidons with a solemn impersonal face. And somehow, with radio and Rachel Field's new book and me and so on, we lulled him on until six. I lay down for a while, weary and feeling a little sick. But supper, except for his fretting, tapping fingers and an occasional strange look in his wide eyes, was fun. And then soon after he washed himself and undressed, and we gave him the little glass of heart drops, and the swig of Niyol, and the tea with a Urotopin tablet in it, and finally the shot of Analgeticum.

And now he is quiet, and I am tired, and I think I'll read a few pages of my green and white book and then sleep. My brain is almost bursting—Noni, tomorrow, Adelboden, La Tour—but I know that before midnight Dillwyn will need me —

October 17, 1938
"D'you know something about my leg?

"It's that, from when it was cut, on down, I can't remember *one goddamn* distinguishing feature!

"It was just a leg.

"It had an ingrowing nail on the big toe—on the inside, I *think*. But I'm not sure.

"Isn't it queer? Simply another leg."

Probably there is in all intelligent people, of whom I consider myself one (perhaps mistakenly, I add without any apparent coyness), a constant warfare between innate delicacy and reserve, and the desire to talk, to tell All. I am often conscious of it, and oftener than not I refuse to indulge in my natural itch to write because of an overfastidious fear of what may be scratched into being, into the light of paper. Often, at night, I don't want to go to sleep when I come into my bedroom from the last business of tea and injection and pillow-smoothing with Dillwyn. I say, Now I can write in my book! Then I add, What? Then quicker than is decent, I add, But what? What can I, what *should* I say? Why in Hell, why in the name of Edith Rex and all the host *should* I write *any*thing? Why should anyone write anything? And so the old hackneyed twice-cursed thrice-monotonous wheel turns once again.

Next week we go to Adelboden. Already I eye the eight weeks' collection of books on my bureau and my table, and count the number of cakes of soap we may need. Of course there'll be an adequate and probably during the ski season a highly sophisticated pharmacy up there, but my pioneer instincts are still adamant, in spite of some thirty thwarted years. The hearts of all my white chrysanthemums are turning brown. I was thinking I'd give them to the little scullery maid with pale hair and hectic cheeks, who came shyly to play the guitar. But they are no longer lovely.

Tonight we went to Doetwylers', and unfortunately it was mediocre. Going up the stairs I spoke, without turning or loosening my grip an Dillwyn's arm, to the shop woman, and Dillwyn very neatly fell back a whole step. It upset him, and me, and the shop woman, and the busboy who leaped up and practically carried . . .

A little whimper —

"What's the matter, darling?"

"Those goddamn mice!" in a deep voice, like Chaliapin.

. . . carried him to our table. None of us raised an eyebrow. Later Dillwyn said that his leg suddenly seemed to grow six feet long, and to search frenziedly all about for a step, like the gigantic proboscis of a moth feeling for nourishment at night.

October 23, 1938

Today, after almost three weeks of fine blue autumn days, it is cold and darkly gray. I am listless, moonstruck. Dillwyn is in greater pain than usual, feverishly ill at ease. We go out, and after peering into several steamy cafs, whose floors, cluttered with dogs and cigar-butts and spittle and a few children, spell disaster to crutches, we go to the Schweizerhof for beer, and a gin-vermouth for me. Home in a taxi, and while I watch Irma massage the smooth white curve of his hip, I am quietly horrified to see a purplish blotch above the bandage. It seems slightly smoother. Is it a bruise from trying on the temporary peg, day before yesterday? I am appalled, and go away without speaking.

Adelboden / October 24, 1938

The first four hours in Adelboden— Yesterday was bad, because of weather, and what is probably a bruise from Timmy's trying on a prothesis, and so on. But last night was fairly good. This morning Irma was like a little excited brown badger, and I became amazingly vague, wandering between the two rooms with my hair down and pieces of packing in my hands. Finally she got us all into boxes and sacks and bundles, like refugees. Tim and I fled to the Café du Théatre for lunch. We had each planned secretly to order caviar or perhaps oysters, and champagne, and we both ordered grilled steaks with pommes chips and a good old Bourgogne.

I drove up to Adelboden. Nigst's friend the Colonel Garagiste, who may be buying our car, sent us a monkeylike little chauffeur in very good livery, who worked hard and well to get all Irma's bundles arranged, and then wedged himself into and under and over them beside her on the back seat. She permitted herself her sole ribaldry by saying, "Oh Madame, there is not even a package between us, and I doubt if there is any danger—but one never knows!"

I drove up, under and then through and then suddenly above a milky October fog, and occasionally saw in the mirror the wan simian face of the chauffeur. He leaned his head with complete relaxation against my gray coat, which was wrapped around the dreadful "protnèse provisioniur," a thing heavy and rigid with plaster and black wood for a peg and wretched canvas straps. Now and then he dragged languidly at a cigarette from one packet Timmy had given him, and looked with slow mischievious eyes at Irma.

Up here all was ready, even to a gay bunch of blue and yellow flowers in the sitting room. We bustled. Timmy and I drank, between suitcases, a flat brandy and water. We kept looking at the mountains, the nearest and most beautiful I have ever seen. Near their tops they are like the mesas in the West, hard and sculptured against an infinite blue sky.

Now, after a good supper, Dillwyn sleeps precariously from Analgeticum, and I sit in my narrow bed, under the strange high feather puff. I hear the slowed autumnal rush of water far below, and even past my balcony light I see the hard prick of the stars. My cheeks burn, my eyes too. I am excited and yet half asleep, eager to wake early to watch from my window the sun upon the mountains.

13:40, October 27, 1938
In a few minutes I go down through thick milky mist to the pharmacy, along the straight sleeping street lined with closed shops and pensions. It is cold. When I look out the window, here in the warm room filled with the staid strains of Handel's *Concerto Grosso* (?), I might be on a ship, fog-bound to the sound of invisible cowbells from below, or in an airship, as well as in this snug Swiss hotel.

I cannot permit myself the doubtful luxury of thought. I am too close to frenzy, to a wild anxiety.

The first day was not bad. The second day, after only Timmy slept well, thanks to Analgeticum and Pantapon, was exciting. The Nigsts came. We had drinks on the terrace and then went down for lunch, with Nigst clucking like a hen over Timmy's agility on the stairs. Timmy overate, to please him. Later the local doctor, von Derschwanden, came for coffee on the terrace. At first he reminded me of a wretched sordid little snob I once knew from Manchester—not so much his manner, which was brisk behind his English pipe—but his mussed and pudgy English slacks and brown tweed coat. (Now I like him, even more than Nigst, I think. His hands are sensitive and investigatory, and he thinks of everything.)

That night was not bad. Yesterday was wretched, with fever for the first time above 37.5° C, and the right leg very painful. Last night was all right—injections, of course.

This morning the doctor came. I could see he was worried—congestion in the main artery of the right leg, general low condition.

Timmy lies for hours with an open book or journal before him. Occasionally he turns a page, but he has read nothing. Slow tears slip down his cheeks, and now and then he shakes violently and clutches me and sobs.

I must go down to the pharmacy.

I stay at the sitting room because I think I upset him a little when I sit in his room. I keep thinking, He may die—other people do—and then I will be sick at the thought of the times I spent here when I could be there. I'll try to begin a book today.

18:45, October 27, 1938
Whenever I start to write, I seem to think of nothing but sadness. Perhaps it is because I never talk of it. Tonight I am almost intolerably depressed. I don't know quite why. I'm not one to be downed by weather that is usually thought to be mournful. But all seems wrong. Of course the main thing is that Dillwyn is not so well. I try to tell myself, and him when I have to, about the effects of altitude and so on. But I cannot convince myself that all those things could make such a difference in him—fever 37.81-2° C now again, and surely higher at 8:00, and pain in the *other* leg, and this general withdrawal from me and life. He looks at me and seldom sees me. Everything he must save, all his various strengths, to fight the weariness, to hold at bay the bouts of pain, to keep himself on the right side of hysteria. I can see it all.

I stay near but away, where he can see me but not have to look at me. Often I keep the radio going. (It plays now, and it almost drives me frantic.) I tried to write, this afternoon, but I couldn't—Irma, a knock, talk, Dillwyn calls me, so on.

I try to play the phonograph. That, at least, I have thought all along, will be wonderful, this wonderful. But it has something wrong, a grinding sound that creeps above everything but jazz. I tried to play *"Es ist Vollbracht."* It was terrible. And even with that grinding it made things seem too sad. Then, when I said, "Do you like that, Timmy?" he answered, "What?"

I found that my favorite album is not here, the Sebelius concerto, and I paid for sending them all from La Päquis only today. Others are missing—and now it is too late to reclaim them.

And the man called about the car, to sell it at 2,700 francs. I said yes, probably unwisely. But it will be one less thing to worry about.

Of course we have often been low before. Occasionally things seemed so bad, at the Victoria, that I wondered if we could stand it. We never spoke about it. And then in the morning all would be well—a decent night, a blue sky, a good letter —

The strange faculty I developed, during my last years with Al, of shutting myself off, has stood me in good faithful stead lately. It is only occasionally, as now, that it *almost* doesn't work. Usually I can shut parts of my realization, of my intelligence off, rather as a ship's engineer shuts off various parts of a sinking ship. I can almost feel doors close—then—then. It is good, for the moment at least. I think it may have turned me into a duller person than I was—but at least I'm safer from myself.

There is much I can never write about. All this is superficial.

November 2, 1938
I just posted, after much deliberation, an order for 115 Tanchnitz and Albatross and Penguin books. Aside from their costing about $80 and so becoming one of the most extravagant actions of my whole life, I felt from the first that they were an admittance of weakness in my nature. It is easy enough for me to justify wanting them, as Dillwyn said today that it was easy to any woman to defend her inability to eat less than she wanted. But the truth is that it is and will be much pleasanter for me to read book after book of silly "mysteries" than to make myself work. Of course if I were a real writer, predestined, dedicated, I'd work in the face of everything. (And even without that fate, I write constantly in my head—stories, paragraphs, phrases, sometimes the skeletons of novels.) But as it is now I feel almost hysterical at the thought of concentration on one thing. I am never left without interruption (Here are the self-justifications!) for more than fifteen or twenty minutes, and when I am in another room from Dillwyn's his door is always open, so that I can hear what he does or says, and be ready to interpret Irma's talk, or help her. I've never held one way or the other with some creative souls' demand for absolute privacy, although Woolf's theory of £500 and a room of one's own seems attractive personally—but I truly don't feel keen enough at this time to be able to put aside all thought of the present while it is moving and moaning ten feet to the left of me.

I notice two things about this life, since the first night at the Brem. Ten weeks ago: my increased fastidiousness and my equally increased gourmandise. Since I can remember, I've been very clean, but now I spend long serious minutes, after my bath, drying each toenail; I wash my navel or my ears as if they were Belleek china teacups; a tiny hangnail sends me hurrying for scissors, oil, all the minutiae of a complete manicure. And I have become almost piggish . . . not in my manners, for I eat slowly and daintily . . . but I eat too much. The food here is good, especially after the tasteless monotony of the hospital. But there is too much of it. Today at noon there was a rich clear consommé with egg cooked in it, ravioli with tomato sauce and cheese, roast chicken with purée of potatoes, and Brussels sprouts, and a chocolate cream with wafers. So rich! I eat in the little sitting room. First I have a small glass of vermouth with D., while Marta is setting the table. Then I take him a cup of the soup, and the crust of a slice of bread broken into bites. Then I sit down, with a book . . . today *High Wind In Jamaica*. I ate all the raviolis, with a glass of wine. Then I took D. a little chicken cut into morsels, and a little applesauce. I ate the Brussels sprouts, and drank another glass of wine, and then some chocolate pudding and three wafers. Then I ordered a cup of coffee, and drank a small glass of cognac with it. Usually I eat a lot of salad, on which I put a spoonful of meatjuice with a strange voluptuous solemnity. I am interested in this slowness, and this solemnity. I suppose it is a desire to escape, to forget time and the demands of suffering.

Another thing is the way I dress: I've always been rather finicky about colors and so on, but now I find myself looking at my reflection in any mirror with a smug satisfaction, noting complacently the way my sweater, my socks, the ribbon in my hair, are the same blue as the shadow on my eyelids, and how the black of my slacks and my sandals makes all the blues more beautiful. It is queer, and slightly boring, but I suppose it won't get any worse.

After a day part cloudy and part sunlit, light from behind the western mountains beams suddenly across the valley, and brings my mountains close enough to lean against. The snow of seven nights ago melts fast, and cliffs I never dreamed of stand out with abrupt starkness from the white slopes, their rock sides cosy in the unexpected light. Lower down the pine trees are oily green-black, clustered like plant lice in diminishing dots up the mountain. At the bottom the foamy, dirt-white ice water rushes, with a steady hissing, to the warm valleys.

November 6, 1938

Before the light of the sun had quite faded from the mountains, the moon rose over them and cast downward its flat shadows, to make everything look like cheap scenery but beautiful, as such backdrops would look to a wise child.

I stood on the balcony, and listened to the lazy melody of a man's call in the far slopes, and the sharp excited bark of a child or a young dog in the village, and beyond all of it the quiet rushing of the river, full from thaw. As I walked toward the rooms, I saw Irma sitting beside Dillwyn's white smooth rump, rubbing rhythmically, and the stiff ruffled curtains framing her in her white cap and pinafore, and then I saw my shadow, faint and clear in the afterglow, by the full moon on the door.

November 7, 1938

This afternoon, after a half-night of wakefulness, I began to write a book. It will be impossible to show it to anyone but Dillwyn . . . if I ever get it that far along . . . because it is about this last summer. Of course all of us, and above all myself, are changed, muted one moment and caricatured the next, by my own licentious mind. If a person could ever be seen truly, it would be by himself. But that seldom happens. Or perhaps, is that rare inward vision of oneself what explains the look of rapturous amusement on a dying person's face, which is always interpreted by good Christians as the first peer at Heaven?

A letter to D. from his mother, fairly spitting and steaming from the envelope with rage that Anne, who had been two weeks home, had not yet come to Claymont, whereas *she* had defied nurses, doctors, and hospital to get home to welcome her errant darling . . . ten days too soon. I can understand her chagrin.

A quiet and prolonged scene with Schwester Irma today, solved finally by petting, cajoling, babying, playfully teasing her into a good humor. God, these complicated middle-aged nitwits who feed on attention! Am I headed for it, too?

After two years of having experts try to fix a gradual crescendo of whir and squaek in our extremely expensive and completely pleasing gramophone, the fumbling, puzzle-witted local radio man came in this afternoon and arranged it as it should be. Of course, I don't know how long it will last, but I enjoy it meanwhile. This afternoon I played a few things, and then the Brahms 2nd Concerto. The 3rd (?) movement of it, I thought . . . my favorite piece of gentle music . . . it will soothe us, it will solace us. But I almost didn't hear it at all, so busy was I trying to keep D. from looking at the clock and crying wildly at the filthiness of a life that is only endurable with *piqures*.

It is 10:00 at night. I'll try to stay awake until D. calls, about 12:30 to 1:30, to give him his shot. Irma has fussed so about how badly she feels, that I'm bitch enough to want to fool her and do the night work myself for once. It's a shot-and-a-half, and I hate the idea of it, but I'm sick to death of her nobly stifled yawns in the mornings. I hope I can work it. *Piqures* make me sick, still, but not actively, as they used to.

It is satisfying, in a queer way, to have written the bones of a book today. I'm puzzled by it, and feel quite doubtful that I can do it as well as I want to . . . but at least I'm working. As I told D. today, I've been proving with so much conversation that I'm through with the lost cause of literature, that at least I can go to work now with the courage of my convictions.

November 8, 1938
It's become almost impossible for Dillwyn and me to talk anymore, except now and then when he is almost human after an injection and I'm not too sleepy. I find myself, after almost eleven weeks of encouragements and quiet words of good sense or jaunty or plain goddamn cheerfulness, so sick of myself that I can't help feeling that he is too. Perhaps I'm hypersensitive. I know that I'm growing a little nervy: the last few days have found me several times cold with exasperation at Irma, or even at the fact that no matter how Dillwyn feels (always badly, but in degrees), or what he says, it is pessimistic. God knows I can't blame him, but lately I find myself wishing that when I ask him if he has slept, he will simply say *Yes*, instead of *Yes, but very badly*, or *Yes, but it was a queer muddled sleep*. I know it could be nothing else . . . but I wish for once he'd leave it at that. And that shows that I am growing cranky. I feel very low today, partly because the few minutes I have had each day with Tim, since this started, have gradually become a listening to his crying and moaning and a fierce battle with myself not to break loose and tell him for God's sake to buck up, when I know that he has no strength left to do it with, and partly because Irma grows daily more cavalier in her behavior toward us, and such treatment always depresses men and makes me feel self-scorn at my weakness in putting up with it. But at the moment I simply can't have any more trouble. If D. were better I'd tell her to go. She's been very good, but she is haunted by the fact that she is in her fifties, and she is of a moody type that thrives on "hot emotional baths" and I can't supply her with them. She would love me (as would not how many other women in my life!) if I'd only weep upon her breast, or scream with rage, or sulk. But I can do none of these things with my inferiors. So *she* sulks, and sobs, in my place. Now she feels unwell, and I hear every detail of her malaise, and heap coals of fire on her wordless resentment of the whole situation by seeing that she has extra fruit, extra rest, by not calling her even once at night, and all *impersonally*. That impersonality is what outrages her preconceptions of being human, of being warm and sympathetic. I regret it, as I often have before. I recognize it, as I should, after so many years of frightening people, of making them feel cheated by my lack of confidences.

November 13, 1938
For several days I've not had time to write, although I have thought a good deal about the book I'm working on. I think I made a mistake to talk with D. about it. Now that he knows, there may be less incentive to work on it.

I read to D. a lot every day, and every night. The sciatica, which is being treated with an unguent made of bee venom that spreads a delightful warm incense in the air, has diminished a lot, and the phlebitus is no longer painful. Temperature and pulse is normal, for the first time since September 1. But the theoretical foot is pure hell, reducing D. to a twitching hysterical wreck unless he can stay mildly doped. Today we gave him ½ cc. of Analgeticum, instead of the whole ampule, and although he was still in pain, he was somewhat soothed. He has been exposing his wound for five- to ten-minute periods to the sun, and that seems to aggravate the pain. The doctor is really deeply concerned, and says that as soon as the one open place is closed he can try injections of vitamin B-1, to nourish the cut nerves, and so on . . . and that D.'s being able to move about will help. But in the meantime there is nothing he knows of, except injections. Last night D. told me he would infinitely prefer another amputation to this pain, if it would be able to retie the muscles or something. It's really terrible.

The weather is beautiful now. We eat lunch on the terrace every day.

I am stupid now. I dozed along, half-dreaming, listening to Irma and D. whispering for my sake, until almost eleven . . . the first time I've stayed in bed since early last summer. I've lost my skill at it, evidently!

ROBERT FROST

EDITED BY MARGOT FELDMAN

◆ ──────────────────────── ◆

Notebook: After England

Robert Frost kept notebooks for over half a century. He kept working notebooks while at Harvard, but after moving to a New Hampshire farm (1900) and into serious apprenticeship, he began a form of notetaking that haphazardly and over many years resolved into a more expansive prose style. Out of his notebook thinking grew the poems, published prose, and talks of succeeding decades. Frost kept notebooks informally, and his sweeping disregard for time (chronology) in them gives the ebb and flow of his ideas sensual patterns: over a thousand pages carry only a handful of dates, and not one physical description of a person or place.

The selection that follows constitutes one notebook that Frost filled between 1918 and 1921. (It contains, uncharacteristically, two dates.) Frost was teaching at Amherst College, riding the wave of recognition that after two elusive decades had broken overnight, upon his return from England at the outbreak of World War I. He had published three books of poetry, and the genesis of a fourth, *New Hampshire*, flares among these pages as the poet moves toward the open declarations on social and political issues that will brand later volumes. Here, the energy and mounting tensions of an industrial power barreling into the century— toward not-so-distant disaster—provoke a barrage of entries. During these years Frost's impatience with academic obligations and what he considered a dangerously liberal academic atmosphere reached a head, and in the spring of 1920 he resigned from Amherst. That fall he moved from his farm in Franconia, New Hampshire, where he spent summers, to South Shaftsbury, Vermont, and the following year to Ann Arbor, where he began an appointment as "poet-in-residence" at the University of Michigan.

Idiosyncracies in grammar and syntax have been preserved. Editorial changes are indicated by brackets. Interpretation of near-illegible words is indicated by [?]. ** indicates the editorial omission of illegible entries and random memoranda. For the sake of readability, standard punctuation has been added. —M.F.

A time when nothing, neither religion nor patriotism, comes to an apex.

Just as we make a reservoir of clay or something that will hold water we are right in taking for our storage class people who will naturally hold money.

We find the parts of religion in everyone, the idea of sacrifice, of submission.

Reasons for wanting to produce at home all we reasonably can: there is safety in peace as well as war in variety of industry—in peace it is from business disaster and famine; there is increase in population and so in strength for the undertakings both of war and of peace—the greater the population the greater the levy of men and of money. Great deeds, great works!

A great many more than half the industrial class are where by a wise stroke of concession they can be detached from the party of dissatisfaction that threatens the state. We are of little faith not to see the simple way to save ourselves from the Russian contagion.

You can't favor the industrial class as against the capitalist without doing it as against the agricultural, and so turning the agricultural industrial.

Realism of the voice.

The king is [rightly?] first over both creative genius and philosopher because he has command of that most worldly part of the world, the deedal part, the first part in importance, whose nature is that it can be sometimes steered forward by the creative genius and sometimes wisely right by the philosopher, but forward or backwar[d], wisely right or unwisely wrong, it keeps going always and must be ridden somehow by one who has special power for keeping in the saddle of it.

America the Luminox of Nations.

Wilson really scorns those whose patriotism he is best able to fight the war with.

The greatest charity is to give way to an occasional inconsistency.

Authority, which is out of ourselves, does hate liberty, which is in ourselves, and viceversa. No one with us cares to personify the authority outright on account of the enmity he would incur.

How authority, which is really no more [than] a projection of our own natures appears first as an actual person of war and [tyranny?] quite separate from ourselves. It was an age of personification (actual) of most of our projections. Something.

Why the Proletariat must rule:
     Because they can take thought for and encourage more human traits.
     Because our new needs have given them the power over us.
     Because all is vanity and of all our ranks, conditions, and degrees not one matters.
     (We talk as if society could be saved by this or that govt. policy. But even society is short-lived.[)]

The Lost Cellar.

I can see that a pacifist must be absolutely sure of his own bravery, so sure that he assumes bravery of everyone—and makes no account of it.

Wealth is just one of the most important ways of getting your self importance.

I met a pacifist who exalted cowardice as the only real hope of ending war.

Whether we win or whether we [lose] we have still the chance to win or [lose] by either loss or gain, and so on a gain to win or [lose] by.

Subjects for next year's lectures:
     Simplicity.
     That we have nothing to do with books except to write them.

Say who's your candidate for king to 'em.

Seeking out your own advantage is something to rise to.

"Nothing permanent achieved by force."

Suicide for spite against the argufier.

What's On.

This little pig turned prophet and told on the whole game. He saw the end of it all in the crash of civilization.

He that has power to hurt and will do none.*

A sad self-knowledge. Ignorance is as good as knowledge. When we lose one part of our ignorance we sigh and say, Oh my lost innocence.

Shaw thinks better knowledge as between nations will bring them together in peace, and yet he thinks families from knowing too much of themselves are nests of hate and must be broken up.

A connoisseur of brave deaths.

Abolishing the capitalist would mean abolishing the farmer included.

The socialist means to abolish the farmer by driving him to work in the cities, and when he has left the farms vacant he will send squads of city industrials on weekly wage into the country for spells to cultivate the land. The president is up to this.

You say you can endure the wading through the waste and rubbish for the little really interesting in a hard subject. But the real professor [feels?] that, to one who knows, there is no waste or rubbish and all is interesting.

We always talk as if the states must go on (when we argue against socialism). But what's to prevent it being that the states and all are doomed and that socialism is only their last illness.

An Intelligencer—one who by travel and current reading and by meeting interesting people calculates to keep posted.

*An allusion to Shakespeare's sonnet XCIV, which begins, "They that have power to hurt and will do none."

Must have interesting people and pleasant surroundings! Oh but these are rewards for those who fear [the] thought that they must have work.

People that can take any side of a question. I think they like to try on other people's ideas as girls try on each other's dresses to see how they seem in them.

Max E. is like a man beside a cannon who makes a throwing motion with his arm every time it goes off and tries to think he is hurling its death and destruction. Or like a person who dips his hand in a terrible flood of water.

Emerson's Mistake about Nature.

The Adoptive American like O'Reilly.

Living Abroad.

European Opinion.

Don't go near anyone till you are strong-selfed enough not to be too much influenced.

Is American literature merely colonial?

Does our literature merely reflect what happens to be going on in English literature?

Poe made the modern short story.

**

Interstices. How the ineffable gets in between the bronze, beads, or language you work in and the thing you try to represent: and again between the thing you represent and the thing you liken it to to represent it.

Education of information.
         "   of criticism.
         "   " rapture.

"   " participation.

Education by joining in with what is done and no questions asked.

The rich have waited to be asked to come and live humbly and meanly with the poor. They have waited to be asked.

The weakness of unity is what it is. Its effect is to break it into competitive parts that again strengthen toward unity.

To flourish is to become dangerous.

Asked your reasons too suddenly you always give a bad one first. Why didn't you go to jail for your conscientious objections? Death and jail are the only defeat. It would be to [lose] the fight. We have to compromise at some point to save ourselves and I compromised there. Because I'm a coward and believe in cowardice. Fear is our greatest hope of ending wars and competition. Third and real reason: because though I believe in martyrdom and going the whole length for a cause, I won't have my country for my cause (the state is an ugly thing). I choose to make my last stand on something else.

The flow of talk goes forward. Words or no words, we must make a sound of voices to each other and we will; but it will be better if we can launch a thought now and then on the stream of words.

Culture is to know things at first hand (at the source).

Special [Privilege?] in Chief: to be out of the Illusion of Life.

Who are the dragged: the disillusioned few or the many disillusioned.

Abnegation. The spoiled daughter as social worker. She will not be better than the worst. Her man and his crimes. Murder.

Got the idea too young that it was not for him to find out and study what others thought but for others to find out and study what he thought.

The teacher said to his writing class, All I am is a straw to catch at. But remember I am that if it seems to you you are drowning. I think most of you are.

Why is it any more sincere and less hypocritical to give up and sink back into what we came out of than to strain forward to what we are going to become?

Tell a well-educated college boy the best thought right out of your own thinking and he accepts it with a, *Do* they say so? He is disappointed when you have to admit, No, *I* say so but they will say so after I show them.

There is this about outside: nothing is so outside that it isn't still inside. Absolute outsideness forever eludes us. But it is there and no one can doubt that from it some virtue proceeds inward to the very center. It may even be more governing than what radiates from the center. Things have ruled in the name of it calling it their divine right. Every elected ruler governs by it who consults his conscience instead of his electorate. He governs from without inward as an idealist, from within outward as a realist.

It is best to be flattered when your thought is taken for what everybody has thought, just as it is when your simile passes for a folk saying from a locality.

Message of May 21, 1919
Pres Wilson says we must be on our guard against our rivals in commerce: in other words we must live in a wholesome fear of them. At the same time he is afraid they are too crippled by the war to be very dangerous. In other words the unctuous man is afraid they are nothing to be afraid of. Ain't that too bad for them or us or which is it?

Only one way to come into this vast hollow with no surrounding walls.

The Real Estate Agent's Inn.
Sets and Sequences.

If a Christian should go on [illegible] with self-abnegation and humility never taking his pay for it forever, where would he come out in the end?

Take the Os and Ohs of a play of Shakespeare. Notice the tones of them and the meaning of the tones. How are the tones indicated unless by the sentences the Os and Ohs are in? The sentences are notations then for indicating the tones of the Ohs. Omit the Os and the sentences still indicate the tones. All good sentences i[n]dicate tones that might be said in Ohs alone or in the Ohs with the same sentences.

You can always get a little more literature if you are willing to go a little closer into what has been left unsaid as unspeakable, just as you can always get a little more melon by going a little closer to the rind or a little more dinner by scraping the plate with a table knife.

Derivative and Original Poetry. Originality depends on [the] faculty of noticing. Strange things happen in us and things not so strange. Cultivate the faculty of noticing or you will notice only what has been noticed and called to your attention before.

Enterprise of Undergraduates. Undergraduates neglect their studies for various enterprises of their own, athletics, society, business administration. (They neglect them for nothing at all, but that is another matter.) The thing is they almost never neglect them for anything more enterprising intellectually, such as the creative in art or scholarship. Modus vivendi found by teachers and those who want to neglect studies more or less for games, society, and administration. Confessed there is something to be said for them.

The Witch of Holts.

Immortality. The Inspector of Mummies. [illegible] The Spoilers. Our loss not their gain.
A Book of the Dead.

Off for the South Seas. His Wife may not go with him. I may go. Who am I? I'll tell you who I am: I'm the original of the picture on the cover of —— magazine just out. Have you seen it? / / Five children to dispose of. Well if you won't take two of them—if you won't accept a fair offer, I'll clear out first—went to France to help in war. Stayed away till the children wouldn't [illegible] on her. / / Heaven is let up.

Explanation of the failure of some people to get on with others. They use the right words and phrases. But they can't get the tones of voice unself-conscious, intimate, and inoffensive. Their tones are offish, uncomfortable, constrained, unconfident, uningratiating. They can't ring true even when they aren't playing a part and when it ought to be easy to ring true. They are the opposite from the great actors who can ring true even when they are playing a part and when it ought to be hard to ring true.

The Latest People.

Couldn't miss the movies in his own town. Would be left out of the talk of the town.

It seems to *Harper's* that Howells deserves to be made a classic.* They have made an appropriation to give him the necessary publicity.

All the accents of meter are alike; at least there is nothing in them to show difference. The accents I speak of are all different. My chief interest is in what we have to indicate this difference.

**

He thought he was prevailing by sheer worldly force and shrewdness, the traits that as a poet he wasn't supposed to have. His wife listened to his ruthless talk and for a long time half-believed him. Reckless of losing her he still talked on. But all the time he was really a good poet and got no inch further than his poetry made way for him. So much for his thinking he could beat the world at its own game. Who was the biggest fool at last?

$60,000 if she would stay true to the boy who died.

Humboldt
Henry Adams
Prioresses Tale
Nonne Priestes Tale
Teodore & Honoria

To make a spiritual parade before the company.

*William Dean Howells had given Frost unreserved praise in Harper's *magazine (Sept. 1915). Frost later (and uncharacteristically) referred to "the great debt I owe to Howells."*

We get on because we have this in common, that both of us are indifferent to money. He doesn't care how large an amount of it he has and I don't care how small an amount I have.

The Buffalo papers said I made an attack on ambiguity. The Syracuse papers said I was suffering from hasty recognition. (false recognition.) I had tried hard to show how unavoidably ambiguous we are most of the time in word, phrase, sentence, tone, deed and even situation. (The position I found myself in on that platform was ambiguous.) I surrendered to ambiguity. / / I had tried to show how the educated suffered from false recognition—from recognizing too hastily a new thing for something known. . . .

Range of playfulness proof of real culture.

Christmas 1921
Give to the poor to make them happy but not to purchase happiness for yourself that night. Do not forget to be wretched with them, your giving cannot reach to touch.

Why give at all?

Life is that which beguiles us into taking sides in the conflict of pressure and resistance, force and control. Art is that which disengages us to concern ourselves with the tremor of the universal deadlock.

The Census Taker—I'll ask you in the train some day.

I met Columbus out in the Pacific beyond the Isthmus.

The New Picture and how to seem interested in it.

The Whippoorwill wasn't saying much—though present.

The mind is given its speed of more miles an hour than even the stream of time so that it can choose absolutely how fast it will go with the stream or whether it will stand still on it or go against it. The great thing is that it can stay in one place for a while and it is probably the only thing that can.

Displacement Due to Poetry. Poetic Displacement.

Poetry brings pollen of one flower to another flower.

He threw the whole machine out of his shop and out of his mind for one fault, and recreated it entire from a fresh conception of what it was intended to do.

The slight lovely hope—what chance has it by itself, unhelped and unfavored from without?

It's not long life that anyone would ever object to, but long death.

Writing Down the Voice.

In tracing back an idea, institution, or species to its origin it is as it were to consider a larkspur, and descending from more flower to less, go right past the stem, and come to an end with the spur. It looks as if the pale point of the spur were what the flower had derived from instead of from the stem, which is not flowerlike at all.

We look for the line between good and evil and see it only imperfectly for the reason that we are the line ourselves.

A good share of hypocrisy is Let's not say till we see.

Regular fellow said all the faculty wanted a literary magazine for was to publish any good themes in [that] they got in their classes.

Reality and unreality in pronunciation. Lesley* persists in saying *a* dog. *The* dog.

Is Poetry Highbrow or Lowbrow.
    The ballads are one and Comus is the other. The distinction in poetry has no significance. Poetry may be either but it doesn't matter which it is so long as it is spirited. Nor ought it to matter of anything else which it is so long as it is spirited.

Lesley Frost, the poet's eldest daughter.

A Prayer before Going Abroad. God help us not to take the English as the English take us.

[Internal evidence in the manuscript indicates a shift in entry order at this point in the notebook. Apparently Frost at some point reversed his order of writing, and began entries from the rear toward the center of the notebook. The reversal is honored here; entries from this point on represent those proceeding from the rear of the manuscript toward the middle.]

The Humanist Exhumed. In re[ading] Mat[thew] Arnold.

Mat's prose says, It makes me mad that people don't see the complete thought involved in their half thoughts. Starting where they do they have got to come out thus and so. They have got to think this. Then his poetry says, After all I don't think it myself. What am I pretending? Their opposition has made me talk myself into a rage of certainty where there can be no certainty. Who am I but a foiled circuitous wanderer to take dejectedly my seat upon the intellectual [throne].*

On Being Funny (like Mark Twain[)] and wanting to assume the dignity of the masterful. The Clown's Wife. Live to right the impression.

**

Remember how we gave to time
The lovely bell we cast
~~Too stately and~~   Too stately and   of
                           note
~~A bell of too~~ prolonged a note reverberance
  For striking fast

~~Time~~
~~Not once~~
So   And how
                       adept
Time struck it like an oldster at the bells
And
But once an hour and then a few

*The allusions to Arnold's poetry ("Sohrab and Rustum" and "The Scholar Gipsy") form the basis of lines 383–385 in Frost's poem, "New Hampshire."

Something that you unexpectedly see a person thinking of himself often makes you dislike him as nothing else in looks or words or actions can make me.

The adjectives words pushed from behind unhelped from the side or from in front.

Digging out what your reason really is for an act already done.

They don't conjoin any more properly than verbs and adjectives.

You must expect to be happy because you are good: but you must contrive your goodness in some way out of your happiness.

Rather a sensualist any day than a sensibilitist—one who makes of himself as a nature framed to enjoy greatly and needing interesting friends and pleasant surroundings but destined also to suffer greatly in a terrible world from the want of these essentials.

There are [t]he clever who consider themselves clever because they deal with urban subjects. The free who consider themselves free because they deal with sexual subjects. The radical who consider themselves radical because they deal with antigovernment subjects. The artistic who consider themselves artistic because they deal with rosy and moonlight subjects. But of course there can't be particular subject matter that makes people artistic, clever, free, or radical.

Heroic in patriotism, in religion.

Government's chief end is to propagate small farmers.

**

The present is more derived from the future than from the past.

No one has really tasted discipline who is only self-disciplined.

Four Layers. The Fobses* have servants who live under the same roof with them and a farmer and his wife who have a home on the place to

---

*The Fobses owned a farm near Frost's in Franconia, New Hampshire. After moving to Vermont, the Frosts sometimes used the Fobses' guest cottage during hay fever season.

themselves. The farmer and his wife have to make a stand with the servants lest the servants should fail to see the difference in their condition and try to drag them down to their level. Now we are farmers too but on our own hook and would you believe it out. When Fobses' farmer's wife sees us with the Fobses as equals she rather resents it, and I am afraid if we had to be much with her we might have to insist on our slight superiority to her, if inferiority to the Fobses who are so of course the top of the stratification because they are so rich.

The Protean Pro German and his Refuge in Pacifism.

The Rich Reformer and the Poor Man's Daughter.

Speculation in Blue Shore Lake Front.

When birding one morning at sunrise, I asked a bird I didn't know if he knew what kind of bird he was himself, and he said he didn't but he could always tell another bird of the same kind when he saw one.

Some people neglect their studies for business, society and government so wholly that they not only stay away from classes, they stay away from college. Everyone has heard of them. I want you to hear of the few who stay away from college and even the intellectual part of college to pursue intellectuality. So very enterprising are they in scholarship or the arts.

The Wherewithal. Where They Got Their Money.
    Revolutionary Funds
    Buying Blue Lake as Agent
    Two Pensions
    Mortgage Fire Telescope
    I'm a Duk for Water

A Poem containing metaphors or a poem that is a metaphor. The latter may be spread thin so that the canvas almost shows through.

There is some living principle in Longfellow like what is cooked out of milk when it is Pasteurized.

AMERICA

How was it nurtured to such bursting forth?
It stole into existence
It stole its growth unregarded by nations, to[o]
great to see realities.
It saved itself whole under the very nose of half-
suspicious England.
And now God discloses it Lo I uncover the West,
discloses it as a power. Shall it be only as a
power and not as an Idea too?

Riches and Thought are remote. Poverty and Toil alone are realizing.

Eating is the primal agression. Beneficent interference is the ultimate agression.

If it is sweet to Englishmen that England though a little island north away should half the lands and all the seas and make them better for her righteousness, why should not Germans wish such glory for their country in their turn. Wish it? Yes. And ask England for it if she dares. But why should not England deny her her request?

Social reform has nothing to do with the war between nations except in every nation to use the predicament to extort from rulers some of its desiderata. The hope of the social revolutionist that the war may mean the end of nations is vain. Nationalism is one thing and socialism another. One does not take the place of the other.

Mechanism or Idealism, what's the difference? By any name all monisms come to the same thing. It is a question of good and bad. If all is good or all bad we were still secure in monism. But we find in experience that there is a division between good and bad. We get both permanently so far as we have gone.

Reason has to be slurred over in every moment of action. Action and reason are two different sequences or lineages that keep pretty well along together, reason just a little behind, catching up by skipping a space at moments of action.

English Dept. ought to be dedicated to the exquisiteness of language which can be experienced only in a mother tongue.

War is the last expression of what we will bear for belief. It is the chastisement that none but the most distant can give us. Near is dear. There must be someone far enough away to chastise you more than the near and dear can be expected to.

Machine-made proletariat. Out of the machines as much as the cloth they wove.

Efficiency in reading. Efficient reading is taken to be the kind that gets the most information out of a book in the shortest time. But mightn't it be the kind that gets the fullest flavor of the book. The eye reader might have the advantage in skimming for salient facts. The ear reader would have the advantage in getting into the subtler facts that lie in tone, implication and style. The ear reader (who is of course an eye reader also) alone has any chance of attaining distinction in knowledge and expression.

The soft surface of the earth is no more than the thickness of a tarnish on a metal ball.

A Book of Kings.

The first state in which a pupil can get a lot done is one of innocence. Keep the pupil there in the long wait for his first accidental success. Make the most of that to make it memorable because the memory is what he has got to live on through succeeding failure.

See how some people always steer the conversation where they have done some thinking of their own. No teacher of course could steer them there by any questioning or set examination.

**

Paul never would go to work for more than $14 a week because he knew he wouldn't get it.
    Sweet Revenge on the Bar
    Paul was Part Human.

Oh boys it's Saturday night
Hooray hooray hooray
Five meals out of the [illegible]
And two nights in the hay
Do lumberjack[s] eat hay? No they're part human.

**

Moving a Brick Chimney across a River.

Three Stolen Apples.

A Dead Orchard.

Sling Shots at Bellows Falls.

On the Town. The Witch of Warren.

Our Troubles. Poor beclouded minds.

Prophetic dreams.

**

His Sister Went Primitive (Indian Guide).

You have to be attractive enough to get people within striking distance.

Our best hopes are our fears according to Sal[ly] Kleg[horn]. The only
thing that will end war is cowardice.

Suppose you came constantly to a class and waited in silence day after
day for someone in it to find something to say. [R]esolved not to help
it one bit. [W]ould they feel embarrassment, get something out of [this?]?

Man in the first seat in room did all the reciting in German class. All you
had to do if you didn't want to recite was keep out of the first seat. Notice
the cunning smile on the face of any American boy you tell that to. Easy
to infer from it that his idea is to get as little as possible of what is the
teacher's idea to give him.

I came to live in the house of a professor who was off in Europe having
what a professor would call a good time. He had left all his books for

me to have a good time with but had taken good care that I shouldn't have too good a time with them. He had marked them all up with a pencil wherever he had found a mistake of any kind just as if they were written by pupils. And he had used the pencil on them for nothing but mistakes. He had never praised anything (I should have loathed his praise), but he had never contributed an idea or interesting commentary.

But not all professors are the same. One who came to [the] rescue for [the] day in a course on the French Revolution when the regular professor was absent, finding that the class had been kept all the time on politics, economics, and the mental diseases of the great and hadn't heard of the Guillotine, said, What, haven't [you] heard about the Guillotine. Why the Guillotine is a very interesting thing, and then went at it with pictures and story to make a perfectly good Revolution exciting.

TESS GALLAGHER

◆ ────────────────────────── ◆

European Journal

*P*aris / *April 5, 1987*

Our hotel is small but comfortable. There's a place for Ray to smoke so
we need only one room. The area of Paris where we've located is on the
Left Bank. Many bookstores nearby. Ray goes into one to see if they
have his book. They don't. At the Café Bonaparte I say: "Well it doesn't
look like you're going to be mobbed here." Ray: "Well, it's only Sunday."

Paris / April 6, 1987.

Lunch with Edmund White who says he'll *take* being pegged as a "gay
writer." He's just written a book on the death of a number of friends by
AIDS. Makes the remark that he wouldn't take up smoking or drinking
again even if he discovered he was dying of AIDS. Death of David Kal-
stone a surprise—from AIDS. I recall reading his books at the U. of
Washington in 1969. Edmund very kind spirited and lively. Ray and I
both like him very much.

Gilles Barbidoux—a critic, also at lunch. Funny, he liked my jokes
because I was very sardonic. Realizing now, as I write, that Ray and I
had come a long, unexpected way to sit at that table. Clear this French-
man has had every advantage. Later Ray said he was sorry not to have
his essays to show Gilles—I said, no, it's better as it is. The minute one
of these French critics *thinks* they can understand you they're finished
with you. Better he's puzzled/expectant.

Some talk about deconstructionist theories. Barthes, Foucault, etc.
Not read anymore in France, Gilles says. Passé. Reduced to a fad here.
But a joke how Americans have taken it all up in the most serious way,
rather like the Russians of Dostoyevski's era, snapping up anything
French out of a sense of inferiority.

Ray is appreciated in same way as Marguerite Duras—for his style,
the particularity of that, not because he's a realistic writer or a minimalist, this last a term he rejects, and rightly so.

White tells us he wants to go back to America so he can write about things there. America—his workshop. *Our* workshop. How things are almost *too* perfect here in Paris for him. He needs the abrasiveness of American life. He's originally from Texas. Describes a grave-tending occasion which reminds me of Missouri and my mother. He also retells a story by Willa Cather which makes us want to reread her.

White walks us over to the Orangerie des Tuileries after lunch and we see Monet's *Water Lilies*. I remember seeing them from my time before in Paris in 1968. The idea of Monet's *growing* the flowers he would later paint—very lovely. Idea of painting the unseen because he was painting light in water. The way an approximation becomes all one needs of the real at certain times.

"I didn't have anybody on my side for years except that dog. She defended me." Telling Ray of Satin—my childhood dog. Remembering the Parisian woman taxicab driver with her dog beside her on the seat. Her covering it tenderly with a small cotton sheet to protect it from the sun. A block later she was swearing viciously at another driver.

Paris / April 8, 1987

A very late evening after Ray's reading at the English Language Bookstore, The Village Voice—Ray reads "Collectors" and "The Father" to a packed upstairs room. People are even standing on the stairs. C. K. (Charlie) Williams is there (living in Paris with French wife). Also Peter Taylor who has just received the Hemingway prize for *A Summons to Memphis*. Williams (very tall!) says he gets writer's block when he finishes a book of poems. Is thinking of starting up a poetry writing group in Paris.

I meet Ray's French translator, François Lascan, and he says he had to do this translation very quickly—too quickly. He would have liked to have gone over it five more times he says. He makes a living as a translator. He'll be with us at the short-story festival at San Quentin. None of his translation was read at the bookstore because it was an English-speaking audience. Two women came up to me after Ray's reading and said how much they enjoy my poems, and when will I have a new book? The proprietress of the bookstore, Odile Hellier, is very lovely, apologizes for not having my books, says there have been several requests.

Paris / April 9, 1987

Short rest at hotel. Then Brigitte, my young poet friend from Syracuse, calls. We agree to meet and go to the Musée d'Orsay. Ray will join us after his rest. We begin on the fifth floor which we've been advised to do. It's crowded. Good and bad painters thrown together. Periods are not respected. The bad pointilists next to Monet. Seeing van Gogh's painting of his room and his self-portraits—this was the most amazing. His intention so firmly impressed into his strokes. *Not* a man of doubt in his painting. The Degas paintings wonderful too and the *manques* of horses in bronze. His ballet dancers so awkwardly balanced in those paintings. Things come alive when they are seen in more than their balanced presentation. The pastels were in such a dark alcove we couldn't see them well. Ray joining us and we see the Gaugins together—*The Blue Horse* my favorite.

Ray and I go for dinner at the Moulin Rouge and take in the "spectacle"—really beautiful girls in elaborate costumes, very fast-paced, but because I've danced I can tell how the girls are sparing themselves. The cancan was most exciting to me—making me remember when I danced it in *The Merry Widow* in Texas in 1966. Was so sore during practice then that I could hardly climb the stairs to my bedroom. The girls smiled a lot and, as Ray said, seemed to be enjoying themselves and in the "seeming," they did. There were acrobats and also a ventriloquist who made people from the audience come up on stage with him and he caused odd, embarrassing noises to come out of their mouths. Then he brought a white dog on stage and made it seem to talk. The audience loved this, of course. There were a lot of Japanese in the audience. Everyone well-dressed. Ray may have been the only one *not* in a suit. But he'd worn a tie. He and I danced two or three times, which was fun, and then he bought me a pink rose.

Coming out, a taxicab driver tried to scalp us. He wanted one hundred francs (about eighteen dollars) to take us back to the hotel. Ray told him to forget it. He found a cab for fifty francs which was probably still about five francs too much.

Once we were safely back near our hotel we went out to the Brasserie Lipp and I had tea and Ray had coffee—just to sit and watch what went on out in the street. Mostly young people, very playful with each other. Some short dresses, but jeans mostly. Strikingly handsome gay men. Not many gay women that I see.

We come back and eat some chocolate. I smoke Ray's pipe. He smokes cigarettes he doesn't like. I read Cocteau's diaries out loud for us.

Ray to Tess: (Paris, Thursday, 9 April 1987) handwritten note.

I'll be glad to get home!

R.C.

Hotel des Saintes-Pères

I promise (intend) to go walking every day, just about, with Tess on the beach in Port Angeles,

R.C.

Wiesbaden / April 15, 1987

Ray and I nap in the early evening after our drive along the Rhine, and then have coffee before going to the casino in Wiesbaden around 9:00 P.M. This is the Spielbank Casino where Dostoyevski won and then lost a fortune. There is even a room in the casino named after him, the Dostoyevski Room! I get fifty marks' worth of five-mark chips. We begin to play roulette at table no. 5. I bet on red with Ray and win a couple of times, then on even and win. I watch a black man who is betting on the numbers by putting chips on the lines between numbers. This gives him more chances but lowers the payoff. I watch for a while, finding it hard to maintain a spot near the table because bettors crowd past me, sometimes gouging me. I bruise so easily I have to take care. I hadn't realized how physically aggressive one has to be to play roulette.

Finally the number 24 occurs to me with such freshness and surety that I feel I *must* bet on it. Dostoyevski is with me! I don't even persuade myself of this. I know it. It is the first bet I've placed on a number. The odds are 35 to 1. My chip (five marks) is the only one left as the others are scooped away. "That's mine!" I tell Ray. There is a sort of sigh that comes from around the table as the croupier says 175 marks and makes a stack of chips (all blue with one red one hundred-mark chip) and asks me to come around. I don't want to leave my place so I motion for him to shift them around to me and smile, but he again wants me to come to him. He's afraid the stack will topple. I start there. But by then he's swiftly pushed them across the table. He starts to retrieve them but by then I've returned to my place near Ray, fearful he has accepted my winnings and I won't get to take them up myself—which seems foolishly important. So, once again, the croupier shoves the chips over in my direction. I give a five-mark tip to the croupier near me who says, "Congratulations." After this I bet on three more numbers but don't win. Then on red and black and win. But I feel exhausted by having won. As if, by connecting up with that strange current of clairvoyance,

I've used up my "normal" energy too. It is exactly 10:30 P.M. and we had agreed to gamble exactly one hour, and then eat.

We go into the adjoining dining room which is very luxurious. Marble pillars, huge chandeliers, candles and flowers on each table. Elaborate gold designs on ceiling. At one corner a flashing display board shows the numbers coming up at the various tables. We get interested in table 3 because many reds have come up in sequence. We watch it all through dinner. A light meal with lobster salad—just the cheeks of the lobster used and slightly warmed. I have quail soup which is mostly broth with some green bits of meat. Quail? Carrots and other veg. cut into marble-sized bits in soup. For dessert Ray has fruit with sorbet and liqueur. And I have a cake in liqueur with strawberries and kiwi, with mint leaves for decoration. Then coffee with cookies. Our waiter is very nice and the place is a real class operation.

Zürich / April 17, 1987

Harold* meets us in Zürich. He seems the same as I remember him— boyish, good-humored, a wry sense of humor that crops up delightfully. But he tells us he isn't sleeping. He has to take a special herbal tea Lynne, his wife, has found, and this seems to work. "It's your move,"† I tell him. And he says "Yes" as if it hadn't quite occurred to him—it was so obvious.

The hotel is exactly right. He has chosen it with care. Very homey. The furniture antique and nice draperies, chandelier over the two beds which are fitted out with the plump down comforters typical for here . . . though many hotels, Harold says, don't use them now. Our breakfast is included in the fee.

We eat lunch with Harold (he takes a glass of wine with me—red wine because white keeps him awake) in the old section of the city. He tells us how well Lynne is doing with her "colorist" job‡ and also that she is taking on doing translations at the University. He has read my poetry manuscript for my book *Amplitude: New and Selected*, and says, "we're going to fight tomorrow"—he wants to take out three poems and put in two others. Also revise the endings on a couple of others.

Ray and I walk together down the narrow streets and stare in windows, then come back for an hour-and-a-half nap. Then a light

---

*Harold Schweizer, our Swiss friend in Zürich who is a poet, scholar and critic.
†Harold had just accepted a teaching position at Bucknell University in Lewisburg, PA.
‡Suggesting which colors enhance the personality and natural coloring of people (for their choices in dressing).

supper of smoked salmon and eggs poached in sauce with shrimp—also asparagus soup, a great summer favorite here. Ray is having a gigantic bowl—goblet!—of fresh strawberries and cream when Lynne and Harold arrive. They have come to see us at the hotel after their church service. We order some local red wine—light and good—a rosé. There is so much to tell—the rough time with L. last summer and with Ray's mother at Christmas. My own mother's bad back. Harold tells the happy story of his job search. For his lecture at Bucknell University he presented Kierkegaard as a contemporary poet!

Zürich / April 18, 1987
Worked with Harold on my poems. Going very carefully poem by poem. He wants some rather overpopular poems out: "The Hug" and "Beginning to Say No" and "Shirts" among them. We also take out "Crossing" and completely rewrite "Time Lapse with Tulips." We run out of time.

Ray and I take a boat ride on the lake. "See"—Zürich See. It's very sunny and many people are strolling along the promenade—a holiday feeling. The Easter holidays are here, so the shops are all shut except for some near the lake—the Café Odeon where Ray and I stop for a while after the boat ride: Pound, Joyce, Lenin, Tristan Tzara (who started Dadaism)—all came here. Last time we were in Zürich the café seemed to be frequented mostly by gays. Harold tells us "it's changed." Ray goes inside, comes out, and says the men are lined up at the bar—as before. One strange dandy of a man at a table across the sidewalk from us who strains to watch every woman as she goes by—he's wearing a thin tie—looks Italian, like out of one of Fellini's films.

Zürich / April 19, 1987
Late morning and it seems hard to get out of the hotel to go shopping before Harold comes at 3:00 P.M. to take us to the Thomas Mann archives at the University. Ray needs to eat at noon so sandwiches of ham and cheese are brought to the room. Arrangements are made for our travel to Rome. I call Nancy Watkins* in Rome and she will arrange first-class train seats for us from Rome to Milan. It has been eight years since she and Gian sat in my little house in Tucson! She says Riccardo†

Artist and publisher (with her husband Gian Franco Palmeri, the poet) of Arsenale, *a literary journal, and of* Labirinto *(the publishing house which will publish twenty of my poems in translation).*
†*Riccardo Duranti, poet and translator.*

hasn't finished his introduction to my poems yet and that summer is a bad time to bring out a book. So maybe they'll wait.

Ray buys me daffodils which are open today on my desk. Harold arrives with chocolate and flowers! Beautiful cut-glass vases are sent up from the desk.

We find the guard at the Mann archives "unusually friendly," as Harold tells us later. He lets us go into areas forbidden to others. Harold picks books off the shelves of Mann's collection looking for handwritten notes. We see much underlining, but *Joseph and His Brothers*—the book he wants—he can't find. Extensive notes in there, he says. The Eastern influence of objects on Mann's desk. A bust of an Indian Buddha. Some horn knives, a photo of his wife. His actual study, which has been re-assembled here, was on the other side of the lake. Goethe actually visited the man who owned this particular house. "They haven't vacuumed these carpets since Goethe walked here," Harold jokes. We see an unreadable letter from Freud to Mann on the wall. Also on a small page, in neat script, the first page of *Death in Venice*. Harold says he regrets he didn't do work on Mann,* since all these materials were here. He takes us into a lovely study room for those who come from around the world to study him—many Japanese, Harold says. We've left the Mann archives and are sitting at a garden café, but I'm still back at the archives in my mind—seeing Harold open a walking stick of Mann's to show us and the guard a flask inside it for liquor.

Rome / April 26, 1987
No time to write in Rome. Too much to see, to do! One of the important meetings for us both has been with Fernanda Pivano who knew Hemingway and was his Italian translator beginning with *For Whom the Bell Tolls*. She shows us photos of herself as a young woman with her husband and Hemingway. We learn she's written an afterword to Ray's book which is just coming out in Italian: *What We Talk About When We Talk About Love*. This will be of great help in securing Ray a good readership in Italy, she tells us. She's a woman who knows her own considerable worth on the literary scene here, I'm glad to see. Formerly she had only been writing on "the beats," but recently she began to follow contemporary American fiction and sees Ray as the "Poppa" of an entire present younger American generation.

*He worked instead on Theodore Roethke, another of our fated connections.

Friday—we meet Nancy and Gian at the "Cemetery for Foreigners," as we understand the local name for the cemetery in which Keats, Severin, and Shelley are buried. It doesn't open until 3:20 P.M., so we go for a sandwich (pizza bread) and cokes and tea. Nancy and Gian order a fruit drink. A kind of frappé. Gian allows his photograph to be taken at the outdoor tables with Ray and Nancy.

Once inside the cemetery we're led into an office where several people at desks look up. A man who speaks English gives us a "rule sheet" which cautions us with twelve rules—one of them is "don't pet the cats . . . they might have rabies." There is a black cat near Keats' grave. "There's always a cat there," Gian says. He also wonders where the other cats are—"There used to be many cats here." Nancy says there are about 300 cats at "the pyramid" nearby.

The grave of Shelley is on a kind of shelf, as I recall it. E. J. Trelawny is next to Shelley. Purple iris stand tall on the graves around. I tell Nancy I've brought from Switzerland bulbs of purple iris for my mother. She says I won't be allowed to take them through customs. I say I've hidden them. She says her mother gave her some chives that had bugs in them, that the rules are made for a reason. I know she's right yet understand how the desire for the strange, the exotic, causes infractions of such rules. The time at the graves is too short since we have to go to the University.

The session goes well—most of the questions are asked by Americans though and one Italian in the back who says that although European lit. has traditionally scorned US writing, there's a change he sees now. As if Europeans are now looking *toward* the US. A University professor denies that *this* (scorn for US writing) has been the perception of "Europeans." "Why do you think there is such underestimation of American literature?" Ray asks the man. No real answer evolves. The man is a writer. Only two people raise their hands when Ray asks how many want to be writers. Quite different from in the States where more than half might have raised theirs.

Before the University session we are beset with photographers. I sit with Ray for a couple of shots.

The room is packed, all seats taken. Some students standing. Afterward a young woman comes up to me and says she doesn't know my work but that she just admires me as a woman, where can she get my poems? She wants to read in English, her boyfriend is English. She says she used to write but became blocked. I say I'll send her a book. She seems astounded, offers money. No, I say, it's for the hospitality of your country. I take her address.

Finally Riccardo breaks up the interviews and we go for dinner at a restaurant within walking distance. There are so many "starters" that I'm full when the time for a main course of lamb comes. Sitting next to me is a very interesting woman who has translated Tillie Olsen and Grace Paley—"to know them," she says. She tells me that translating is terribly undervalued. A lot of work and it doesn't pay. You have to do it because you just have to do it, she says. She has two daughters, is divorced, has been evicted from her house after many years. Has just had to move. Lives in the same building as Kathleen Frazer, a poet from San Francisco whom Ray and I both know. We agree to meet next morning at 10:00 A.M.

Fernanda Pavino sits across from Ray and me at the dinner. She doesn't stay long, doesn't eat. Is there just long enough to talk a little. There is so much happening I only remember her smile and her lime green outfit—very cool and smart and comfortable-looking. She's still wonderfully handsome, vital.

Milan / April 29, 1987

Dinner with Mr. Bondechini, editor for Mondadori. He has arranged this meal so as to pre-empt our meeting with the Garzanti* staff. He is feeling sheepish about having allowed Garzanti to "pick up" Ray's books previous to Cathedral (which Mondadori brought out but which didn't sell). Now Ray's work has caught on and Mr. B. is sharking around us to see what he can "pick up" himself, to get back into the action. He wants to scalp Fires of its stories and put them together with new stories. (Ray and I just listen, don't say much.) I dislike him immediately so I go overly much in an agreeable direction to hide this. He jokes about the head of the English Dept. in Rome where we spoke—how he studied with this man and how the Professor mistakenly thought he (Mr. B.) was doctoral material, so the Professor was disappointed when Mr. B. went into editing and publishing. He is anxious to find out who is *in* in American writing. It's clear he decides a lot by what other people "think" and not by reading himself.

Garzanti publicity representative calls at 10:00 A.M. and at 10:30 is at the hotel. Anna Drugman—one of the top people of publicity for the

---

Garzanti publishing house has brought out What We Talk About When We Talk About Love, *while we were there.*

press . . . if not the top. And the editor-in-chief, Piero Gelli. They are very welcoming and we immediately like them. Gelli is dark, frosty-headed, trim. His English has a few bumps but he's sharp in a sincere way which comes through. He's scheduled to the minute and doesn't stay long. Anna D. wastes no time in letting us know in a nice way that since we went to Rome first, there is no way for her now to make a "big splash" with the media in Milano. She wishes we'd come to Milano first. But . . . she has still managed to get a full schedule of interviews and photo sessions on for Ray. I hardly see him for the next two days—until evening. We apologize about Rome, perhaps insincerely since we wanted to go there first, media be damned.

London / June 1, 1987

We're met by Mark Crean, Christopher MacLehose's* assistant. He's shy, driving Christopher's car because his own is "in the shop in a comer" (coma). He drops us at our flat at 13A Clarendon Rd., which is off Bayswater Rd. near the Holland tube station. The flat has a narrow but bright kitchen area, dining area, little study, bedroom, and living room with electric fireplace. We don't locate heating until after a visit from the maid who lives nearby. The furnishings are a few modest antiques, wicker and unfinished wood. Living room is lemon yellow. A huge bouquet of flowers has been arranged on the dining-room table, compliments of Collins-Harvill.

Paris / June 26, 1987

Reading at French Center for Writers: Maison des Ecrivains (rue de Verheuil) was the main activity of the day because it meant a reunion with François (Ray's translator) and also Laurence, both of whom we'd met on our Paris trip before.

After the reading and reception we walked to the house of Beverly Gorday whose husband, Michel, was married to Chagall's daughter. They remained friends even after the end of the marriage. Chagall used to give them the little drawings as presents, until they had children. Then he gave them chocolates. Many paintings no one has ever seen are there. Michel is a retired journalist, one of the first allowed to visit USSR when journalists began to be allowed in again. Beverly told a story about arriving newly married from America in France with Michel's luggage and trunks. In one was a tuxedo shirt with a drawing on it. "What a

*Ray's editor at Collins-Harvill.

shame," she thought, "someone has ruined this perfectly good shirt." So she threw it out. (She knew nothing about who Chagall was: "It's an awful story to tell on myself," she said.) She is a rather elegant American, tall and well-dressed. Michel is many years older. He told me he was rereading John Dos Passos and really loving it.

Story Olivier* told of his father taking him to Deux Magots and pointing out Albert Camus: "You see that man over there? That's Albert Camus. He is a writer, and someday he'll be recognized as a great man and a great writer and everyone will know his name. You don't know who he is now, but you will later." And Olivier has remembered and because his father was right about Camus there is a sense of literary history being in some sense aware of itself *as* it happens, but also a wonderful secret waiting, always waiting to be told later.

*Ray's editor at Mazarene.

MAVIS GALLANT

◆ ─────────────────────── ◆

French Journal

*A*pril 25, 1987

Country weekend. Yves is thin and frail and resembles an Indian, as Frenchmen sometimes do when they grow old. Lean face, Iroquois profile. We walk along a road that skirts the woods. He tires quickly; we keep stopping on the side of the road so that he can pull together a little more strength. If we kept going we would come to Fontainebleau. Gray sky, scenery flat and green. He talks about Cocteau, Malraux, Yourcenar, says he rereads, that trying to read new work exhausts him. Remembers incidents that took place when he was five or six years old, before the First World War: recalls a particular Sunday at the Coupole, in Montparnasse, with his father. Yves wore a sailor suit and hat, laced boots, white stockings. A waiter in a long white apron set a tall glass down on the table and said, *"La grenadine à l'eau, c'est pour Monsieur."* It was the first time anyone had ever called him that. He still thinks about it—the first "monsieur." His father had a goatee and mustache and looked something like Napoleon III. Men passing by tipped their hats. Suddenly his father said, "Look carefully at that man, over there. His name is Lenin. You will hear his name again." He had been to a meeting and had heard Lenin speak. (Later, I repeat the story to Hélène. She says, "Yes, I know. It is a true story, but it happened at the Dome, and the man was Trotsky.")

I mention Klaus Barbie. Some people of Yves' generation are against the idea of a trial: Barbie is mischievous, has nothing more to lose, and will try to slander the Resistance movement by naming "traitors," men who worked with the Gestapo. Names are already making the rounds. Y. does not agree. His older sister was arrested by the Nazis and he never saw her again. He hates Germans, all Germans, and believes they should be made to carry their guilt to the last generation. He won't see a German film or read a German book. The Nazis came to arrest him, he says, and failing to lay hands on him took his sister.

I see him home and go on alone to the village. Main street ugly and dull, an unbroken wall of houses, all alike. Enter café and ask for Paris newspapers. Customers (men) stop talking and stare. No papers. Church shut tight. Sign on door: "There will be no evening Mass on Saturday and probably none for several weeks, the Abbé having suffered an accident (broken tibia)." On a corner two old women stand gossiping, holding sheaves of bread. I say, "*Bonjour*." One covers her mouth and snickers, the other pretends not to hear. I am thankful I do not have to live in a village, anywhere. They are all Eboli.

But the house is charming, full of Hélène's flowers and books. Abundance of a house where guests are welcome and cosseted, everything supplied or at once replaced, as in a fairy tale. They have elderly habits now, quiet routine of meals, TV, slight friction over newspapers. (He gets *Le Monde* first and hangs on to it for twenty-four hours.) Yesterday they told me about a poodle they once had. Hélène bought it when her son got married. He returned from his honeymoon and said, "You've replaced me with *that?*" When they talk about the dog their faces change. They seem younger, and give the impression of being in a different period of life, faraway and innocent, like youth before a war.

Sunday, April 26
At breakfast, conversation about de Gaulle, the liberation of Paris, etc. Yves suddenly exclaims, "But you weren't even born then!" He can't mean it literally. From the standpoint of great old age any other adult belongs to an undefined and inexperienced generation. I remind him that the year Paris was liberated was the year I started to work on a newspaper.

Wednesday, May 6
Cold spring. The heating in my apartment building has been turned on, after a bitter and argumentative vote, and much conspiring in hallways and in the elevator. All foreigners vote for heating and being comfortable, and hang the cost. The richest occupants, with the largest amount of floor space, vote for sore throats and influenza. Some write the number of square meters they own next to their name, in the "No" column of the voting list, stuck to the concierge's door. An unknown hand scratches the figures out. My neighbor, aged Mme D., wears a long woolen scarf and is quietly freezing, waiting for the heating to take effect. She wants me to vote about a different matter, or, at least, give a written opinion. A majority of occupants wish to sack the concierge—a poor muddled woman with nowhere else to go, and no hope of finding another job or roof. Americans in the building (three) seem revolted by the plot to evict

the concierge: "She delivers the mail and takes out the garbage. What more do they want?" Told that she is accused of not giving "service," and that the halls and stairs are very dirty, they look puzzled. "Service" vanished from the American vocabulary a long time ago.

Take my stopped watch to "Fred," on rue Royale. A superior young man with a large mustache twiddles the needles and says, *"C'est une montre ancienne. Je ne sais pas si on peut la réparer."* The watchmaker, once famous, has vanished from the face of Switzerland. He holds the watch by the strap at arm's length, as if he had found it lying in a puddle: "I shall see what I can do. If you have not heard from me within a week, come back in a month's time." I remark that people used to buy a watch for life; I have windup watches that still work. A statement that does not rate a reply.

Friday, May 8 (V-Day)
Sign on door of bank, rue Littré: "Because of the Armistice" the bank is closed. There was no armistice in 1945. It was an unconditional surrender. No one remembers.

The Klaus Barbie trial begins on Monday.

Saturday, May 9
Hot summery day. Trees in bud and blossom. Lunch in Place des Vosges with O.W., who takes prodigious amounts of medicine, Europa style, between and during courses. After lunch, drop her off on her doorstep. The taxi driver, who has blue black hair and beard, and speaks with an accent I cannot place, comments on how thin and fragile she looks. He overheard some of our conversations and asks what was meant by "camps." I say, "My friend spent eight years in Soviet camps." He says, "Soviet camps? Who ran them? Russians?" Because of the Barbie affair there are a number of TV programs now about deportation; he thinks I mean Nazi camps. I start to explain. He interrupts: "Was it at the time of the Czars?" I ask if he means to be funny. He says, "Well, I did not know the Germans had camps in Russia." Later, I call O.W. to report this conversation. She is not surprised. When she and her husband arrived in Paris, in the fifties, and when it became known they had been deported to far corners of the Soviet Union, it was taken for granted they must have been Fascists. The idea that only Fascists were imprisoned or deported was so entrenched, even after the 1956 Congress, that they were shunned and dropped by the intellectual class. Even today she still meets people who ask if they were deported because they had *done something*.

Only lately, "an educated man" asked her if Soviet camps had been run by Germans. The trouble is, she says, we take it for granted that everyone reads what we read, knows what we know. Suddenly she says, "What was my life about? The long deportation and my husband's broken health, and his death, and my solitude. What can happen to me now? What can I expect?"

Barbie affair: Reporters arriving in Lyons receive a gift package containing a watch and other goodies, and public relations stuff about the city. There are tickets to theaters and concerts, and guided tours, and (according to Paris papers) majorettes. A restaurant called "La Tour Rose" offers a Barbie menu, with "gâteau de carottes Vichy." (N.B.: this story, widely circulated in the French media, turned out to be false. "La Tour Rose" had never featured a "Barbie menu," or anything like one.) Heard the deputy mayor of Lyons on the radio, saying that Lyons is a good city for foreign investment, and he hopes it will be associated with something more positive than the Gestapo and the Milice and Klaus Barbie.

Sunday, May 10
Conversation at dinner with widow of American diplomat who was taken hostage (and released) in Latin America, many years ago. U.S. policy was "no negotiation," and she was afraid she would never see him again. When he was set free he called from a café. Because of the café a rumor spread that he had been drinking. The terrorists stole his watch and clothes, but gave him something to wear before turning him loose. I ask, "Were they Communists?" "Of course." "I mean, were they members of an organized C.P., or were they *gauchistes*, Trotskyites?" She says, "What's that?"

Concierge greatly heartened: an actress in the building (large floor space) has come down on her side. The other day the wife of the Prime Minister, Mme Chirac, came to tea with the actress. Concierge is convinced the two ladies talked about her. If she is evicted, she has nowhere to go. Her unmarried son, eighteen, is leaving for military service. Her married children have modest means, and no spare room. Today I ran into the most vocal of the anti-concierge faction. He had been drinking and kept waving his arms. "We're throwing her out," he cried. His wife smiled as if to say, "You know how men are."

Sent by S.B., a woman arrives to see about mending the rush seat of a kitchen chair, and ends by taking away four chairs, an armchair, and a stool, all of which she says are in terrible shape. Examining the stool, she says, "*C'est de la merde, ça.*" She is a gypsy, aged thirty-three, nearly toothless, has seven children, a mop of curly dark hair, quick bright eyes. Says she can't write her own name. She writes mine, and spells it, "Guylan." I do not bargain over the offered price. She seems disappointed, and brings it down. Leaving, she forgets a bunch of keys. Downstairs I find an attractive girl of about twelve, in gypsy dress, posturing in front of the mirror in the entrance hall, and a charming little boy helping his mother carry chairs. Parked outside is a new-looking and very clean camping car.

Saturday, May 16

Early this morning the gypsy brought back my chairs. With her was a different child, a sturdy and handsome boy of about ten, well-dressed, green eyes, reddish hair, one of those tufted haircuts, standing almost as tall as his mother. I ask his name. "Jimmy." "But what is your real name?" "Jimmy." I ask if his name, at his birth, was registered as "Jimmy," knowing how sticky French law is about given names. His mother nods her head. Her eyes dance: there is no other word for that quick, joyous, ever-moving glance. "It's an American name," she says. Jimmy checks the column of figures on her bill, and quite solemnly watches me write a check. The kitchen chairs are fine, but the armchair has been given a cane seat instead of rushwork. I say nothing, because it would never end.

Long lunch with my godson, who is working on a film set in Paris. The director recites anecdotes about how he was once young and hard up and used to go to official parties just to eat the canapés. The sort of story successful middle-aged men adore telling the young. The Prime Minister visited the set last week and was taken across on a dolly, unaware that many of the people looking up, smiling, were moonlighters. "Who are the moonlighters?" "They are all called Anja, live in the Marais, have little flats, are thin as rails, and eat like horses."

Friday, May 22

Strong north wind blows along the street, still soaked with last night's rain. Boys from the school across the street in leather jackets buttoned to the neck, hands in pockets. Voting list still posted on concierge's door. Names are added, scratched out, replaced, as occupants change their mind, according to the morning weather.

Heard on the radio this morning (France-Inter, state-owned FM and LW station) a panel of journalists and critics on the subject of "*méchanceté*" (spitefulness, nastiness, unkindness), at which they are presently seen to excel. The program's host offered one name after the other—a politician, a writer, a singer—and the panel (all men) supplied every degrading and filthy remark they could think of. Of Charles Pasqua (Minister of the Interior) and Michel Droit (a right-wing and highly controversial writer): "When they go to the toilet they wipe their face—the wrong thing." Of Bernard-Henri Lévy (author, philosopher, subject of frequent interviews): "It must be useful, sometimes, nowadays, to be a Jew." ("*Ça doit servir parfois de nos jours d'être Juif.*") This is probably an indirect reference to the Klaus Barbie trial and the renewal of interest in deportation, concentration camps, and the plight of French Jews during the war. Some people have already had enough. Tolerance on the subject is perhaps rather low. Nobody wants to know too much. (Etc.) When the pop singer France Gall, is thrown to them, they attack her because she is small. It is not teasing, but angry, ferocious, as if her height were (1) her own fault and (2) a moral flaw. (Actually, she is slight, blonde, pretty, and talented.) The contemptuous laughter of these infantile grown-ups calls up a hideous memory: the retarded girl in that Canadian schoolyard, her back to the wire fence, the fear on her sad face, and the half circle of beastly little boys taunting her.

Alain G. arrives promptly at five. Looks slightly English, a Tenniel drawing. Low voice. Is starting a new review to be called *Journal Littéraire*. He is so shy and silent that I am driven to chatter. Stares, like a child, but may just be daydreaming. He comes from near Toulouse, is Protestant in origin, and, like me, spent some time in Catholic schools. I wish him luck with his venture, but I can't write for a French publication—that is, I cannot write *only* to be translated. It would turn me into an émigré writer.

In the evening, long conversation with A.B. about her Oblomov son. No longer a literary joke, but alarming, now. He won't dress, seldom washes himself, spends the day sleeping or staring at the ceiling. The other day he was persuaded to come to lunch with her, but he neither ate nor spoke, except once, when he unbuttoned his shirt and said, "This is where the butterfly is," meaning the anxiety. I tell her to stop blaming herself. We all have millions of ancestors. If she could examine her family tree she would find others like him. She says that the long persecution of Jews in Eastern Europe has probably created a genetic weakness. On her father's side there was Cossack blood. She inherited from her father, along with her high cheekbones and Cossack eyes, a kind of brutal vitality (her words) and a ruthless will to live. "But I was not able to pass it on to my son," she says, sadly. And her father's native temperament did not save him from dying in Treblinka.

Monday, May 25

Lunch at the Coupole with B.C., the worse for wear after drinking wine with his translator all night. Talks about his late mother. Once, when she was so ill, his father called and said, "I can't find your mother." They looked all over the house and grounds, and walked down the street to a ravine with a footbridge over. Without a word they went on the bridge and looked down. He all at once thought that if the worst had happened it would be a deliverance not just for her, but for his elderly father. This thought had all the shock of a revelation. He gave a kind of gasp, and his father quickly looked down again, thinking he had seen something. But she had locked herself into a sunporch and gone to sleep; the pain had been unbearable in the night, and she did not want to keep waking his father up.

We sat talking until about four o'clock.

Ascension Thursday

Another long spring weekend. Street empty and quiet. Argument at lunch about the Barbie trial. Some think it is indecent to ask all those old, sad people to relive their past. And Barbie not even there to listen: he was brought in to court for fifteen minutes, so that a witness could identify him. He sits in a cell (he has two, a day and a night cell) reading newspapers, working crossword puzzles, watching television, while the appalling memories spill out across the city. Golo Mann has declared from Switzerland that it is useless to try an old man for crimes committed forty-five years ago. But it may be our last chance to hear the voice of living witnesses.

Tuesday, June 2

J.A., now eighty-one, is giving a lunch for seven men—champagne, lobster salad, *boeuf en croûte*—in the private rooms of a state museum. The curator is a close friend, and has lent his beautiful dining room. I ask (teasing) if she was ever the mistress of some or all of the seven. She turns her head aside and says, *"Certainement pas,"* then adds, unexpectedly, "Only two are homosexuals."

Thursday, June 4

Vernissage, Right Bank. R.K., unrecognizable, sits on a velvet settee, drinking champagne out of a tumbler. Says that she virtually lives in hospitals now. Remembers "Parsifal," all those years ago, says it was one of the great moments. I can think of nothing comforting to say (her boundless depression, the eclipse of her beauty) and sit beside her, holding her hand. She survived an inconceivably awful childhood in one of the small, peripheral death camps. Nothing showed. She seemed to float through art galleries. Ten years ago something broke. About Barbie, she shrugs, says, "*C'est inutile.*" I try to find M., to congratulate him on the show; look everywhere in the crowd and see a man with snow-white hair and thick glasses standing outside in the street. He is close to tears as we embrace. Talks about the sixties, when (as he now recalls things) everyone was good-looking and having tremendous conversation and love affairs. He is wholly in favor of the Barbie trial, but does not expect a lasting impact. Says even now he hears more about the French Tennis Open than the case.

Thursday, June 16

Rainy and cold. Registered letter delivered by streaming wet girl with curly hair. Thanks to the new rental law, I am offered a three-year lease with guaranteed annual rise. By 1990 I shall be ready to live under a tent in the street. Call the agency. Man says, "You can negotiate. It isn't a one-way affair." "Negotiate how? With whom? With you?" "That is up to you," he says. "I can't be your advocate and your landlord's too. It is a fair rent for a street near the FNAC." (The FNAC, anagram of the name of a former association of *cadres*, now a record and book shop and purveyor of electric and hi-fi equipment, occupies a converted department store on Rue de Rennes.) I ask if the FNAC building is considered a cultural landmark. No answer. Call landlord, in Orléans. He sounds unhappy; but not unhappy enough. Says, "I don't want to lose you, but I am told it is fair rent for a street near the FNAC." I wonder who starts these stories.

Tuesday, June 23

Having accepted the new lease, I hear on all sides that tenants' groups are up in arms, and that many people are refusing the new rents. But rent strikes are nearly always followed by eviction, and I would rather have matters settled—at least, until 1990. Turned on TV just now and there was a man holding up a renewal-of-lease form, and saying, "Insist upon this . . . ," etc. Fat chance.

Thursday, July 1

Last week of the Barbie trial. *Shoah* three nights on TV. One of my friends, who until now has shown slight interest in the trial, makes cassette recordings for her future grandchildren. Verdict on Saturday. A formality. No one doubts the outcome, and that is why some people think it should not be called a trial. Barbie seems wholly isolated. What isolates him? It is not madness, like Hess, or unthinking belief, like Winifred Wagner. His mind must be a dim room at the end of a dim corridor. Perhaps it is a room full of mirrors: just himself. My neighbor in the Midi, Roger S., was interned in a transit camp run by the Milice. Germans turned up once a week and the Milice handed over the consignment for deportation, with as much emotion as if they were handling parcels. He (R.S.) was imprisoned, with other Frenchmen, Resistance and black market, mixed, in classrooms of what had once been a boarding school. Jewish prisoners were shut up in a coal cellar, with windows boarded over. When they crept out to be taken away, they were black with coal dust. He (R.S.) never showed the slightest compassion when he talked about it. He seemed to think it normal that their conditions of detention were so much worse than his. He once told me that that they did not mind what was done to them, and I am sure he believed it.

Sunday, July 4
Barbie guilty and sentenced to life imprisonment. In a summer night, brightly lighted for TV, a crowd boos and chants as Jacques Vergès and other defense lawyers leave the courtroom. Vergès speaks of public opinion worked to fever pitch (probably he means *Shoah*) and *"un climat de lynchage."* Last night cars rushed around Lyons, horns sounding, as if the local football team had won the World Cup.

The BBC asks, "Was it a fair trial?" Answer: "By our standards, no." A BBC journalist: "There are Ukrainians and Balts in Britain who killed more innocent people in a day than Barbie in a lifetime. But they will never be brought to trial. What is needed are quiet, dignified trials that stick to the point, and not flamboyant showpieces."

What has been served? The feelings of survivors, of some of the innocent people whose lives are damaged forever, of Resistance figures dragged in the mud by rumor and innuendo. The relatives of dead children: will some of their anguish be lessened? Apparently, yes. It is impertinent to speculate about the private thoughts of old people, eaten up by grief. As to a fair trial, well, jurors in English-speaking countries do not read newspapers, talk to their families, watch TV. Here, the jurors saw (or were able to see, if they wanted to) the three long evenings of *Shoah*, a few days before they came to a verdict. Barbie watched the French Tennis Open, day after day, until his guards protested and got permission to take the set away. And so he did not see *Shoah*. Perhaps he should have been sat down in front of it; but I suppose it is not part of his punishment.

He continues to show indifference and, they say, incomprehension, and most certainly no remorse. He is sure he did only the right thing; and we—the winning side—contributed by hiding and sheltering him for years. He did not say a word at the trial, or mention the so-called Resistance traitors, or even try to justify himself. In that sense, nothing happened. A sick old man, with an undecipherable conscience, his future is this: for the last years of his life, he will get proper food and good medical care; he has no more need to carry a false identity or be afraid of strangers, and has no more understanding of why he has been put in prison than Don Juan knows why he was dragged to Hell. In a way, he is already dead. The day we turn on the news to hear, *"Klaus Barbie est mort,"* it will seem a delayed announcement.

GAIL GODWIN

◆ ——————————————————— ◆

Journals: 1982–1987

FATHER

Pawley's Island / May 30, 1982
The ocean was so close and loud last night. 1955 summer. When my
father, on his vacation, drove north to Baltimore with his wife Mona, to
"rescue" me from my life. We went to Carolina Beach where the Buies
had lent their cottage for the week. My father, whom I had not laid eyes
on since I was eight, lay tanning on the beach beside me. Said in his
musing, never-far-from-sarcastic voice, "I'm glad you're good-looking."
At night the three of us went out to eat, then walked the boardwalk and
played miniature golf.

My legs got a deep shade of brown. I remember Mona, who only
reddened and splotched, exclaiming, "Gail, your legs!" Poor Mona. All
that youth and *claim* walking into my father's life.

I was reading, at eighteen, *Bonjour Tristesse*, written by a French girl
at my age. I was gloomily jealous. I wanted everything, played both
ends against the middle, and . . . always, always . . . had my eye on the
main chance.

I don't know what my father felt, don't know what he expected.
But surely, a man who had little to do with young people, who had a
well-deserved reputation for being selfish, he must have found me scarify-
ing: both in the sense of my being selfish like him, and in the sense that
I was not the malleable, appreciative daughter I am sure he thought he
had the right to expect.

I had no idea that his disappointments were accumulating like
waves, which, in three years, would drown him in the high tide of his
despair. I do wonder what he hoped for—from me—as we lay there on
our stomachs looking at each other, our backs to the ocean.

That I would be a credit to him—no, that might rankle. That I
would be made happy and fine by coming to live with him and that I
would let him know I owed my sheen to him. That we would look good
together and people would say: "Look at Mose and his daughter. He

went and found her and gave her what nobody else could in the way of style."

AN OLD MENTOR

Asheville / October 8, 1982

Well. Full of old hurts and aches. Where to begin? I am as shy as if someone were reading this over my shoulder. Oh God. Well let me begin.

Yesterday it began to rain just as I was driving out to the convent. I was sorry for the rain because I had hoped we could walk. Though I doubt we would have walked because she was dressed up.

Anyway. I got to the convent about ten minutes late. You don't even enter the school grounds the same way anymore. All the *pines* along the old drive have been cut down. She was waiting just inside the door. Oh damn. I am so full of . . . I don't know what. As if my muse had answered my prayer to let me feel thirteen again. She was wearing a rust-colored blouse—one of those drip-dry ones. A light-brown skirt that did not fit quite right at the pockets. A small silver crucifix. Stockings. Rust shoes with stacked heels. Very nice legs. Looked as if she'd walked on them a lot. But smooth.

She seemed pleased that I'd brought her a flower (Persian violets) and we hugged and she took me into a terrible room—the visitors' room. Small, hot, stuffy, with new furniture that does not sink when you sit on it, but resists you.

She shut the door.

(As I made a new paragraph for this sentence, I thought: see how skillful I've got; manipulating moods with my paragraphing. All these years it took. Yet I am still the same old suffering me. I am still power-less, powerless. It is like Father Webbe said in his book: you can't just work hard and love hard and "get" God's attention. You can't pull him down to you; you have to go up to him and understand what *he's* thinking. It was the same with her yesterday. Yet during the whole visit I was afflicted with double vision. I saw the woman who had enchanted me when I was thirteen and I saw the woman sitting next to me, playing absently with the horrible scratchy sofa cushion, twisting her silver ring, and occasionally reaching over and touching me with her dry hand to emphasize a point.)

I had brought her an inscribed copy of *A Mother and Two Daughters* because she had asked me to bring the book along so she could read it.

So, as she was shutting us into the room, she said, "I'll return this to your mother as soon as I've read it." "No, this is for you," I said. "Oh!" And then she opened it. "Oh, it's inscribed," and came over and hugged me. "Don't read it until after I'm gone," I said.

Then she sat down beside me on the god-awful sofa. She asked me about myself and I was not forthcoming. I even forgot to tell her I was rich. I did not know how to bring up R., so didn't. Also, she is "deaf as a post" as she puts it, and wears a hearing aid in each ear.

So she began telling what she did. And I watched her and listened to her, meanwhile watching and listening to myself.

What was it about her? What *was* it? The gift of the gab. The narrative art. The shaped anecdotes that young people find irresistible. The low caressing voice addressed to you alone. The melody and the challenge, as Pat expressed it. And the facial movements: the lips drawn tight as a purse, little wrinkles above the mouth as she expresses distaste for the unhygienic state of a village street in France. The hard, healthy teeth, the little chip between the two front ones. The laugh: a surprised intake, a bark, the face coloring like a girl's, as if she's delighted to be taken by surprise.

She told me about her trip to Europe. The Jesuit she met on the Irish train whose father lives in Asheville; about staying at Farnborough Hill, the English convent that used to be the home of Princess Eugenie; about changing a grandniece's diaper for the first time in her life. About her brother's farm and the horses he and their father raised. How next year she will celebrate the fiftieth anniversary of her profession. She went to Belgium from County Galway as a girl of eighteen, to enter a convent where her entire novitiate would be in French. I wanted to ask her what had made her decide to be a nun, but was too shy. I only asked if her parents had approved. She said, "Our family was the sort to support you in whatever you wanted to do, but they weren't wild about the idea."

We went to the kitchen to make some tea. There were no tea bags, so we made instant coffee. Perfunctory, joyless kitchen where food is obviously not important. A crazy sharp-eyed old nun, still wearing the habit, spoke to us with thick irony.

Mother W. to me: "This was my school mug. I've gotten attached to it."

Old nun (eyes snapping malevolently): "Imagine! Getting 'attached' to something." By the time we had poured our coffee, the old nun had found us some tea. But we took our mugs back to the constricted little visitor's room. Every once in a while, during the remainder of the visit, she'd ask me: "But what about *you?*" And I stumbled and halted and agreed that yes, in New York I sometimes went to concerts and museums.

DREAMS AND SPLEEN

Woodstock / December 4, 1983
A thick steady snow providentially canceled The Lunch.

The *New York Times* did not include *Mr. Bedford* in its list of notable books, although small fry like —— and —— got included. But I wasn't hurt and stunned as I used to be. I thought: well, I am not one of their favorites and I will exist in spite of them. I may even outlive the *New York Times*. And I feel—it is difficult to express—less and less of their world and more of my own. Maybe this is part of the cantankerous pleasure of getting older and skilled at what you do. You rejoice at thick snow so you don't have to have lunch with an ass who happens, at the moment, to be an important somebody in publishing.

Upsetting dreams. Mother selling a small piece of jewelry I felt was just right for me because she needs money for Rebel's car. And last night a strange dream. I was rooming with a girl like Gwen P. She suddenly avoided me and then I realized she had rented her part of our apartment to an awful woman, a combination of the Woodstock woman with the frizzy hair who double-parks in the middle of the street, and those feminists who hate me for my "elitism." And this woman moved *in:* it was just a fait accompli. Gwen had done this to me. So I went, still in my slip, to the owner of the apartment, who was that ugly woman who eats at Schneller's, and begged her to do something. She said I could instigate legal proceedings since Gwen hadn't told me. But the new roommate only laughed, said it would take time, cost me money . . . as for herself, *she* would qualify for Legal Aid. I got madder and madder. Couldn't work. And my new roommate simply settled happily in. "I don't trust you," she said to me, "but I don't hate you either." I said, "I wish you did hate me, but you can perfectly well trust me." I got a goody-goody feeling as I said this last.

Gwen. In college she was a pretty but very insecure girl who roomed with me for half a semester. Then, suddenly, she moved out without telling me. Took her mattress down the hall and slept with some other girls. I was hurt by it. She finally told me that she felt erased by me; when I was around, nobody noticed her. She had very red hands and Jack M., whom I had dated for a while, bought her a tiny little diamond for their short, doomed engagement. I think she later had a nervous breakdown.

Now what does it mean in my dream when "Gwen" leaves and the charmless, contemporary, proletariat-feminist moves in mockingly without a qualm? Do I fear being invaded by such a person?

Or is my existence threatened (or diminished) because I won't acknowledge such a person?

BEST FRIEND

Woodstock / March 29, 1984
Pat and her former student/protegée, "Little Pat," here for their spring break. This morning as Pat and I sat in our white nightgowns drinking R.'s strong Viennese coffee and flinching occasionally from the sight of the snowstorm driving right at the tall expanse of north windows, she said: "I choose to see this snowstorm as a symbolic message. Just now I am depressed by exterior things, I am fighting aging, the inevitability of the physical life, and this storm is saying, 'Baby, you'd better just accept me. I am the way it is.' Whereas, for you, the storm rages internally. Everything in your life is going well, but your storm is inside. After what Tommy did in October, I was really afraid for what would happen to you when you returned to New York. Not that he and you were that close, but his death was such a senseless thing, a thing you wouldn't have allowed into the careful world you have structured for yourself. But it has turned out that your world was stronger than what happened down there in Asheville."

"Little Pat's" younger brother Corky is a mortician-in-training. She tells us how he sleeps in the attic room over the big clock at West's Funeral Home. He first wanted to be a preacher. All her brothers are very religious. He turned twenty-one two days ago and the family celebrated with something they call "Long Island Iced Tea." Iced tea with four kinds of liqueurs. Once last month Little Pat went with Corky to pick up a corpse. A woman had just aborted a full-term baby into the toilet. The police were taking her off to jail and Corky was left to decide what to do with the baby. He put it in a small box and talked to it all the way to the funeral home. "Now you're going on your first car ride." When the box slid around on the seat, he'd reach over and stroke it and say, "It's okay."

Corpses are dressed, she says, on a tilted slab after they are washed and embalmed. The clothes are split in back, but the family never sees. (Monie's blue robe split. Tommy's gray pinstripe suit of which he was so proud!) "The whole viewing is for the sake of the family." There are lights hidden in the ceiling to give the body a rosy, healthy look. The hairdresser works from a photograph if there is one. Corky's eighteen-year-old brother is studying cosmetology and hopes to go into business with Corky later.

For the first time I've been aware that Pat could die. Leaving me old and best-friendless. The way she puffed, walking up the hill after they had pushed their car out of the snow. I told her, "You made me promise about suicide." She said, "I know, I'll go on a serious diet. But I have good lungs and look at my skin. Healthy! Do I look like someone who is losing oxygen?"

READING AND WRITING

Woodstock / January 30, 1985
Everyone seems to be writing novels about poor white trash or downtrodden working class people who are too tired to have any interesting thoughts. My dinner table scene with intelligent people is more eventful than ——'s upstairs barroom sex and Sears parking-lot scene. It's fashionable now to see how well we (who are educated, who are not poor) can imaginatively intrude on the lives of the ignorant and the destitute. I will go back to *A Southern Family* tomorrow and have Julia think of what the Quicks *are*, in the larger sense. . . .

February 2, 1985
Thinking about the character of Clare made me slightly nauseated, but she does not have to be the main character. There are no main characters. I must find some kind of interweaving process so that the reader never minds leaving one character for another because s/he knows that there will be more (and perhaps contradictory) things to be learned *about that character* through switching to another character's mind. . . .

November 26, 1985
Why is it I can read Mrs. Gaskell's *North & South* every few years, and just finally put down that big Czech's novel I really wanted to read? I can't stay interested because, although the writer lived in interesting times before he immigrated to Canada, his novel is too slow, too mean-

deringly self-indulgent, and has that smartass, showoffy quality I so frequently find in (usually) men's novels. Robertson Davies is above all this. He delivers it all: erudition, humor, surprise, the satisfying story of the quest for the whole man, the man's quest for his wholeness.

May 5, 1986
Tonight, while I was reading some nervous-serious essays about minimalist fiction, a mouse poked his head out from behind the stove. I sang to him in a kind of reassuring rhythmic keening and he completely lost his good sense and came out and danced on the kitchen floor.

September 18, 1986
Have trudged through, dipped into, abandoned, gobbled, sighed over, so many novels while judging for the Book Awards.

· the precocious first novel, in which the writer is discovering before your eyes how to put words together to make an impression.

· the sensibilities that, no matter how worthy, I just can't warm to.

· the books I wanted to like and can't admire as much as I'd hoped. The ——, for instance. I could feel him on every page gritting his teeth and grinding out his masterpiece.

· the ones I read greedily for *information about worlds I didn't know and/or didn't want to enter*. David Leavitt's novel about homosexuality. Daphne Merkin's cold Orthodox Jewish childhood.

· the ones I read despising the philosophy and admiring the art.

· the ones I read feeling comfily at home: my kind of memories of how things once were. Yet, in some, despite their beauty and rightness of tone, knowing I am reading about a dead society. Peter Taylor.

So many of these books are about family.

December 3, 1986
Wrote my absolutely-must letters, Guggenheim recommendation for P.H., sent money to the Save St. Genevieve's Fund. Balanced my checkbook. Then packed my swimming bag for Kingston and drove down the hill in an eerie cloud. Decided to skip the swim . . . bought coffee, a piece of chicken, and pasta from Maria, wine & dishwashing liquid, and came home and ate, drank three glasses of wine and finished a book about a nun's life, which, despite its terrible writing, gave me a feel for the day-to-day life of a postulant, novice, and newly professed. Which I hope will help with my Sister Patrick chapter. I also read most of Merton's *Sign of Jonas*—he's a *writer*, but after a while, I confess, this religious life

does stick in my throat. In Merton's case, maybe because religious ecstasy doesn't lend itself to description. In the other book, because much of that so-called discipline seems medieval and petty, the product of too many centuries of discipline perverted, or just too primitive ideas of discipline.

I don't know what I've got upstairs in those eleven folders in different colors. I thought of going up and looking through those eleven chapters, just skimming and pretending I'm someone else. But I just can't bear it. It was one thing, three years ago, to look *forward*, holding it in my head, what it was going to be. Actually, it seemed clearer than it does now. Am I being too hard on myself? Could the baggy masterpieces I admire stand up under this kind of tormenting scrutiny?

OK. Why did I want this chapter in the first place? I just *knew* from the beginning that it had to be the end. Why did I want these two women to get together? The mother and the nun? Well, they mirror the "Olympians" chapter, where two women go up to a mountain on the day Theo dies. But why should two more go up to a mountain on the anniversary of his death? *Symmetry* is not enough.

The mother is the nun. The nun is the mother.

Irish:

Oh, now!	at beginning of sentences:
to be sure	"Now . . ." "And . . ."
Now, I ask you	"And little thanks you
Straight up to his face	get for it."

"That's a nice how-do-you-do."
"That's all very fine"
"Just go round and see her a little, won't you?"
"Takes three mortal hours to dress herself. . . ."

August 15, 1987
Trollope is first-rate in depicting human politics. The scene in *Framley Parsonage* where Sowerby allays the (rightful) suspicions and accusations of young Lord Lufton is masterful. You can see how effective a really convincing swindler can be.

Or this:

"Mrs. Harold Smith was not, perhaps, herself very honest by disposition; but in these latter days she had taken up a theory of honesty for the sake of Miss Dunstable."

August 23, 1987
From Max Frisch's *Montauk:* "More and more often some memory comes along and shocks me. Usually these memories are not shocking in themselves, little things not worth telling in the kitchen or as a passenger in a car. What shocks me is rather the discovery that I have been concealing my life from myself."

August 25, 1987 (Rebel's 29th Birthday)
From V. S. Naipaul's *The Enigma of Arrival:* "That solitude of Alan's as he walked about the garden and grounds was like a demonstration of the psychological damage he had suffered once upon a time. There was a part of him that hurt, a part where he could never be reached and where he was always alone; and the nature of his education, his too-literary approach to his experience, his admiration of certain writers and artists of the century, his wish to do again, but for himself, what they had done, all this conspired to conceal things from himself. The solitude of the manor grounds was a solace. Outside that was threat and the vision of his own inadequacy."

PHILOSOPHY AND POLITICS

Woodstock / August 27, 1987
. . . I am *waiting* for something. I feel I may be turning into something else. Just before sleep last night and today I sent out a sort of beseechment: tell me what to do now, tell me what I am. . . . It struck me today that the world might really be changing, mutating into something else. I had a vision—from half-sleep—of people in a crowded place, milling around in some vast place like Penn Station. I have been brought up to believe that each person is *alone* in that crowd, but I now saw how, one day, they might all be connected and *know themselves connected.*

The next step would be: if they are mutually aware of this connection, would they be able to influence anything as a *group*, as well as changing something as an individual? An individual can walk across the floor and purchase a magazine. What kind of thing-activity would a group-mind, a group-body be capable of?

September 1, 1987
Dreamed last night I was campaigning for office. A group of people, including our plumber Bill Heckeroth, asked me to define my political platform. I thought hard and then told them, "Constructive sorrow. My platform is constructive sorrow." No one seemed very impressed. Heckeroth, as I remember, tried to argue me down.

MARY GORDON

◆ ──────────────────────── ◆

Notes from California

I

M. takes me to the grave of Marilyn Monroe. The roses on the grave
are held together with pink ribbons. On the ribbons are messages in gold
paper letters. The letters say:

> Sweet Angel Marilyn
> With God in Heaven Forever
> In Heaven Your Home
> Pray for me Here
> I Love you only forever.

On another grave are the words:

> Leesa de Bois
> December 25, 1977
> What Shall We Do With Our Lives?

I I

In the evening, in the room where I work, not in the historic room where
I can see the tower, in the blank room, here, I read this in a book by
Kierkegaard: "I knew a person who on one occasion could have saved
my life, if he had been magnanimous. He said, 'I see well enough what
I could do but I do not dare to. I am afraid that later I might lack
strength and that I might regret it.' He was not magnanimous, but who
for this cause would not continue to love him?"

I cannot think what this could possibly mean.

I I I

A local artist has created an installation of *retablos* and ex-votos, images
of saints, expressions of gratitude for favors granted. But his *retablos*

commemorate unanswered prayers. Among the flowers and the images of saints, such things as this are written:

> Because my mother who cared so much for us and who we really loved felt depressed to see us without home or money, she killed my little sister Summer and my little brother Brian while they were asleep and then she killed me in spite of my screams, and then she committed suicide, I ask Saint Dominic Savio, protector of the poor, Why did she do this to us? And I will ask him for all eternity.

I V

A man I sat next to at dinner tells me this:

"I was traveling from Denmark to Germany. It was 1959. I took a ferry into Germany, and after that a train. From the train you could still see the devastations from the War. I don't read German or Danish. The papers, the immigration papers were in German and Danish. I made a mistake on the immigration form. I wrote in the place of entry for the place of exit and vice versa. I knew I'd made a mistake but I didn't feel like changing it. When I got to Berlin, they told me there was trouble with my papers and they put me in a detention cell. I was guarded by a Russian soldier. I didn't feel in danger. I lit up a cigarette. The Russian soldier knocked it out of my mouth. But I knew he was only pretending to be angry. I knew he only wanted to communicate. I gave him a cigarette. He looked around to see no one was watching him. He lit the cigarette. He put his gun down. He smiled at me. Then he said: 'Jack London.'

"I smiled back and said: 'Tolstoy.'

"He said: 'Mark Twain.'

"I said: 'Dostoevsky.'

" 'OK,' he said.

" 'Spasibo,' I said. 'Da.'

"I knew that he could have killed me but that he was not going to kill me."

V

I am waiting to get my hair cut, reading a crumpled copy of *Life* magazine. There is a picture of an old Greek woman standing behind a church. She is wearing the traditional old woman's garments: black kerchief, black shoes, long black dress. She is toothless, grinning. She is

holding in her hand a grinning skull. In the back of the church there
is a graveyard. Against the walls of the church there are piles of bones,
sorted by type: skulls in one pile, leg bones in another. The old woman
asked the photographer to take her picture holding this skull. She could
tell, she said, that it was the skull of one of her old rivals. She did not
say how she could tell. But she wanted her picture taken, she said to the
photographer. "Because she is dead and I am not dead. You can see me
here, alive. I want everyone to see me here, alive."

V I

Everywhere I have been I have thought at least once a day of my dead
father. He has been dead for over thirty years. In a book he inscribed for
me are these words, in his handwriting, a translation of a line of Virgil:
"Among the dead there are so many thousands of the beautiful."

V I I

At the cemetery where Marilyn Monroe is buried, some of the grave-
stones have inscribed on them the likeness of a mountain and a lake.
Two people, a husband and a wife, have inscribed their signatures in
bronze. A dentist has his name and D.D.S. A famous drummer has below
his name "One Of A Kind." Flowers grow in pots on the flat gravestone
of a famous murdered girl.

People are buried with their nicknames: "Fannie, Muzzie, Poppy."

People are buried with testimonials. "She left the greatest legacy of
all. She left us love."

The famous dead of movies, and the dentist, and Leesa de Bois,
December 25, 1977, Christmas, no other date inscribed.

Did she die on the day of her birth?

"What shall we do with our lives?"

The famous dead of movies lie in the shadows of green buildings
that seem made of bottle glass.

An art collector has constructed for his death a mausoleum bigger
than a house.

DONALD HALL

◆ —————————————————————— ◆

Working Journal

August

Eric Gill: "Work is sacred, leisure is secular." Georgia O'Keeffe: "The days you work are the best days." Matisse: "Work is paradise." Rodin: "To work is to live without dying." And then Flaubert, to keep us honest: "It passes the time."

I get so pissed off at the plain-talk people—who claim that Whitman wrote street talk and that William Carlos Williams let it all hang out— that I forget the beautiful *art* of simplicity. When I read a stretch of short, simple, powerful things by Jack Gilbert, I remember how utterly moving plainness can be: "Divorce":

> Woke up suddenly thinking I heard crying.
> Rushed through the dark house.
> Stopped, remembering. Stood looking
> out at the bright moonlight on concrete.

Everything is there: exact adequacy, intelligence that withholds comment, and the luck (or vision) of the natural symbol. There is also that invaluable thing—with luck you hit on it five times in fifty years of writing—when you say something that everyone has experienced (waking up feeling, not knowing why) which is not common literary property.

If you find yourself telling an anecdote or a fantasy, to illustrate something, more than seven times in your life, try writing it out and see what happens. Like photography draining color from the landscape.

T. called to say that J. died Monday evening. She was euphoric; the dreaded thing was over. He died quietly drifting in and out of sleep for two days. Until the Thursday or Friday before, he spent at least eight hours a day sitting up in his chair, downstairs, trying to read. The hospital bed was upstairs, and T. slept in the same room. No IVs. The

Doctor said: If he complains terribly we will do it. There had been no eating or drinking, I suppose, as the tumor filled his throat. Did he have a tracheotomy? I don't know. A day or two before he died T. interviewed a nurse; she didn't know if she could handle it alone. J. said, "No," emphatically, and followed: "We've been through this before." T. laughed as she told me, "Not exactly through dying." (Through many things, I suppose, without the help of others.) An hour or two before he died he said it wasn't so bad. "Amen," he said, "amen"; then: "It's coming. It's coming."

T. told me all this on the telephone, as she must have been doing for two days straight. The years of his dying—except for the beginning, the announcement—have been good for them; more open affection from J., more connection to world and family. The last four months, when he knew it had come back, were especially good; a honeymoon, she said. Just the two of them. Children and grandchildren visited but mostly they were alone.

They did his dying as well as they did their living—mostly. Models: J.'s combination of gentleness with a resolute aversion to compromise—his courage in effect: skeptical, loving, in love with poetry, without ambition, with insufficient self-regard, brave without bravado. T.'s relentless ongoing scrupulous examination of *everything*, inside and outside.

Reading Ruth Stone's poems, wonderful with that ending zag which is unpredictable, exact, repeated, yet it never becomes mannered.

A disaster of a reading! All day I heard how G. read to an audience of *two hundred* the night before. "Don't tell me about it." In an auditorium seating five hundred we pulled maybe eighty. M. led off and read badly, passive and throwaway, scattery, without concentration. So I read badly too. Flat, flat. I couldn't have picked a worse bunch to read new poems to. They sat there like dandelions on a lawn. So I went to the Tried and True, and I still felt flat. I tried harder, I strained—and everything came apart. I gave up, and played the tape: angry, contemptuous, miserable.

Afterward they told me I was great. With one of them—maybe the second or the third—I argued, which is stupid; it begs for praise. Imagine the reasonable discussion: "You were great." "Actually I was ghastly." "Ah, yes, I see. You have a point. I must have been mistaken."

Some who praised seemed sincere. So? They could have lousy taste in poetry readings or stars in their eyes. And of course I could be wrong—just reacting to empty seats, like old Robert Frost.

L. preaching again. Although he is rational or humanist, he becomes a vehicle for spiritual energy, maybe because he loves ritual and the centuries cast themselves through its shape. He has a clear vision of Jesus, historically clear, uncluttered by decorative plaques or pious archaism. Something speaks through him that is holy whether he is conscious of it or not.

Poetry fails, in each poem, to be as good as poetry ought to be—or as I somehow think it somewhere is, somewhere I'm not looking. Every flesh is flawed and poems are flesh.

The last few days I've dredged through old boxes of photographs, finding things for the Gale book. Depressing—and tomorrow is the service for T. I feel volatile, continually nauseated. I fear coming apart—and more than that I fear the lunch before: strangers, small talk, anxiety. Less and less do I want to be with people, especially strangers; or with more than two people at once, even friends. In the photographs there are so many who visited us here ten years ago, whom I photographed—and I forget their names. Then there are all the dead cats and all the dead people: Reuel, Caroline. Maybe the gallery of aging bothers me more than the dead. My own, my children's.

Looking for pictures I found dozens of letters and postcards to my grandparents, and my grandmother's annotations, and the Sunday school program, 1931, when I first went to Sunday school, with the crayoning I did there, and my mother's postcard to my grandmother after I got home telling how I talked all the time about New Hampshire. I was brought up to love New Hampshire! There's a postcard I wrote to my grandparents about Fluffy and another, 1944, about the death of my blind chick. Typed letters from Exeter talk about track, busyness, poems in magazines.

Somebody writing about Garrison Keillor's essays: ". . . they are a throwback to a time when America was genuinely innocent."

When was that? Everyone confidently refers to a time when this country still had its cherry. The time when America was innocent is always twenty to fifty years ago. Lately it's mostly before 1945—before victory, before Hiroshima. But sometimes it's before Kennedy was killed, before Chicago in 1968, before Watergate. I'm old enough to remember people saying that it was before the Depression, before prohibition, before the Great War. There are always fine reasons, always fatuous. Reading history when I was a kid I thought variously that it was before the Spanish war, before the gilded age, before Grant and Reconstruction, before the Civil War, before the Fugitive Slave Law, before the Mexican War . . .

But go read Henry Adams about Jefferson's lies and Madison's chicanery. What innocence? We imported black captives, Yankee ships, and Virginian customers, through the horror of the middle passage to work and die raising tobacco; then we turned Virginia and Maryland into breeding farms exporting forty thousand black slaves every year to work in the deep south. Some Eden. No nation was ever innocent.

When we think that our country was innocent in the past, we are thinking of latency when we were five years old. As ever, the personal is laundered into the historical.

October

In *Publishers Weekly* a week later someone claims that the 1939 World's Fair, New York version, is memorable because "of American innocence, now gone the way of the passenger pigeon. It was the last flowering of our optimism . . ." Hah! That World's Fair was whistling in the dark against Depression on the one side, with its threat of revolution, and on the other World War II with Fascism howling out of Europe. Innocence! In 1939 only the wretchedness of a terrible war—which many of us optimists thought that Germany would win—began to raise wages and provide jobs. Innocence and optimism and bullshit.

Granted that most writers are bipolar—established by statistics, confirmed by reading biography—this characteristic blood chemistry is compounded by the volatility of reputation, or even by the melodrama of the daily mail. Independent (largely) of the writer's bipolarity are the extraordinary ups and downs of book reviews, like the good luck or bad of the *NYTBR* assignment. And in the mail a young editor of an old house in New York introduces herself and wants to reprint two out-of-print books in a new series. In the same mail an old friend screams that my new work is total disaster. The telephone rings and I have won a prize I never thought about, $10,000. A week later the young editor has eloped to Syracuse and abandoned her projects. Next day I am included in a new anthology, seven poems, and my name goes unmentioned in a history of my own generation.

One *wishes* one never thought of such matters. However, one is equipped with two lungs, one liver, one heart, and two kidneys. Needless to say a single disappointment (insult, bad luck, snub) is equal in intensity to five hundred triumphs.

Multiplying mutability by bipolarity accounts for the compulsiveness of writers, a proneness to pencils sharpened in a row, to schedules, to lists and numbers. We hear so often: "I get up at four and work until noon." "I do five hundred words a day." Rituals are magic, and every writer plays magic games with paper, pads, pencils, pens, or computers; with magic chairs and with magic coffee cups. Control of time by schedules and lists supports the manic depressive beset by mutability, by instant heaven and hell in every mail and every shrill of the telephone: Routine, routine, you can *count* on it. We graph our moods against the repeated grid of The Day.

Last night I read my poems at a small town library nearby. When I did it ten years ago, ten or twenty neighbors showed up, mostly elderly and female. They were still there last night but another hundred and thirty added themselves and the reading moved to the Town Hall. Many of the audience had never heard of New Hampshire ten years ago. Lots of older people (my age) but some younger ones also. I got some star stuff: "I only found you two years ago!" "I couldn't believe it when I read it in the paper . . ."
  Of course I want it; *I also don't want it.* It's disturbing in this place because it is alienating. And the change is upsetting: Ten years ago, people talked not about me but about the things I was writing about; now the writer is more important than the place. Vatiphages have arrived and settled in like tent caterpillars. Of course as people they are all right; they like it here and they want to read their neighbor. But I feel them *deferring* to me, like people at universities. They're not my cousins; of course I am more like them than I am like my cousins.

November
Reading an awful essay about the kitsch of the suburbs. A row of sitting ducks. Vulgarity is everywhere and this essay has been written for sixty years. Mencken did it with a sense of where he was attacking from, not only to proclaim himself superior. This fellow puts forward a familiar notion: The past (which means his own youth) was rough, raw, sexy, poor, and (therefore) virtuous; he's another smart aleck showing he is better than the people he lives among. Eighty percent of human endeavor exists in order to prove that we are better than somebody else.
  I do it too. I've done it all my life. And "everybody does it" is no

comfort. Who wants to be everybody? When I harangue about the McPoem or the bodilessness of critics and teachers, I praise myself. Depressing! When I was a teacher I proved myself better than business-men and now that I free-lance (which is being a small business) I rail about academics. I've always screamed about the suburbs because I was raised in the suburbs and you always remain what you were raised as. Therefore I'm like the woman who belittles the feminine in order to separate herself and kowtow to men—or in order to be what she cannot be.

The alternative to self-deceit is silence.

Just lately, in her eighty-fifth year, my mother tells one story over and over again: The man who always took out her storm windows and put them back was kind and courtly to her. "Tell me what I can do." She liked him; she often spoke of him. This October as he took out the storms they were talking together about my father; my mother said that he had died just after his fifty-second birthday. The man kept shaking his head. "That's my age," he said, "and that's too young to die." He looked fine; he felt fine. The next Thursday she read his obituary.

Never feel pity for anybody else; it's your turn next.

The pleasure of writing is that the mind does not wander, any more than it does in orgasm—and writing takes longer than orgasm. I can't stand movies because I cannot pay close continual attention. While I watch baseball I read a volume of letters between pitches. Even reading a good book—which is the third best thing—my mind sometimes wanders; or I watch myself reading. When I write I *never* watch myself writing; I only *am* the struggle to find or make the words. I am fundamentally boring with a boring mind until, I hope, the word with its sounds and associa-tions becomes a texture in front of me for working over, for shaping, for cutting, and for flying on.

It's the medium not the matter which affords this concentration. If I am working on a headnote for an anthology I am wholly engulfed by concentration on the rhythm and phrase, syntax and pitch, though I write nothing more than "John McPhee (b. 1930) writes . . ." It is the grain of the wood, not the image of the Madonna, that concentrates the mind.

The poetry's in the redundancy. Reduction to message is reduction to concept, the abstract fallacy. Essence of vanilla! So redundancy is never redundant (the nominalist's self-contradiction) but minutely varied in ways both visual and audible—the thousand tongues of style.

Chief among the activities that bore me—because I cannot give sufficient attention and my mind wanders and I want to be doing something else—is talking with other human beings. When my friend sits across the room from me I become impatient. I complained to A. about this reclusiveness, and he imagined a scene I had already thought of. As I am sitting in the living room talking to my friend Z., with whom I enjoy a correspondence, after twenty or thirty minutes I become bored and restless. I want to go off into my study, close the door, and be alone—where I would be perfectly happy to write a letter to Z.

Work is style, and there is style without thought; not in theory, only in fact. When I take a sentence in my hand, raise it to the light, rub my hand across it, disjoin it, put it back together again with a comma added, raising the pitch in the front part; when I rub the grain of it, comb the fur of it, re-assemble the bones of it, I am making something that carries with it the sound of a voice, the firmness of a hand. Maybe little more.

On the other hand there is no thought without style. Unless language taps chisel into stone, nothing is being thought. By itself the stone is only the blunt opacity of an area for thinking in; the stylus does the thinking—by cutting, by making clean corners, by incising. When we believe in translation into concepts, philosophy or poetry, we do not really think. Of course, when you use the stylus you are not necessarily thinking. But *unless* you use the stylus you are *certainly* not thinking. It is not always necessary to think. When it is necessary to think, poetry, because it is the most controlled stylus—because it makes more facets to control—is the ideal instrument of thought.

I understand that this notion is not generally accepted. "Poetry is for decoration and prose is for thought." Piss on that. Some philosophers know better, like Cavell not to mention Wittgenstein or Heraclitus. The stylus cuts word into stone, therefore the apothegm and the fragment. Emerson carved in stone; they were small stones and hard to build with but they were carved stones as Nietzsche understood.

In making sports analogies to the arts, the mucker knows no limits. Therefore let us dismiss poets of impeccable technique and nothing else: "Good field no hit."

Vatiphagy again. There's a knock on the front door, which my daughter answers, startled because the front door opens only once every forty years, for a coffin. She interrupts me at my desk to tell me that someone wants to see "Donald Hall." The quotation marks which she distributes allow me to understand that the object which it is desired to see is some sort of institution, possibly architectural, surely out of the way; or perhaps a rare bird, appropriate for a life list. When I meet the woman at the door I note that another sits in the car, the shy one, as the bold one tells me with triumph that they have spent the entire day looking for me; she expects felicitations on their accomplishment. I do not ask them in. I allow myself to be led to the car, to meet the shy one, and I nod my head and smile falsely for a minute before I pull myself away (work ended for the day) and as I leave them I am congratulated: "How wonderful that you have this place, with all your solitude and seclusion."

December

Remember when I had a poem in *Poetry* and a month later received an envelope forwarded from Chicago, "personal and confidential," with a sheet of paper inside. A tiny unsigned note praised a poem—and when I unfolded the note a twenty dollar bill fell out.

Dream of Little Joe Jesus.

Work and the materials of work. In March of 1986 we left here for seven weeks to travel in China and Japan reading poems and lecturing. I knew that I would stop working, the longest patch in the ten years since we moved from Michigan to New Hampshire. I thought it would be good for me to break my routines, and that I would build energy for work when I returned. (It worked that way; when I got back, after two days of feeling awkward at the desk, unused muscles, I let loose in a tidal wave of joyous work.) For weeks we traveled, talked, banqueted, and read. The trip was exhausting, exciting, consuming. Toward the end I felt restless with the desire to be home and to write, but the circumstances seemed too jumpy for work. Over seven weeks I wrote nothing but a hundred and two postcards.

Our last stop was in Sapporo, on the northernmost Japanese island of Hokkaido: birch trees, snow, Holstein cattle; amazingly like New Hampshire. After a day of public talk, we visited the Hokkaido historical museum where the director showed us around and took us on a tour of a reconstructed village, a Japanese nineteenth century Williamsburg, and then bought us lunch. As we finished our noodles, the director shyly and apologetically reached into his pocket for a sheet of paper with two lines of typed English on it. He needed to write a caption in English, for a photograph, and would we mind terribly glancing at it to see if he had made any errors? His English was fine and in his two sentences he had merely omitted an article. I marked the page. Then I noticed that the second sentence trailed off, that if I reversed the order of clauses, its order would be more vigorous. I fiddled with it. Then I noticed that I could collapse the two sentences together into one complex sentence, using only two-thirds of the words he had used, making a sentence that mounted vigorously, with the lowered pitch of a parenthetical clause, to a firm conclusion. As I messed with the director's manuscript and prose style—ignorant of his subject, with no interest in his subject—my heart pounded with excitement.

JIM HARRISON

◆ ——————————————————— ◆

From the Dalva Notebooks: 1985–1987

The thirteen-year-old girl walks out into the damp moonlight. It's after midnight and I'm trying to imagine the freshness of her emotions.

Only when I'm fatigued do I worry about being vindicated.

I explained to Ms. —— that life was a vastly mysterious process to which our culture inures us so we won't become useless citizens.

I'm inventing a country song, "Gettin' too Old to Run Away." In the middle of these sloppy ironies I remembered the tremendous silence of the midday eclipse last summer. Nature was confused & the birds roosted early. I was full of uncontrollable anger because I had to leave for L.A. in a few days for a screenplay conference. No one liked my idea of the life of Edward Curtis except me.

In a dream a ranch foreman named Samuel Creekmouth appeared to me and told me how to behave. I became irritable but in the morning had a lush & jubilant vision of what the novel was to be.

On the walk there were two small beaver, a huge black snake, a great blue heron feathering into a S.W. wind, sand dunes caving into a furious sea, on a rare hot day in late April.

Hard to keep the usual inferior balance when the dream life is kicking the shit out of you during, as usual, the waxing moon. In the same place I saw an actual wolf last year I found a female wolf in a dream, her back broken. I went to her, knelt down and gathered her up, and she disappeared into me. This experience was frightening.

That peculiar but very beautiful girl I saw in a dress shop in Key West ten years ago reappeared. She told me you can't give up Eros. Then, as with most of my dream women, she turned into a bird (this time a mourning dove), and flew away.

Awoke in the middle of the night and wrote down that it is important not to accept life as a brutal approximation. This was followed by a day of feeling quite hopelessly incapable of writing my "vision" of the novel which I haven't begun to compose.

In New York City staying with my agent Bob Dattila over by the river on East 72nd. We are trying to make business deals on the phone, and play gin rummy though we can't quite remember the rules of the game. Bob asked me what was even deeper than the bedrock in the huge excavation next door. I told him watery grottos full of blind, albino dolphins. Then in the night, in a dream, I climbed out of the excavation in the form of a monster: my eyes were lakes, my hair trees, my cheek was a meadow across which a river ran like a rippling scar. In the morning it was a comfort to walk the dog up to Ray's for a breakfast slice of pizza. Since I have three at home it is a considerable solace to have a dog friend in NYC, and when I come to town Bob's dog knows she can count on me for a slice of pizza. In short, we make each other happy.

What I don't want for myself is called a "long ending" with the vital signs not altogether there. This thought occurred to me after reading a biography by John Dos Passos.

Upset that this novel is going to make me too "irrational" to earn a living. In my background it is inconceivable for a man not to offer the full support for his family. A half dozen years ago I made a great deal of money but didn't have the character appropriate to holding on to any of it. This must take training. Now the accretion of beloved objects & images in my life and dreams has become more totemistic & shamanistic: grizzly bear turd & tooth, coyote skull, crow and heron wings, a pine cone from the forest where García Lorca was executed. Probably nothing to worry about as it began when I was half-blinded as a child, and for comfort wandered around the forest and lake and you don't find any trinkets there.

Always surprised on these days when the mind makes her shotgun, metaphoric leaps for reasons I've never been able to trace. Remembered that Wang Wei said a thousand years ago, "Who knows what causes the opening and closing of the door?"

Alliance: Nebraska reminds me of what America was supposed to look like before it became something else. Along Rte. 20 the almost unpardonable beauty of desolation. I could live along a creek in the Sandhills. I've established no strengths outside the field of the imagination, which is a fancy way of saying I'm hungover from an American Legion barn dance a waitress invited me to. She disappeared with a cowpoke who could wrestle a truck. Woke at first light laughing. Stepped on a steak bone.

Re: the banality of behavioral and emotional weather reports. My life is still killing me but I am offering less cooperation. I want to know what you do, rather than what you quit doing.

Up at my cabin more attacks of irrationality. Been here too long in solitude. Blurred peripheries so I "am" the bitch coyote that killed the rabbit in the yard. My longest & strongest literary relationship is with McGuane—twenty years of letters and we don't even see each other once a year.

Rode an enormous crow, flying down to the Manistee River to drink from a sandbar. Used a martingale. Easier to stay on than a horse and a better view! James Hillman says that dream animals are soul doctors. Bet I'm the only one around here who reads Cioran & Kierkegaard after working his bird dogs.

Disturbed that I am creating this heroine because I'm lonely and wish to have someone I can utterly love. Relieved of sanity fears by reading Angus Fletcher on the subject of the borders of consciousness.

There are many hidden, unnumbered floors in the apartment buildings in NYC, or so I have thought.

My coffin was made of glass and she ran out of the woods and shattered it! She is E. Hopper's girl at the window.

This must be a novel written from the cushion—silence, out of water, the first light, twilight, the night sky, the furthest point in the forest, from the bottom of a lake, the bottom of the river, northern lights, from the clouds and loam, also the city past midnight, Los Angeles at dawn when the ocean seems less tired having slept in private, from the undisturbed prairie, from attics and root cellars, the girl hiding in the thicket for no reason, the boy looking in the wrong direction for the rising moon.

At the cabin the fog is so dense you can hear it. A rabbit near woodpile, fly sound, crackle of fire in the hush. Can't drink much or my heroine escapes, evades me. The voice just beyond hearing.

Hot tip from Taisen Deshimaru on the writing of this book. "You must concentrate upon and consecrate yourself wholly to each day, as though a fire were raging in your hair." Reminded me again of the injurious aspects of protestantism for an artist—one's life as inevitable, or predestined, causing a looseness in the joints, the vast difference between Calvin (and John Bunyan). You must transfer these banal energies toward self-improvement to your work.

The postmodern novel suffocates from ethical mandarinism. It is almost totally white middle class, a product of writer's schools, the National Endowment, foundations, academia. The fact that this doesn't matter one little bit is interesting. Who could possibly give a fuck during this diaspora. The literary world is one of those unintentionally comic movies they used to make about voodoo and zombies.

Who said, "You can't do something you don't know if you keep doing what you do know." Drinking prevents vertigo and that's why I can't get her voice if I drink. A trip to NYC restored my vertigo. If you enter a bookstore or a publisher's office your life again becomes incomprehensible. Fear refreshes. Luckily you can head immediately for a good restaurant.

Back home the troubling dream image of myself emerging like the "Thing" from a block of ice full of sticks and leaves.

In another dream she ran backward nakedly into history which was an improbable maze. Another night an unpleasant visit with Herman Melville who didn't look well.

Went up to my winter retreat at a hotel in Escanaba to edit *Paris Review* interview. Can't get beyond first page by the second day because I'm not currently interested in anything I've ever said, what with a hot eyeball from being two-thirds done. Zero degrees and a five-hour walk in the woods because I got lost, followed by rigatoni & Italian sausage, and two bottles of red wine. Next day I walk miles out onto the frozen harbor ice—a marvelous polar landscape of glittering sun & ice as far as you can see. Fishermen have driven their pickup trucks out on the ice and are pulling nets where the ice was divided by a fuel oil tanker. They are Chippewas and offer me a partially frozen beer that thunks in the bottle.

A strange March walk: broke, can't write, sick from new blood-pressure medicine, out in an area of juniper, dunes, pine culverts out of the wind. Thoughts about the degree to which I'm a slave or lowly employee of the system I've created: cigarettes smoke me, food eats me, alcohol drinks me, house swallows me, car drives me, etc.

"She" comes and goes. I had to talk to Hollywood today (to say why I was fired from the last project) and she fled top speed. An utterly enervating & fatal game of pursuit.

It seems that severe emotional problems, neuroses, are born, thrive, multiply in areas where language never enters. The writer thinks that if he can solve these problems his quality of language will vastly improve. This is the fallacy of writing as therapy. Dostoyevski maintained that to be acutely conscious is to be diseased. One could imagine a novel that murders the writer. You don't want to discover a secret your persona can't bear up under. But then you can't rid yourself of the hubris of wanting to create a hero or heroine of consciousness.

Completely flipped from nervous exhaustion on page 430. Take my wife and daughter to Key West, a place I had feared returning to after so much "disorder and early sorrow" from a dozen previous trips. Turned out pleasantly. Good chats with Brinnin, mostly on how to determine pathology when everything is pathological. Studied the giant ocean river, the gulfstream, where Duane committed suicide on his buckskin horse. We forget we have blood in us until it starts coming out.

All your aggression is directed toward discovering new perceptions, and consequently against yourself when you fail to come up with anything new. But then I "made her up" knowing very well we will abandon each other.

Bernard Fontana warned me about getting the "Indian disease." It takes a great deal of discipline not to shatter into fragments. The wonders of negative capability & allowing her to decide what she's going to do next. What Fontana meant is the intense anxiety I felt at the Umbanda session seventy miles outside of Rio de Janeiro when the ladies went into their whirling trance to heal the black drummer who was a drunk. If you've seen and lived the supposed best the white world has to offer it's "harmless" to check out the rest of the world. We are all in the *Blue Angel* in that respect. The actual world is Dietrich's thighs.

Startled to read in Jung that violently colorful dreams & psychic events occur to people in psychic flux who need more consciousness.

At the cabin just saw a chipmunk leap off the picnic table & tear the throat out of a mouse, lapping vigorously at the blood. I am chock-full of conclusions. Must write Quammen to find out what's going on here. Lopez told me the only way to feed ravens is to gather road kills, a rather smelly business. Peacock has studied bears so long he has become one, not entirely a happy situation. Dalva is probably my twin sister who was taken away at birth.

Nearly finished. It's like going outside to estimate the storm damage. Want to avoid stepping into a thousand-storey elevator shaft. As a ninth grader I was very upset to discover that Ross Lockridge committed suicide when he finished *Raintree County*.

My friend —— thought that all of his concessions, like the Eucharist, were rites of passage. He forgot how easy it is to earn the contempt of your fellow writers.

Was amused to realize that the mess I am always trying to extricate myself from is actually my life. The other night I played ranchero music & thought how different the music is in areas of fruit, hot peppers, garlic, hot sun, giant moths, & butterflies. An old woman in Brazil had a worn photo of a group of men ice fishing in Minnesota which she thought was amusing. We drank rum and I tried to explain away the lugubrious masochism of life in the upper midwest.

For almost ten minutes I looked forward to the second volume when Northridge's voice will become mangled & intolerable, a prairie Lear.

Finishing any large piece of work makes one dense and irascible. I cooked the fucking brook trout too long! I demand more of myself and life than it is suited to offer. I look for the wrong form the reward is to come in—thus it is a full year before I realize how good a certain meal was: during bird season we stopped by a river, started our portable grill and watched four English Setters and a Lab swim lazily in an eddy in the October sunlight. We grilled woodcock and grouse over split maple, had a clumsy salad, bread, and a magnum of wine, napped on the grass surrounded by wet dogs.

Nearly done at the cabin, a specific giddiness. Last night wild pale-green northern lights above scudding thunderheads. On the way home from the tavern I saw a very large bear on the two-track to the cabin, thus hesitated to take a midnight stroll, possibly disturbing both of us. He was not my friend, but a great bear, a Beowulf, trundling across the path & swiveling for a look at me, his head higher than mine was in the car.

Hard to develop the silence and humility necessary for creating good art if you are always yelling "look at me" like a three-year-old who has just shit in the sandbox.

Postscript. Finished the novel in July and have since driven 27,000 miles to get over it. Perhaps it is easier to write a novel than survive it. Driving is a modest solution as the ego dissipates in the immensity of the landscape, slips out into the road behind you. Watched an Indian, Jonathan Windyboy, dance seven hours in a row in New Mexico. That might work but as a poet I work within the skeleton of a myth for which there is no public celebration. Publication parties aren't quite the same thing. I can imagine the kiva late at night under a summery full moon; the announcer asks the drum group from the Standing Rock Sioux to play a round from the Grass Dance for Jim's beloved Dalva! But perhaps our rituals as singers are as old as theirs. Caged my epigraph from Loren Eiseley's tombstone—"We loved the earth but could not stay."

NICHOLAS HENDERSON

◆ —————————————————————— ◆

A Weekend with the Rainiers

*P*alais *de Monaco* / *May 14, 1978*

Princess Grace had been our guest in the British Embassy in Paris at the fashion show last autumn. She may have been impressed by Mary's flower arrangements there, designed to reflect in silver the spirit of the Jubilee. Anyway, she wrote a month or two later inviting her to take part, either as a judge or a participant, in the annual Concours International de Bouquets in Monte Carlo in May. Mary accepted saying that she would like to participate. The two categories of the competition for which she entered were "Fleurs Imposées," where they give everyone the same collection of leaves and flowers, and, secondly: "Un Petit Déjeuner," an arrangement that, according to the rules, has to be "realisé sur un plateau," but is otherwise up to the whim of the exhibitor. So we took down with us from Paris the raw materials for this breakfast setting. We had with us cardboard boxes containing jars of various sorts of flowers. It had been a problem picking them at the right time in the garden in Paris. I packed them in ice and we kept them fresh on the long drive down. From time to time as he drove, Jacques, the chauffeur, would lift the layers of sopping newspaper beside him to peep, with a certain air of disdain, at the little plastic containers of lily of the valley, pansies, euphorbia, sweet williams and black tulips, peopling the leather seat of the car in front. "*Ça va*," he would reassure us. Tommy the night guard at the Paris Embassy had been most eager the previous evening to help with the packaging of the flowers for their long journey. He could not suppress his surprise that we should be taking flowers from Paris to the Côte d'Azur. "You will find plenty of 'em down there," he assured us. We would, but Mary was quite right that they would be shop flowers, like iris or birds-of-paradise, not at all what she needed for the arrangement she had decided upon.

We also had with us on the journey a large silver tray and the luster tea set that we collected from the cottage at home last weekend. These were essential props for the exhibit.

We were greeted and treated at the palace with great hospitality.

Our initial worry was how the flowers would weather the night. Mary snipped off the ends of their stems and, resorting to the gold mosaic hand basin in our bathroom, changed the water in the plastic containers. Sensing a crisis, the English housekeeper at the Palace rose to the occasion and insisted that we leave the flowers in the passage where they would be cooler and she could keep an eye on them.

I had an interesting talk with Princess Grace at dinner. She said that her father, an Irish politician, had preferred her elder sister to her. She had been very conscious of this and it had hurt her. I wondered, though did not ask, whether this had had anything to do with her decision to go on the stage. Feeling insufficiently appreciated, as she thought, by her parents, had she sought to compensate for this by looking for attention elsewhere? I was not sure that this was so, because she seemed so undemonstrative, almost self-contained, with no apparent wish to strike a pose or seek the limelight. That may be because she has had so much notice taken of her without having to make a great effort.

She said that her mother had brought her and the rest of the family up very strictly. She had tried not to spoil her own children but it had not been easy. I asked when they did the washing up and the housework. She said Rainier, which is how she calls him in conversation, had begun with big yachts, but they had got smaller and smaller so that there was now no crew to look after them on board. It was there that the children had to do the chores.

As we sat beside each other at another dinner, one which was held at the Hotel de Paris following the Flower Exhibition, the conversation got round to wine. She is an enthusiast. I said that Mary regarded me as a wine bore, indeed my nickname now in Paris was WB. She said that she did not agree. She would love to own a vineyard. I asked myself why not. It is difficult to gauge the extent of their wealth. I also found it hard to gauge with her, as it is with other minor royalty, what was the correct degree of formality or informality to maintain. In doubt I plumped for being formal.

She and the Prince are extremely free-and-easy and unpompous. Neither of them puts on airs at all. He took part in the flower competition, in two categories. One of which was "One of the Twelve Months of the Year" and the other "Adventure and the Sea—Illustration of a Text from Jules Verne."

He worked away at his exhibits just like all the other competitors with no extra help and no ceremony, clad in an open shirt and espadrilles. I was not even sure that the Japanese ladies alongside him, bent over their contorted little creations, were aware whom he was. He had a nom de guerre for his presentations which was: "Monsieur Louis de Rosemont." He arrived and left in a Land Rover, driving himself. It was piled high with garden equipment as well as large bits of rusty iron to help recapture Jules Verne. Apparently one of his many hobbies is welding. Whenever any metal breaks up at his farm behind Monaco he insists on doing the smithy work himself. His naturalness and enthusiasm are engaging. There is nothing remotely ceremonious or blasé about him.

Certain court formalities are in contrast with the Rainiers' personal informality. For instance before meals the guests have to assemble before the arrival of the Rainiers, and then to curtsey and bow, for all the world as though they were attending a formal ceremony at Buckingham Palace. It is the same before setting off to the town in convoy. The non-royals, i.e., the guests, have to foregather at some predetermined point ten minutes before the Prince and Princess are due to appear. They have, as it were, to be in attendance—in waiting.

Yesterday I went for a swim in the Palace pool before lunch. The meal was to be served alongside the water, beneath the palm trees, mimosas, and nisperas. I was about to get into the water when an elderly courtier approached me to say that we would be lunching in ten minutes' time. I said that, given the coldness of the water, I would have plenty of time. In fact I was not ready on the dot, was not wearing a tie, and was putting everyone into stitches of embarrassment when the Prince arrived before me. Mary rushed over to say that I really must behave and that I could not possibly appear without a tie. So I hurried to my room followed all the way by my valet who seemed to have a ceaseless vigil to watch over me to try to ensure that I was turned out correctly and punctually. I found it odd that, eating beside a swimming pool, one has to be dressed as in a restaurant. However, I see that appearances must be maintained. The Palace has to avoid becoming like a jet-set pleasure dome such as the Marbella Club, for instance. That would be fatal. So I agree that it is I who must conform. From now on I shall be on time and with a tie. But for the visit to the zoo? Will it really be necessary then? Will the baby tiger, and the diminutive seal—the Prince's pets— show their bare teeth if I show my bare neck? I shall soon find out.

All yesterday morning Mary worked at her flower arrangements. I was employed as a runner and, when she saw the paraphernalia used by the Japanese and other competitors, she asked me to do some shopping for her in Monte Carlo. Firstly I was asked to fetch some croissants; then to buy a bunch of dark grapes; and finally a flower holder, because one of the rules was that each flower had to be in water and she wanted to tuck a flower under the breakfast plate. As a finishing touch she grasped the daily newspapers that I had under my arm and slid them under the corner of the tray. Thanks to her talent for design and, I hope, of mine for delivery, she won two prizes. One of them was a first prize for Harmony of Color; the other was for a breakfast arrangement.

There was heavy Japanese competition, twenty-six of them having flown from Tokyo to take part. They went to enormous pains in their presentations. I was told that many had been on three-year courses devoted exclusively to flower arrangements. No wonder the products were so unspontaneously awful, so far removed from the wayward changeability of nature. Three Japanese ladies were there in the exhibition hall, which was decorated elaborately but unconvincingly to simulate the world of the sea, when we arrived at 7:45 A.M. They started cutting up and contorting the leaves and flowers provided by the "Fleurs imposées" competition. They were still at it four hours later when the exhibits had to be finished and the judging started. None of them won a prize; indeed the Japanese invasion was beaten off all round. They did not win a single medal. One received a mention honorable and her name was called—after a fashion—at the prize giving, but to her evident disappointment she had nothing to take back to Toyko to mark the distinction. As I watched those inscrutable but unmistakably downcast faces, I could not but wonder whether the Japanese contingent would be quite so numerous next year.

We made a lot of new friends over the weekend. Among them, the Montague Meyers and the De Lesseps. At the first dinner in the Palace I sat between the Princess and Mrs. Meyer, alias Fleur Cowles, an old friend of the Rainiers. When the ice cream was served she said: "I don't know what it is, but at least it will make us fat."

She talked about the Prince. One of his passions is the circus. He takes a special interest in clowns and animals. He had planned once to follow a circus throughout its summer tour and had had a Mercedes adapted as a caravan for the purpose. Alas, at the last moment, he had been dissuaded. He has a zoo at the foot of the rock which he has promised to show me round before I leave.

Fleur complimented me on Mary's dress and on her appearance generally. She continued to do this throughout the weekend, whether in relation to her petit déjeuner, her straw boater, or her performance of the charleston, saying, with a thrust of her face toward her hands, that she just couldn't stand such competition. Indeed Mary's charleston and the late nineteenth-century decor of the Hotel de Paris dining room were the highlights of the ball for most of us.

With Meyer I had an agreeable talk about Ernest Bevin, who had been a great friend of his father's, the owner of a successful timber company that had always done a great deal of business with Russia. After Bevin's death, as I remembered, Meyer had been generous to his widow, Flo, who had been left almost penniless.

Another friend we made was Rory Cameron, who lives in Provence—about which he has written a book. I had the impression that the Princess was delighted he was there. People kept telling me that he was Lady Kenmare's son, as though that would explain everything. Mary and I both found him delightful, liking and hating all the same things as we did. Recently he has sold his mother's beautiful house and garden, La Fiorentina, just west of Monte Carlo. The crowds had become impossible. He has now established himself near Avignon. From his personal accounts and those in his book, *The Golden Riviera*, describing inter-war visitors and neighbors like Somerset Maugham, I gained the impression that his life must have been like that depicted in Cyril Connolly's *Rock Pool*, before this part of the Riviera had turned from gold to concrete. I suppose those towering blocks are essential to the livelihood of Monaco, but they do present a horrifying picture to the eye. One can, of course, have a lovely view of the sea from them, but it is the view from an airplane. There is no feeling of direct contact with the sea, which is indeed practically impossible, so overbuilt is the whole coastline.

Sunday morning with Rainier was most agreeable for me. The rest of the school went off to flower arranging demonstrations given by some professional, apparently, hailing from Yorkshire. His arrangements that we all saw when we arrived at the Sporting Club for lunch were startling. "You'd love to take one of these home," Fleur Cowles whispered to me. They confirmed my growing antipathy to the whole business of flower arranging. My only interest had been in picking up tips on how to keep flowers alive for as long as possible. I cannot say that I am intrigued by the process of torturing flowers into unnatural shapes around bright stands of plastic and twisted ironwork. Indeed there was scarcely an exhibit in the competition that had not struck me as unfortunate, as being just the opposite of what should be done with flowers.

So Mary and the others had to listen to two hours of expertise and to watch the creation of one more grandiose bouquet after another—all of them photographed by the Japanese for future detailed study and, alas, perhaps for imitation, so that in years to come, instead of the customary Japanese flower settings of a bare twisted branch and a dried petal adorning a piece of black lacquer, we will have a new outbreak from the east of vast contraptions of gladioli, streletsin, salvia, and begonia.

A courtier came to my room to tell me to be in the Cour d'honneur at 11:30 where Son Excelicisimo would join me to take me to see his motor museum and his zoo. He arrived and we shook hands. "Good morning, sir," I said.

"Good morning, sir," he said.

Showing me round the lovely old cars he told me which were his favorites, and which Grace's. He intends starting a museum open to the public.

He then drove me in a Ford Fiesta down to the zoo. There was no nonsense about a police escort. The Prince observed the traffic lights and the instructions of the policemen on point duty. The only departure from the ordinary was that the policemen saluted the Prince as he drove past.

The zoo is in the hands of an Austrian who was formerly a bear trainer until he got mauled, and of a French couple, of whom the woman was a former dentist's assistant and the man previously an employee of the estate. The Austrian's face wore scars that did justice alike to his courage and inexperience with animals. "The trouble is," the Prince confided to me, "that they get too confident." He told me of a particularly nasty accident when the female of a pair of anteaters, who had been as docile as a lamb for years, suddenly attacked the keeper and took a joint out of his thigh. I asked knowingly whether this had happened when she had been on heat and the Prince confirmed that this was so, though the keeper had not known it at the time.

We stared at an enormous young gorilla bleeding from its paws. "The trouble here," the Prince explained, "is that she will eat her feet. We cannot think why."

I asked—again with extreme sagacity—whether she had had children and was told that she had not. I also enquired whether the Austrian and his wife and the French couple had children. They had not either. They certainly had plenty on their hands with all these shrieking animals. The monkeys seemed particularly talkative that morning.

As we went round the zoo, built on the edge of the rock below the Palace, the Prince gave instructions to the attendants. He pointed to a light that needed mending. He suggested putting those two chimpanzees together. He asked for a bucketful of carrots and apples to be brought for the elephant. He then fed the elephant tenderly by hand inserting the food deep into its mouth while it thrust back its trunk. "She's got a very good character," he explained, "never complains."

I asked the usual question about its private life and was told that there was no room for more than one elephant. "But she seems quite happy. . . ."

In fact we left Monaco after our weekend feeling that everyone there, whether visitors or staff, were bound to be happy—so long as they were not too involved with the female anteater or a Japanese flower arrangement.

EDWARD HOAGLAND

◆ ———————————————————— ◆

Learning to Eat Soup

Learning to eat soup: Like little boats that go out to sea
                                    I push my spoon away from me.

At my parents' wedding in Michigan, one of Mother's uncles leaned over
before the cake-cutting and whispered to her, "Feed the brute and flatter
the ass." The uncles threw rice at them as they jumped into their car,
and Dad, after going a mile down the road, stopped and silently swept
it out. That night, before deflowering each other (both over thirty), they
knelt by the bed and prayed to consecrate the experience.

To strike a balance is everything. If a person sings quietly to himself on
the street people smile with approval; but if he talks it's not alright; they
think he's crazy. The singer is presumed to be happy and the talker
unhappy, which counts heavily against him. . . . To strike a balance: If,
for example, walking in the woods, we flake off a bit of hangnail skin
and an ant drags this bonanza away we might say that the ants were
feasting on human flesh; but probably wouldn't. On the other hand, if
a man suffers a heart attack there and festers undiscovered, then we
would.

Baby inside M.'s stomach feels like the popping and simmering of oat-
meal cooking, as I lay my hand across. Pain, "a revelation to me like
fireworks, those comets that whirl," she says in labor room. She lies like
a boy-under-stress in the canoe-shaped cot, the nurses gathering gravely,
listening to the baby's heartbeat through the stethoscope between con-
tractions—heart like a drumbeat sounded a block away. Baby, with bent
monkey feet, is born still in its sack. Doctor is unlocatable. The interns
gather. A nurse picks up both phones simultaneously and calls him with
urgency. The crowd, the rooting and cheering in the delivery room—as
if the whole world were gathered there—after the solitary labor room.

Very old people age somewhat as bananas do.

Two Vietcong prisoners: an American drew crosses on their foreheads, one guy's cross red, other guy's green, to distinguish which was the target and which the decoy to be thrown out of the helicopter to make the target talk.

Winter travel: snowbanks on river ice means thin ice because snow layers shield the ice from the cold. And water is always wearing it away from underneath; therefore keep on the *inside* of curves and away from all cutbanks, where the current is fast. Travel on barest ice and avoid obstacles like rocks and driftpiles sticking through which also result in a thinning of the cover. Gravel bars may dam the river, causing over-flows, which "smoke" in cold weather like a fire, giving some warning before you sink through the slush on top and into the overflow itself. Overflows also can occur in slow sections of the river where the ice is thick and grinds against itself. A special danger area is the junction of incoming creeks whose whirlpools have kept the water open under a concealment of snow. If the water level falls abruptly, sometimes you can walk on the dry edges of the riverbed under solid ice which remains on top as though you were in a tunnel, but that can be dangerous because bears enjoy following such a route too.

You butter a cat's paws when moving it to a new home, so it can find its way back after going out exploring the first time.

My friend Danny Chapman, the Ringling Bros. clown, had a sliding, circus sort of face, like the eternal survivor, marked by the sun, wind, pain, bad luck, and bad dealings, the standard lusts and equivocations, like a stone that the water has slid over for sixty years. Face was much squarer when not in august-clown blackface; it seemed smudged by reacting to all he'd seen, and holding so many expressions in readiness that none could be recognized as "characteristic" of him.

Success in writing, versus painting, means that your work becomes *cheaper*, purchasable by anybody.

The *New York Times* is a vast democratic *souk* in which every essayist can find a place to publish his or her voice. But otherwise, for a native New Yorker with proud and lengthy ties to the city, it's not so easy. The *New York Review of Books* is published by a group of sensibilities that give the impression of having been born in this metropolis, but of wishing they were Londoners instead. And *The New Yorker* traditionally has been the home of writers and editors born in Columbus, Ohio—who yearned so much to seem like real New Yorkers that their city personalities in print had an artificial, overeager sophistication and snobbery.

I ride my stutter, posting over its jolts, swerving with it, guiding it, if never "mastering" it.

At the annual sports show at NYC Colosseum, "Stay straight with sports," says a poster, a picture of a girl wearing a tee-shirt with that slogan over her breasts. An exhibitor tells me he just saw two men fondling each other in the men's room—"It just turns your stomach." A woman wearing a huge odd-looking hat made of dried pheasants' heads is cooing affectionately at a cageful of pheasants. A skinning contest is held in which three taxidermists go to work on the carcasses of three Russian boars.

If two people are in love they can sleep on the blade of a knife.

Karl Wheeler used a baby bottle until he was five years old, whereupon his mother said to him, "That's your last bottle, Karl. When you break that one you'll never get another one!" and he began to toss it idly in the air to catch it, but he missed.

First white men in British Columbia sold some of the Indians their names: $10 for a fine name like O'Shaughnessy, $5 for the more modest Harris.

At 6:00 A.M. I shoot a porcupine in the garage (knew about it from seeing Bimbo vomit from a fear reaction after his many tangles with porcupines). It goes under the building to die but not too far for a rake to reach. I take it to Paul Brooks' house. In his freezer he has woodchucks, beaver, bear, deer, bobcat, and porcupine meat (he is a man living only on social security), and he cleans it for me. We see it's a mamma with milk in her breasts. His mouth fills with saliva as he works; he's also preparing a venison roast for lunch with garlic salt, Worcestershire sauce, pepper, onions, etc. Says this time of year, first of June, the woodchucks are light as your hat, the winter has been so long for them; you can feel their thin legs. Porcupine liver is a delicacy, the rest not so much. The porcupine had been chewing at my garage; I eat the porcupine, therefore

I'm eating my garage—dark drumsticks that night by kerosene lamp. Game tastes herby even without herbs—best is bobcat and muskrat, in my experience, not counting big meats like moose. One countryman we know had his ashes scattered on his muskrat pond. The porcupine had chattered its teeth and rattled its poor quiver of quills as I had approached with my gun. Was so waddly it could not even limp properly when badly wounded. Lay on its side gurgling, choking, and sighing like man dying.

At the Freifields' one-room cabin with snowshoes hung under steep roof, I read Larry's father's hectic journal, written in Austro-English, of desperate orphanhood on the Austrian-Russian front in WW I. He, adopted by the rival armies as they overran the town, living in the trenches with them, living off stolen crusts otherwise, surviving the bombardments, dodging the peasants who hated Jews, but cherished by Austrian soldiers, who then were killed—saw one's legs blown off just after he'd changed places with him. That night peed in his pants in the trench and froze himself to the ground.

"Old Bet," the first circus elephant in America, was bought by Hachaliah Bailey from an English ship captain in 1815, but was shot eventually by religious fanatics in Connecticut as resembling the biblical Behemoth of the Book of Job (as indeed she did).

My first overtly sexual memory is of me on my knees in the hallway outside our fifth-grade classroom cleaning the floor, and Lucy Smith in a white blouse and black skirt standing above me, watching me.

My first memory is of being on a train which derailed in a rainstorm in Nebraska one night when I was two—and of hearing, as we rode in a hay wagon toward the distant weak lights of a little station, that a boy my age had just choked to death from breathing mud. But maybe my first real memory emerged when my father was dying. I was thirty-five and I dreamt so incredibly vividly of being dandled and rocked and hugged by him, being only a few months old, giggling helplessly and happily.

Had supper at a local commune where they have a fast turnover and have made life hard. They buy $20 used cars instead of spending $200, use kerosene instead of the electricity they have, and a team of horses to plow. They got 180 gallons of maple syrup out of their trees but they washed 1,400 sugaring pails in the bathtub in cold water, never having put in a hot water heater. Much husky embracing, like wrestlers; and before they eat their supper they have Grace, where twenty-some people clasp hands around the table, meditating and squeezing fingers. Bread bakes on a puffy black wood stove. Rose hips and chili peppers hang on strings, other herbs everywhere and pomegranates and jars of basic grains. The toilet is a car on blocks up the hill. Supper is a soup bowl full of rice and chard and potato pancakes with two sour sauces and apple butter, yogurt for dessert; and we drink from mason jars of water passed around. And the final "course" is dental floss, which everybody solemnly uses. A dulcimer is played with the quill of a feather accompanied by bongo drums. The women ended the public festivities by each announcing where she was going to sleep that night, which bedroom or which hayloft, in case anyone wished to join her. Clothing is heaped in a feed bin near the bottom of the stairs, and everybody is supposed to reach in in the morning and remove the first items that fit them and come to hand, without regard for which particular sex the clothes were originally made for. The saddest moment of the evening for me was when a little girl came around to her mother carrying a hairbrush in her hand and asking to be put to bed. The mother lost her temper. "Why run to me?" she said. "Everybody in this room is your parent. Anybody can brush your hair and tell you a story and put you to bed."

Manhattan, now 14,310 acres, was 9,800.

Bernard Malamud speaks of writing as a battle: "go to paper" with a novel. At this age, sixty-one, is trying to "write wise," new aim, and hard. Being between books, I say I'm in a period of withdrawal and inaction like that of a snake that is shedding its skin.

On the crest of Moose Mountain is an old birch growing low and twisty out of the ruins of a still older, bigger bole, surrounded by ferns, and it's there that the deer that feed in my field bed down during the day.

There is a whole literary genre which consists, first, of foolish writing and then later capitalizing upon the foolishness by beating one's breast and crying *mea culpa*. Why *was* I a white black panther, a drug swallower, a jackbooted feminist, a jet-set-climbing novelist, a 1940s Communist? How interesting and archetypal of me to have shared my generation's extremes.

Busybodies are called in Yiddish a *kochleffl*, a "cooking spoon," because they stir people up.

The hollow in the center of the upper lip is where "the angel touched you and told you to forget what you had seen in heaven."

Wife of F.'s uncle, to prevent him from going to work one morning when she preferred he stayed home, set the alarm so that it seemed it was too late for him to make the train when he woke. But he did rush so terribly he got to the station, and there collapsed and died, and she, only twenty-seven, never remarried.

Joyce consulted Jung, who diagnosed his poor daughter as incurably schizophrenic partly on the evidence of her brilliant, obsessive punning. Joyce remarked that he too was a punner. "You are a deep-sea diver," said Jung. "She is drowning."

The cure for stuttering of holding stones in one's mouth works because of the discomfort of them rattling against one's teeth. Stones from a crocodile's stomach were thought to be the best.

Amerigo Vespucci said that Indian women enlarged their lovers' sexual parts by applying venomous insects to them.

After losing her virginity at seventeen, she felt unstoppered on the street, like a hollow tube, as though the wind could blow right through her.

The sea, at the village of Soya on Hokkaido Island in 1792, was so fertile that twelve quarts of dry rice could be bartered for 1,200 herring, 100 salmon, 300 trout, or 3 seal skins.

How Davy Crockett kept warm when lost in the woods one night: climbing thirty feet up a smooth tree trunk and sliding down.

Am drunk from soft-shell crab lunch with Random House's Joe Fox, but stutter so vigorously with William Shawn as to obscure both from him and myself my drunkenness—stutter through it and give myself time to recall names like Numeiry and Assad, necessary to win Shawn's backing for the trip to Africa. He, as reported, is excessively solicitous of my comfort and state of mind; insulated and jittery; heated by electric heater (in August), yet fanned by electric fan; in his shirtsleeves, and immediately suggests I remove my coat. He has an agonized, bulging baby's head with swallowed up eyes, like that of the tormented child in Francis Bacon's painting *The Scream*. Questions me effectively, however, on my knowledge of the Sudan and the prospects for a salable article there. Says okay. Lunch the next day with Alfred Kazin, my old teacher. Kazin as always is a veritable tumult of impressions, like H. S. Commager and other busy intellectuals I have liked, but in Kazin's case it is enormously in earnest and felt. Expresses hurt at Bellow's recent inexplicable anger. Otherwise an outpouring of talk about his new book on the forties, when he published his first book and met the literary figures of the day. Played violin with drunken Alan Tate. Advances the idea that William James, a hero of his, is a better direct heir of Emerson than Thoreau; also the view that students now resent the fact that a professor knows more than they do, want him to learn along with them in class, as in group therapy, and when caught out on homework facts, get offended instead of trying to fake through, as in the old days. On Ph.D. orals, the candidates seem to have no favorite poem, no poem they can quote from, when he asks them for one at the end.

I like easterners more than westerners but western geography more than eastern geography; and I like the country more than the city but I like city people more than country people.

Essays, the most conversational form, have naturally drawn me, who have a hard time speaking in ordinary terms.

Tail end of hurricane rains buckets, flooding Barton River. Then the sky clears with nearly full moon, and I hear the deer whickering and whanging to one another gleefully, the mountain behind them gigantic and white.

Bellow says in Jerusalem journal that "light may be the outer garment of God."

Oil spills seem to attract aquatic birds; the sheen may resemble schooling fish. Also oil slicks calm the surface, look like landing area.

Roth speaks of his debt to both Jean Genet and the Fugs for *Portnoy*.

Roth a man who wears his heart on his sleeve, thus rather vulnerable to insult and injury; part of his exceptional generosity. Tells story of man bleeding in front of God but trying to hide blood from His sight apologetically.

William Gaddis: jockeylike, narrow-boned, fastidious Irishman, clever and civilized, with none of the usual hangdog bitterness of the neglected writer.

Warhol: keen, Pan face with tight manipulated skin that makes it ageless except for his eyes. Bleached hair hanging to his leather collar. Fame based upon being immobile.

Pete Hamill, bursting personality, does columns in half an hour, movie script in three weeks, discipline based upon not drinking till day's stint is through. Fewer bar brawls now, more empathetic, though still lives from a suitcase. "Irish Ben Hecht," he laughs.

Malamud: not at all the "Jewish businessman's face" I'd heard about, but a sensitive, gentle face, often silent or dreamy at Podhoretz's, disagreeing with the host and Midge, but holds his tongue and hugs him at the end with professional gratitude to an editor who once published him. When he speaks, his voice is young, light and quick, an enthusiast's, idealist's. Hurt by attacks on him in Jerusalem *Post*, for dovishness. Extremely solicitous of me, as kind in his way as Bellow, though style of it is modulated lower. Both of us distressed by Israeli's grinning description of Arab prisoners being beaten up. William Phillips says he thinks the Palestinians probably have a point but that he's not interested in hearing what it is.

Grace Paley; short stocky woman who at first sight on the Sarah Lawrence campus I mistook for the cleaning woman; asked her where the men's room was. We rode rubbing knees in the back seat throughout that semester in the back seat of a car pool. She'd been marching in protests since high school (Spanish civil war), but her exhilaration at being arrested in Washington peace march in midterm reminded me of my own exuberance at completing the hard spells of army basic training. Yes, we were good enough!

Heard MacLeish at YMHA. Afterward unrecovered yet from defeat of his play *Scratch* on B'way. Sweetness and bounce of his voice, however, is unchanged in twenty years; sounds forty, a matinée tenor, and the old lilt to his rhetoric. Face like a sachem's, too wise, too heroic, with a public man's nose. Talks of friendships with Joyce and Hemingway and imitates Sandburg's *O* very well. Talks of Saturday Club in Boston where Harlow Shapley monthly debated Robert Frost. Reminisces of artillery-lieutenant days in World War I, "making the world safe for democracy," where his brother was killed. Five years later he and other non-dead *did* die a bit when they realized it had been a "commercial" war and they had been lied to. He is a man of Hector-type heroes. Says Andrew Marvell poem was written while going home from Persia after his father's death.

Berryman given $5,000 prize at the Guggenheim reading, wearing a graybeard's beard which hides tieless collar. Reads best "Dream Songs," plus two sonnets and Rilke, Ralph Hodgson and eighteenth-century Japanese poet. Emphatically, spoutingly drunk, reads with frail man's grotesqueries, contortions, and his own memorable concoction of earnestness, coyness, staginess, name-dropping, and absolutely forceful, rock-bottom directness. Becomes louder and louder at the end of this floodlighted moment after long years of obscurity and hardship. Here was the current Wild Man, people thought, successor to Pound, there being one to a generation, though many others may have been reminded of Dylan Thomas, as he fell into the arms of Robert Lowell, punching him affectionately, when he finished. His whole life was thereupon paraded before him, when old mistresses and chums and students like me came up, expecting recognition, and one of his old wives, presenting him with a son whom obviously he hadn't laid eyes on for a long while. He boomed with love and guilt, with repeated thanks for letters informing him that so and so had had a child or remarried, till one was wearied of watching. One felt guilty too, as though competing for his attention with the neglected son. I felt Berryman had not long to live and I ought to be content with my memories of him and lessons learned and not join in the hounding of him. Nevertheless, I did go next afternoon to Chelsea Hotel, with bronze plaques outside memorializing other tragic figures like Thomas and Brenden Behan. He'd said the son would be there, so I was afraid that I would be taking time away from a son who needed to see him much more. But the son had left—all that remained was a note in Ann B.'s handwriting. Instead a *Life* photographer and reporter were talking with him, plying him with drinks, though he was holding back dignifiedly, talking of fame, of Frost, and his own dog Rufus. Frost was a shit who tried to hurt him, but he quoted the wonderful couplet about God forgiving our little faux pas if we forgive Him His great big joke on us. Is bombastic in his total commitment to words. Legs look very small but chest inflates with importance of uttering snatches of poems, till he collapses in coughs. Rubs beard and hair exhaustedly, recklessly spendthrift with his strength, and begins harder drinking; leads me to bar, where waiter, thinking from his red face and thin clothing that he is a bum, won't serve him till he lays a ten dollar bill on the table. I soon leave, but he was hospitalized within a couple of days. "Twinkle" was his favorite word at this time. He used it for commentary, by itself, and irony, or expostulation, quoting an enemy like Oscar Williams, then merely adding a somber "Twinkle."

Turgenev's brain was the heaviest ever recorded, 4.7 lbs.; 3 is average.

Child's tale about a man who suffered from shortness of breath. Afraid he would run out, he blew up a bunch of balloons as an extra supply for emergencies. Blew up so many that he floated away holding on to them.

Updike comes to U. of Iowa for first workshop session in three years (hasn't really taught for sixteen years), but handles himself in a classy manner nevertheless, and very well prepared with students' manuscripts beforehand, and in the exhilaration of reading his own work in front of 1,000 people in McBride Hall (which we call Mammal Hall because it's part of Nat'l Hist. Museum) freely sheds his private-person role that had made him a bit stiff before, when he'd refused even a newspaper interview. Signs autograph cards for eleven-year-old boys and physics texts for Japanese students and mimeo forms for students with nothing better to offer him. Wife is ample, attractive woman with large intense face, obviously both loving and sexy, a relaxed, close companion—he is wearing a wedding ring and ignoring the ambitious students who show up for his morning class wearing cocktail dresses. We talk of Africa—both finishing Africa books—and classmates and lit. hierarchies. He mentions Cheever's drunkenness, whom once he had to dress after a party like dressing a father. Our mothers are same age. "Poor Johnny," his said, watching a TV program about senility with him recently.

Updike says he quit teaching years ago because he "felt stupid," seeing only one way to write a given story properly, not the endless alternatives students proposed in discussions.

Indians used to scratch small children with mouse teeth fastened to a stick as a punishment for crying in front of white men. (White man, of course, a "skinned" man.)

Short stories tend to be boat-shaped, with a lift at each end, to float.

Yates says art is a result of a quarrel with oneself, not others.

Five toes to a track means it's wild, four toes means cat or dog.

Writers customarily write in the morning, and try to make news, make love, or make friends in the afternoon. But alas, I write all day.

Bellow says he spent the first third of his life absorbing material, the second third trying to make himself famous, and the last third trying to evade fame.

"A woman without a man is like a fish without a bicycle": tee-shirt.

People say they'll take a dip in the sea as if it were like dipping into a book, but I nearly drowned in surf's riptide off Martha's Vineyard's South Beach. Repeatedly changed swimming strokes to rest myself as I struggled in the water, surf too loud to shout over and I'm too near-sighted to see where to shout to. Reaching beach, I sprawled for an hour before moving further. Spent next day in bed, next week aching.

New England is "pot-bound," says Charlton Ogburn; thus superfertile.

Petrarch, climbing Mount Ventoux in 1336, began the Renaissance by being the first learned man ever to climb a mountain only for the view.

Rahv told Roth, "You can't be both Scott Fitzgerald and Franz Kafka."

People who marry their great loves sometimes wish they'd married their best friends; and vice versa.

Trapeze artists some days complain "there's too much gravity," when a change of the weather or the magnetic field affects their bodies. Elvin Bale bought his heel-hook act from Geraldine Soules, who after a fall started doing a dog act instead. Soules had, in turn, bought it from Vander Barbette, who, walking funny after *his* fall, had become a female impersonator and trainer of circus showgirls.

In old-time Georgia you ate mockingbird eggs for a stutter; boiled an egg for jaundice and went and sat beside a red-ant anthill and ate the white and fed the yolk to the ants. For warts, you bled them, put the blood on grains of corn and fed that to a chicken. Fiddlers liked to put a rattlesnake rattle inside their fiddles.

The fifties are an interim decade of life, like the thirties. In the thirties one still has the energy of one's twenties, combined with the judgment (sometimes) of the forties. In the fifties one still has the energy of one's forties, combined with the composure of the sixties.

The forties are the old age of youth and the fifties the youth of old age.

Adage, "God sends meat, the Devil sends cooks."

Carnival stuntman whom Byron Burford banged the drum for used to swallow live rats and ping-pong balls, upchucking whichever ones the crowd first asked for. Stunned the rats with cigar smoke before he swallowed them.

> The intellect of man is forced to choose
> Perfection of the life, or of the work,
> And if it take the second must refuse
> A heavenly mansion, raging in the dark.
> —Yeats, "Choice"

Lying to my lieutenant as a private at Fort Sam Houston as to whether I'd shaved that morning before Inspection; or only the night before—he reaching out and rubbing his hand down my face.

Glenn Gould liked to practice with the vacuum cleaner on, to hear "the skeleton of the music."

Nature writers, I sometimes think, are second only to cookbook writers in being screwed up.

Deer follow moose in these woods, says Toad. I say maybe they look like father (mother) figures to them.

At Academy-Institute ceremonial, the big scandal is Ellison's lengthy introduction of Malamud for a prize, and Barbara Tuchman's brutal interruption of it. Ellison had tried to speak of blacks and Jews. Stegner very youthful, as befits an outdoorsman. Cowley very food-hungry as always, as befits a 1930s survivor. Commager tells my wife that his daughter loved me and so he loved me. Lots of cold-faced ambitious poets cluster around each other and Northrop Frye; Galway seems likably unaffected and truthful next to them. Ditto Raymond Carver.

Joe Flaherty's line for the Brooklyn Bridge: "the Irish gangplank."

Whale mother's milk would stain the sea after she was harpooned and the calf would circle the ship forlornly. "I do not say that John or Jonathan will realize all this," said Thoreau, in finishing *Walden;* and that's the central and tragic dilemma as the environmentalist movement fights its rearguard battles.

In starving midwinter, foxes catch cats by rolling on their backs like a kitten ready to play.

Warblers average eight or 10,000 songs a day in spring; vireo 20,000. Woodchucks wag their tails like a dog. Blue jays like to scare other birds by imitating a red-shouldered hawk.

My bifocals are like a horse's halter, binding the lower half of my eyes to the day's work.

At my frog pond a blue heron circles low overhead while a brown-muzzled black bear clasps chokecherry bushes and eats off them thirty yards away from me.

Only six hours old, a red calf stumbles toward the barn as mother is herded in by Hugh Stevens on ATV vehicle, and is eventually tied to its mother's stanchion with hay twine, while a six-inch red tab of its previous cord still hangs from its belly. It's as shiny as a new pair of shoes, its deerlike hooves perfectly formed, including the dew claws. Mother and calf had had a brief wild idyll under the summer sky before they were discovered by Hugh—the last sky this vealer will ever see.

Old people seem wise because they have grown resigned and because they remember the axioms even if they've forgotten the data.

"When you come to the end of your life, make sure you're used up."

I trust love more than friendship, which is why I trust women more than men.

"All hat and no cows": Texas saying.

"Eat with the rich, laugh with the poor."

Buying a new car after thirteen years, I discover why country people like to keep the old one about the yard. First, it makes the house look occupied. Second, it's a nesting site for ducks and geese and a shelter for chickens during the day. Third, it reminds you of *you*.

EDMUND KEELEY

◆ —————————————————————— ◆

Going to the Border

Bangkok / December 15

I took a walk over to Wireless Avenue to see if I could find the American
Ambassador. It was a long, complicated walk, because my map shows
only the major thoroughfares and not the many little side streets which
hold the real life of the city. I would turn into one of the side streets
occasionally to try and get a feel for the place. The people you run into
there seem to be relatively poor, though maybe well-dressed in local
terms, some of the women very handsome, their features regular, strong
lips and eyes, cheekbones high, and the men more mixed, some faces
drawn, pinched, others what you might call handsome, though often
slight in build, without giving you the sense that they are underfed. In
fact, eating seems to be the city's main public entertainment. Eating and
driving, generally in old cars that breathe out bad air or three-wheeler
taxis called tuk-tuks.

I went down Wireless Avenue without any clear idea of where I was
and suddenly came up against the American Embassy's Residence, quite
grand, with tall palms on the right and left of the road curling up through
the front garden to the door. I asked the Thai guard at the gate if the
Ambassador was in. He either didn't understand me or thought me a
crazy tourist (I was wearing my fisherman's cap from Mykonos). The
guard just stared at me, then looked away. I continued down the avenue, and that's how I found the Embassy, several blocks away. I
managed to convince the man at the desk that my brother had been the
Ambassador's deputy in Cambodia some years back, and that got me a
pass to Ambassador's office.

When I went in the Ambassador was looking over a speech he had
to give the next day, glanced up, greeted me very genially, told me how
much he admired my brother, a courageous Foreign Service officer, he
said, even if he did have a temper on occasion and had to be calmed
down when Washington did something awful or stupid in the days before
we pulled out of Cambodia. Just like his father, I said, another career
diplomat who had a temper when it came to dealing with Washington.

The Ambassador smiled, asked me what I was up to in Thailand. I told him I wanted to go to the border, wanted to get to know the territory out there because I was writing a novel about the fall of Phnom Penh. He stared at me the way the guard had at the Embassy Residence. Then he said that it could be arranged, anything could be arranged for the brother of my brother. And he started to phone people who might be able to help. He thought it would be relatively easy under the circumstances, he said, because a refugee relief expert was arriving from Washington to look over the camps along the border, and I could probably hitch a ride with him the following day.

I walked back from the Embassy to the Hotel Erawan hoping I would find my young friend Jason there, due in from the Nong Samet camp north of Aranyaprathet, where he was setting up an experimental station for small-scale agriculture to give the refugees from Cambodia a way to raise some of their own food and fight against boredom. At the corner where you turn off Wireless Avenue heading for the hotel, I came across a shrine of some kind, and four young girls were dancing in front of it, barefoot, in costumes that were topped by a pointed crown like the steeples on some of the local pagodas, the movement of the dancers slow, jagged at times, the shape of it ritualistic but not predictable to Western eyes, and the hands always delicate birds in flight.

Jason wasn't at the Erawan Hotel when I got there. I went out on the hotel balcony that overlooks a swimming pool, and there were four or five foreigners sitting around the pool, all very white. That seems to be the going color, or absence of color, at this hotel: white suits, white decor, the talk careful and accented toward the British, everything very laundered and sanitized, including the toilet bowl with its paper band sealing it shut as in an American motel, but then a bit of relief on the snack refrigerator, where there is an exotic fruit bowl with bananas, green tangerines, something reddish that could be a local pomegranate, enough to remind you that this is Thailand. Jason arrived wearing his Khmer bandanna and a T-shirt that shows how brown he's gotten on the border, and he says we have to move out right away, this place is too uncomfortable, too white and expensive, so we're heading for the Nana Hotel down the road, half the price, where the lower floors are reputedly set aside for massage parlor entertainment by charming ladies of the region but the upper floors are as ordinary and neat as you could want, and they give you a broad view of the cement landscape that is gradually rising to dominate the city.

Yesterday Jason took me sightseeing to the far side of Bangkok, a five-hour trip through this city's Chinatown, into the lavish temples and beyond to the river, where we picked up a fast, sharp-nosed, narrow boat called a baht, two to a seat, the kind used by the local commuters to get to the smaller canals, or "klongs," that cut away from the main canal like side streets, each lined by houses on pilings that hold the living barely above water, the pattern of houses broken here and there by a shopping area or a wat with saffron-robed monks on a garden stroll. The water was a thick coffee brown, and where it settled along the banks it had an oily glaze. We sliced through it at a speed that kept it at a safe distance except when there was a wave created by the wake from a boat running counter to ours. You could see people of both sexes washing in that water, children swimming naked, one man using it as a giant sink to shave, but Jason said you should do what you could to keep from swallowing it or even wetting your lips with your tongue if any of it got there—just hold your lips sealed tight and let the saliva gather until you had to spit it out—and anywhere else the water hit skin, you could eventually wash it off with Mekong rice whiskey. Later he said he'd only been kidding, but I didn't talk much during that trip because I was splattered fairly regularly; and when we got to shore we lit out for the first open-air bar we could find and had a little baptism in rice whiskey: the whole head and anyplace else above the waist where skin was showing. The commuters waiting to go home at the table next to ours were stunned, then seemed amused, then just looked away.

We headed for the border early this morning in a volunteer agency minibus that the Embassy arranged for us to hop a ride on. We had two companions for the trip, one of them an old hand out here working on the resettlement of refugees, an American named Crawford now married to a Thai woman and well versed in the local culture, the other a refugee relief expert named Colonel Hopwood, on loan to the State Department from the Pentagon. The fact that the man was on loan from the army to review relief work along the Thai–Cambodian border made Jason suspicious of him from the start, but the Colonel—of course crewcut and square-jawed—kept his own counsel most of the time, his opinions low-keyed, more cynical than reactionary.

Crawford was really the man in charge of the trip: his bus, his insane driver. The ride out to the border town of Aranyaprathet was thrilling at moments because this Thai driver of his seemed much distracted and a bit lean on talent. He came close to killing us twice while dodging other cars—he's with the majority out here when it comes to pride in holding fast to the center of the highway—and one time late in the trip he didn't seem to notice that the road up ahead was blockaded by a new military check point and nearly got us machine-gunned off the road before Jason yelled something sharply obscene at him in his native language to bring him to a desperately sudden stop.

Three and a half hours into the trip we had a midmorning lunch of greens and noodles and dried fish fried up for us by a very solemn lady at a roadside stand, and while we sat on a bench there helping the stuff go down with Singha beer, Crawford told us a bit of local history to fill us in on the border situation, in particular the changing attitude of the Thais toward hundreds of thousands of refugees who had been camping along their border without much hope of going home or elsewhere year in year out, some there since shortly after the fall of Phnom Penh in 1975, many since the invasion of Cambodia by Vietnam in 1979. The Thais had been reasonably tolerant of their dispossessed neighbors at the start despite the long tradition of bad blood between Thailand and Cambodia, but the refugees had gradually come to be resented by the farm workers in the region as cheap competitive labor and by the Thai authorities as a destabilizing threat that might encourage Vietnam to use their border skirmishes with Cambodian resistance fighters as an excuse for an incursion into Thailand.

The whole thing apparently came to a head in June of 1979 when the Thai government, run by some general, suddenly decided to initiate a policy of "forced repatriation," which meant that recently arrived "illegal entrants"—the official name for the Cambodian refugees seeking asylum—had to go back across the border into the Cambodia they had left after the harshest kind of crossing. Going back proved harsher. Some one hundred and fifty buses transported forty-one thousand of them from the border camps to the Preah Vihear region farther north in Thailand. The refugees were led at gunpoint by the Thai military to the edge of an escarpment on the border, almost a cliff, and were then forced to climb down it and head off into Vietnam-held Cambodia across a mine field that was supposedly protecting Thailand from invasion.

I don't know how many died trying to make it across—everybody has his own figures—but some got through by stepping on the fallen bodies in front of them and others were guided out finally by Vietnamese soldiers. And some managed to scamper back up the escarpment and hide in the woods at the top until they could make it out safely, a few ending up in Bangkok a month later almost starved to death, one woman having dragged her son behind her until he was raw wherever his flesh showed. And—this is the hardest to believe—some of those who got through the mine field made it back to one or another of the refugee camps many months later, even years later, looking for a second chance at repatriation to a third country, which now seems to most out here less than the last chance they have left.

Crawford told of one couple that he thinks is going to make it. A woman who reached the bottom of the escarpment sent her brother out to get some water so they could boil the uncooked rice they'd been given as a parting ration, and the brother never came back. While she sat there weeping on the edge of the mine field a man she had never met before came up to console her, went after the water himself, somehow made it back through the mine field, then led her across the way he had come, and the two stayed together after that for the months it took them to make it back to Thailand and are now going to a third country, probably Australia, though not yet officially married. "There's no way you can have the heart to fight against luck like that," Crawford said.

This bit of history put a pall on the trip until the driver got our juices going again with some kamikaze maneuvering on the outskirts of Aranyaprathet, known as "Aran" to the locals. Anyway there wasn't much to fill the eye on the way out. Most of the villages you pass through on this highway are nothing more than shacks, garages, repair stops for motorcycles or small trucks, and the Thai version of fast food restaurants on both sides, maybe a house or two hiding beyond the main drag, but what you see is meant to serve the highway traffic. The land seemed out of use as we approached the border—fallow fields, orchards that appeared to have turned wild, some planted fields with the rice stalks gathered up and waiting but others burnt clean, as though their season was already over. And few animals in sight. Once we spotted a water buffalo, black mother with a light-brown calf, both caked with mud. You wouldn't have called either healthy.

Coming into Aran gives you the feeling that you've arrived at the end of the line. I had expected something between a town and a city, but it's really a large village, a market village that must have grown out of nothing with the arrival of refugee relief. Few buildings more than three stories high, though there are some new concrete shells rising higher, the lower stories filled mostly with booths selling vegetables and fruit—cabbage, cucumbers, lettuce, other kinds of greens a Westerner would have trouble naming, pineapples, oranges, bananas, limes, potatoes, and roots in shapes you wouldn't believe. Between the booths there are places where you can eat whatever is sold next door, cooked in woks or boiled, along with chunks of meat or fish on skewers. Then there are the grocery stores with goods that must have been brought in from faraway places—Rome, Paris, London, maybe New York—because many of the labels are familiar, and so is the liquor in the shops: Johnny Walker Red or Black, Courvoisier, Hennessy. Who but the foreigners in town—the volunteer refugee relief workers, or "volags" as they're called on the border—or maybe the Thai military could possibly afford what you see in some of those shops.

The feeling of being at the end of the line doesn't really come until you pass beyond the two streets with brothels—doors apparently shut until it gets darker—and the street of parked tuk-tuk taxis where the concrete road abruptly turns to dirt and you head out for the camps to the north and west: Kao I Dang, Nong Chan, Nong Samet. We decided to make a quick tour before returning to Aran for dinner. Not far north of the town we hit the first checkpoint and stopped to get our clearance for moving on to the border area. While we were waiting there a truck-load of Thai soldiers drove up, all in the black uniforms belonging to the special border patrol, I was told, but reminding me of what I'd read the Khmer Rouge—at least the more regular of them—were wearing when they moved in to empty Phnom Penh. Now the Thais allow the Khmer Rouge guerrillas to keep as much ground as possible free of a potential common enemy, the Vietnamese, who claim they invaded Cambodia merely to clear out the true enemy: the genocidal Khmer Rouge.

The first of the camps we checked out briefly, Kao I Dang, seemed more solid and clean than I'd expected, the barracks fairly new, the roads separating them dusty but some of them broad enough for a bus or truck. It is apparently the camp where those with the best chance for resettlement end up, where the interviewing takes place, and the long wait before the few who are approved for another country finally move on. I'm told that solid as it may seem, it's still meant to be temporary, but not as temporary as Jason's camp, some kilometers up the road and actually laid out across the border a short distance inside Cambodia so that the Thais don't have to consider it their territory when the Vietnamese move in to wipe it out, as they are expected to do any day now (the Vietnamese apparently like to use the Christmas season for their annual wipeouts, some think because that is meant to send a special message to Westerners supporting the Khmer Rouge and other guerrilla groups).

On the way to Nong Samet we heard what sounded very much like machine-gun fire, just beyond the second checkpoint, the only evidence of a border anywhere near, and that sound drove our driver more insane than he already was by nature. From then on there was no bump in the road, no hole or rock or wayward branch that he missed in his hurry to get us to that refugee camp and back out to the main road again before we were caught up in this imminent imaginary incursion by tanks and armed men that was tormenting his perception of things, so that even Crawford finally had to give him a few intensely quiet words in his native language to calm the man down.

Jason's camp was clearly makeshift: a vast gathering of flimsy huts, some with blue plastic sheets for walls, the roofs not wood or tin but a loose thatch, open mephitic gutters for drains, paths rather than roads between the huts and the paths sometimes very narrow because most huts now have a bunker cut out of the ground in front of the entrance, roofed by any scrap of metal or wood that can provide protection. When the shelling out of the jungle starts, that's where the whole family ends up, in a space that looks as though it would hardly do for a latrine.

Jason led us to the far end of the camp where his agricultural project—a pond for ducks and fish, some young pigs in a pen, several kinds of chickens that he's brought up from chicks, a few plots for cultivating whatever will grow in small strips of ground between the edge of the camp and the no-man's-land where the mine fields and the jungle begin. He told us that he has to keep experimenting with new things to put in the pond and in the pens, because whatever fish he brings in for breeding usually disappears mysteriously before it gets to the water, the ducks and sometimes the chickens just as mysteriously wander off into the jungle, and the pigs survive in their pen only as long as the refugee guard he posts there remains incorruptible, which is generally something between a week and ten days.

Jason's been out here on the border—beyond the border—for eight months now, and he says he sometimes gets so discouraged he can't think straight enough to go on experimenting seriously, but then he figures you have to be a little patient, maybe look on it more as a private food distribution program than an agricultural training center and bear with it until the agency he represents loses its patience. Anyway, it's clear that he's very popular in the camp, and the really surprising thing about that miserable place is the cheerful way people greeted us, Jason of course in particular, as we moved back between those huts to the road out, a lot of smiling and nodding and rising up from a squat to greet us, even those with legs missing from having crossed the mined no-man's-land beyond the camp as they escaped from their homeland or from having strayed too far beyond the camp's cultivated areas in search of wild things to eat or the pot some of them have planted where no one less desperate for it would dare to go.

We went back to Aran for dinner after Crawford, the Colonel, and I dropped our things off at the motel "bungalow" that the government agencies use out here, closer to the border than the town—so close, in fact, that a short way off the main road you run into the tank trap that the Thais have set up on their side of the border mostly for symbolic purposes ("No self-respecting tank would pause to worry about that ditch for two seconds," Crawford said), and a mile or two straight up the road you come across a huge Thai flag on a pole and twenty-five yards beyond that a heavy barrier in front of a bridge that has an equally huge Vietnamese flag at the other end of it, all signals grand enough to let you know that this is without question the end of the line. We had dinner at a small place in town called "Maxime's," where I picked my way through a broiled fish that I thought was some kind of red snapper but that turned out to be carrying the green death, which hit me in my motel room half into the night. I'd spent the early part of the night killing the mosquitoes that had moved in to take over my bathroom and bedroom, tens on tens of them, all of course carrying that particularly virulent new strain of malaria that, according to a headline in the *Bangkok Times* the day I arrived in Thailand, was raging through the camps along the border because there was yet no antidote known to man. I whacked away at those mosquitoes from a safe distance with a towel every time one would land on the wall until I was too tired to care. The following morning, this morning, Crawford came into my room from his next door to say that he'd had another one of those bad nights you get on border, the sound of artillery in the distance coming into your sleep, an intermittent thud thud thud that just doesn't seem to end, like the last time he was out here for the night and heard the steady sound of tank treads moving in on the motel, what turned out to be the sound of an air conditioner with a squeaking wheel in the room next door. I didn't tell him about the green death that had visited me, but I felt I had to mention my murderous orgy with the mosquitoes. He looked at me and shook his head. "One day on the border and already you've got a touch of the dread volag madness. Think of what it's like for those of us who have to keep going year in year out. Or think we do. Which is part of the disease."

I didn't really understand what Crawford was getting at with that remark three? four? days ago. I think I have a better idea now, after watching him in action at Kao I Dang, where he spent two twelve-hour days interviewing candidates for repatriation to the States in a crowded administration hut called the Conference Center, thatch on the outside, paper walls on the inside, with a sort of wicker window through which those outside could watch the action. That room was just the front line for a waiting horde that curled around the building and far back into the camp's byways. Section leaders in the camp would bring in their candidates to Crawford's desk, he would talk to them quietly, patiently, review their documents if they had any, try to explain why there had to be documents, try to explain why they had to have relatives of some kind in the States before they could qualify for repatriation there, do the best he could to show his sympathy for those—and these were the majority—who said they didn't have any relatives left because they'd all been killed in the Khmer Rouge massacres under Pol Pot.

One old lady was brought into the hut, stood there a while waiting, then turned and left without a word, apparently assuming she'd been rejected again as in the past—an example of what one of the volags out here calls the "rejection syndrome" among refugees. Crawford had to insist that the woman be escorted back in to have her say, present her petition for resettlement after three years of waiting, and when it turned out she too didn't have any relatives, Crawford walked her to the door, tried to explain, then went off to have a cigarette, shaking his head.

While he was gone I had a chat with the young Sino-Khmer refugee who has the job of being Crawford's official camp interpreter even though Crawford doesn't need one. Where the interpreter learned his English, I don't know, but it was good enough to give me a ghastly image of what he had gone through as one of those who had been forced back into Cambodia over the Preah Vihear escarpment in 1979, when he was fifteen and close to dying from malaria. He had to be carried across the mine field on a friend's back—he was light from malnutrition and his mind at the time "sicker than my body"—the humpbacked pair inching along a path in the footsteps of those in front who succeeded in making it out and then the two of them off into the woods beyond where they could crawl unseen to the road that took them eventually to Battambang and on to Phnom Penh where the Sino-Khmer tried to track down his parents and one or another of his nine brothers. He found nobody there, because Phnom Penh didn't exist any longer at the time.

But he gradually got his health back by working in the countryside here and there, and now, three years later, he's back on the Thai side of the border where he found one of his brothers in a camp up the road, both of them now waiting for repatriation to the States, where one of their older brothers somehow managed to make his way.

I stayed in the Conference Center as long as I could, listening to one broken story after another, some told as though by rote, others too fragmented to be entirely comprehensible, though the gist was always the horrors Pol Pot had brought to his people and the hope that I might help in getting the speaker out of that camp and into a third country. I didn't have the heart to explain that I was just an observer. When I left the Center I had in mind taking some snapshots of the camp as inconspicuously as I could, but everywhere I went I was trailed by somebody who had a new version of the old story to tell me—the history of Pol Pot's four years of terror, then the three years of suffering under the Vietnamese occupation, then the escape across the border, and now the need for my personal help—a kind of catechism that must have been the essential English lesson everyone in the place eventually learned by heart. The one succinct version I got was at the far end of the barracks rows, where a kid who couldn't have been more than twelve and who had been tugging at my sleeve so that I couldn't get set for the long-view picture I wanted of that god-forsaken camp, got me to stop: "Hey Mister," he said. "You take me home now, we buy a car, we go to California, OK?" I was trying to smile—"OK," I said, "OK"—but he could see that there was something wrong with my face, and then I couldn't look at him, so he just shrugged and turned away.

Aranyaprathet / December 23
I spent yesterday afternoon touring the Old Aran Camp (as it's now called), the place where the first refugees who came over after the fall of Phnom Penh in 1975 were put, now as empty as their city was when they left it. My guide was Jason's assistant, Lim Than, a young Khmer who came out of Cambodia in 1976 when he was seventeen, part of a work force of 300 laborers called a "mobile group" because they moved wherever the Khmer Rouge needed them most, always under guard, like old-time convicts condemned to hard labor though in fact merely junior citizens of the new Democratic Kampuchea. One day their leader, who had been selected by the Khmer Rouge, did the impossible: he spread the word that during the next work detail they were to head for a river nearby, cross it, then go for the border, each man on his own. For some

reason they believed him and the whole group took off. The Khmer Rouge went after them. Fifty-six made it across the river, the others, including the leader, were either shot on the near bank or were executed back at their base camp. It took Lim Than and the small group he ended up with twelve days to reach the border. He lived on leaves from a jungle tree the group knew about and on what little water they could find in holes—it was January, the dry season—and then on his own urine, which he kept in a small alcohol bottle next to his chest, secretly rationing it out hour by hour so the others wouldn't steal the bottle. They came across the tracks of wild animals—tigers and elephants, he said—and at night they would light fires to ward them off, but they never actually saw any. When they finally got to a mountain where they expected to join guerrilla resisters—Mountain 1014 on my map—there were no guerrillas there: something better, the Thai border at the bottom of the mountain, and Thai soldiers waiting to give them food.

He settled into Wat Koh, now the Old Aran Camp, what has become an informal monument to the desperation of those early days, with the look of an abandoned concentration camp: a fence all around the place, two rows of wooden barracks with rusted tin roofs, the floor a platform three feet off the ground, each barrack divided into a number of segments that are now marked only by two-by-four pillars that must have once supported the cardboard walls lying around flat, and under the platform what remains of life from the old days: broken crockery, discarded shoes, bits of clothing, a picture of an American naval officer cut out of a magazine, a notebook with primitive English scribbled in it. The English and French lessons at the deskless YWCA School in the center of the camp are what saved Lim Than, got him eventually to France where he was educated enough to return as a relief worker so that he could find his brother, who, he is convinced, is in one of the camps somewhere along the border. He's been looking for him six months now.

My tour of that old camp and its ghosts demoralized me in a way even Nong Samet and Kao I Dang hadn't, so that when Jason came back from his agricultural station late yesterday afternoon, I talked him into going for a spin with me in his truck just to get a change of scenery. We headed out of town to visit a Buddhist shrine on a sort of knoll overlooking the border, high enough so that you could see the whole vast spread of the Thai valley where the camps in this region are located, the view of salvation, however temporary, that greets those who come over the range behind us and who make it safely through the border mine fields. On the other side of the knoll, the Cambodian jungle.

While we were up at the top sitting on the roof of a bunker the monks guarding the shrine must have built, I asked Jason what exactly he thought Crawford had meant by the dread volag disease. I could tell that my question had touched a danger spot, because Jason didn't say anything at first, then went on talking some time after I'd gotten his point, finally ended up telling me a few horror stories to underline his evident worry about what might even get to him someday. One lady— the sweetest nurse in the world, he said—had gotten so caught up in refugee relief work that she'd decided to head back home and get a degree in rural sociology. She came back to the border and within two months she found that she had trouble driving, kept easing off to the side of the road, finally cut a path into the jungle that took out a number of trees and broke many of the bones in her body and got her sent back home permanently. And just the past week two guys were cooking a pizza for themselves in the headquarters of a local relief agency north of Aran, one guy a returning volag and the other about to move on to Bangkok for reassignment the following day, both hard workers with a lot of experience, and they started drinking vodka, got a bit rowdy, began throwing eggs at each other and slices of pizza, things like that, and when a doctor at the headquarters came down to see what the hell was going on, they got in a fight with him, laid him out, then went for the headquarters, dumping over filing cabinets, clearing the shelves of medical supplies, trashing the place completely. An extreme case, Jason said, but indicative, indicative. He was looking off into the Cambodian wilderness as he said it. I decided at that point that we both needed a vacation, so tomorrow, Christmas Eve, we head south for the sea.

Bangkok / December 25

When you take the road out of Aran for Chantaburi and the southern shore you have to go through a stretch of the main road to Bangkok, very flat, very boring, maybe because it's too familiar already, but once you turn south on highway 317, you're in another country. The land is often green, and there are sudden mountains, half cliff and half slope, rising straight up from the plain, one a small-scale Yosemite with caves in its rock face and a giant Buddha to keep your mind in the right climate. And the farther south you go, the more distinctive the trees become, palm trees, some high umbrellalike pines, acacias, teak, God knows what, and there are houses by the road with gardens, the wash hanging out, a sense of the old quotidian domestic atmosphere that makes you forget completely how close you still are to the border that parallels the highway off to the left.

Another thing that makes you forget is Jason's pipe, which moved back and forth between us for a while on the way down, rich stuff in it from a small plot on the far edge of his agricultural station at the camp but not part of his official experiment, fine for giving the excursion a glow to go along with the softening sun before we hit Chantaburi and switched to Mekong rice whiskey. Chantaburi is not Aran; the aura is still provincial, but there are billboards advertising whatever the housewife needs, or the husband out for classy transportation, or the children looking for violent movies. There are also lakes in the area, inlets from the sea that cut right through my glow with a sharper longing.

We made a stop in Chantaburi to look in on some Irish nurses that Jason is particularly fond of, a whole house full of them assigned to the Kamput refugee camp on the southern border not far to the east, most of them full of good cheer and blarney, their accents enough to break a lapsed Irishman's heart. One of them gave us each a rubber suction device that she said was used to help new mothers get their milk going, the one thing the girls could come up with as a Christmas present for us, and Jason left a little package of his experimental pipe tobacco on the mantel that was serving for their Christmas tree. Jason wanted to stay on there, but I was hungry for the sea, and I finally managed to drag him away from a plan he was working on to link up for the evening with a red-headed beauty who knew her Yeats and her Joyce but, as I finally persuaded him, clearly had no mind for what he had in mind on a first date.

We rode along the coast without being able to see it while the sun was nearly down, high on the prospects ahead as much as on the glow inside us, riding faster than we should have been, the road lined by tall trees that seemed to have gathered in the afternoon light so that they could now give it back in thin slanting rays that dappled the highway in front of us. Suddenly Jason spotted something and swung sharply to the left, barely slowing down, cut off the highway and into a dirt road I hadn't even noticed, went down that road as though something deadly was after him but driving well enough to keep us out of the gullies along the side, and within five hundred yards he took another sharp turn and slammed on the breaks to stop a foot or two short of the cleanest white beach I've ever seen.

There was no talk. We were out of our clothes and in that water swimming hard for the horizon without stopping to look back until we had to for breath, and that's when I first saw that we'd parked by a bungalow complex still half-built but with several of the finished sections rented because there were people now standing out on their balconies, I suppose watching to see how far we would get before the sharks moved in. That was the first swim. The second came about an hour later, some miles down the road, where we settled in for the night in a small, isolated group of beach bungalows with a gathering of Jason's friends who had come down from Bangkok after a call from him the previous day, mostly border relief workers no longer on the border, Americans, Brits, Thais, one Khmer lady, an Australian, all restless for the sea and some new talk.

I went for the water again right away. It was warmer than any I remembered from the Mediterranean or the Caribbean, God knows cleaner than the former, and there were green islands in the distance, something you could at least aim for if not reach, though I swam out and out and felt I could go the whole way given a bit more life to live than the too much I'd already spent. When I finally looked back I could see clean sand stretching for what looked like miles, no jellyfish, no sudden garbage floating by, no speedboats or windsurfers or other signs of the tourist trade, just that bright water and the palm trees and the white sand. Except that something always comes in to spoil things like that with too much reality. At the far end of the beach on the border side, maybe a mile from us, there was a metal structure that might have been a power-line pole, only this one had wings at the top of it, curved metal wings turning and turning with a silent wha wha wha wha: radar tracking the border. Tomorrow was Christmas Day. There had been new checkpoints on the road down here, unexpected barriers, so somebody must still be thinking that today or tomorrow or the next day the Vietnamese will finally make their move, as they did when they invaded Cambodia over Christmas in 1979.

I turned away and swam slowly in. I could see figures moving against the dusk between the bungalows and on the small lawn in front where they were setting up the table for dinner—what turned out to be all Thai food, fried watercress, lemon grass, lime leaf, some kind of mushrooms, stir-fried beef and pork, curried chicken, crispy fish, the best you could find in the region. One of the figures I could see was Jason making a Christmas tree out of a stake six feet high and whatever palm branches he could get to stick to it with tape—a scrawny, unreal thing, but it had to do. And then others started putting candles on the table and in a circle around the tree. I came out of the water and stood there dripping in air that now gave out only the slightest chill, thinking that these young volags had somehow managed to scrape up the feel of Christmas Eve however beautifully inappropriate and ungodly the territory they had to work in.

URSULA K. LE GUIN

Riding Shotgun

From a diary written in the right front seat of a diesel VW on the way east
from Oregon to Georgia in June of 1981, and on the way west from
Georgia to California in July.

*I*ndiana and Points East
We're doing 55 on Indiana 65.
  Jasper County.
  Flooded fields.
  Iroquois River spread way out, wide and brown as a Hershey
    bar.
  Distances in this glacier-flattened, planed-down ground-level
    ground aren't blue, but whitish, and the sky is whitish-blue.
  It's in the eighties at 9:30 in the morning, the air is soft and
  humid, and the wind darkens the flooded fields between rows of
    oaks.
    Watch Your Speed—We Are.
Severely clean white farmhouses inside square white fences painted by
  Tom Sawyer yesterday produce
a smell of dung. A rich and heavy smell of dung on the southwest wind.
Can shit be heady?
La merde majestueuse.
  This is the "Old Northwest."
Not very old, not very north, not very west. And in Indiana
there are no Indians.
  Wabash River

     right up to the road and the oaks are standing
     ten feet out in the brown shadowmottled flood,
     but the man at the diesel station just says:
     You should of seen her yesterday.

The essence is motion being in motion moving on not resting at a point:
and so by catching at points and letting them go again without recur-

rence or rhyme or rhythm I attempt to suggest or imitate that essence
the essence of which is that you cannot catch it.
Of course there are continuities:
the other aspect of the essence of moving on.

The country courthouses.
Kids on bikes.
White frame houses with high sashed windows.
Dipping telephone wires, telephone poles.
The names of the dispossessed.
The redwing blackbird singing to you from fencepost to fencepost.
Dave and Shelley singing "You're the Reason God Made
      Oklahoma" on the radio.
The yellow weedy clover by the road.
The flowering grasses.
And the crow, not the Indian, the bird, you seen one crow you seen
      'em all, kronk kronk.

CHEW MAIL POUCH TOBACCO
TREAT YOURSELF TO THE BEST

on an old plank barn, the letters half–worn off, and that's a continuity,
not only in space but time: my California in the thirties, & I at
six years old would read the sign and imagine a Pony Express rider at
full gallop eating a candy cigarette.

    Lafayette
    Greencastle
    And the roadsign points: Left to Indianapolis
                            Right to Brazil.

              Now there's some choice.

Another day
Ohio, south Ohio, Clermont County.
Cloudpuffs repeat roundtop treeshapes.
Under the grass you see the limestone layers, as if you drove on the
ramparts of a fallen castle the size of Clermont County.
    Ohio 50, following Stonelick Creek.

Daylilies dayglow orange in dark roadside woods
Brick farmhouses painted white, small, solid, far between.

Owensville founded 1839
Monterey
Milford
Marathon   Little towns beads on a string
Brown County
Vera Cruz   A Spaniard in the works?
Fayetteville   founded 1818 by Cornelion MacGroarty
        on the Little Miami River
Nite Crawlers 65 cents a dozen

There's a continuity, though the prices change:
Nite Crawlers crawling clear across the continent.

Highland County
Dodsonville
Allenburg   The road dips up and down in great swells like the
        sea
Hoagland
The Mad River, about one and one-half foot wide
Hillsboro, home of Eliza Jane Thompson, Early Temperance
        Crusader
Clearcreek
    Boston
        Rainsboro
Ross County
    Bainbridge
        Paint Creek
Seip —

But Seip is older than Eliza Jane, and older than Ohio.
Seip is a village twenty centuries old.
Posts mark the postholes of the houses within the encircling wall; all
walls are air, now; you rebuild them in your mind.
Beyond the little houses stands the long, steepsided mound, silent in the
sunlight, except for the bumblebee of a power mower circling it, performing the clockwise spiral rites of the god Technology, the god that cuts

the grass; the long, sweet grass on the enormous, ancient altar. A church half the age of Stonehenge and twice the age of Chartres. A country church.

Onward past Bourneville, Slate Mill, North Fork Farm, to Chillicothe.
     At Chillicothe, the Hopewell Burial Mounds.
The people whom the white invaders dispossessed had been living here
for several hundred years; they called the ones who built these mounds
the Old Ones.
Walk in the silence of the vast sacred enclosure among the green mounds
built above the bones and ashes of the illustrious dead
laid between levels of mica, sheets of mica
transparent and glittering as eyes, as souls.
The pipes are stolen
The sacred pipes are broken
The beautiful carvings of Bobcat, Prairie-hen, Raven, Turtle, Owl
The sheets of pure thin copper cut in the shape of the Bear,
     of the Falcon, the soul-falcon,
     of the falcon's foot
     and the human hand.

So, back to the New World, the thin, sick skin we laid on this land,
     the white skin. And onward past Londonderry, Salt Creek,
     Ratcliffburg, Allensville, Zaleski Freewill Baptist Church, Lump
     Coal for Sale,
and you can see the streaks of coal in the shaley yellow soil. Prattsville.
Dingers Motel in Prattsville. Athens County. Greysville. Coolville.
Hey man I come from Coolville. And cross the brown Ohio
into WEST VIRGINIA.

And another day
Now here are Allegheny names as we went in the early morning
with the red sun rising over the misty heads and chill fog-filled
hollers of the hills:

     Buky Run
     Ellenboro
     Pennboro
     Burnells Run
     Spring Run

The sun is robed in a glory of mist enrayed by tree-branch shadows
shooting like arrows down.

Snow Bird Road
Smithburg
Englands Run
Morgans Run
Buckeye Run
Dark Hollow
Fort New Salem
Dog Run
Cherry Camp
Raccoon Run
Salem Fork
Flinderation.

After breakfast at Lums', the Entire Lums Family Thanks You,
comes the Child Evangelism Camp, and Harmony Grove,
and Pruntytown, 1798, Founded by John Prunty.
And we come over Laurel Mountain and from the top see all the misty
    ridges
and coming down we're into the Eastern Seabord smog, that yellow bile
that you see from airplanes, the yellow breath of our god.
Nite Crawlers 75 cents a dozen,
beside the Cheat River, a misty mirror for the hills.
Into Maryland at Backbone Mountain
and then right back into West Virginia, a state all backbone, loyal to
    the union.

Mineral County.
Mount Storm.
The Knobley Farm, 1766, on knobbly hills
Ridgeville village on the hogback ridge
Hampshire County, 1754, we keep going back
The Stone House
Little Cacapon River
Paw Paw, on Short Mountain. Where ye bin, honey?
    I bin to Paw Paw, maw.

WELCOME TO VIRGINIA!   *Jesus is coming ready or not*

And it's left one mile to Mecca, and right one mile to Gore.
We'd better go straight on.
So we went on to Georgia.

Far West Going West
WELCOME TO UTAH early in the morning.
The sunflowers are confused, haven't got turned sunwards yet, face every
    which way.
Juniper. A good, strong, catspray smell of juniper in the high dry air.
Sagebrush, chamiso, the little yellow-flowered clover that's been along
    our way from Oregon to Georgia and back. And crows.
Suddenly we descend from mountains into desert
where there are monsters.
A potbellied Mexican waterjug two hundred feet high
turns into a sphinx as you pass it.
A throne of red rock with no seat, a hundred feet high.
Red lumps and knobs and kneecaps and one-eyed skulls the size of a
    house.

The sunflowers now are all staring East like Parsees,
except a couple in the shadow of the roadcut, which haven't got the
news or received orders yet.
      There aren't a whole lot of names, in Utah,
      but here's one: Hole in the Rock:
            big white letters on a big red bluff with a hole in it, yessir,
            and also Paintings of Christ and Taxidermy.

A lone and conceivably insurgent but probably uninformed sunflower
stands in the shadow of a cliff, facing southwest, at 7:41 A.M.
Well the last time *I* saw the sun it was over *there* and how do I know
where the damn thing's got to?
    Arches National Monument, near Moab. Red stone arches. Red stone
    lingams, copulating alligators, camels, triceratops, keyholes,
    elephants, pillows, towers, leaves, fins of the Ouroboros, lizard's
    heads. A woman of red stone and a man of red stone, very tall,
    stand facing the falcon-faced god of the red stone. Many tall,
    strange stone people standing on the red sand under the red cliffs;
    and the sand dunes have turned to stone, and the Jurassic sea that
    lapped on these red beaches dried and dried and dried away and
    shrank to the Mormons' bitter lake. The sky is as blue as fire.

Northward, stone dunes in white terraces and stairways pile up to the
violet-red turrets and buttresses of a most terrible city inhabited
by the Wind. A purple fortress stands before the gates, and in front
of it, four tall, shapeless kings of stone stand guard.

Next morning
Heading out of green and gentle Delta to the Nevada line, early, to get
across the desert in the cool.
        Jackrabbits flit
        on the moonlit salt pans
        to the left of the mountains of dawn.
        Jackrabbits dance
        in the moonlit sagebrush
        to the left of the mountains of dawn.

        Four pronghorn drift
        from the road into the sage
        in the twilight of morning
        to the left of the mountains of dawn.

Nevada
There are no names here.
        The rosepink shadowless mountains of dawn now are daylit,
        deep-shadowed, and the moon has lost her dominion.
        In this long first sunlight the desert is grayish-gold.
By the road as straight as an imaginary canal on Mars are flowers:
        Michaelmas daisies, Matiliha poppies white as the moon up there,
        milkweed, blue chicory. The green lush South was flowerless.
There are
five fenceposts
        in the middle of a vast sagebrush flat of which the middle
        is everywhere and the circumference nowhere.
Five crows
one crow per post
soak up the morning sun.
                Only Crow's been with us all the way,
        north, middle, south, and west. Even the redwing blackbird
        gave out in Nevada, but Crow's here, Crow of the Six Directions.
Jackrabbits go lolloping off like wallabies
        with magnificent blacktipped ears.

Gabbs Luning. There's a name for you!
At Gabbs Luning there's a Schneelite Mine.
I don't believe anything in Nevada. This is pure Coyote country.
A vast lake that holds no water
is full to the brim of glittering light.
Far out, toward the center of the lake,
lie the bones of a wrecked ship
that struck on the reef of the mirage
and sank through heatwaves down and down
to lie now bleaching fathoms deep in blinding light,
all souls aboard her drowned in air.
Probably a potash mine. Who knows? We drive on West.

NORMAN MAILER

◆ ——————————————————— ◆

Lipton's

The Journal from which these excerpts are taken went on for close to one hundred thousand words. I would usually write in it on Mondays and Tuesdays after a heavy pot weekend—marijuana was referred to by the not very opaque alias of Lipton's. Begun on December 1, 1954, the Journal has entries until March 4, 1955. Anyone more curious about the origins might take a look at the Fourth Advertisement in my book *Advertisements for Myself* (Putnam, New York, 1959).

December 1, 1954
Perhaps the writer is less sensitive than his audience. That is, he reacts with less intensity to experience than people who are not creative. Thus the writer, seeing coldly, but able to see, touches upon matters which move him very little, and move his audience much. It is perfectly conceivable that the stupid man feels worlds of experience he can never communicate; he is actually far more sensitive than the intelligent, "sensitive" man.

December 1, 1954
The reason "insensitive" people very often react negatively to sex or shocking matters in books is because it is actually more real to them. They are more sensitive to it. So, Stanley Rinehart. He must excise the presence of *The Deer Park* because he reacts to it more than I do.*

December 8, 1954
Medicine may be witchcraft as fully as psychoanalysis. There is still no understanding of why the germ flourishes in this human and not in that at any moment. To say that the resistance is low is merely a fancy, societal, and untruthful way of describing X. But the idea of "germs" accomplishes much—including other things, it gives intellectual backing to the sexual inhibitions which society must generate to protect itself.

Stanley Rinehart was the publisher who broke the contract on The Deer Park *when it was in galleys.*

December 17, 1954

What worries me today and other days is that I am playing an enormous deception on myself, and I embark on these thoughts only to make myself more interesting, more complex to other people, more complex to myself. My vanity is so enormous. Perhaps I do all this to demonstrate to my audience that I too can create mystic spiritual characters. But on the other hand, these remarks can be merely my fear of what lies ahead. I love the world so much, I am so fascinated by it, that I dread the possibility that some day I may travel so far that I wish to relinquish it. What is important is that I think for the first time in years I'm growing quickly again.

December 17, 1954

Jazz is easy to understand once one has the key, something which is constantly triumphing and failing. Particularly in modern jazz, one notices how Brubeck and Desmond, off entirely on their own with nothing but their nervous system to sustain them, wander through jungles of invention with society continually ambushing them. So the excitement comes not from victory which is the pleasure of swing (more later) but from the effort merely to keep musically alive. So, Brubeck, for example, will to his horror discover that he has wandered into a musical cliché (society) and it is thrilling to see how he attempts to come out of it, how he takes the cliché, plays with it, investigates it, pulls it apart, attempts to put it together into something new (for in every cliché there is an ocean of truth once we truly look at it) and sometimes succeeds, and sometimes fails, and can only go on, having left his record of defeat at that particular moment. That is why modern jazz despite its apparent lyricalness is truly cold, cold like important conversations or Henry James. It is cold and it is nervous and it is under tension, just as in a lunch between an editor and an author, each makes mistakes and successes, and when it is done one hardly knows what has happened and whether it has been for one's good or for one's bad, but an "experience," (a communication between the soul and the world) has taken place. It is also why I find classical music less exciting for that merely evokes the echo of a past "experience"—it is a part of society, one of the noblest parts, perhaps, but still not of the soul. Only the echo of the composer's soul remains. And besides it consists too entirely of triumphs rather than of life.

January 25, 1955

It is no accident so many socialists came from the middle class in this country. They hate our society, and the Soviet even more, if, like me, they are anti-Stalinist leftists, but what leaves them so unappetizing and so unsatisfying even to themselves, as I was always so dissatisfied with the yawning holes in my intellectual structures, is that they wish to replace society by another society. Their thoughts, programs, predictions, and analyses invariably have a square, blunt, brick-building quality. Even Malaquais, who is the best Socialist thinker I have ever come across, thinks in finite blocks. His thought, of course, has the nobility of a cathedral, but he's filled every square inch of the cathedral with a tile, and so his new thought can merely replace one tile by another, but he will never build a cathedral which dissolves into light. For all the beauty of his conceptions, a dark oppressive gloom breathes out of the doors and no one wants to enter poor Malaquais' cathedral. He is left the gloomy caretaker of it. One reason he cannot chase me away entirely is that I'm the village boy who wandered in one evening and stayed to admire the cathedral for many years, asking the caretaker every day, "Don Malaquais, tell me about the saints, and why is this stone this color?" I was a naughty boy, and I was forever quitting his lessons to throw stones at the bats, but what he cannot bear, dear Malaquais, is the silence now that I am gone. Timidly, terrified, like a shy old miser, he is making the endless preparations necessary to go out and buy a new hat. He has no real hope he'll be detained in the village and find a place to build a new cathedral, he knows he'll go back to the old one and watch the bats multiply, but it is so gloomy in there. Even Fra Jean has to get a bit of air.

January 25, 1955
Prose on wings, tra-la, tra-la. What I started to say in the previous note is that radical socialists present tools of analysis that bourgeois society unaided could never have come up with, but because socialists think sociostatically, so capitalists can turn their thoughts to their own advantage. Norman Thomas is always complaining that the Republican and Democratic parties have stolen his program, and indeed they have. Marxism for all its grandeur and its revolutionary ethic—its ultimate anarchism which nearly all socialists have forgotten—approached the problem of society as a materialistic conception. But capitalists are also materialists. So they could adopt Marxism to their needs, improve their sociostatic techniques, shore up the crazy house and keep the warped mirrors from cracking . . . yet.

January 25, 1955
So, modestly, I see my mission. It is to put Freud into Marx and Marx into Freud. Put Tolstoy into Dostoyevsky and Dostoyevsky into Tolstoy.

Open anarchism with its soul-sense to the understanding of complexity, and infuse complex gloom with the radiance of anarchism. As Jenny Silverman said of me once, "The little *pisherke* with the big ideas." Pint-sized Hitler. Yes.

January 26, 1955
The pompous man, the extraordinarily pompous man, is trying to teach people. He wears a mask which is the caricature of himself. (Indeed, *one's personality is always the caricature of oneself*.) So the pompous man is at bottom a loather of society, a potential destroyer. He is so bound to society that he cannot express himself in another way, but a part of him is always saying, "Look at me, look how ridiculous I am. If you are taken in by what I once believed, then you will look like me, and will be able to teach only by driving people away."

January 27, 1955
For some time I have wanted to write a note about the Negro prejudice of southerners. I wonder if their rage at Negro advancements is due to their unconscious belief in the myth—which may well be right—that the black has a happy sex life, happier than the white, and so is recompensed for his low state in society by his high state in the fuck. The scales are balanced. Therefore, to the white southerner, an improvement in Negro rights is to tip the scale in the Negro's favor. People of lower status are considered to have equal status when the private benefits are added in.

January 27, 1955
Word mirrors! (Better word for echo than reversals.) Be and ebb.

January 27, 1955
. . . on Sunday morning I could remember nothing of the tremendous insights I felt I had had on Saturday night. Again I felt depressed, and the *Dissent* meeting was hanging over me. That came on Sunday afternoon, and was deeply depressing. I felt I didn't belong there. All these bitter rationalists, with their rationalist talents—they would turn on me if they knew what an anarchist I am. And indeed Lewis Coser spoke approvingly of how Clara Thompson and the Sullivanites were riding Reich out of business under the auspices of the Pure Food and Drug Act. (What a perfect title for a law for once.)

Anyway, the meeting was unbearably dull. I kept despairing of socialism. These people are well-meaning, they are even courageous, but they are pale, they are scholars, bitter scholars, they are deeply middle-class, they are the essence of social democracy even when they are to the left of it. Their socialism is not a desire for justice, a passion for equality, but the intellectual urge to order society. I kept feeling I should speak up, and kept deciding not to. It would have been disruptive, and I would have been defeated. After all, if I had won—which is inconceivable—I should have had to take over the magazine, which I certainly don't want to, and so I felt merely a spoiler, a wrecker, a renegade. I knew that I could stay with them only by accommodating my personality, giving articles to *Dissent* which would be stimulating for them because I would only go a very small distance.

Yet with Howe and Coser I get the feeling that they are deeply dissatisfied, that they wish to move on, and I expect more tolerance from them than from the others. Anyway, before the meeting was over, I left—my only suggestion which was more than a joke being that the *Dissent* covers remain the orange-red of the last issue—which was carried. But all afternoon, first in the delicatessen—what else would Jewish socialists do before a meeting?—then in Plastrik's home, I felt a stranger and alien. I fled with Mike Harrington who is a Catholic Anarchist masquerading as a socialist, tried out a few of my milder ideas on him in the taxi, for which I got half-response, half-worry, and then home to Adele.

January 27, 1955
24 pages today—To my memory, the greatest number I've done in a day.

February 1, 1955
Depression is coming on, distrust of this journal, distrust of myself and my ideas. Again I worry—Is this all a monster rationalization? Am I full of shit? Also, I'm hungry again. I interrupt to go down for supper.

February 1, 1955
Jesus, I'd rather be a genius than a saint (but in my mind the sentence kept coming out reversed—I'd rather be a saint than a genius). The psychopath, I'm afraid reluctantly, I must relinquish—at least temporarily.

February 2, 1955
I've spent the last few hours rereading the Journal and find it less exciting than I thought, and quite unpublishable in its present form (which had been at the back of my mind). But there is a lot in it. I have

to develop it. One thing I notice is that the wild mystical plunge of the early pages simmers down after a while. I think the early pages merely express the great relief of being able to use words like God, soul, saint, genius, and so forth—at last I was going to allow myself to revel in the cliché. But I write this note totally off everything. Off Lipton's—it's three days now, off Seconal—two days. Feelings of sexual vigor are returning, and with them, more quiet confidence. One thing which bucked me up is that in going over *The Deer Park* I found I could add sentences to it which had the nice literary style of the book. So, apparently, I'm not stylistically drained. What I felt as I was writing Deer Park lines this morning was the old feeling of a fine tension.

I can probably generalize on the effects of Lipton's and Seconal. Lipton's releases vast amounts of exciting material and trivial material with very little selection. It enables me to work at a tremendous rate, but everything is equally exciting to me. Which is mystically, philosophically valid, but is almost impossible for a novelist to deal with—at least in my present stage. That is, I could not write novels on it, although it might be good to turn to it when I got writing blocks. The Seconal is what is bad for it is beginning to give me bad letdowns and deep depressions. Except I know how to handle those too, now. If I can't sleep. I must just sit up and read instead of trying to fight myself into sleep. Enough for today. I think I'll lay off the Journal for a few days.

February 7, 1955
After lunch, and how I hated giving up time for lunch. So many ideas I had while I bolted my food, and so many of them must be lost.

February 8, 1955
Hemingway's peculiar weakness is that he's a Taker, his heroes are all Takers. His idea of courage is that you can take it. It never seems to have occurred to him once that courage might also consist of giving.

February 21, 1955
Saw *Mutiny on the Bounty* and some Keystone Chaplin films last night. What a genius Chaplin is. How he expresses all the body frustrations of sexual repression. He wipes his nose on a rag, wipes the rag on a dish, hands the dish to a whore in a dirty restaurant. He hitches his ass, he *rolls* his eyes, he strikes and is struck, and always, sex, sex, sex. We laugh in roars and waves. (Roar, horror, aura.) And the captions are incredible. In one skit, standing before his wife who dominates him completely, he

grins sheepishly, struts and says, "Every day I get better and better, but every night I get worse."

February 21, 1955
And Laughton. What an incredible sense of the homosexual sadist, the sex-repressing officer. *Mutiny on the Bounty* is the source of *The Caine Mutiny*, but with what a dramatic difference. For Fletcher Christian is the man who goes native, while Bligh, totally sadistic before sexual expression (the most minor infraction of discipline) is also the great mother figure once he gets in the boat with the men who have elected to come with him. Now he knows sex will not be in the air, and so he can be a great seaman.

WILLIAM MATTHEWS

◆ ———————————————————————— ◆

Travel

In Siena I tugged a drawer in my hotel room and it slid toward me with that smooth rumble that means good cabinet-making. Empty. There's a Truffaut film (*La Peau Douce*?) in which a traveler headed for an assignation strides into his hotel room and one by one switches on every light, as if he were filling the blank dark of the hotel room with the glare of his own fantasy life. The erotics of travel, with their powerful undertow of melancholy, are most intense in a good hotel room. Lovely, one thinks, but something's missing. Could it be me? I began to fill the drawers. I would be there four nights.

Six in the evening. Haze hung in the burnishing light like a scrim. From one window I could see the glittering pool and from the other birds swirling and darting above the juts and slopes of the town's tiled roofs, a whole landscape in themselves. Time to shower, time to sit in the garden and wait for dinner, as if for an assignation.

In the morning I'll set out to find a place where I can sit outdoors, sip a cappuccino, and read the *Herald Tribune*. The farther you are from home, the shorter the articles in the newspapers available in your native language. A line score stands for a whole baseball game, and in six lines from Reuters hundreds die in a plane crash. My father loves travel and loves to read of transportation disasters. He's lived for years in England, unrepentantly American. Once, he told me, he sat outdoors on a warm spring day in London with a milk shake, a rare treat, and read contentedly about a plane crash at Tenerife. I was, he said, about as happy as one can be. To travel is to engage the fantasy that one can be at home anywhere, though Rimbaud wrote home from Ethiopa, "What am I doing here?" But, turning the pages of the *Herald Tribune*, I'll know what my father meant. One is like a tic on the flank of a huge and, for now, hospitable animal. Somewhere else, hundreds of tics may perish, but here? Mmmm. Warm fur. Good blood.

"The word travel is the same as the French *travail*," writes Bruce Chatwin. "It means hard work, penance and finally a journey."

One morning we were aloft by seven and flew in a hot-air balloon over San Gimignano, counting the famous towers. Thirteen. Everywhere in Tuscany you can see the hills rising from the rolling land to the walled towns, like clenched fists. In the thirteenth century San Gimignano fought off barbarian invaders, as non-Tuscan hostile forces were called, and also fought their neighbors: Poggibonsi, Volterra, Colle Val d'Elsa. In 1300 Dante went to San Gimignano to make a speech urging the unity of all the Guelph cities in Tuscany. They went on fighting each other. By 1301 Dante was exiled from Florence for life.

But you have to struggle to think of such things in a balloon. Fully inflated, ours were 100 feet high and seventy feet wide. You could be dangling from a flying building. You're traveling with the wind, so you can't hear it, and pass through a preternatural calm above one of the most beautiful landscapes on earth. One of the three burners emits a frequency humans can't hear, but which drives dogs crazy. Everything is calm and beautiful and seen from a distance, and below the dogs snarl and twist and yelp.

Back on the ground, in San Gimignano, you can stare up at the towers. They were often built in pairs, joined at the tops by wooden bridges. These are long gone. For the great families in San Gimignano fought each other. The towers were not, like the giraffe's head in the savannah, the high outpost of watchfulness over the countryside, but brooding emblems of vanity and hatred. You climbed as high as you could go in one of your towers or the other, and when someone tried to come up, you killed him.

Of course now the town is as famous for its towers as it is for Vernaccia, its crisp white wine, and for Ghirlandaio's fresco of the Annunciation in the cathedral. It can all become part of a mesmerizing wash of sensations, which you float somewhat through but mostly over.

I value my hours in the balloon. But finally to travel not through a benign daze but by your own curiosity and with some love for the emotional life of the place you're passing through, you have to brood long on those dogs.

We're straggling along the *autostrada* in the slow lane. The BMWs and Volvos swirl by at 160 km/h. Now and then a Maserati growls past even faster, and in our rented Fiat Panda we feel more and more like passengers on a roller skate with delusions of grandeur.

"Who lives in Gubbio?" A. asks.

"Gubbians," I tell her.

Here's a tiny mystery for which I'm sure there's an easy solution, but I can't find it. Once I quoted a nostrum to a friend, who liked it. "Where's it from?" he asked.

"It's from the Confucian Analects," I said authoritatively, because I thought it was.

Later he was interested to find it exactly, to use it for an epigram in a book. He couldn't find it in the Analects and neither could I.

The mystery isn't where did I find it, nor whether I made it up. If I could say what the mystery is it wouldn't be a mystery. I think mystery may be too grand a word for it. Go on too long or too grandly about anything and it becomes silly. No doubt that's why I'm addicted to writing poems, with their illusory endings. But I think their silences are like the self-deceptions by which we live.

Here's the nostrum. "The way out is through the door. How is it nobody remembers this method?"

The day before San Gimignano we landed in a field to the east of Siena, and as we came down the balloon's shadow startled a small herd of goats. Also we flushed from cover behind a windbreak of poplars two middle-aged lovers who had somehow made it to the outskirts of town, undressed in a tiny Fiat little bigger than a bathtub, seen a balloon drift silently down from above them, dressed frantically and spurted back toward Siena dragging a roostertail of dust along the unpaved road—all before 8:30 A.M. Then busloads of Italian army parachutists came roaring through the dust the other way to use the field for calisthenics and maneuvers. The officers wandered over to see what we were up to and wound up helping us deflate the balloon, roll up the envelope, and stuff it back into the chase van. We offered them *spumante* but they were on duty. They gave us chocolate in dun-colored government wrappers— dark, intense, wonderful bittersweet chocolate. The field was formerly an airstrip, the biggest open space for miles around. Balloonists love open spaces and hate power lines. "You hit a power line," A. loved to say, "you're toast."

Every family is a conspiracy of heartbreak, and thus a family traveling together becomes a small band of smugglers. You wait and wait. One of you smokes and another of you hates it. The people who go by probably belong here and have ordinary lives. Then the train stutters and rolls off. Customs agents pass through the train like a combine through a field. Instead of a heart you have a rabbit in your chest. But it's no use. They come and go. You'll never be discovered. It will always be like this.

Every morning the balloon pilot released a trial balloon, the kind you'd buy for a child at a dime store. The verdict was swift: where it went our balloon would go.

The day after San Gimignano we took off west of Siena and drifted over the city's heart, the Campo, the piazza shaped like a clamshell where the three hills on which the city has been built meet. In the Campo dirt was being laid for the Palio.

Siena is divided into seventeen *contrade* (an exact translation would be a word that occupies a space equidistant from "parish" and "precint"). Each has a name, colors, a budget for running the Palio, and a master strategist.

The Palio is a bareback horserace, two and a half laps around the periphery of the Campo. The race is run July 2nd and August 16th. Ten *contrade* compete, so each race includes the seven excluded from the last race and three chosen by lot.

There are no rules of good conduct for the race. Horses are assigned by lot, but a *contrada* must buy the services of a jockey. There's room and board for the horse, naturally, and what's left in the budget goes for bribes.

It's best to win, but worst that your enemies win. It's widely assumed that most bribes are tendered in hopes of insuring another *contrada*'s defeat, but since bribes are by nature sub-rosa, who knows?

Before the race each *contrada* blesses its horse, led in colors to the altar.

A balloon is as close as a human gets to know how a cloud feels. We tufted languidly over the city. Below us—please don't photograph the prison yard—deals were struck over coffee.

A *contrada* is usually named for conventionally impressive animals (eagle, panther) but there's a caterpillar, too, and it hasn't won in thirty-seven years. The silks and banners of each *contrada* are sumptuous. The long fevered wars between the city-states are rehearsed here, and the vitriolic isolations of the towertops, and by such flurry some pilot light is tended that can ignite in any of us the sanctimonies of home and thus the need to travel.

To dawdle is at the center of travel. To eat outdoors on a warm night in Rome, let's say, and linger over the last of the wine, is not only to soak in one's own pleasure as in a tub, but to live out the open secret of pleasure: it spites time. Good meals last long. The purpose of sexual intercourse is to get it over with as slowly as possible. The function of rhythm in poetry is to manipulate time, to prefer rather than the steady onslaught of actuarial time, 4,200 heartbeats per hour, the lulled trance in which good poems insist that they be read.

Ours is an age which measures time most accurately by the rate of decay of radioactive matter. This method is not only an improvement over the methods of earlier ages, but also a convulsive embrace of a powerful metaphor. There are arts that happen in "real time," like music and film, and part of their authority for heartbreak is that they do. Poetry refers by its every formal wile to our urge to go slower, and that longing is part of poetry's authority for heartbreak. Travel is like that. You walk for a while. You sit there and sip. You stand there and look.

Is travel, whatever else it is, a kind of narrative, a picaresque, I suppose? How did W.M., a small-town boy with a smattering of Latin, get to Orvieto on this particular sweat-drenched afternoon?

Probably travel is not the path of explanation and causality, but, whatever else it is, the path by which we act out an impossible longing for explanation and causality. The dog of emotional life, narrative comes ever at the heels of experience.

The early raptures of reading are the first travel.

But what if I should go back to Troy, Ohio, and retrace the path I rode and rerode on my bike, to and from the public library? Back at the old house the sentinel hollyhocks, with their dusty carillons, no longer grow against the toolshed.

How much of the work of leaving Troy was done by reading. Leaning against the base of that tree, and in that high window, the work of the rupture was slowly and stubbornly performed in the silent thrall of reading.

So that when I finally left I took with me as much of what I had learned to love from reading, even my sorrow. No wonder this small county seat looks freshly cleaned, as if for company. I look down McKaig Ave. past the porched white houses toward the pebbled playground infield that surely is still but three minutes' fevered ride away.

To love this place again as I did then I'd need to re-invent it, and in order to leave again re-invent the travail, the working through, the penance.

Florence is hot and saturated with tourists. The youngest of them, college age, carry plastic bottles of Evian water and trade travel tips: "The lines are shortest at the Uffizi at lunchtime." Older tourists are distractedly sweeping the Via Tornabuoni, it seems, for one last leather good. I can feel a distasteful sourness building in me that I recognize, not happily, as a traveler's greed and fatigue akin to the teacher's pleasure in walking across campus on vacation, when the students are all gone.

The Boboli Gardens are cool and people sparse there. I wander around the gardens for two hours and then head back to my air-conditioned hotel room. It's a day when the active, animal alertness of travel just wants a day off. OK. I switch on the TV to see if there's any coverage of Wimbledon and see that the Palio is being telecast.

They've been running the race since 1656. The ten horses are tensed between the two restraining ropes. The front rope goes slack and in ninety seconds it's over. Three jockeys are thrown; two horses go down. The winning *contrada* is *La Selva* (the forest), named for something that can't move. It must have come straight from the Latin *silva*, I think idly. The TV is showing reruns of the race but I'm no longer watching. I sit in a cool room sipping a glass of Prosecco from the frigobar, shut off from and yet in thrall to the vast world, *silva rerum*, the forest of things.

From a letter from S.M.: "Travel is, for me, the most beautiful intoxicant. The words of travel, *valise*, for example: what couldn't you pack into that? Where couldn't you take it?"

Where couldn't you take it? We travel in order to find out.

THOMAS MERTON

◆ ——————————— ◆

Alaskan Journal

August 22

A picture of Mount McKinley in front of me under the lamp—(came today as a feast day greeting for Sunday)—I cannot believe that I may see it. Or even find myself one day living near it. Is Alaska a real option? One would think not. And yet there's that Bishop. . . . Certainly it is not the place I myself would spontaneously choose (full of military!).

For myself—Bhutan! Or that tea plantation I heard about yesterday near Darjeeling!

August 27

Letter from the Archbishop of Anchorage. The Vicar General will meet me at the plane—Northwestern Flight 3 from Chicago is the best—several pieces of property in mind. I can live in a trailer at the (contemplative) Precious Blood Nuns. . . .

September 17

"Hermit cells" in P. C. monastery. The Red Barn nearby. The man in the gray shirt crouching in the wood (Cleveland—a bar owner, bartender, whore & another, kidnapped, shot in the park, found by joggers). The old P. C. convent. Sister with an ulcered leg feared that if the convent were left unguarded teenagers would break in the graveyard & dig up the dead.

A while ago we were over miles of Canadian lakes, blue, blue-green, & brown, with woods between, an occasional road. Still three hours from Anchorage. Two—probably—from Alaska. Clouds again, packed thick, quilted, beneath us.

I borrowed the letters of Miller & Durrell from Ron S. & don't feel like reading them. The first one, with Durrell putting down *Ulysses* (saying *Tropic of Cancer* was better) turned me off.

(More lakes down below, between clouds. Olive green, wild stretches of watery land.)

Flight yoga. Training in cosmic colors.

Dull, concise bronze of ginger ale.

Last night, choosing the Scotch Fr. Xavier offered was as silly as a choice of smoke, & I had smoke in my head when I awoke.

Ginger ale has in it perfume of stewardess.

First sight of mountains of Alaska, strongly ribbed, through cloud. Superb blue of the gulf, indescribable ice patterns. Bird wings, vast, mottled, long black streamers, curves, scimitars, lyre bird tails.

September 18

FIRST ECSTASY OF RAMA KRISHNA

One day in June or July when he was six years old he was walking along a narrow path between rice fields, eating puffed rice from a basket. He looked up at the sky & saw a beautiful storm cloud, & a flight of snow-white cranes passing in front of it, above him. He lost consciousness & fell into a faint at the beauty of it. A peasant found him with rice scattered all about & carried him home.

September 19

On the morning of the 10th I went down to the monastery for the last time to get some money, pick up mail, say goodbye to Fr. Flavian, Bros. Maurice, Patrick. No one else much knew anything about my departure. Ron Seitz came about ten. A gray, cool fall morning. We drove into Louisville. I got traveler's checks, medicine in St. Matthews. An AWOL bag for camera, second pair of shoes, etc. Afternoon—a shower & short rest at O'Callaghan's, in the evening a supper send-off party that probably could have been better done without. But no matter. Dan Walsh was there & I hadn't seen him for a long time. I slept at St. Bonaventure's Friary & got out early in the morning. Flew to Chicago then Albuquerque.

I was met at the airport in Albuquerque by Tom Carlyle, a very likeable hippie type who is staying at Christ of the Desert & working for them. A really good, sincere, spiritual person. One of the best. We drove up in his Volkswagen—dragging a plaster mixer with which he plans to make adobe brick for the monks.

Two days' retreat in the canyon. Swam in the cold Chama.

Then to the Jicarilla Apache encampment feast on the reservation near Dulce. A feast of Tabernacles. Booths of boughs, tents & campfires everywhere. Then the race the next day. Back to Santa Fe. Slept at the Devereux's in Reyena Madre. Low adobe house. Supper at the Pink Adobe—good curry but too much of it.

Flew from Albuquerque to Chicago (last sight of distant Pedernal quite clear!). Rain in Chicago. Went to the new Poor Clare convent & gave them a talk; I liked the architecture. Ed Noonan, the architect, came for mass next day—I concelebrated with Fr. Xavier Carroll, who took me to the plane—with one of the sisters who was leaving.

The Northwest plane for Anchorage, Tokyo, & Seoul was late getting started. Crowded with families, American & Japanese, returning to Asia. I felt for the first time that Asia was getting close!

My flight to Alaska was mostly over clouds. Quiet. A soldier on the outside seat: the middle seat of the three empty, we didn't talk much except for a little bit just before landing. (He said Anchorage wasn't any colder in winter than Syracuse, NY, but that there was a lot of snow.)

The clouds opened over Mt. St. Elias & after that I was overwhelmed by the vastness, the patterns of glaciers, the burnished copper sheen of the sun on the bright blue sea. The shoreline. The bare purple hills. The high mountains full of snow, the dark islands stark in the sun—burnish on the water.

We swung slowly down into Anchorage & got out into cold, clear autumn air. Everywhere the leaves have turned. Gold of the aspens & birches everywhere.

Without actually going into Anchorage, we (Fr. Lunney met me) drove out on Route 1 to the convent, at Eagle River.

It is a nice house among the birches, at the foot of low mountains, looking out through the trees toward Cook Inlet & Mount McKinley— the nuns may move in a few months as the place is not quite suitable.

I have a sense of great warmth & generosity in the clergy here. The archbishop is away at Juneau, but will be back next week—all are very eager to help & I feel they are eager to have me settle here. Meanwhile I'm busy on a workshop with the nuns. They are a good community, & like all, they have their troubles.

This afternoon—in the sun at the foot of a birch, in the bushes near the monastery, at a point where you can see Mt. McKinley & Mt. Foraker—great, silent, & beautiful presence in the afternoon sun.

September 22
Sunday. 6 A.M. on KHAR Anchorage; Alaskan Golden Nugget potatoes respectfully suggest that we worship God since we are a nation under God & want to build a stronger America. Nugget Potatoes are glad of this opportunity to "voice this thinking." A good thought from a respectful potato.

Yesterday—end of workshop—visit of P. Blood priests—not without a song & "Ole Man River." Evening—to the army base at Ft. Richardson—like city of shiny apartments—bourbon on the rocks—tarpon fishing on TV—wild ducks in slow-motion flight—memories of Brooklyn. And supper at the AF base at Elmendorf (like city of shiny apartments). Heated argument between conservative & progressive clergy & laity: which is better: to kneel for communion or to stand?

Cordova / September 23
Landed at the cool, lovely airfield shortly after dawn. Still freezing. I rode into town on the airport bus—a school bus—with a bunch of duck hunters, very voluble about their luck & about the good weather which is bad for them as the ducks & geese have not begun to move south.

I find St. Joseph's Church, no one around. I walk in the rectory & after a while Fr. Llorente arrives—a remarkable person, a Spanish Jesuit who got himself sent to the Yukon thirty years ago & has been in Alaska ever since—has become a sort of legend in the region. He was going to leave to work with Mexican migrants in California, but was needed for Cordova. . . . He stayed.

A small fishing town between steep mountains & blue water—a highway on one side, & Eyak Lake around at the back.

I have no hesitation in saying Eyak Lake seemed perfect in many ways—for a place to live. The quiet end of it is several miles back in the mountains, completely isolated, silent. Wild geese were feeding there. Great silver salmon were turning red & dying in shallows where they had spawned (some had been half-eaten by bears). Bears would be the only problem, but Fr. Llorente said they were not grizzlies. A few cabins nearer town were attractive. Also the bay was impressive.

Valdez (Valdeez) / September 24

Most impressive mountains I have seen in Alaska: Drum & Wrangell & the third great massive one whose name I forget, rising out of the vast birchy plain of Copper Valley. They are sacred & majestic mountains, ominous, enormous, noble, stirring. You want to attend to them. I could not keep my eyes off them. Beauty & terror of the Chugach. Dangerous valleys. Points. Saws. Snowy nails.

Anchorage / September 26

Today I fly to Juneau with Archbishop Ryan. Then to Ketchikan tomorrow & back to Anchorage Saturday.

Sound of chapel door closing as Bishop comes down to say his office before breakfast (Mass tonight—concelebration in Juneau).

The bishop's house is warm & quiet. It smells of bacon.

Haircut in Anchorage Westward Hotel. Manuel, an artist in hairstyles, found little to do on me, but spoke of what he had learned about wigs in Heidelberg. "Inexpensive!" He emphasized this. A nasty hint!

Behind Palmer: Pioneer Peak, badly named, tall & black & white in the snow—mist, rugged armatures, indestructible, great. It vanishes into snow cloud as we retreat up the valley into birch flats. McKinley hidden.

The log house of Mr. & Mrs. Peck by the windy lake. Clouds of blowing aspen & birch leaves fly across the lawn. Mr. Peck with an army field jacket & a good Dutch cigar—brought by the big silent boy from KLM who sits with a bottle of bourbon in the shadows of the kitchen.

Yakutat / September 27

Bay with small islands. Driving rain on the docks. A few fishing boats. Beat-up motorboats, very poor. An old battered green rowboat called *The Jolly Green Giant*.

It is a village of Indians, with an FAA station nearby. Battered houses. A small Indian girl opens the door of the general store. Looks back at us as we pass. Cannery buildings falling down. Old tracks are buried in mud & grass. A dilapidated building was once a "roundhouse" though it is a large rectangle. After that, all there is is a long straight gravel road pointing in the mist between tall hemlocks out into the nowhere where more of the same will be extended to a lumber operation. The woods are full of moose, & black bear, & brown bear, & even a special bear found only at Yakutat—the glacier bear (or blue bear).

Frank Ryman had in his lodge the skin of a wolf—as big as a small bear.

Yakutat has plenty of wolves & coyotes, besides bears.

And in the village are many murders.

Tlingit Indians.

Here there was once a Russian penal colony. It was wiped out by the Indians.

Yakutat—one of the only—perhaps *the* only place that is on Yukon time. All the other places have adopted one of the other timebelts, Anchorage or Pacific.

Juneau / September 27
This morning—we flew in bad weather to Yakutat, came down out of thick clouds on to a shore full of surf & hemlock & muskeg. Desolate airstrip.

Frank Ryman drove us into the village to show me the village. Broken down houses, mostly inhabited by Tlingit Indians, an old fish cannery, & a small dock with a few fishing boats on a lovely broad bay with islands. Everything seemed covered with hemlock. Driving rain, mountains invisible. Frank Ryman has a quarter acre of land he offered me—& it is enough to put a trailer on. But it is right at the edge of the village. If I lived there I would become very involved in the life of the village and would probably become a sort of pastor.

Juneau / September 28
Blue-green Juneau. The old cathedral. The deserted hospital. The deserted hotel. The deserted dock. The deserted school. We met Senator Gruening in the airport & shook his hand. Famous people are never as tall as you expect.

St. Michael / September 29
Talking of the changing of nuns' names (at Mother House) Sister Charity said: "Those who have mysteries have to change." Others were interested in the rigors of Trappist life, sleeping in underwear. A Kodiak

gray nun knew Abbott Obrecht. There's always someone, somewhere, who knows a Trappist.

"All the Sisters who have mysteries have to be changed?" And they are delighted at my monastic nickname "Uncle Louie." But the Bishop would prefer more reverence, more decorum. However, he says nothing. At Mass today I did not give the nuns the kiss of peace for fear of the Bishop. Several of the Precious Blood Sisters came with bangs—a slightly different hairdo.

There were three or four copies of *Ave Maria* on the table but I did not get to look at them to see if my statement on draft record burning was there. Nor have I had any repercussions. A letter from Phil Berrigan (Allentown Prison, Pa.) was forwarded from Gethsemani. He does not mind prison life. But demonstrations & draft card burnings are not understood: they help Wallace. Is it possible he may be President? Yes, possible.

September 30
Flew to Dillingham in a Piper Aztec (two engines), a fast plane that goes high. Bristol Bay area—like Siberia! Miles of tundra. Big winding rivers. At times, lakes are crowded together & shine like bits of broken glass. Or are untidy & complex like the pieces of a jigsaw puzzle.

Two volcanoes: *Iliamna*—graceful, mysterious, feminine, akin to the great Mexican volcanoes. A volcano to which one speaks with reverence, lovely in the distance, standing above the sea of clouds. Lovely near at hand with smaller attendant peaks. *Redoubt* (which surely has another name, a secret & true name)—handsome & noble in the distance, but ugly; sinister as you get near it. A brute of a dirty busted mountain that has exploded too often. A bear of a mountain. A dog mountain with steam curling up out of the snow crater. As the plane drew near there was turbulence & we felt the plane might at any moment be suddenly pulled out of its course and hurled against the mountain. As if it would not pull itself away. But finally it did. *Redoubt*. A volcano to which one says nothing. Pictures from the plane.

In Dillingham some time ago (a year or two) the sister of the Orthodox priest went berserk & tore through the Catholic mission with an axe, breaking down one door after another as the Catholic Father retired before her from room to room, calling the State Troopers on various telephones.

October 2
Big black mouths of the jet engines open in silver fog. We bounce high over the Chugach lifting out of Anchorage.

We come up into the sunlight, possibly over Cordova.

Perpetual mist grant unto them O Lord. The seatbelt sign is on "Please Fasten your Seatbelts Thank yo!" What is this "Thankyo!"? Is it west? Is it only Alaska?

NINE RULES FOR AIR TRAVEL

1—Get the last window seat in the back, next to the kitchen.
2—Get Bloody Mary when the girls start off with their wagon.
3—Read Hermann Hesse, *Journey to the East.*
4—No use looking out the window. Fog all the way up to 36,000 feet.
5—Get second Bloody Mary when girls come back down the aisle.
6—Expect small dinner, racket of which is right beside you (slamming of ice box doors, etc.).
7—Sympathy & admiration for hardworking stewardesses.
8—Cocktail almonds in pocket for Suzanne who is supposed to be at airport in San Francisco—assuming we make some kind of connection in Seattle!
9—"We had brought the magic wave with us. It cleansed everything." (Hesse)

The sky finally opened when we were over British Columbia & all its islands and on the way down into Seattle we flew over at least six big forest fires and a lot of small ones that were nearly out. But the big ones were by no means out and now south of Seattle the whole lower sky is red-brown with the smoke of big distant fires. Volcanoes stand up out of it. Mt. Hood, etc.

October 3
Then there was Portland (where we were not supposed to be) & the plane filled up & I finished Hermann Hesse & Paul Bowles & looked

out at the scarred red flanks of Lasseur Peak and as we landed in S.F. a carton of Pepsi cans broke open & the cans rolled around all over the floor in the back galley & even a little bit forward, under the feet of some sailors.

Stewardess 1—"When her eyelashes began to fall out I . . ." (inaudible).
Stewardess 2—"Real ones?"
Stewardess 1—"Yes!"

LEONARD MICHAELS

◆ ───────────────────────────── ◆

Journal Entries: 1976–1987

1976

Berkeley dinner party. Mrs. R. kept asking Z. how her son got into Harvard, as if it had nothing to do with his gifts, but were some kind of trick or fluke. Z. laughed, virtually apologizing, though she's very proud of her son who is a good kid and also a genius, which I tried to suggest, but Mrs. R. wouldn't hear it because her son didn't get into Harvard and she was too miserable or drunk merely to agree that Z.'s son would be welcome at any university. Mr. R. left the table, went to the piano and started banging Haydn on the keys so nobody could hear his wife raving about Harvard, but she raised her voice and talked about her glorious days in graduate school when she took seminars with Heidegger and then she asked Z., "When exactly did you stop loving *your* kids?" Instead of saying never, and never would, whether or not they got into Harvard, Z. sat there laughing in the sophisticated style of Mrs. R. and feeling compromised and phony and intimidated. Mr. R.'s Haydn got louder, more torn by anguish and humiliation.

N.Y. Mother's apartment. Moritz visits, tells a story. One freezing morning everybody had to go outside and watch a man be hanged. He'd tried to escape the previous night. Beside Moritz stood a boy, the man's brother. "His nose became red. It was so red," said Moritz. "That's what I remember." Moritz's eyes enlarge and his voice becomes urgent, as if it were happening again. His excitement isn't that of a storyteller. He can recite long passages from *Manfred* in Polish, but he isn't literary. The experience is still too real to him. His memories are horrible and very dangerous. He fears another heart attack, but he tells about the camps. It should be remembered as he tells it. Freezing morning. The boy's red nose.

The Trip, 1976

●I stopped at a roadside grocery near the Oregon border. A huge fellow with the face of a powerful dullard stood behind the counter. He turned for items on the shelf and I saw that his pants had slipped below his hips where he was chopped sheer from lower back to legs. No ass to hold up his pants. His bulk pushed forward and heaved up into his chest. He had a hanging mouth and little eyes with a birdlike shine. I bought salami and oranges from him.

•Iowa City. Breakfast with David near campus. A strange woman joined us at the table. She smoked my cigarettes and took my dimes for her coffee. In her purse she had a fold of bills compressed by a hair clip. "My tuition fee," she said. David smiled and carried on as if she weren't there. He said one of his colleagues felt happy when he turned fifty. He no longer desired the pretty co-eds. He would concentrate on biochemistry, get a lot of work done, not waste time fucking his brains out. David laughed. He sympathized, but didn't believe in this lust for biochemistry. The woman, pretending to study for a German class, looked up from her grammar and said, "I will learn every word."

•Drove from Des Moines to Kansas City where the amazing beauty lives. She wore baggy pants, a man's sweater, no makeup. She had violent opinions about everything as if to show, despite her exceedingly beautiful face and body, she damn well had a mind. Then I drove west through Missouri and felt sick with regret at having met her, ready to forgive every fault, half in love with a woman I'll never see again.

•At a place called Truck Stop, I ate lunch. Truckers lean toward each other, eating pills, coffee, and starch. They looked fat, vibrant, seething with bad health.

•Checked into a motel in Manhattan, Kansas, and got the last room. Though it was midnight, people were still arriving. The highway was loud throughout the night. American refugees seek the road, the road.

•Infinitely clear sky and prairie of Kansas. I felt vulnerable, easily seen, as in the eye of God.

•A farmer came into the diner. He wore a baseball cap with a long bill. He was very tanned and dusty, and moved ponderously with the pain of this long day. His hands were much bigger than the coffee cup in front of him. He stared at it. In his eyes no ideas, just questions.

"What's this?" A coffee cup. "What do you do with it?" Pick it up. Between the first and second question, no words. No words even in the questions.

•Eyes are questions.

•In the town I saw wide streets, old brick, kids in high-sprung cars with wide wheels. I saw tall girls and a theological bookstore that sold phonograph records and radios. Starlings had left the pavements white with shit.

1979
On the train from Poznan to Warsaw, a young couple sat opposite me. The woman was long and pale. Her husband not as tall as she. His double-breasted suit and dark shiny tie were very ugly. He'd tried to dress impressively, perhaps for an official occasion. She was with him for the ride, the visit to Warsaw. She wore a handknit gray sweater, setting off her lovely pale complexion. She could have improved her husband's taste, but was maybe indifferent to it. He had thin, colorless hair and red-rimmed obedient eyes. They flicked nervously in her direction, hoping for a command. He suggested a small town bureaucrat whose every action is correct and never spontaneous, but he was in love with his wife and lived in agonizing confusion. He looked to her for sympathy. She offered none. She had what she wanted in life. It included this man, or such a man. She made him feel ashamed of himself, his needs.

Feelings come for no reason. I'm terrorized by them. I see in terms of them until they go away. Also for no reason.

Berkeley. Denis is building his patio, laying bricks meticulously. The sun beats on him. Heat rises off the bricks into his face. I'm in here writing. He'll have built a patio. I'll be punished.

X. tells Y. Y. repeats it to W. and thus betrays X. The moment of telling, for X., felt like prayer, almost sanctified. He thinks the betrayal was evil, but evil lay in the telling, in daring to assume one could.

Spoke to her on the phone. She cried. Said she missed me. I feel like a ghoul wandering in this southern darkness.

The secretary said a long goodbye. A minuscule flake, like a fish scale, trembled in her right nostril. Her face shone with cosmetic oils, as in feverish sweating.

I go to the park and play basketball with the black kids. My body knows what to do, but does less than it knows. After a bad pass and a bad shot, I overplay a kid out of exasperation and bump him too hard. "I'm sorry," I say, "I'm too old." He says, "Don't say that, man. Look at me. I'm eighteen."

1984

"Do you think it's possible to have fifteen sincere relationships?"

"Not even one," she says. "Let me tie you to the bed."

"No."

"Why not?"

"Because I don't want you to."

"But I'll stop when you tell me. Just don't say 'stop.' That only excites me. Say 'tomato' or something."

Natural light passes through murky glass windows in the office doors and sinks into the brown linoleum floor. It is scuffed, heel pocked, and burned where students ground out cigarettes while waiting to speak to their professors. The halls are long and wide, and have gloomy brown seriousness, dull grandeur. You hardly ever hear people laughing in them. The air is too heavy with significance. Behind the doors, professors are bent over student papers, writing in the margins, "B+," "A—."

He comes to my office. "Free for lunch?" I jump up and say, "Give me a minute." He glances at his watch. I run to the men's room, start pissing, want to hurry. The door opens. It's him. Also wants to piss. He begins. I finish. Seconds go by and then a whole minute as he pisses with the force of a horse. He would have gone to lunch with me carrying that pressure.

His wife was a virgin, he says. She came the first time they had sex. Worse, he says, she came every time after that. He watches my eyes to see if I understand why he had to divorce her, but he has never said anything about the woman that makes her seem less than adorable. Why does he want to depress me?

1986

They say, "Hi," and kiss my cheek as if nothing terrible happened yesterday. Did they already forget? Perhaps they have no memory of anything besides money or sex, so they harbor no grudges and live only for action. "What's up?" Just pleasure, distractions from anxiety and boredom. Impossible to sustain conversation with them for more than forty seconds. The attention span of dogs. Everything must be up. They say you look great when you look near death. They laugh at jokes you didn't make. They say you're brilliant when you're confused and stupid.

X.'s Story

"I can tell by how he looks at you that he does it," says Y.

"Does what?" says X., imitating herself asking, puzzled.

"Goes down on you," says Y.

"Ha, ha, ha," laughs X.

"I'm jealous," says Y., and then says, "Jeff only does it on my birthday or Christmas."

I love X.'s little stories, but I'm still angry.

Some subjects, if they require discussion, are already dead—love, fidelity, etc. Poetry needs death. Emotion recollected in tranquillity. After a while nothing is lived except with a squinty eye to making. Nothing is lived. They even fuck to have poems later.

The woman pressed my leg with hers under the table. Conversation stopped. She continued pressing, then pulled away abruptly. Conversation resumed. She'd done it to excite herself; no more.

You know your feelings so you mistrust them, as if they belonged to an unreliable stranger. He behaved badly in the past, and is likely to do so again. But you can't believe that. You believe you've changed. Then it happens again and the same feelings surprise you. Now you're fearful of yourself.

She comes to my office, sits, looks me in the eye and says, "Girls like to be spanked."

Ortega says men are public, women are private, mysterious. Montaigne says, if you want to know all about me, read my book. They say the same thing.

A man writes a letter, then decides not to mail it. Maybe someday he'll use it in a publication. One of Byron's letters reappeared as a poem. Such intimacy is for the world, not a friend.

If there are things I'd never tell a psychotherapist, I would only waste time and money talking to one. It would feel like a lie. I need a priest.

He's talking and eating a turkey sandwich. A piece of turkey falls out of his sandwich onto the floor. My life stopped. What will he do? Something told me that he'd go on talking as he picks up the piece of turkey and pops it into his mouth. He did exactly that. I felt we knew each other. At his funeral, I thought, I would cry.

"She can't understand any experience not her own. She's Irish." She didn't mean because she's Irish. She meant thin, practical, cold. She meant not like herself, dark and warm. She meant blonde. In effect, the way people talk is what they mean. It is precise and clear—more than mathematics, legal language, or philosophy—and it is not only what they mean, but also all they mean. That's what it means to mean. Everything else is alienation except poetry.

I said to Margaret, "When we talk we make a small world of trust." Quickly, she says, "There are men so loose of soul, they talk even in their sleep." She laughs, surprised by her good memory and how wonderful Shakespeare is. It no longer mattered what I was going to say.

He laughs at his unexpressed jokes, then gives me a compassionate look for having missed the point known only to himself.

1987
Every wildness plays with death. Washing your hands is a ritual to protect against death. The small correct things you do every day. Aren't there people who do nothing else? They have proper sentiments and beliefs. They are nice people. I wanted to do dull ordinary chores all day and be like nice people only to forget death, only to feel how I'm still alive.

Port Townsend. Disorienting landscape sliced by water. Excellent light lasts long on summer afternoons. Time slows and pools in this light before seeping imperceptibly into twilight. One day replaces another like cards in a deck, so you feel you're always in the same place, the place you were yesterday, only it's today.

The sweet crazy student gave me shells he'd collected along the beach, and a piece of green glass honed by the waves. "This is the truth," he said. He put the shells in my hand. I said, "Thank you," feeling embarrassed more than touched, and carried it about all day in my pocket, broken shells, a bit of glass—his poem.

Bodega Bay. Want to write, but I sit for hours looking at the dune grass. It is yellowish green and sun-bleached. It sparkles and changes hue with the changing light. It is more hue than color, like the whole north coast. Now the dune grass has the sheen of fur. I need to be blind.

CZESLAW MILOSZ

◆ ──────────────────────────────── ◆

Fragments from a Journal

*P*aris / *May 10, 1987*

Musée d'Orsay. It's difficult to define my impressions as aesthetic. Besides, I don't know what people mean by aesthetics. My reflections go in two directions: (1) All that has been occurring since the middle of the nineteenth century—those innumerable lives of human beings submitted to physiological changes but also to fashions and shiftings or leaps of history, of beings who died, every one by his or her own kind of death—that immensity eluding imagination, *yet*, condensed into an extract. For instance, *Dancer* by Degas. That girl is herself, but she also is accompanied by her whole ambiance, her family, family conversations, beds, habits, Paris of the epoch, a year, a day. Degas moves me, for what transpires through his painting is pity. Pity for a frail body, for the aspirations of those girls, for their lovers, husbands, for their own subsequent adventures, of unknown nature, of *bourgeoises*, of *poules*, of great ballerinas. Time stopped here, now, together with its potentiality. In Musée d'Orsay I turn to realistic painting, from before impressionism. (I am also walking through these halls with a practical purpose, searching for a picture to be reproduced on the paperback cover of my volume *Unattainable Earth*. And I find it: a landscape by Antoine Chintreuil entitled *L'Espace* from the salon of 1866.)

Thus (to return to my subject), painting condenses and fixes this human time of rushing decades that is otherwise evasive, untouchable. Though people may say, And photography? Perhaps. Let others answer the question as to why it is not the same. For me it is important to see here a date under every canvas.

(2) To reflect seriously, it is hardly believable that from a distance, when we do not know as yet the name of a painter, we are able to distinguish and say whose work it is. For instance, that a given landscape is by Corot. This means that there exists—How to call it?—a tonality, a shade, a melody proper to one being only and to no one else. A sign of person. And painting provides a particular means to realize it. A painter may succeed in expressing that something of his own, though this

does not mean other people are deprived of that peculiar tone. Possibly this is the only proof of the immortality of the soul, provided however we accept an additional metaphysical premise: some*thing*, strictly individual, unrepeatable, cannot ever be destroyed, because that would be senseless and unjust.

Berkeley / August 6, 1987
Adventures of my life. "A revolving bard," as I have called myself. For thirty years in Poland an Orwellian non-person, then a reception in my honor at the Summer Royal Palace in Warsaw given by the Minister of Culture, and soon after, at the time of martial law, again to an attic. Yet my adventure with Oscar Milosz is even more surprising. A couple of months ago, on May 24, 1987, I take a train from the Gare de Lyon to Fontainebleau. After a few minutes I recognize to the right of the track familiar escarpments and trees; my station, Montgeron, flashes by, and later, when the train passes Brunoy and runs through the fields, I search the horizon for the cathedral tower of Brie-Comte Robert.

The first time I sat in a train to Fontainebleau was in 1931. I was twenty. A young elegant woman, a Parisienne, on the opposing seat intrigued me, a provincial. It is not so that now, in this train, I do not give her thought. On the contrary, I am counting: she might have been around thirty then; to add fifty-six years makes eighty-six, so probably she has already died.

Then, in Fontainebleau, Oscar received me in his room at the Hôtel de l'Aigle Noir. The birds he kept in a cage (or cages) were African sparrows which could not be released in the park. After all, he would not keep local birds as prisoners.

For me: apprehensive respect, snobbish affection for a French relative, genuine admiration for *Miguel Mañara* in Ostrowska's translation—and complete ignorance as to how our fates were going to be linked several decades later. For, after all, I was going to discover in the Princeton library his correspondence with Christian Gauss, and later, considering it my duty to propagate his writings, translate into English *Ars Magna* and *Les Arcanes*. I would not have encountered difficulty in publishing them could they have been classified as fashionable, cheap esotericism, which was impossible. Moreover, their prophesy of the triumph of the Roman Church antagonized many. Yet at last both these works entered the huge volume of his writings, *The Noble Traveller*, with my introduction, published in 1985 by Christopher Bamford.

Learning about the Nobel Prize, I thought it was a providential decree, to make his name known. And in some Berkeley bookstores *The Noble Traveller* stands on the shelves together with my poems.

Thus, May 1987. La Societé des Amis de Milosz celebrates with an annual luncheon precisely in the Hôtel de l'Aigle Noir, and I go there as a newly elected *président d'honneur* after the death of Jean Cassou. Probably the only sunny day in this May. We depose flowers on the tomb which bears an inscription in Lithuanian and in French: "The first representative of independent Lithuania in Paris." A little crowd is composed of Frenchmen and Lithuanians. Andrzej, who arrived from Warsaw a few days ago, startles the latter by addressing them in pure Lithuanian. After that, a visit to Place Milosz and to the house where Oscar died, at rue Royale, with a garden surrounded by a wall, where we are allowed to enter by the present owner, a retired shoe merchant. A long luncheon, speeches, next a promenade in the Parc du Château, where I wonder whether I am identical to the young man guided here by my cousin fifty-six years ago.

Berkeley / August 9, 1987
In Walnut Creek at the wedding of Ewa, then a party arranged in Danville at a park. When I came to Berkeley in 1960 with Janka and the children and Alfred Tarski was driving us around to show us the region, east of the Berkeley Hills there was only the country—in valleys, the orchards of walnuts; higher, slopes of straw color throughout most of the year, dotted by black oaks. Now the city is everywhere: streets and houses amidst the green, lawns, tennis courts, pools, parks. Also, a metro line, here not underground, leading from San Francisco. I am not sure whether I am strongly for conservation and against development. These landscapes were once rather sterile: dry grass and prickly oaks. The climate is different than in Berkeley, the fog from the sea does not reach here, the sky is always blue, everything is parched, and only people bring water and verdure here.

My childhood differed from childhood today. Mainly because of clouds of insects which buzzed, jumped, stung, bit, entered your eyes. Naked legs covered with scars and blisters from constant scratching. Crickets sputtered in the grass, beetles were running, plenty of red ants (those had the strongest sting), black ants of various sizes; on leaves caterpillars of many colors and shapes were spotted; in the kitchen or in some rooms, for instance those by the dairy, walls hardly visible under a moving fur of flies; glass fly traps filled with whey made dense by layers of drowned bodies. Chemicals have gotten rid of that swarming multiplicity which distinguished my childhood by one more thing: a great number of birds. Today insectivore birds have a hard life, though their scarcity probably does not strike people lacking comparisons.

Berkeley / August 10, 1987
There is a peculiar quality of light in the north and I discovered it after we (Janka and me) lifted our tent in the Canadian Rockies, at Jasper National Park, from where (in August) we had been chased by the first snow. The year was 1969. The road to Edmonton goes first north and only later turns east. There, by the Athabasca, I met this quality of light, so normal for many inhabitants of our planet that they do not even notice it. The first time I had that perception was shortly before World War II when I came from Warsaw on a visit to a small town, Glebokie, where my father was working. Glebokie is not farther north than my native district, but much farther to the east; thence, possibly, a difference. I have never described that town. It was surrounded by the most essential Byelorussian countryside; it had two baroque Jesuit churches and a *shtetl*, known from Yiddish literature and Chagall's paintings. But I have never seen, before or afterward, such an agglomeration of wooden shops. They looked like one barge or ark divided into small cubicles.

Accustomed to the light of California, probably I would now adapt myself to the light of the north with a certain difficulty. Already I found the last gray May in Europe depressing. Yesterday a blue sky (from around 1:00 P.M.) assuaged various despairs to which I bar access. Though I guess I would also like the climate of the Caribbean, those violent rains lasting a few minutes and again the splendor of wet, glimmering verdure in the sun.

Berkeley / August 15, 1987
Reason for my black moods. If somebody's life is marked by the sign of public and private misfortunes, there are some reasons. Strangely enough, since my childhood I lived in countries just coming to their end. First, Tzarist Russia. Of course, then I was not aware, but perhaps there were some fluids foretelling the end; I felt them so distinctly in Rzhev on the Volga in the revolutionary autumn of 1917, and later I tried to capture them in my youthful poems, unsuccessfully. Next the war of 1920, images of a lost battle, escapes, fate reversed in the battle at the gates of Warsaw, though only for a short time. Then, my school years were exceptional, i.e., normal, but as an adolescent already I was aware that the whole order of things was provisory. I knew that everything

would fall to pieces, yet, curiously, there were two levels: one, of the apocalyptic war; another, which at least in my consciousness, took precedence, of the ideological vacuum, and in that vacuum—here again I must refer to currents, fluids, signs to be interpreted—Marxism as the only force potentially charged with reality. To Poland it announced defeat, yet I did not see any counterbalance to it and I spoke frankly about that to my director at Polish Radio, Halina Sosnowski. She took my words seriously. Soon I saw with my own eyes the end of the independent countries: Poland and Lithuania. Also, the end of Europe cut off from its trunk. Whatever the fate of the Western European peninsula was to be, my perception of its transitory existence in the first years after World War II was not unlike what I had felt in the 1930s (as a consolation, one should remember that Europe lived for a long time under the menace of Islam, first of the Sarazzins from the south, then of the Turks from the east). This was a kind of postmortem existence: in the case of Western Europe, a transformation of live countries into a museum and a tacit readiness to accept slavery (according to a classic Hegelian formula, a slave is whoever wants to live at any price, even at the price of losing his freedom).

Berkeley (after return from Castel Gandolfo) / August 25, 1987
A conference on "Europe and What Came Out of It" in Castel Gandolfo, together with my jet lag and inability to sleep because of the Italian summer heat. Every morning a little bus takes the participants from our *pensione* to the papal palace; enters the gate, saluted by the Swiss guards in colorful dress; then a session in the presence of the Pope lasts from 10:00 A.M. to 1:00 P.M.; downtown again to our nuns for lunch and my only chance to sleep, the siesta. The afternoon session, also in the presence of the Pope, from 4:00 P.M. to 7:00 P.M. The walls of the palace are thick and provide some protection from the sun, but there is no air-conditioning. The room opens into a long terrace from which there is a view of the lake; a breeze moves the curtains. We are seated at a long table before the microphones, the table of the Pope is in the corner, loaded with books which he looks through, listening.

The Europeanization of the planet is the subject, but overly specialized papers lack the larger vision that I do find in Professor Robert Spaeman's and Professor George Kline's paper (Russia and the West). The Germano-centrism of the Germans forces me to take the floor and speak of a permanent German tendency (preceding Nazism and explaining the lost war of Hitler against Russia) to treat areas east of Germany as "external darkness." After the session I am comforted by words from the Pope ("this was the proper moment to bring in this necessary issue"). I also speak of "Shoah" (its accusation of Christianity) and of a corrosion of the religious imagination as a consequence of the European scientific revolution, asking how that corrosion acts and will act upon particular great religions of mankind.

Berkeley / August 28, 1987
In Castel Gandolfo somebody told me about the Pope's visit to the Turkish assassin, Acsa, in a Roman prison. In the photograph it looked as if Acsa confessed to the Pope. In reality, he shared with him his apprehensions. He had shot from such a short distance that the Pope's survival could be explained only by the intervention of the Holy Mary of Fatima; that day was the anniversary of her apparition. Acsa, superstitious, was now afraid she would retaliate. The Pope had to calm him down, assuring him that to take revenge is not Holy Mary's way.

Berkeley / August 29, 1987
"The inevitable extinction of the human person appears to us as the ultimate defeat of being; unlike the biological decomposition of the organism, it does not belong to the natural order of the cosmos. Indeed, it violates this order. Order, being empirically inaccessible, may be spoken of only when the *contingentia rerum* is related to a necessary and thus external reality." (Leszek Kolakowski, *Religion*, p. 157)

According to Kolakowski, one cannot believe in God without believing in immortality, for such a disbelief abolishes God; one cannot believe in immortality, without believing in God, for such a disbelief abolishes the very probability of immortality.

When we feel that our death is real, we are able to appreciate the argument of Leibniz about the world: certainly imperfect but the best of the possible worlds, for who would have we been if not for pain and death?

Berkeley / September 20, 1987
The partition separating life from death is so tenuous. The unbelievable fragility of our organism suggests a vision on a screen: a kind of mist condenses itself into a human shape, lasts a moment and scatters.

Berkeley / September 23, 1987
Nearly every day, educational television films for the young on Nature—on spiders, fish, lizards, coyotes, animals of the desert, of mountain meadows, etc. Technical excellence of photography does not dissuade

me from ranking these programs as *obscoena*. Because what they show offends our human, moral sense; not only offends, annihilates it, as the thesis of these programs is: Here you see how it goes on in Nature, and for that reason it is natural, and we, too, are a part of Nature, we belong to the chain of evolution and we have to accept the world as it is. If I turn off the television, terrified, loathing the images of mutual devouring and also the mind of the man who films them—is it because I am able to imagine what these images mean when translated into the life of human society? And those children, do they look without incurring any harm? For, do they not associate anything with the cruelty of Nature? Or, without being aware of it, are they being poisoned slowly, systematically, by these masters of photography who do not know what they do?

Berkeley / September 25, 1987
The makers of these films profess a scientific *Weltanschauung* and they show truth, nothing but truth; besides, they appreciate the splendidly photogenic features of Nature. It is difficult to raise objections. And yet they are not eyes alone, the lenses of their cameras film in the service of what inhabits their heads, i.e., of theory. A tale presented by them in images is an illustration in motion of the theory of evolution, of natural selection, etc. Notwithstanding whether that theory is scientifically valid or not, it organizes and composes the material.

Balzac lived at the time when so-called natural history began to reign, there was no need to wait for Darwin. In his *Human Comedy* he wanted to present various species making up a human society. And he presented them. We were passionate readers of Balzac under the German occupation, for the brutalized reality that surrounded us was mocking more lofty works, while it confirmed the brutalized France of the first half of the nineteenth century found in Balzac. Of course his way of writing is a model of the realistic novel and so on. Thanks to him we are able to understand much of the everyday patterns of relations between people. Yet in truth, *Human Comedy* is a big fantasy not unlike Theodore Dreiser's America. As much realistic as invented.

Berkeley / September 26, 1987
I remember in the period of the greatest ideological frenzy, Soviet discussions about Darwinism, when instead of natural selection through the mutations of genes they introduced the inheritability of acquired traits (Lysenko). A cooperation between animals was opposed to the blind struggle for existence (even invoking the anarchist Kropotkin). Who

knows, perhaps the main goal of that discussion was pedagogic, i.e., to secure for new generations "a happy childhood," protected from reality by a serene indoctrination. Darwinism is too gloomy for this purpose.

Higher culture, i.e., written, and lower culture, i.e., oral. I use this distinction of Ernest Gellner's when preparing a paper on nationalism for a conference at Ann Arbor. I am also prompted by Allain Finkelkraut's *La Défaite de la pensée* bought this year in Paris and by an Isaiah Berlin essay on nationalism. Political romanticism as a moment of the passage of human masses from oral culture to culture inculcated in school. The consumption of native literature as a "national heritage." This is confirmed by my own education. A textbook of the history of Polish literature by Professor Chrzanowski was primarily a nationalistic indoctrination.

What do we serve, we who work in language? Is it not possible to imagine an aircraft carrier named *Pushkin* or a submarine *Dostoevsky* or an interplanetary vehicle for a conquest of distant planets *Gogol?* Poor Gogol. He did not want this. He did not know. And we, do we know how we will be used?

Berkeley / November 8, 1987
I would like to read a novel on the twentieth century, not one of parables in which human affairs appear through metaphor, but a novel, thus a report on many characters and on their actions. It should be an international novel, as the century is international in spite of the flourishing of many nationalisms. I do not find such a novel, so as yet it has to be written—and I wonder whether somewhere there is a writer sufficiently sure of himself to attempt it. The techniques of narration fashionable today—in the first person and about one's own self—are an obstacle. It should be a panorama shown through delegated characters—as in Thomas Mann's *Magic Mountain*. And the characters should not be average, gray; on the contrary, models could be provided by colorful and eminent personalities, and these are not lacking.

As a place of action I would choose Rome or a monastery like Our Lady of Gethsemani, Kentucky, where people of various professions and views used to come to visit Thomas Merton. Merton himself, with all his contradictory desires, would appear in the novel, not only discussing Duns Scott with Maritain (who visited him, too), but also thrashing around politically. In Rome a quite good model would have been Cardinal Poupard, whose views on the state of faith among Catholics, particularly among the clergy, divulged during a dinner at Mme G's, were so dismal that even I felt uneasy. Also in Rome or in Gethsemani a philosopher could act, modeled for instance on Leszek Kolakowski, as well as a writer, probably put together with a few known names and treated not too kindly—for who else, if not writers, allowed themselves to be seduced by foolish ideologies and then busied themselves with seducing the minds of the public?

The work would not be limited to clashes of views and attitudes, though the Naphta-Settembrini quarrel in Thomas Mann would probably resurge in a new form. The book would not do without a romance, and women must be introduced. Here we are in trouble, for why should a female protagonist be good only for bed? But where are those intellectually prominent women of the century, able to stir the imagination of a chronicler? Undoubtedly the most famous was Simone de Beauvoir, yet she does not bring honor to the promoters of feminism and the sooner she is forgotten, the better. She does not qualify as a model, the caliber is too low—after all, my novel would not be satirical. When she published her novel *Les Mandarins*, gossipy, with "a key," in a Parisian provincial mode, I asked Albert Camus whether he intended to answer. He shrugged: "One does not answer a gutter." He was right.

Two eminent women, both philosophers: Hannah Arendt and Jeanne Hersch. They would have merited to be introduced, together with the master of both, Karl Jaspers, and, perhaps, in the background, the not-at-all-innocent-ideologue Heidegger. I met Hannah Arendt in Paris through Jeanne. A contemporary pen should have dealt with them, but Hannah Arendt is no longer alive, and I have not even attempted to draw a portrait of Jeanne.

San Francisco Airport / April 21, 1988
On misanthropy. People can say of us: he is a misanthrope; we don't say of ourselves: I am a misanthrope. And since misanthropy has many degrees, I confess to only a certain amount of it, which inclines me to keep people at a distance and doesn't facilitate permanent submergence in a mass. For that reason America is better for me than the Slavic countries, and my hilltop Grizzly Peak home protects me to some extent. A true misanthrope should live in a castle. The main character in Jules Verne's *Le Château de Carpathes* lives precisely that way. His castle, at the top of an inaccessible, wild mountain in Transylvania, is surrounded by a moat, but that's not enough; an electric current in the hidden wires would have knocked down a daredevil attempting to enter. There are

no daredevils, though, for the owner produces, with the help of electricity, presumably supernatural phenomena, so that in the valley the castle is considered to be inhabited by ghosts. The misanthrope lives alone with his old faithful servant, he spends his time listening to a voice from a phonograph, the voice is of an Italian cantatrice, once his love, and he looks at her movements on a screen. (Foretold invention of television!)

Misery of the human species. Physiological, but also the misery of myths we incessantly create together, which makes it impossible to read reality and see how everything really happened. These myths are gathered into so called "culture"! Hardly a few years—ten, fifteen—and people spin threads to swaddle a person, events in a cocoon for their own use.

I have read a number of poems in a couple of languages on Osip Mandelstam as a martyr for freedom. I have also heard a cassette of a Polish theatrical spectacle in his honor. All this has very little to do with the real Mandelstam.

Question: Is the transformation—simplifying, vulgarizing—inevitable? Is it so that the larger the spread of fame, the less complications are allowed to subsist? And what is our part, of us already bygone, in encouraging a myth: i.e., What traits of ours favor it?

Paris / June 3, 1988
In Paris I try to follow the trail of Jean Le Louet, without result. Yesterday, at a dinner at Pierre and Betty Leyris's, I read his poem "Attitudes" from my just published book of essays *L'Immoralité de l'art*. All agreed that it is a fine poem. Yet it is a translation from my translation into Polish. The French original is lost. Its author, Jean Le Louet, from the second wave of surrealists, found himself in Warsaw in August 1939, perhaps for romantic reasons; he was gay. Vaguely, I remember that he knew Iwaszkiewicz and even visited him at Stawisko. The outbreak of war caught him in Warsaw; then the Germans sent him, as a French citizen, to an internment camp at Bodensee where he had for a fellow mate another French citizen, Stanislaw Dygat. There he wrote this poem, perhaps immediately after the fall of France in 1940. Dygat, when released, brought it to Warsaw and gave it to me. I translated it and published it in my anthology, *Independent Song*, in 1942.

Leyris, very old and familiar with all of literary Paris, told me that his remembrance of Le Louet was scant: slim, delicate, nearly feminine, suffering from a throat illness and the loss of voice. From somebody else (Pierre Boutang, Jr.?) I heard that after the war he led the life of a hobo.

When he died nobody knows. This is all. Completely forgotten as a poet with only this claim to memory, a poem in translation into Polish. An extraordinary poem, having nothing to do with surrealism, as Leyris justly pointed out, going back to a biblical tradition (as if written by a Polish romantic poet), prophetic, for who could in 1940 foresee collaboration? Any anthology of the best texts written during World War II should include it. It is better than poems of young underground poets of Warsaw, more concise, dense, like a Gospel parable.

Paris / June 6, 1988
Continued search for traces of Jean Le Louet, for, as it transpires, André Silvaire knew him. Before the war Le Louet edited a revue, *Les Lettres Nouvelles*. His poetry volumes bore strange titles. They were not published by Gallimard, for his revue was in competition. Some, including Jean Cassou, greeted Le Louet as a young genius, as a revelation of a new Rimbaud. He received a fellowship for a voyage to Poland. Silvaire, after the *débâcle*, met him in Toulouse. Le Louet then intended to get out of France. He spent the rest of the war in Spain. I asked myself, When was he released from the internment camp at Bodensee and when did he write the poem? I do not remember when Dygat was released, besides, Le Louet could have been released earlier. He could have written the poem immediately after the fall of France. If, however, it was written before, which seems more probable, it refers not to the French situation but to the Polish situation, as visualized by the author, and it is in fact a Polish poem by a French poet.

After the war Le Louet did not return to literature. Those few who knew him talk of his downfall with horror and pity. He was a hobo, a *clochard*, in the literal sense, and lived for a long time in that manner; he died only a couple of years ago. So, I would have found him.

DMITRI NABOKOV

◆ ─────────────── ◆

Close Calls and Fulfilled Dreams:
Selected Entries from a Private Journal

22 *Nestorstrasse, Berlin / Early 1935*

My knees are completely green, because I have been crawling on the emerald rug of the apartment where I have lived since I was born last year. The apartment is that of my mother's cousin Anyuta, a beloved auntlike friend who will fulfill multiple functions in my upbringing. She will share her lodgings with us until we leave Germany in 1937. Her life, like those of many Russians, has been overturned. She is a talented pianist, but will never be able to pursue her studies. In 1939 I shall go with her to Deauville, far from the approaching thunder of Hitler's bombs. She will take me to two double features a day when I travel from Boston to visit her in New York in the 1940s, and, when I sail for Southampton in 1959, will come to my New York flat to collect a last load of my belongings for safekeeping. Those belongings will be stolen from her West Side cellar, and a few Nabokov first editions, with butterflies Father has drawn for me, will probably be chucked into the trash by some semiliterate scoundrel. In 1968, very ill and nearly blind, she will be rescued by Mother from her nightmarish New York existence, and spirited to Switzerland, where her life will be extended by a few happy years. She will be buried in 1973 in a verdant Swiss cemetery overlooked by the tower of an ancient castle and, in 1977, my father's ashes will be interred nearby.

Nestorstrasse, Berlin / May 1936

I have discovered the primordial pleasure of taking aim and throwing. My first missiles are spoonfuls of spinach, aimed at my nursery wall. I soon progress to lofting the toys received for my recent second birthday toward a smaller target: a window opening onto the street below.

Berlin / Fall 1936

I have progressed from the comfort of my baby carriage, an elegant beige vehicle with fat tires, and am now walking fairly well. The focus of my gaze has shifted from overhead foliage passing as I was rolled along sun-dappled lanes; it is a new thrill to observe my surroundings from a vertical posture as Father guides me by the hand into the mysterious Grunewald and the infinitely rich world that still awaits me.

Berlin / Winter 1936 – 37
I have begun cataloguing cars. The parent walking me along a city sidewalk is required to follow my finger as it indicates passing vehicles of special interest, and record them mentally for a detailed report to the one who will greet me on my return. The elaborate coach work and fender-mounted spares of imposing sedans have first priority; also high on my list are the thunderous exhaust and gear whine of large trucks, for which I have invented the onomatopoeic appellation *blombabakht*.

Rue Saigon, Paris / December 25, 1938
Its color is an appetizing metallic red. It is sleek, heavy to hold, and an incredible thirteen-and-a-half inches long. It has removable rubber tires, a battery-operated headlight, and a powerful clockwork motor. Its front axle can be positioned in one of five notches to make it travel in a straight line or in circles of varying radius. It bears the inscription "Renault" in black letters on a yellow background, and is driven by a plump figure with white suit and helmet and an expression of amazed delight. We give car and driver the collective name Belov, from *belïy*, Russian for "white" (I am as yet unaware that a Captain Belov appears in *The Real Life of Sebastian Knight*, Father's recently completed first novel in English). I have loved cars more or less since I was born; I have already been given countless small toy vehicles, plus a drivable approximation of a silver Mercedes that I named Lemba and once pedaled into the middle of Berlin traffic at the age of two, and that, to my grief, I rapidly outgrew. But now I have received my first substantial model car. Belov will survive a war, some twenty moves, and years of semi-oblivion in a remote warehouse, to recross the Atlantic and rejoin me in Switzerland, practically intact. I shall one day learn that it is a faithful reproduction of a prototype designed for an attempt on the Land Speed Record.

I know that Father is a "writer." For now the word connotes only vague impressions: mysterious smoky discussions, in which I am not qualified to take part, with people named Fondaminsky, Hodasevich, Bunin, Aldanov; red-bound volumes on high shelves that attract only my sense of touch; Father withdrawing into the bathroom of our cramped quarters to work undisturbed by the child of the house. My first inkling of what he really does comes when I listen with delight as Mother reads to me his Russian translation of *Alice in Wonderland*.

Cannes / 1930s

I love the cherry-colored buses of the Riviera, and the sky-blue, gasoline-powered railcars whose clicking and whistling I call *dagadaran-dagada-ran—day-you*. I am told such a train is known as an *otoray*. I live with my own Russian-based Esperanto. Later, when I begin discovering the oddities of French phonetics, I shall be surprised to learn that it is spelled *autorail*. I call the vertical clusters of red aircraft beacons at Antibes "geraniums." I also love riding out into the sea on Father's shoulders. One day we set out for a closer look at a twin-engined flying boat, in olive-and-tan camouflage livery, at anchor off the Fréjus beach. A snapshot taken by Mother at that beach contains a hidden surprise: a crane in the background, hoisting an airplane. The crane will fall into German hands during the approaching war, and Mother will send that snap from Cambridge in response to an appeal from the U.S. authorities for chance photographs of strategic value. Her paramilitary activities will end there, even though I shall learn one day that some lunatic believes she was once a member of a terrorist hit squad.

Another photograph, of Father and me in front of two urns outside the pension Les Héspérides in Menton, will also survive, and will be retaken on a 1959 visit to the still standing Hésperides, but then I shall tower over Father's six-foot frame.

Fréjus / Summer 1939

I am five and in love. Her name is Anny. She is a blonde child somewhat older than I, whose family occupies a neighboring spot on the beach. This name is associated in my senses with anise, which I have never tried but for which I have invented a flavor. The color associated with my Annie is red, from the hue my colored vision has assigned to the letter A. When I am eight my father will test me for the colors of the alphabet. M will be a robin's-egg blue, and so will Mother. F will be tan, C yellow. He will record that test in one of his little diaries. The loci of my childhood sojourns on the Riviera will blend into a sunny haze but, when I consult that diary forty years later, I shall find that the colors of my letters are unchanged.

Paris / May 15, 1940

We are leaving Paris today. I have a fever of 104, but there is no choice: by a stroke of luck our passage to New York has been shifted from the last to the penultimate scheduled sailing of the *Champlain*, for war has broken out in earnest. My parents know what will make me feel better: three of my favorite small toys—two automobiles and a truck—have been retrieved from among belongings we shall never see again, and set out as a surprise for me this morning.

Saint-Nazaire / May 20, 1940

My fever has miraculously vanished. I have been led by my parents to a square from which they can show me, as if offering a splendid present, a glimpse of an enormous yellow cylinder that turns out to be the funnel of our ship. Even amid the turmoil of departure from a disintegrating Europe, a departure uncertain until the last minute toward an equally uncertain future, I live in a cocoon of love, even-tempered optimism, and sundry amusements. I have never before seen a real ocean liner, and the image will remain indelible.

Aboard the Champlain */ May 1940*

Two guns on rotating mounts have been installed on the deck as protection against German submarines. They are manned by young and nervous seamen, who fired today at a whale's spout. No submarines have been seen.

Morning, May 28, 1940

We shall arrive today. I had a dream last night, so vivid that I shall be able to play it back many years later: skyscrapers have been promised in order to give me something exciting to look forward to, like my first glimpse of the liner; but we are nearing a dream New York and, unlike the ship's funnel that did materialize in St.-Nazaire, there are no skyscrapers to be seen, just a dreary assemblage of low, nondescript structures. My disappointment is bitter.

Afternoon, May 28, 1940

We are approaching real New York. My faith had been shattered by that dream, and it is a splendid surprise to see the promised giants emerging from the mist! We dock at the French Line pier, on whose opposite side is another wish come true: the huge, three-funneled *Normandie*, with wonderful oval portholes amid the round. Ever since I received its miniature rubber-tired replica, this particular ship has been my concept of the ocean liner (the prototype, alas, will burn and capsize at its berth while being converted into a troop transport). We have arrived poorer by a flask of French cognac and a bottle of champagne, last-minute gifts from a family friend thrust into an unlocked portmanteau (*"Il ne faut jamais laisser les hommes seuls avec de l'alcool,"* a ship's officer tells Mother to exculpate his men). We shall narrowly escape remaining poorer by most of our funds, a hundred-dollar bill that Mother, mistaking cents for dollars, proffers to a very honest taxi driver. The *Champlain*'s next voyage, on which we were originally booked, will indeed be its last, but not only for the Duration: it will be sunk, with all aboard, by a German submarine. Forty years later the term "Duration" will long since have lost the meaning "duration of the war," a war that, for now, is but a vague collection of impressions—a child-sized gas mask I donned during air-raid drills in Paris, shelters in that city's bowels, the distant drone of what I was told was a German airplane. Only a handful of bombs will fall on Paris, but one of them will destroy our apartment after we have safely reached America.

My future contains predawn sailings by tugboat into the same harbor's waters, to board incoming troopships and process arriving troops. That will be only one of the agreeable adventures I shall one day have as an American soldier.

New York / September 1940
I am home from my first day at the Walt Whitman school. I proudly announce to my parents that today I have learned English.

New York / May 1941
The fruits of my first year's classroom labors are mostly messy watercolors, but I have begun to receive some real education at home and on exciting excursions with my mother to the sights of New York: the Statue of Liberty, the Aquarium, the Bronx Zoo, the push-button model railroad in the bowels of Rockefeller Center, the streamlined summit of the Empire State Building, swaying slightly on a windy day. I have decided the only things I really like are those that are either larger or smaller than life.

Wellesley / September 1941
In New York Mother would take me to school. In winter I walked with her through the fresh morning snow of Central Park, my Flexible Flyer

sled in tow. Now, along a tree-shaded lane, I ride my balloon-tired bicycle to a neighborhood school on my own. We live in a shingled house on Appleby Road, whose name will remain mnemonically entwined with the green apples that grow in the leafy depths at its dead end, and that serve as missiles for elaborately staged battles. In the spring I shall be initiated into the rites of marbles by the girl next door. Her mysterious femininity at twelve, ideal perhaps for a future Humbert Humbert peering through the opposite end of the telescope, will appear unattainably mature to me at eight, and my crush will remain undeclared.

Cambridge / September 1943
I have begun attending a school around the corner from Craigie Circle, where we now live. I assume that my score on an IQ test is inadequate, since I find myself relegated to a "remedial" class. It will be explained to me later that, according to the dictates of Progressive Education, the happy medium of a perfect youngster is best attained by leaving the fortunate average group alone, and blending, in special classes, the excessively gifted with the moronic. My parents will not leave me in this school for long, but one wonderful thing will happen here. Mrs. Ruedebush, the music teacher, is a rare, truly dedicated educator. She will notice that I, a European child with no grounding in traditional American singing, have trouble carrying the tune of hymns sung during the school assemblies. She will take me under her musical wing, give me lessons in solfège and piano, and begin training my high soprano voice. Enthusiasm will replace frustration. I shall go on to sing in choirs and student performances, and eventually reward her early efforts by becoming a professional operatic basso.

Brookline / June 1947
I sit on the lawny grounds of Dexter School. It is the day of spring sports awards. I entered Dexter three years ago, still quite unequipped for life as an American boy. The school's headmaster, Francis Caswell, has been the second superb pedagogue of my life. He has taught me not only Cicero and Caesar, but also how to bat a ball and throw a block, how to give a firm handshake while looking the other squarely in the eye, how to be a "citizen."

I am surprised to find my parents present at the ceremony. I have managed to win maroon Dexter Ds in various sports, but still think of myself as a skinny, imperfectly coordinated outsider when it comes to athletics. I am in mid-reverie when I hear my name announced as overall winner of the spring sports contest, a cumulative competition comprised of track and field events plus such things as baseball throwing. I look around, thinking I have misheard, then, in a mist that has not yet become joy, stand up to receive my prize. Francis Caswell will remember me—and probably all the other boys who have been under his tutelage— with birthday cards for the rest of his life. He will always include a short Latin phrase, and a personal recollection. His favorite memory will remain the occasion when, during the half-time break of a school soccer game, he played my father one-on-one and Father scored a goal from the opposite end of the field (part luck, part skill, for he had always loved soccer, and played both at his University in England and with an amateur team in Berlin). The Rev. Caswell will die, after a long life of service to others, at the same home for the elderly to which he has volunteered the years of his retirement.

Jackson Hole, Wyoming / July 1949

After many trips with my parents to our marvelous American West, I am, for the first time, on my own. I have been deposited at the Jenny Lake campground, equipped with a small tent and a sleeping bag. I shall cook over an open fire, bathe in the lake's chilly waters, and attend the Petzoldt-Exum Climbing School. Ever since my hands felt their first rocks in a city park I have had a strong urge to clamber up anything climbable. One day I shall even scale Harvard's Memorial Hall, though not during a lecture of my father's in that building, as someone has said. I shall eventually attempt things that do not appear readily climbable, and make a couple of first ascents in Canada.

For now I am to have my first taste of technical mountaineering and the thrill of my first rappel, a backward leap from an overhang followed by a fast slide down a double rope. I shall do a few guided climbs before joining the fellow alpinists camped at Jenny Lake in progressively more difficult ascents, then begin to lead myself. My guide on my first serious climb is Art Gilkey, who will soon die on an American expedition to K2.

Ithaca / May 1951

My boarding-school career has survived some bad skids, and would have ended in disaster but for the intervention of another splendid headmaster, Edric Weld. I have lived on the perilous border between success in various school endeavors and minor clandestine delinquency: beer in the woods, secret nighttime excursions, even a first-year episode of petty thievery to impress my classmates (to two of whom I shall remain forever grateful for making me return contritely to the store, purloined merchandise in hand). A superb teacher named Charles Abbey has taught me the rudiments of Shakespeare and guided me to state and New England debating championships. My voice turned into a low bass, and I became a soloist in school performances. I discovered the joys of skiing and hiking in the New Hamphire hills. I had already been accepted at Harvard, and was to sing and speak at the Commencement ceremony. Then came an indignant protest from a group of village mothers, claiming I was a menace to their daughters. It had all been pretty innocent: as one of the school drivers, I had volunteered to chauffeur a spastic fellow student on regular visits to the local osteopath, discovered that the doctor's office-cum-home contained a flirtatious daughter, and taken advantage of the opportunity for a few groping trysts. Thanks to the Solomonic Reverend Weld I have been allowed to leave with dignity, take my final examinations on the honor system at home in Ithaca, and even bid a hasty farewell to my village sweetheart on the way to the station. For a few weeks I shall receive neat letters with upside-down stamps, signifying that I am still loved. Then there will be the final, upright stamp—for I have been replaced.

Cambridge / September 6, 1951
Today, as I shall learn much later when preparing his letters for publication, Father has written to his sister in Geneva:

> Mityusha is already attending Harvard; he is seventeen and enormous, he sings bass in an Episcopalian church choir, and he is interested, in the following order, in: mountain climbing, girls, music, track, tennis, and his studies.

I have, in fact, discovered that one can easily survive at college with a minimum of application, and am taking less than full advantage of Harvard's splendid opportunities. When I am not too exhausted from daily track practice, it is enough to focus briefly on a page for it to register photographically. But the image fades quickly, alas.

Perhaps my most entertaining course this first year is an obligatory one intended to bring all freshmen up to a minimal level of literacy. I have the good fortune to be in the section taught by John Ciardi, who relieves me of all formal assignments on condition that I submit to him one story or poem per week. I fulfill the obligation religiously, even though most of those early attempts, when reread later, will turn out to be embarrassingly bad.

Cambridge / March 1952

The family rule now is that I must work to earn pocket money. I have had interesting part-time jobs: mailman in the Harvard Yard, with the neat, symmetrical sensation of replacing incoming envelopes by the outgoing in my pleasantly professional satchel; partner for tennis and French conversation to an odd, ruddy-faced little Bostonian bachelor who would fetch me in a Jaguar, play decent tennis and speak bad French, and most of whose conversation concerned the details of boarding-school locker rooms; then, after the Dean of Freshmen warned me that the chap was notorious for placing the tennis-and-French ad in the Harvard *Crimson* every year, and had compensated the earnings I would forego with an obscure seventeenth-century grant "for hungry students," my last and best freshman-year job: walking, or rather running, a creature named Pedro—half boxer, half great Dane—who grew most fond of me after a strained initial meeting (keys left for me, academic owners absent), but who considered all other dogs his mortal enemies, so that I would occasionally conclude these exercise periods with hands bloodied from separating frenzied canine mandibles.

Wyoming / July 1952

I am eighteen. Since fall I have had my first car, a 1931 Model A Ford in middling shape. I have hammered the dents out of its dark-blue fenders, and driven West by myself this year. I have whizzed down a long incline into one town with no brakes, entered another aflame, and arrived in Laramie with an ominous knock in my motor. My parents have prearranged various meeting places and mail drops, since my trip coincides with theirs, and have christened my jalopy Kubik. Mother does not believe I shall make a profit on the $70 I paid for it by "selling it to the Indians."

I must make climbing money, so I find a gardener's position at a vacation motel near Laramie, where I can visit my parents on free days. I have a brief romance with a California girl called Glenna, and go with her to my first auto race. That little hill climb on a dirt road in Wyoming is very different from the high-speed mountain events that await me in Europe, but it awakens my interest: for the first time I see Jaguars and MGs in competition.

My hedge trimmer cuts its own umbilical cord and my duties are changed to those of lifeguard at the motel pool, temporarily replacing a comrade whom I shall take up Long's Peak and the Grand Teton. My work obligations completed, I climb much of the summer with a friendly Park Ranger. On the West Face of the Middle Teton with him, I slip off a ledge while dodging a falling rock, and land on my back in a boulderfield some thirty feet below. My pack cushions my fall, and I seem not much the worse for wear, but the damage I have done to a vertebra will return to haunt me after many years. Solo climbs are strictly forbidden by Park rules. To show off before a comely girl who is working this summer at the Jenny Lake Store, I climb an easy spire alone. In the summit register I proudly write my name followed by the word "solo," which I had seen inscribed in the Teton guidebook after accounts of first ascents by such early climbing greats as Frytiof Fryxell. I am summoned to the Head Ranger's office for an amiable but convincing dressing-down. Yet there is an alpine poetic justice, for the day will come when my name, too, will make an occasional appearance in mountaineering journals and guidebooks. At summer's end I do sell the car (which would have never made it back to Cambridge) for $30 to a girl camped at Jenny Lake. Unable even to make it start, she resells it to a local tinkerer, who combines it with two of its siblings to yield a perfectly functioning Model A.

Jackson Hole, Wyoming / August 1952
I am climbing a peak called Teewinot with a partner I have met here. The sky darkens unexpectedly and a lightning bolt strikes within ten feet of him, leaving a large black scar on the rock, which will later seem a kind of portent. Chris, who would have inherited a tobacco fortune, will soon be killed on a California mountain.

Nighttime, Camp 2 (15,600 ft.), just below snowline on Mt. Orizaba, Mexico / December 1952
I am abruptly awakened by a massive whoosh passing over the two-man tent where I have been sound asleep. I peek out. The night is starry, and the immense white volcanic cone reflects the light of a nearly full moon. All seems still around me and in the depths below. The following morning we shall discover a ten-foot crater in the snow on a direct vector just above our camp. We shall conclude that we had been narrowly missed by a caroming meteorite, even though I never heard it hit below. We shall go on to the summit, which a satellite survey will later pinpoint at

18,855 feet. I shall gaze down at Veracruz and the hazy shimmer of the ocean, and think of Keats's stout Cortez, who should have been Balboa. During Christmas break, Bernays, Merrihue, three others, and I have traveled here, first in an elderly Packard hearse whose motor we lovingly rebuilt in a dim garage, and which we have equipped with bunks, bucket seats, and B-25 tires; then in an open truck, drinking Tequila with the natives; and finally by burro to our second camp. This trip will remain a sunny memory of adventure, my first real expedition. Only as the years pass shall I begin to wonder whether, at eighteen, I had not thoughtlessly taken something for granted. I shall read of the ghostly "third man" that accompanied early Himalayan climbers at high altitudes, and of the strange fogbows Whymper saw on the first ascent of the Matterhorn. One day an old Zermatt guide will reveal to me certain personal mysteries of his. I shall wonder what really flew over me that night.

Cambridge /September 29, 1953
I shall find out that today Father wrote to Aunt Elena:

> [Our son] has run his third car into the ground and is getting ready
> to buy a used plane. During the summer he took part in a Harvard
> expedition to almost totally unexplored mountains in British Co-
> lumbia, before which he worked building highways in Oregon and
> handling a gigantic truck. [. . .] We found him in his bivouac tent
> on the shore of a lake in the Tetons (Western Wyoming), and from
> there he drove off to Colorado. He does up to 1,000 miles a day in
> his car—it's unbelievable!—sometimes driving twenty or thirty
> hours at a stretch. Vera and I spent the spring in Arizona, and the
> summer in Oregon, worrying constantly about him—I doubt if we
> shall ever get used to it. We saw him the other day at Harvard; he
> has grown a splendid blondish, shovel-shaped beard and looks like
> Alexander III.

Father has taught me not to complain and not to give up. Self-control and courage, even in the direst circumstances, have always been his norm. That is both his innate character and the result of the British stoicism instilled in him amid Russian luxury by his exceptional parents. I have not expressed the internal struggles between will and fear when, climbing alone in Colorado this year, I clung for thirty minutes to a precarious hold trying to convince myself that a jump could propel me to a narrow ledge, and that what appeared to be a finger-sized crack would allow me to keep my balance on that ledge.

My parents have encouraged me in all forms of sport. Father has taught me the rudiments of boxing, soccer, tennis, and skiing. The adventurous facet of his nature is contagious. One of his few unfulfilled dreams is to own a motorcycle, but his motoring career ended in a ditch on a family estate when, at the age of twelve, he surreptitiously appropriated grandfather's Benz. On a May day in Italy in 1966, without Mother (who may always tell me to slow down, but, in her twenties, flew in a stunt plane and is no slowpoke at the wheel herself), he will ask to be shown if my new ISO Rivolta will really do 150 miles an hour on the *autostrada*. Mother has listened with rapture as I told her of my exploits, and of the sense of poetical purification a day in the mountains gives me. And they have never mentioned their anguish, as they will not years later while awaiting my phone call from an Italian race course, or while I travel in obsolete airplanes above distant jungles on the way to singing engagements in Medellin or Caracas. Instead Father will write me, on May 30, 1970:

> If you fly high over the tropical forest, you may notice what looks like shimmering little light-blue mirrors—*Morpho* butterflies flying above the trees.

And, when he learns that I ran out of fuel between Sorrento and Capri while leading in a 1975 offshore powerboat race, he will berate me for my improvidence.

The road-building machinery I operated last summer did not always come to a good end. A gravel truck in marginal condition, driven with excessive brio, dumped its load like the toy trucks of my childhood on their sandlot roads: by being overturned. Then there was the Dumptor, a massive diesel-powered contrivance, with catastrophically inadequate brakes, that would be loaded by power shovel, then driven at maximum speed to the edge of a precipice, abruptly stopped, and emptied by the momentum acting on its hinged bed. My amiable foreman called it a "dumpster." When I cockily corrected him, he replied "Well, I didn't go to Harvard." It would have been more logical if he had, for a tempting assonance with Harvard's Dunster House might well have justified the error. The day came when the dumpster's brakes failed to stop it at the designated spot, and only a hasty bailout kept me from finishing my workday at the bottom of a deep ravine.

After those entertaining interludes of labor I traveled in my stately 1938 Buick—much like the vehicles I had admired in childhood—to a

Canadian rendezvous with a Harvard hearse, thence to British Columbia to climb with a university expedition, and on to Alberta to repeat for the first time the original snow-and-ice route on Mt. Robson, the highest peak of the Canadian Rockies, with Bernays and Merrihue. My good friend Craig Merrihue will become an astrophysicist of brilliant promise, and have time to glimpse the mysteries of Black Holes before he dies on a winter practice climb in Mt. Washington's Huntington Ravine.

Cambridge / February 1956
I successfully, if not very diligently, finished Harvard last spring. The subject Father had suggested for my History and Literature honors thesis was Shakespeare's influence on Pushkin. My advisor was Richard Pipes, who is also to become one of our government's most competent advisors. I started on it last summer in Taos, but procrastinated dreadfully on my return to Harvard, and finished in a nonstop fourteen-day sprint. On the morning of the day the thing was due, three Cambridge ladies were still typing industriously from my untidy manuscript, while a crew of friends assembled pages into three binders until the final minute. I could have done much better. The honors awarded to my thesis were demoted by one notch because, as one of the official readers put it, it was done "in such terrible haste that even the name of the author's father is mistyped in the index."

I am now at the Longy School of Music. My first MG has been wrecked, and I drive my second. It was bought used, has been modified to go fast, and possesses no top or windshield wipers. It is often parked near Harvard Square, and usually contains, amid sports paraphernalia and snow, an open copy of the first book I shall translate: Lermontov's *Hero of Our Time*. Father, who is my collaborator, is in Cambridge. Each time he comes upon the car, he carefully notes the page number to see how far I have progressed, and reproachfully reports it to me in the evening. When I finish the job he nevertheless allows me to begin work on a long series of his own Russian works, beginning with *Invitation to a Beheading*.

New York / March 29, 1959

> The pang comes from a faded diary,
> the date is Easter, fifty-nine.
> You were Hellenically earthy,
> you were becoming not quite mine.

The cause of parting was a detail,
a detail made the parting last:
my rage at your request for freedom
to meet a beau out of your past;
our reconciliation party
—the date was Easter fifty-nine—
at an unlisted someone's townhouse,
the jotting lost (was it a sign?);
the little turquoise roadster circling,
its driver's burgeoning distress—
the vain hope that a secret magnet
might draw me to the right address.

Milan / December 1959
I have crossed from New York on the S.S. *United States*, whose true top
speed has never been revealed because of its military potential. I have
picked up a Triumph TR-3A (my first brand-new car!) in Southampton,
driven through Chartres and over the Bardonecchia Pass, and nearly
killed myself upon abruptly entering a solid wall of Lombardy fog, a fog
I shall soon know well. On my second evening an operatic snowfall has
transformed the dullishly gray city, setting a perfect scene for the pretty
young prostitutes cavorting near the park under their proplike umbrel-
las. I must return to the Principe e Savoia for dinner with my parents,
who are in Milan to participate in *Lolita* festivities and help organize my
operatic training. I lose my way and ask one of the girls for directions.
Before I know it I have been lured to a friendly nearby *pensione*. She is
clean, unwilted, and agreeable (*"Lo lavo io?"* she asks, afterward), but
this is to remain my only experience of the kind in the strictest sense of
the term. Professional help is unnecessary, for I am in the magical land
of Ginas, Zanzes, Magalollis, and AIDS has not yet unsexed the world.

Milan / January 1960
After a stay in Sanremo and Menton, where that childhood, prewar
snapshot with Father was restaged, I am back in Milan. Mother has
found me a pleasant if oldish hotel near the Scala, whose amiable manager provides me with a comfortable long-term room. The resonant bass
next door turns out to be that of Nikolai Ghiaurov, here to make his
Scala debut as Varlaam in *Boris*. We shall become good friends and, with
his charming wife Zlatina, he will even give me a few lessons. He will
become one of the great bassos of the century.

I shall learn eventually that an entire floor of the hotel is reserved for collective orgies with exotic call girls. The friendly manager will pursue me with proposed *partouzes* even after I move to my own apartment, and it will take patience to convince him that I can think of few things less appealing than a member of my own sex sweatily toiling away at intercourse nearby.

The apartment search will, however, yield a bonus: a chance encounter with a quite special girl. All my adolescent reveries will suddenly become reality, for she represents an ideal synthesis of beauty, sensuality, and kindness. It is *una questione di pelle*—a question of skin—but with the integument including, by extension, her almond eyes, her long blond hair, her convex lips, her special lithe compactness, her innate ability to project sexuality through the most elementary movement or the simplest attire. We shall part, over the years, to meet again, and each meeting will be made exciting by its newness (I doubt, for now, if I am cut out for the routine of continuous cohabitation). She will be one of a series of such supremely sensuous Mediterranean girls, but will remain the best. The relationship, enhanced by its cadence, will endure for a long time.

My new Milan apartment, in a central cul-de-sac, will also be the scene of something I shall not be very proud of. A self-styled publicity agent who has made himself extraordinarily useful in other fields will propose the following scheme: a "Lolita" contest (even though Stanley Kubrick has long since selected Sue Lyon for the forthcoming film) with national newsreel coverage, a jury of Scala singers and other acquaintances, and a predetermined winner. I shall watch as a procession of decidedly postpubescent would-be nymphets, some with provincial mothers in tow, invades my digs. My father, who has pointedly kept out of the casting process, will happen upon a magazine photograph of the bevy of "finalists" surrounding me on my oversized, satin-covered bed, and will cable with justified indignation: "STOP LOLITA PUBLICITY IMMEDIATELY."

Reggio Emilia / April 1961

I have sung in a few provincial concerts and made my first professional recording: madrigals by Gesualdo di Venosa, sung *a cappella* with five other solists. The disk will win a major prize, but the impression that will remain most vivid in my mind is an incidental one. We recorded in a hall of Milan's Institute for the Blind because of its excellent acoustics. The institute's students played soccer during their evening exercise period, accompanied by the eerie clinking of a special ball. I once opened a door, and realized they were playing in a pitch-black gymnasium.

Now, by a fluke, I have won first prize among the basses at the Reggio Emilia International Opera Competition. The winning tenor is named Pavarotti. The reward is a debut in *La Bohème* in this most demanding of venues, where opera is as much an everyday passion as soccer, and where real tomatoes are still thrown. As opening night approaches, I feel increasingly unprepared and uneasy. I shall have a private recording made of Acts One, Two, and Four, in which the bass Colline appears. And that recording, joined by a third act of unknown provenance, will be issued commercially by an Italian firm twenty years later to the day (i.e., upon expiration of possible copyright claims under Italian law). I shall experience a familiar queasiness—the horrid insecurity of that evening in 1961—when I put it on my turntable, and shall realize with retrospective relief how narrow the line between success and disaster had been on that distant evening. I shall also be touched to recall that the small role of the toy vendor Parpignol was sung by Pavarotti's father.

Lugano / April 1964
It is white with a blue stripe—American racing colors. It has been custom-tailored, and is the only one of its species with bubbles in the roof to accommodate my height. This time it is full-scale, my first true racing car. In order to facilitate certain formalities, I am taking delivery at the Alfa Romeo garage near Lugano. This is the culmination of two dozen or so automobiles of gradually improving age and quality, and the fulfillment of a need I suddenly understood when I got behind the wooden wheel of the first of my MGs—a technically antiquated vehicle, but possessed of a nimbleness unknown in normal American cars of the day. I have had my first races in the Triumph, kit-modified by mail order from England. I am discouraged with my singing, for I know I can do better, yet cannot find anyone to show me how. This is the right time for the racing adventure. I shall, for the next two years, travel with Alfa TZ and brilliant Italian mechanic in tow. I am a bad tourist, and only the prospect of an exciting purpose—be it singing, climbing, or racing— will move me to visit fascinating corners of Europe, with names like Castell'Arquato or Gaisberg, that I might never have seen otherwise. And I shall meet special people—artisans who take old-world pride in their work with metal; true sportsmen of presponsorship times who live for the next race and pass the intervening week studying every meter of the racecourse and having the latest innovations installed in their ma-

chines; charming villagers like the old female caretaker of a remote castle who will suddenly appear with flowers for my Brazilian traveling companion. I shall compete alongside machines bearing names destined to grow "exotic" with time—Ferrari GTO, Porsche 904, Ford GT-40—and accumulate my modest treasure trove of trophies. I shall fly over the embankment at Monza because I refuse to back off for the Parabolica Curve before Deserti, who will be killed on this track during his tryout for the Ferrari team a few months later. Bandini, orphan garage errand boy grown into official Ferrari driver, will tell me before the start of a 1,000-kilometer race that his love of racing has been stifled by the professional pressure, and, not long after, will burn to death on the Monte Carlo Grand Prix course because the organizers refuse to stop the race so that he may be extracted from his wrecked car.

Monza / July 17, 1965

I shall not move to Monza until fall, but I already have friends here. I have spent the night with them after last-minute testing at the Autodromo. I have parked my race car on its trailer in their front yard, since I must leave early tomorrow for a hillclimb in Trieste. They will not unlock the gate. They are a famous tenor and his wife, who insist that I must forget about racing and get back to singing, under their guidance. I shall persuade them to release my car, and shall come back with my trophy, but it will be my last serious auto race.

Sanremo / August 1967

Some dreams should remain dreams; others are best if they unexpectedly come true. While studying voice somewhat haphazardly in New York in the fifties, I used to lull myself to sleep with a reverie: the thought of performing the Death of Boris before a large, cheering audience. For a time that dream evaporated into would-be land, and was no longer evoked to stage a blissful bedtime. Last night, with full chorus and orchestra, I finally sang the Death of Boris in a full, enthusiastic amphitheater.

My second great lyric dream has existed ever since the summer of 1954, when I shared with my parents an adobe house in Taos they had rented from a pair of opera-loving gentlemen. Its painful quaintness was amply compensated by two unexpected extras: a WW II Jeep in which I chauffered Father on lepidopterological hunts, and the first recording I had ever heard of Verdi's *Requiem*. That would become my favorite piece of music. The bass on those early LPs, Augusto Beuf, would be one of my first teachers in Milan. My dream of actually singing the *Requiem* will come true in Duluth in 1975.

Varese / November 1966

I am doing the final scenes of my first and only film. It is not very good, although it will run on late-night TV well into the eighties. Its chief claim to fame is a starlet who once worked with Fellini. Everyone is a villain, and I am the chief villain, a dashing British gangster with a bum leg and a switchblade cane. It is fun, and I do pretty well, but spring clothing is madness when snow must be blowtorched off the lawns of the palatial old villa that is our set. I am soon to leave for Tulsa and Hartford for my first serious U.S. performances. I shall arrive in Oklahoma with an incipient sore throat, and, on opening night, watch myself being optimistically interviewed on television during the previous evening's dress rehearsal, when I already knew I would have to cancel. My U.S. debut will be postponed until next year.

Hartford / December 16, 1967

Last night I had the joy of singing a major part with a fully professional American opera company. I have made my U.S. debut as Friar Lawrence in Gounod's *Roméo et Juliette*. My principal colleagues were Anna Moffo, who had been one of the judges in the misbegotten Lolita contest in Milan, and Franco Corelli, a superb tenor whose fragile nerves will put an untimely end to his career. I feel that I am finally on the first rung of the operatic ladder. In future seasons I shall have the honor of performing with many of the great artists of my time in North and South America and in Europe. I shall collect a repertoire of true anecdotes with which to lace my interviews. I have already fallen into the prompter's booth, flustered by the formidable Molinari-Pradelli during a rehearsal for my Reggio Emilia debut in 1961. I shall risk serious injury when, in the Banquet Scene of a Puerto Rico *Don Giovanni*, an absent-minded stagehand leans against a buzzer causing a trapdoor to open prematurely as I, the Commendatore, solemnly back over it, to be saved in extremis by the quick-witted, much regretted, Fernando Corena. No one will believe a Milan newspaper's report, on the eve of my departure to sing *Rigoletto* and *Trovatore* in Barcelona, that a briefcase, containing the scores of those operas, has been stolen from my car near Piazza Duomo, and recovered, so help me God, by an opera lover named Trovatore, which means both "troubador" and "finder."

Lausanne / July 2, 1977
The worst news comes on idyllic, sun-drenched days, and cheerful summer is a more poignant setting for a funeral than the stereotyped chill drizzle of so many books and films.

I have returned from Munich in time to be with Father when he dies. He expires with a triple moan of descending pitch, just like Boris Christoff on his *Boris* recording. The echo is so strong that I imagine for an instant that it is indeed all staged, that he will soon speak again. He has had time to tell me, one sunny day on a Swiss mountain, that his creative process was simple: writing was like developing an exposed film stored in one's mind. And he was happy, for almost all the film had been developed. I have not had time to tell him that I have learned to edit my own dreams while dreaming them. Is this perhaps but a nightmare that I can rewrite?

Father will leave me an unusual legacy, the best I can imagine. It is the legacy of inspiration. The first thing I shall ever write that pleases me will be a memoir about him for a British volume. My best translations are yet to come: the posthumously published *Enchanter*, and his French article on Pushkin. And my best lectures about Father and about working with him will be given in future years, at Cornell, Harvard, and the University of Geneva.

The Gulf Stream, East of Miami / June 1980
I have gambled in order to stay in the lead, and narrowly missed a traversing freighter's rampartlike bow as, with my two teammates, I pound over the waves on the outbound leg to Bimini. My hobby of choice now is racing a thirty-four-foot, twelve-hundred-horsepower offshore powerboat. The passion evolved gradually, beginning with my first boat, a Molinari tunnel-hull outboard on Lake Como; on three lakes and then the Adriatic with a fast ski boat before it was stolen one night, lock, stock, and trailer; then during forays from Sanremo to race my twenty-five-foot Fletcher between Naples and points south. The passion is now full-fledged. I have acquired a base in Palm Beach, and my Coyote prototype lives at its maker's just north of Miami. It travels to distant race sites such as New Jersey and Detroit on a large trailer pulled by a crew-cab truck called a "doolie" for its dual rear wheels. I have a throttleman, a navigator, and a full-time mechanic. Today I am running in the Bacardi Cup, with the team airplane taking pictures overhead. The final picture will be that of dejected arm-waving, for we shall break down short of Bimini. I shall have a long stay on the island, since the

flying boat that is to bring out spare parts will be commandeered by a deranged chap who, atavistically perhaps, wants passage to an African diamond mine. He will eventually be persuaded that the airplane's range is but a few hundred miles and that it has no toilet and no air conditioning, and the parts for my engines will finally come.

Early Fall / 1980

I have been happy with only a few of my performances—those blessed occasions when the complex physical and psychological variables allow the sensual tingle of voice production to blend with the artistic thrill of drama. All the while I have searched far and wide for the "right" teacher so I can make further progress. I am at last on the verge of a true, full-time career, my voice mature, my technique pretty secure, and some twenty serious engagements for the season, but everything is about to come to a skidding, flaming halt.

Chexbres, Autoroute *between Montreux and Lausanne / 1045 hours, September 26, 1980*

Last night I returned from Paris where I sang, for French Radio, in the first European performance of Barber's *Antony and Cleopatra*. My Ferrari was at the Lausanne dealer's for a periodic checkup, and my mechanic brought it to the Geneva airport to meet my plane. I am staying with Mother at the Montreux Palace. It was late, I was tired, and for once I decided to leave the car outside in the hotel courtyard. I am on my way to the dentist in Lausanne, a fifteen-minute drive. There was an odd electrical malfunction this morning and, for the first time, I had to call a nearby mechanic to help start the car.

I have just lost directional control, and am skidding toward the center guardrail. The impact is oblique, the front hood, beneath which there is only a spare tire and a battery, pops open, and a small tongue of flame leaps out. The car spins and travels backward. The steering response that would have allowed me to induce a counterspin is gone. I turn off the ignition, tug at my seat belt, and travel backward for an infinitely long time. The only sensations I perceive are a strange calm, and curiosity as to what will happen next. At last the car slams sideways into the opposite, outside guardrail and grinds to a halt. I disengage my belt. The door on my side is jammed against the steel railing; the right door cannot be opened either. I notice orange flames blowing back with surprising violence from the slightly open front-hinged hood. I ponder my options, and begin working with a kind of desperate determination on the top part of the driver's door; finally it yields sufficiently for me to squeeze through and over the guardrail. I notice that the nylon T-shirt inscribed "Bimini" that I have worn this Indian-summer day is burning. To put out the fire I somersault down an embankment just beyond the guardrail. Several good Samaritans soon gather, and one nurselike woman restrains me from climbing back up to extinguish the fire and retrieve a briefcase with every essential document I own. I cannot do so anyway, since my legs will not sustain me. As I am loaded into an ambulance I warn the attendant to be careful, for my neck feels oddly disconnected after my tumble. As if in a dream, I hear the driver ask, "Where to, sir?" I propose Montreux. He recovers from what is apparently a shocking sight even for him, and suggests that the Burn Unit at the Lausanne Hospital might be more suitable.

My neck is, in fact, fractured at the odontoid, and I shall learn later that one uncautious move would have instantly paralyzed my diaphragm. But only now do I begin to realize what else has happened. It was just shock that made jelly of my legs, but the third-degree burns that cover 40 percent of my body will keep me in the greenhouse-like, totally sterile burn center for three months, and nearly a year will pass before I am sufficiently repaired and re-educated to go home. Every other day, at first, I shall be dipped by a cranelike device with webbing into a potassium-permanganate bath, and two energetic nurses will scrape off the burnt flesh with washcloths. On the twelfth day, for a short time, I shall be clinically dead. I shall be deliciously enticed by a bright light at the far end of the classic tunnel, but restrain myself at the last instant when I think of those who care for me and of important things I must still do. I shall have six major operations, including microsurgery on my left hand, which, originally, was to be amputated. I shall be surrounded by the screams of others, dreadfully burned by accident or by intent, and some of them will die. I shall imagine and indelibly record in my mind a surreal new way to stage the last act of *Don Giovanni*. I shall have a curious, multiple, trancelike dream in which a pretty, real-life Canadian nurse will appear in different guises—geisha, squalid trailer resident—and turn out, at each dénouement, to be one and the same girl.

Poor Mother, whom I called as soon as I was installed in a Hovercraft-like bed to say I would not make it home for lunch because of a small mishap, will see me only through a window and speak to me only by intercom for those first months of isolation. I shall keep the light off. She will be shocked to see how I look when she is allowed near me the day I move to the rehabilitation hospital. Like a child, I shall gradually be taught the most elementary motions. Soon I shall be sneaking from my room at night to climb stairs (first night three, second night four), then out to jog (which is strictly forbidden because there are doubts about the mending of my neck). My best therapist will be an athletic Swiss girl who, after a short time, will improvise a ping-pong table. Her competitive instinct will quickly overcome any therapeutic indulgence, but I shall still beat her first time out, and that will be an important victory in a struggle whose outcome I shall never question. I shall have a hired car sent as soon as possible and drive, in the evenings, to the therapist's table-tennis club to play with the local aces.

I shall emerge from the hospital with new priorities, having decided that I can make my best contribution by dedicating myself to writing, both my father's and my own. Against all predictions, my physical condition will eventually be better than before the accident, and I shall very soon resume tennis, climbing, and skiing. I shall in fact devote most of my time to literary pursuits, but shall gladly accept certain special singing engagements that come my way, such as a Turkish festival or Dvořák's splendid *Requiem* for Israel State Radio. The scars on my arms, neck, and back will heal quickly. I shall learn that my car was sabotaged. I shall acquire, and sometimes race, a faster Ferrari of a slightly darker blue.

Büyükada, Turkey / August 1986
I have been invited by the Turkish government to give a recital in a festival on this small island in the Sea of Marmora. After a rocky start (policeman who was to meet me at the airport asleep in a back room; attempts to reach people I don't know, in an unfamiliar language, over cranky pay phones voraciously consuming Turkish tokens; finally a two-car caravan to a dock on the Asian side of the Bosporus and the island mayor's launch from there), I am comfortably installed in a nearly completed building, with meals at the Parliamentary Beach Club next door, and a two-horse carriage to transport me through the charming, carless landscape.

A surprisingly well-read Nabokov translator has tracked me down and invited me to spend a day in Istanbul. He will be waiting on the quay like a secret agent, with a copy of *Sebastian Knight* to signal his identity.

After a five-day struggle, I have picked up barely enough Turkish to decipher, in a local paper, the news that Nabokov has suddenly been declared *persona grata*, and is being published in Russia. A handful of brilliant scholars will gradually surface amid the apparatchiks of the Soviet literary establishment, and will strive to safeguard the integrity of Father's texts. No talk, of course, of royalties, but publishers of all kinds—first a chess journal, then mainly obscure provincial periodicals and minor Party organs with names like *The Young Leninist*, and finally the big literary guns—will hasten to produce all the Nabokov they can before (*a*) they run out of paper, which is high on the list of endangered commodities, or (*b*) the window of *glasnost* is slammed shut. I shall learn of a projected bowdlerization of *Lolita*. Before launching an international appeal, I shall cable *Inostrannaya literatura* for verification. To my astonishment, they will answer by return cable that, if they print *Lolita*, they "will use Nabokov's translation, thank you."

Cambridge / December 1986
I have returned to Cambridge for the first time since my departure for the Army in 1957, to read from and comment upon *The Enchanter*. My arrival in Harvard Square evoked in me a combination of what must have been felt by Pnin, when the wrong train he had boarded to travel to a teaching engagement reached its actual destination, and by another protagonist of Father's, who enters a provincial French museum to emerge in a Russia with a new orthography and a frightening regime.

Cambridge appears to have changed more than a little, but a morning amble has reassured me that the Yard and Lowell House have retained their timeless tranquillity, and that there are still public conveyances named "Huron" whose orange ancestors, many years before I entered Harvard, would carry me toward our Craigie Circle apartment. I also note that the fluorescent illumination of Lamont Library's cubicles, where I have spent many hours, hums on as evenly as time itself. I have had an additional satisfaction, a kind of regression to my student days: a courteous chap of thirty-eight or so, letting me pass first through a door, said "There you are, young man." I do, after all, belong to the class of '55. The evening gives me such pleasure that I resent the walleye of time. A miniskirted girl whom I fleetingly admired during my afternoon walk turns up at the reading to interview me for a student paper. I sup at the Faculty Club with several fine scholars, including an entomologist who, in 1988, will organize a Nabokov exhibition at the Museum of Comparative Zoology, where Father once peered into "the wondrous crystalline world of the microscope."

The Enchanter is doing well, and would be doing even better were it not for the publisher's parsimonious blundering. Most of the critics write with enthusiasm. One reviewer is complimentary in my regard to the point of skepticism, for he suggests I have invented both *The Enchanter* itself and the reality of my capsule biography. I have never given it much thought, but now wonder if some things about my life might not indeed seem implausible to a stranger.

Jerusalem / January 1987

Some years ago my parents and I were invited by Mayor Teddy Kollek to visit at an artists' colony here, but Father's illness made that trip impossible. Now I am finally in Israel, to sing with Aronovitch, the most brilliantly original conductor I have ever encountered, in the Dvořák *Requiem*. He is so exacting in preparing his very personal interpretation that only during the microphone tests, on the morning of the performance, do we rehearse the final sections of the difficult 225-page score. It is to be a nationwide live broadcast, in front of an audience of three thousand. During this hurried run-through of the previously untested music I twice botch an important solo phrase. As that passage approaches—inexorably—in the performance, I know I shall need more courage and concentration than on the most precarious mountain pitch. When it has gone by without problems I have an instant for reflection, and feel sure it is the discipline learned in many domains that has carried me through. Then I take such a deep breath of relief that the diaphragm button pops off my dress shirt. I seize it in midair like a mosquito. No one is the wiser about this minor accident, or about the torment that preceded it.

The following night I am invited to a party with some of Jerusalem's best talents. I am told, among many interesting things, that if I chose to go to Russia, I would doubtless be received as if I were the son of Pushkin.

Milan / October 1987

I am back in my old haunts, and happy that I have held onto my tiny Monza penthouse with its immense roof garden. My trees blend with those of the vast park beyond. From the Autodromo in its depths comes the unmistakable howl of a Formula One motor. The pitch rises with spine-tingling speed, only to be plucked down again by each gear change, and there is an odd visual association: telegraph wires watched from the speeding trains of childhood, their rhythmic rise punctuated by periodic poles. It is comforting to know that, in a few days, there will be a Ferrari gathering, and I can run a few quick laps. But I am here principally for two other, happily concurrent, reasons: I shall sing the Death of Boris and other compositions to commemorate the anniversary of Pushkin's death, and, shortly thereafter, present my Italian translation of *The Enchanter*.

Father visualized the Hegelian triad as a spiral. If singing is the thesis, and literary work the antithesis, then things have come full spire and this is the perfect synthesis.

V. S. NAIPAUL

◆ ──────────────────────────── ◆

Congo River Journal

On the Congo steamer *Major Vangu*, Kisangani-Kinshasa.

When I bought my ticket the ticket-seller worked out the fares and supplements on his adding machine, repeatedly, as though on one occasion he might catch the machine out in a wrong answer.

The steamer crowd had begun to arrive since Wednesday for the Thursday steamer, sitting outside the dock and the Onatra office with their bundles and hens—and even a black goat. Their many crates. On Thursday afternoon we saw the steamer arrive, a great flat-iron affair with people crowded between, as it seemed, caged low decks; then a gap; and a white superstructure at the stern. It was in that superstructure, I hoped, that the *cabine de luxe* was. The hotel boy (really a small old man) went with my luggage (a suitcase, a small condensed-milk box with supplies I had bought for the journey). The crowd was massed at the gate and it wasn't easy to penetrate. Someone else attached himself to us and eventually we went to another gate, guarded like the first by soldiers. They told us that embarkation time was 9:30. I said I had been told it was 9:00. The smell was indescribable: Africans, salt fish, chickens. Some higher rank was appealed to; he said I would have to wait like everybody else; everybody here says no the first time. Eventually I was let through the gate, as a favour; and as a further favour my luggage was allowed in. The hotel boy, faced with the soldiers, had said that his duties were over; I had paid him off. The idler who had attached himself to us now took charge of my suitcase and we walked down the dock to the gangway.

The *cabine de luxe* made a good impression at first. It was very much better than I had expected. It made a bigger impression on the boy with the luggage, who asked for 3 zaires, $6. He settled ungraciously for $3. Then the cabin which had made such a good impression began to reveal its terrors: an unmade bed, a dirty floor, filthy bathroom with a stained washbasin. The cistern of the lavatory never ceased to fill: the stupid boy to whom I pointed this out said, as though speaking of an irrevocable fact of life, *"C'est pas bon."* The air-conditioning didn't work. It was very hot. Palaver; shouting; a growing despair on my part. But somehow the *mécanicien* arrived and the room was cleaned out. (After many false starts and false approaches: where no one wears a uniform it is hard to distinguish passenger from crew, idler from officer.)

The maître, a little unsteady, eyes a little beer-glazed, but anxious to display his authority, came to the cabin and was courteous, asking what I wanted. He said he didn't really belong to the steamer. He knew grander things; he knew aeroplanes and European ships. He suggested a menu of soup, *oeufs à la Russe, poisson, pommes nature* or *frites*. I asked about the coffee; he said he would make mine apart from the rest.

At 11:00 we began to leave. In the distance, clearly visible from the dock, were the Stanley Falls, impeding navigation further up the great river. How grand the Hotel des Chutes looked, as perhaps it had been grand in the old days of "Stan." All the time dug-outs, some with outboard motors, were crossing and recrossing the river, passengers sitting sharp and distinct on the thwarts, showing up beautifully and a little comically in silhouette against the river.

The steamer, moving off, showed things in the city I hadn't seen: the Roman Catholic cathedral, and ruins on the bank. The green! Green grass spilling over the banks, the earth showing red. It was stormy. A storm light lit up the green; the dark sky, silver in patches, smudged with gray, made the green stand out. Then the wind made the water wrinkle, abolished the reflections of greenery, and the rain came. The Congolese beside me on the deck said, *"Il pleut déjà."* The rain was welcome to him.

The accommodation on the steamer is so arranged that the passengers who were waiting outside the Onatra office were hidden from view. To look down on them one has to peer through the dining room windows; and then a great covered area—a kind of travelling market, as it turned out, with WCs—blocks the further view, so one is hidden from *them*. But it is there that the life lies.

After lunch and a sleep I woke to the sight of boys swimming in the river, greeting the boat. Dug-outs were moored to the steamer and were being pulled along by it: there were sellers of cane chairs and stools, decorated mortars, neatly tied up bundles of cassava and manioc, basins of big pineapples. The price of a stool was half a zaire, 50 makuta, an armchair 120 makuta. I bought a pineapple for 20 makuta. A lady told me that her stool was half a zaire; I thought she was selling; she said with a laugh that she had just bought.

The river is so charted now. Black and white directional signs are nailed to trees, and the steamer swings from one side of the river to the other.

The time came for the dug-outs to push off and this was interesting to watch. So skilled the people. Though recently, as I heard, there had been an accident: which explains why, at night, the searchlights from the bridge, operated by someone who obviously delights in the drama of his job, sweep the river. Moths show white in the light; the smoke; and the hyacinthlike plants that root in this river (with pale lilac flowers) show white also.

The banks are alive. From unlikely places dug-outs pull out to join the steamer, the marketplace that travels. That first afternoon, when the dug-outs brought chairs and stools, I should have bought, but I didn't, not thinking of the furniture as temporary and disposable, as the Africans did.

Today the dug-outs bring fish and monkeys, some monkeys roasted in their skins, blackened and stiff, shapeless bundles. Others freshly killed, red and gray. They are tied up by their tails and easily carried about in this fashion: a holdall of dead monkeys, a portmanteau of dead monkeys. On the throbbing steel deck the monkeys can appear to be still alive; the wind ruffles their fur. The paws of the red monkeys, facing this way and that, suggest a deep contented sleep, their forepaws sometimes loosely held together, sometimes their heads bent forward, their forepaws stretched out before them. The big fish: they look like a kind of dogfish. I suppose this is what I will get for lunch today.

Sights: a shrivelled baby monkey, wet, kept as a kind of pet by a young man. One girl having her hair done. Another, her hair plastered flat, being deloused by another girl. Music. The WCs never cease flushing: the water runs off the steel floor continually. The stalls offer: razor blades, batteries, capsules of various sorts, soap, hypodermic syringes, vitamin B capsules and even thermometers. Cigarettes, pencils, copybooks. White grubs in baskets of dark earth covered with wet straw: obviously these grubs, an inch thick, like softer lobsters or crayfish, will only survive in damp conditions. The dug-outs are smaller today.

The dead trees of the forest, bare white trunks standing out against the green.

Monkeys always cause great excitement when the market dug-outs offer them for sale. The monkeys are cooked in this way: first held head down over a wood fire, so that the fur is burned off; then disembowelled; then roasted. Sometimes ready-roasted monkeys, black sculptural objects, are offered. (Monkey looks, when smoked, like smoked fish, which can also look like smoked snake.)

On the forward part of the ship I fall into conversation with a man in salmon-coloured pyjamas. He spoke very correctly and well. He works for Onatra, the steamer corporation, and had just been spending a month in Kisangani at the Zaire Palace hotel. He travels free, and if he didn't have a *nombreuse famille*, as he said, he would have been travelling first class. He told me there was no difference in price or flavour between gray monkey and red monkey; price depended on weight. A good monkey here on the river fetched about 3 zaires; the same monkey would fetch 6 zaires in Kinshasa. All the while, the man's *nombreuse famille* was in a little steel cabin with a curtained doorway; he was sitting just outside in his pyjamas watching the market scene; he seemed quite happy, part of the crowd.

Some Australian hippies, one of the tiresome groups travelling round the world seeing very little, asked to use the bathroom of my *cabine de luxe*. They were denied this facility. They thought Africans were inferior: it seemed a very stupid conclusion to come to. One wonders why they bother to travel.

The landscape slowly changes. The bamboo and the wet lushness of Kisangani gives way to palms; and now to low secondary bush, with ruined, bare, dead tree trunks. The water is muddier, the dug-outs are smaller. It was cool after the storm at Kisangani; the wind cool and moist. Today the river glows in a heat mist and the wind is warm and enervating. My taste for the food diminishes. My reaction to Simon, the cabin attendant, squat and barefooted and sweaty and stupid and dirty, becomes increasingly hostile.

But I tell myself this is no longer a Belgian steamer. This is an African steamer, serving the African people who live along the banks. (Though the Onatra man and someone else as well were anxious to assure me that the huts we saw on the banks every so often were not villages but temporary fishermen's settlements. The villages were bigger places, with *rues et avenues*.) The size of the country remains something hard to grasp. We have travelled perhaps 400 miles through unchanging scenery. I tell myself it is a privilege to be doing this, winding through a complex primitive world, witnessing, noting. The life is complex; the goods are complex (they have taken only those Belgian products that they need). The complexity of the life is surprising. And this morning, going out briefly to the bows—briefly because of the heat which quickly makes one sicken and feel faint—I saw many young people reading magazines. Another dimension.

The green of the river at Kisangani. It is the same green now, only the big trees are darker. This green is accented and given depth only by distance: then it turns blue and gray. Unchanging green, but there is nonetheless change: bamboos disappear, blasted tree trunks appear, palms sweep down low over the smooth water, brown branches brushing the water. A kind of savannah country behind: so many dead trees. (But no snags in the river.) Always, near the huts, little plantings of bananas. And all the time the dug-outs appear: carrying away beer, returning crates of the empties.

Banda in Malawi. Nyerere in Tanzania. How odd this situation, in which the most revealing thing is that every country produces only one man who is known. The leader, the leader. Nobody else exists.

I was wondering today whether Uganda, as I knew it in 1966, was more corrupt than this is. Makerere College at the heart of that particular corruption; the foreign publishing houses seeking African markets; the whole bogus European-managed cultural thing, creating a kind of bogus man, acting for the expatriate. Perhaps it is better as it has turned out here, this starting from scratch.

A small smoked crocodile today.

We stayed for some hours at the town of Mbandaka. A few Belgian colonial buildings line the river. Green corrugated-iron roof, red corrugated-iron roof; two-storey concrete buildings, with arches. How melancholy rusty corrugated-iron looks. And those iron barges in the Chantiers Onatra look as though they will never move again.

The teacher was telling me about the wonders of the Congo peace. It was marvellous, he said, to be able to go from his village to a small village north of the river and to spend five days there. I remarked on the absence of policemen in the streets of Kinshasa and Kisangani.

The Intercontinentals of Africa—the outposts of progress. In *Jeune Afrique* I see that there is one in Libreville in Gabon as well, and it is very busy, as busy as the Kinshasa Intercontinental.

More about the ambitious young. The young man who greeted me in the bows came up to the first-class deck last night. He carried a briefcase—I daresay all his valuable possessions are there—and he had his girlfriend. He said in English, "Good night." He is twenty-four. He is interested in psychology, with special reference to personnel relations in industry, I believe. He spoke English well. He said he suffered because his scholarship was small, 35 zaires a month. Some of his friends were lucky. People from Europe, well-wishers, sent them money. Reminds me of Uganda and the begging young in 1966.

The river—so green the banks, so whole-looking the vegetation at Kisangani. But then the river widens and becomes full of islands and the vegetation becomes battered, full of blasted trees, the first line of trees distinct against a background of tattered vegetation that blurs in the distance. Then the river widens more, and the land becomes more cut down and flat: grassland, bright green, with darker blobs of trees and far away the low blue wall of forest on the bank, beyond the flat islands on which, so often, there are little homesteads, thatched huts in yards scraped smooth because, as I learned from the English engineer this morning, there is a great fear of snakes and of soldier ants. So this is the great surprise of the Congo: the river does not move through primeval forest, as in the highlands of Guiana in South America, but it moves through flat, flat land, which is peopled and has known cultivation.

The river gets wider and wider, the islands more numerous, flatter, less covered with vegetation, becoming mere sandbanks, and the receding line of vegetation gets lower and lower. Enormous, like a sea, the river here, one day out of Mbandaka.

In heat and haze the swallows skim the water, migrants from the Scandinavian winter. The hawks pounce, fishing with their feet.

The air-conditioning in the *cabine de luxe* broke down this midday. The great heat was oddly exhilarating. The African word for the grubs they like to eat is *makio*. For the water hyacinth, *Kongo ya sika*, the new thing *(sika)* in the Congo. The plant appeared in 1956 at Kisangani, and the teacher told me that if the Belgians had not gone away in 1960 they would have got rid of it.

School history of the country, from the teacher. It begins in 1484 with Diego Cao discovering the mouth of the Zaire river; then it moves straight to the missionaries of the nineteenth century.

From the teacher: to travel first class in the Belgian days, an African had to have a *carte de mérite civique*, a certificate of civic merit.

The air-conditioner remains unmended. I decided in the end to go to the captain. I went up to the bridge and found him *occupé* and bad-tempered after last night's accident when some students were capsized in their dug-out. It was the first I knew of this accident: all that I saw at the time were the two passenger barges adrift when the steamer stopped suddenly. Searchlights: we lost three hours trying to lash the barges to the steamer again and looking for the boys, about whom we still know nothing.

A boy I met told me with some pride that he was from the Batatela tribe. They were slave-hunters for the Arabs.

And there is the man who said that his father remembered the cutting-off of hands. The father was born in 1900. I also heard more about the rebellion of Pierre Mulele in the eastern Congo in the early 1960s. "Mulele was against everything. He wanted to start from the beginning."

Everyone speaks with admiration of Mobutu. His cult is widespread.

They tell me that in the Belgian days the African passenger barges were towed at some distance.

Sunset, with clouds. Wipes of pale blue, ochre, streaks of gray. Rose and pink and smouldering flame. The wind whipped up the water and where the sunset lit up the water the colour was violet, below a violet sky. Away from that the colours ranged from pale blue to dark gray. The low islands with scattered trees—dark green silhouettes against the distant and now hilly bank. The land is smooth here (near Kinshasa), sculptured, with sharp edges, with pockets and patches of vegetation. The green, green grass against blue low hills. The violet sky. Fewer dug-outs here, where the river is like a sea. On the hilly bank, smooth, the patches of vegetation are darker, where soil has run down from the igneous rocks.

Arrival. The rust. The launch: white and gray, banged about, roughly painted, old paint. A general rundown air. The waiting crowd massed in the terminal; the colours of the ladies' clothes.

The passport of one of the foreigners was seized by the small fat man in blue as we came off the *bateau*. Then examined by the ugly, coarse-featured man in a flowered shirt. Then we were led into a cage, concrete blocks on one side, metal gates on two sides, metal bars on top. The beginning of the shake-down. The little man in brown pretended to be in a bad temper. He shouted to the American to take his knapsack off his desk. Empty at first, the office fills up with foreigners from the steamer. The man in brown strikes the desk in pretended rage. The man in the flowered shirt, eating a kebab, laughs. That laugh tells all: it is makuta time, time for the passing of money. The sense of nightmare, after these days and nights on the river. The paralysis of the Englishman, the silence of the Americans. The money passes outside. It is necessary to learn how to pass the money.

The nervousness, the sense of danger, comes later. The game need never have been called off. Where there is no law there is no illegality or legality. No logic.

JOYCE CAROL OATES

◆ ——————————————————— ◆

Selections from a Journal:
January 1985–January 1988

There is a common folk belief, I can't testify to its accuracy, that a tree's
height is matched by its depth; that is, the surface of the earth divides it
neatly and evenly . . . the many-branched trunk, a visible but seemingly
infinite little galaxy of limbs, stems, twigs, and leaves is matched by its root
system: an invisible twin galaxy of branches hidden in the earth. So too,
I've always thought, with us. With what is called the "social self" and
the "private self." The self "out there" (seen and known by others) and
the self "in here" (never seen and never known—at least by others). The
journal is the ideal place of refuge for the inner self because it constitutes
a counterworld: a world to balance the other.

Of course, writers and poets are always constructing counterworlds.
If not artful these worlds are art—"artificial." A sequential polygamy of
a kind. Sometimes zestful, sometimes desperate. Sometimes the small
bell-like voice of utter sanity. And sometimes—sanity's opposite. The basic
fact of the journal is that it is constructed out of language; it acquires, or
records, a voice. If the journal is not inevitably stories we tell ourselves,
it is propositions of a philosophical kind: What *is* this proposition I seem
to embody, in finite perishable flesh?

What is *this* proposition I seem to embody, in finite perishable flesh?

In 1971, when my husband and I were living in London, on Park
Lane just opposite Hyde Park Corner, I began a journal with the self-
admonition: to tell only the truth; and never to revise. This journal is
hundreds of pages long by now (the "now" of this writing being December
31, 1987) and most of its pages, merely glimpsed into, cast a chill of
mortality upward . . . I feel so little kinship with the "I" of those years.
The meticulous recording of events, including conversations with men and
women of enormous charm, merit, and complexity, the frequently bulldog-
gish self-analyses, self-assessments, self-dissections . . . all so remote, so
somehow melancholy and curious. *I have written, therefore I must have
existed.* But the proof lacks conviction.

So preparing this selection has been no easy task. Much has to be
censored, yet much (more) isn't worth censoring. The instinct is to toss it

all away, and forget. But once gone this personal history will be forever gone—there is that somber practicality to keep in mind. If I am delighted to read others' journals why not my own? If I am rarely bored or impatient with others' journals why with my own? Is it the novelist's habit to value others (ah, any others!) more than she values herself? Or is this itself merely a novelist's subterfuge?

Selecting passages from a journal that covers so many years means either gallumphing through the years in vertiginous giant steps or concentrating upon one period. The latter seemed more sensible, the results possibly more readable. Contemplating the journal as an ongoing phenomenon I saw myself on an upper storey of a corkscrew staircase, a staircase of nightmare, looking over the bannister at a ghostly figure making its way upward in my wake—"Is that me? But who *is* it?" The task was forcibly accomplished just past the winter solstice (shortest day/longest night) at the very end of the year, as day waned to New Year's Eve, most desperately hopeful of all human celebrations.

*J*anuary 4, 1985

. . . . Very much out of contact w/ this journal; w/ caring enough to write in it. A sort of revulsion re. the ego: who cares? So much data! so many hours, minutes! Yet life has been remarkably varied, rich, lively, fun . . . last night at Ed & George's for instance talking & laughing until midnight w/ the Hales (Sir John Hale & Lady Sheila Hale: bright, well brilliant, Sheila is a NY'r though now very British having lived twenty years in England, John is visiting at the Institute this year, a Renaissance historian), I felt sparked up one might say, funny, witty, the very reverse of a sort of leaden feeling I've had re. this novel—though not recently, recently things have gone smoothly, excitingly. . . . AND ALL THIS IS SO FAMILIAR.

. . . . The problem lies in the very nature of the journal. If I tell the truth the truth *is* likely to be petty. If not demoralizing, comical in all the wrong places, crushing in its dullness. If I don't tell the truth I lose all interest in writing. Fiction isn't a reflex action but a highly conscious craft, discipline, whatever, it's my entire life, more serious perhaps than my (external) life, I won't waste time on a journal at the expense of that, "And so on, and so forth," she said not knowing why she was angry.

. . . . (Sometimes I think: it's an error trying to write a novel about suicide. I'll regret it. I will. Then I think: Oh no I won't—*I'm in charge.*)

. . . . The luxury of revising Part I, trying to cut it back. Now I am on p. 88 for the second time. Enid *is* me but I'm not Enid, not quite. (Oh yes the sense that having been born in this world, *this* pain-filled world, was some sort of error that only diversion—activity, work, friendship, love—can disguise. But no more of that! no more.) Where Enid differs significantly from me: she isn't going to be a writer; she *is* going to have a disastrous love affair at an early age.

. . . . Strange, sad letter from G. I sat reading & rereading it thinking how to reply. And my reply isn't adequate. I hear "my" voice going all chatty & ebullient & sensible whereas I am in G.'s position I suppose— though not so distressed about not knowing "answers." G. is a naturally religious person, she wants to believe, has an instinct to believe, whereas to me (as to Enid) it's all implausible & faintly comic. I *don't* have the slightest instinct to believe in abstract Platonic unlikely things.

. . . . Does disliking or distrusting a journal mean I dislike/distrust myself: I don't know. Don't think so. Life moves too rapidly now, is filled w/ too much excitement & pleasure, to be typed out in this form. I think that's it. Yet as it slips away I feel a distinct regret, a fear of loss, for I'll forget everything that isn't somehow recorded. & there is so much of sheer simple happiness these days/domestically I mean/ & w/ friends—I wish I might preserve forever. The very antithesis it occurs to me of Enid's life.

May 29, 1985
. . . . These lovely days: & my feeling that even "failure" doesn't matter since so much has fallen into place lately and all the anguish/dread/ strain/anxiety re. *The Green Island** seems to have been worth it. I think. Now that I am nearing the conclusion and can breathe again. Now that I can look forward to the revisions for much of the summer.

. . . . ("Her curious gift to her self: a hard-won 'early' draft of a knotty work to be untangled.")

. . . . Is this the prime of (the writer's) life!

. . . . Reading through Peter Manso's pseudobiography of Norman Mailer, a wearying task that provokes skimming, a sort of headachey

Original title of You Must Remember This.

imagining of that "other" life—extroverted, engagingly self-centered, cheerily egotistic, brawling, silly, generous, spacious, daring, reckless, willing-to-take-on-all-contenders, and so forth; the experience of reading the book is like hunting through the trash for something you've lost, an earring let's say, demoralized by the hunt but certain it's worth it. Mailer in my experience has been only warm, gracious, funny, unpretentious, interesting; but I didn't know him in the prime of his raw manhood and during his years of drinking and drug-taking—obviously "another" Mailer, less congenial to my taste. (At the American Academy we were talking of boxing; I think Norman's "The Fight" is extremely good; he recounted in amazing detail the first round of the Ali/Foreman fight—the first round!—while observers listened puzzled or bemused or frankly incredulous—why are Norman Mailer and Joyce Carol Oates talking about Ali/Foreman?—but I was quite fascinated. I don't think Norman sees in boxing precisely what I see, obviously he's a man, how could he "see" through a woman's eyes, but I rather think (am I being too self-assured?) that I can "see" through a man's eyes—my identification with men as men is an easy, even comfortable one, since obviously I am not a man, nor would I (I think) like to be one.)

. . . . (I'd like to eat Mailer's heart—is that it!)

. . . . Having just finished a difficult chapter of *The Green Island* (Felix's rapid decline after Enid's abortion: ending w/ his being beaten savagely); having finished two weeks ago the final—final!—revisions of *Marya;* having just had a productive conversation w/ my editor (Don Erickson) at the *New York Times Magazine* re. the essay "Boxing: The Tragic Sport"; having learned that my parents will come visit for a week in mid-June; having had a number of other professional bits of good news lately (being chosen for the *Best American Short Stories 1985*, a very long rather grim & weighty story at *Kenyon Review*—"Little Wife"—and "Testimony" at *Southern Review* of all places (!)—and, yes, the *N.Y. Times Book Review* will publish "Beginnings" of which I'm so fond sometime soon)—I am feeling heartened, cheerful, happy, well in motion as I need to be & love to be—the sense of things getting accomplished to some purpose.

June 29, 1985
. . . . Taking down my map of Port Oriskany; disposing of my time charts; mailing out the manuscript of *The Green Island* one day and the manuscript of *Raven's Wing* the next; now things are oddly cleared away

and my "study" isn't a special place any longer but just a room I suppose . . . these usual postnovel feelings. Lying not hurt or unhappy but perhaps stunned, numbed, on the beach, trying to recollect how I got here.

. . . . The subterfuge of blankness. Pretense. Temptation.

. . . . Each novel an exorcism. Layer upon layer. In Enid and Felix however—did I strike bottom? Words enhance, romanticize. An anthropologist's chilly definition of love: "the over-estimation of the individual."

. . . . (Pursue the thought, however elusive!—"words romanticize." The very act of writing on any subject is a romantic act, and results in the "romanticization"/"over-estimation" of that subject. For one thing, all other subjects are bluntly excluded. To write of boxing, for instance, is to romanticize it, however neutral one wishes to be.)

. . . . Industry that came to very little. So many book reviews—review-essays—elaborately tricked out with quotes, dates, facts, evidence. But when I consider bringing together a collection of essays these reviews don't interest me at all. I scarcely want to reread them—don't in fact reread them. Who cares? The authors of the reviews probably care; I don't. Nor can I even remember why I ever did.

. . . . The problem being, expenditure of energy, enthusiasm, time, hope. Poured into a thimble! My instinct is simply to begin again, to assemble new people, imagine a new setting (now lovely gritty Port Oriskany is gone forever—but can it be gone!!!). (God I feel like Felix Stevick driving up along Stubb Blvd. looking at the city, the waterfront, he loves—he's going to miss it, he thinks, he's missing it already, and he's still alive.) (Meaning: JCO will miss it, is already missing it, though "Felix Stevick" is still alive as a fictitious character.) (These "fictitious characters"! How much life *they* possess, in contradistinction to the rest of us.)

. . . . Patches of hot blazing sunshine. Storm clouds too. "Showers likely." I'm so wired up, I can't resist the impulse to go outside; run a mile or so; see what awaits *(what can possibly await)* when I return.

June 30, 1985

. . . . Rereading Thoreau, re-experiencing old memories, feelings. How beautiful his language, how convincing while one reads. But afterward . . . ? I have the sense that Thoreau lived his physical temporal life during the day, then turned himself inside out to write in his journal, and in his "formal" work, creating a personality as one might create with zest and excitement a fictional character. To this fictional character he gave the name "Henry David Thoreau." And why not?

. . . . (Still, it isn't true that the "social" self is a fiction, surely not a lie. I *am* as much in company as I *am* alone. If the company is congenial, lively, funny, provocative—like last night's: our dinner party here—I am as much drawn out of myself and as likely to surprise myself with things I say as during these solitary mind-probing mind-exhausting hours. One without the other is in fact unthinkable. One without the other—an aborted life.)

. . . . Knocked down by an "invisible" punch, the young boxer's instinct is to stay down. His trainer must then train him to overcome his instinct by way of his will—or another's will.

. . . . (If I am knocked down by a blow out of the invisible, how then do I anticipate the next blow out of the invisible.)

. . . . The writer's superiority: she knows that her stories are inventions, attempts to express some sort of truth obliquely, while other people, non-writers, imagine their stories (their tales of themselves) are true.

. . . . Not even the most devastating truth can be *told;* it must be *evoked.*

. . . . ("You have robbed me of my story," the inarticulate might claim. Again & again. Because Kafka's "The Metamorphosis" is the story of so many lives, usurped by the artist.)

. . . . (Sometimes I think: *I* am usurping my own life. Anticipating the future. Living through emotions beforehand which, when I finally experience them, will arouse only a sense of déjà vu. Or second-hand—they've belonged to my fictional characters.)

. . . . (Bemused by accusations in the *N.Y. Times* re. certain writers—I was not named—who "fail" to explore the moral, social, political aspects of contemporary American life. So what? Who says? Why? By what authority? Writers write what they want to write. It isn't our task to provide the world with a meaning the world has never had—that belongs to propaganda.)

. . . . (The writing I like to attempt does deal with the connections between the private and public life; but then it's my temperament, my inclination. I don't make my practice a principle for others.)

. . . . Writing in defense of one's powerlessness; also, in defense of loneliness.

. . . . In fiction the writer lays herself bare, memories, insights, emotions, impulses, all to what purpose: to construct a fictitious self in which to live. Then she forgets what is fiction, what not. And no one else knows either—naturally. So she must consider that the "life" is mainly fragments of a personal history of some pragmatic literary use. What is not "literary" is discarded as of no worth. (Yes: but to be retrieved at unanticipated moments. "The punch flying out of invisibility.")

. . . . (Once I saw a fight. I think I saw a fight. Or was it narrated to me afterward; or did I overhear its narration, afterward. The men, shirtless, drunk, swinging at each other, furious, clumsy, was there blood on someone's face?—and my father trying to hold one man back? Or was my father one of the men who were fighting. A tavern, the canal (?), summer, dusk, waiting in the car reading comic books (?)—but no I can't remember. I would have to invent in order to remember and then, having invented a "world" to encompass this stray little thread of a memory, I would be totally incapable of knowing what was fiction, what "real." I must put my faith in fiction as the only honest activity of which I'm capable.)

. . . . Team sports/solitary sports. How I loved the former—in high school in particular; have never felt comfortable with the latter. (And no longer play tennis.) I don't like games either. Competition to no purpose. Imagination to no purpose. A Rolls-Royce to drive to the corner store.

. . . . Boxing as the very emblem of madness. That must be what fascinates—the spectacle of it. An image of mankind's collective insanity small enough to be contemplated.

. . . . I want to work with different material, now that I've exorcized certain elements of the past. To try to come to terms with something elusive, mysterious, that reflects more accurately my life now. But I don't really want to do any fiction for a while. It's so exhilarating/exhausting emotionally; such a risk. (For which boxing has come to seem a poetic metaphor.)

. . . . The predicament of the artist: all artists (?): that the energies of childhood and adolescence are likely to be more powerful, because more painful, than those of adulthood, and certainly of mature adulthood. But these energies feed upon memory; upon the past. And the past is ever-receding. To live *now*, to reflect upon life *now*—that would be a consider-able challenge. (As I suppose I've done in *Solstice*, to a degree. In some of the Cecilia Heath stories. Some of the very brief stories.)

. . . . Intense emotional experiences, these past months. The extraordi-nary demands of *The Green Island* in unfolding. Also the boxing essay. (Which I continue to expand and revise, two weeks after its appearance in the *Times*. Now it must be perhaps forty pages long. And my "dia-logue" with the subject isn't yet over.) The emotions attached to writing are analogous to the image of a tree whose roots go as deeply into the soil as its branches reach into the air. The more strain, effort, desperation, sheer hard work, the more happiness afterward; the greater the sense of accomplishment. So I must not press myself to begin something new so quickly. I must let myself breathe. I must take comfort and even pride in the fact that, yes, some things get finished, and finished to my satisfac-tion. . . . A day doesn't have to exhaust me to seem worthy of having been lived.

July 1, 1985
. . . . So much air to breathe! it's vertiginous.

. . . . (Boxing & pornography. Let me speculate—since I know very little about pornography: each mesmerizes the spectator with the sense that something *crucial, important, serious* is happening. Something *real*. But boxing *is* real and pornography is simulated. Boxing focuses upon a public ritual, pornography upon a private ritual. But each makes a voyeur of the spectator.)

. . . . These lovely summery days. I don't really feel homesick for *The Green Island* because I am still thinking about it so much. And as I tell myself, I can rewrite any page any time I want; sink myself back in Enid's or Felix's consciousness again. Any time I want.

. . . . Very strange very long yet touching letters from a youngish man who lives in Selmer, Tennessee. He is my "ideal" reader!—seems to have read everything I ever wrote and to think about it a good deal. A lonely person. I throw the letter away, retrieve it; throw it away in impatience (the handwriting is nearly illegible), then retrieve it. Perhaps I made a mistake in sending him a postcard a few weeks ago: now I seem to have unleashed a torrent of confidences. He believes I may be like him inside: "sort of lonely and always searching." A fair guess.

. . . . I keep thinking I don't want to write any fiction for a while. But my thoughts are a din of ideas, abortive little tales, voices. How long should I keep them at bay? (I'd love to write something under a pen name.) (Yes but you've had such notions before.) (*Yes. But.*)

July 2, 1985
. . . . Metaphysics, says William James, follows a primitive quest. "Unlawful magic." "Words." If you have the name for a thing or a creature you have control over it—in fantasy. The universe is an enigma "of which the key must be sought in the shape of some illuminating or power-bringing word or name. That word names the universe's *principle*, and to possess it is to possess the universe itself."

. . . . (One of these extraordinary summery days. All sunlight, silence. And I am here in a place suddenly so familiar—the white-walled glass-walled room. Looking out into the courtyard, or, to the rear, to the lawn. Roses, day lilies, begonias, geraniums in large black tubs. It's as if I have been transported from Port Oriskany to a paradise of a sort, under the authority of people I have never met and could not name.)

. . . . (*Is* this my place? Do I own *this?*—yet it's what visitors see, what they attribute to the people who live here.)

. . . . Ideas brush past fleeting & insubstantial as moths. But I let them go, I don't want them. What I want is a voice.

. . . . The scar in X.'s cheek, vertical, perhaps three inches long. Not disfiguring but startling—you look quickly back to his eyes hoping he won't have noticed (but of course he has) where you'd looked. *What caused that scar*, I won't ever ask. Because the answer would be banal and the scar itself is not.

July 7, 1985

. . . . These most perfect of days. How to describe them (but why even try: if you can't evoke the emotion, you can't set down the truth).

. . . . Convalescing from *The Green Island* (I suppose: a benign version of "athlete's kidney"—Joe Frazier collapsed after his fight with Muhammad Ali which he'd won) and working here in the guest room. White walls & glass & the courtyard of roses, geraniums, hanging plants, flagstones, wisteria, the glass of a facing wall twenty feet away & my own study to the right, its glass wall & hanging plant & lushly blooming African violets. And to my left the sliding doors looking out onto green, & daylilies (yellow, deep red, orange), wax begonias, roses (mauve, yellow, red, white, deep deep red). How after finishing a difficult work I feel that I deserve the world again. And here, splendidly, the world *is.*

. . . . Writing poems. Reading poems. Reading books on Magritte, Burchfield, the Sufi poet/mystic Rumi. Letters of Sylvia Plath to a girl friend Lynn Lawner proving that the Plath we believe we "know" existed only in part; there were, still are, others. (How reluctant the world is to grant complexity in us. I mean how reluctant we all are. Though knowing ourselves mysterious, subtle, complex, self-contradictory. Weedy logic. Of which I want to write.)

. . . . Weedy logic. Wm. James & not Plato. *This is a world in which I can breathe.*

. . . . (Magritte photographed, 1960, aged then sixty-two, with a tuba for a hat. A solemn expression.)

. . . . N.B.: how Magritte, during the Nazi occupation of Belgium, responded (emotionally) by painting lush Renoir-like Impressionist paintings. (Subsequently denounced by his admirers. But why: they don't seem to me bad.) 1942 etc. For Magritte the attempt to counter the reality of Hitler by "pitting joy against world tragedy & the horrors of the military." To celebrate sun, plenitude, flesh (especially female flesh à la Renoir). His belief that poetry & painting could change the world. Where, always, his art had expressed the darker & more mysterious emotions—anti–false optimism, bourgeois sentiment—now the dialectic swung him the other way. Work as counteroffensive.

. . . . What this suggests: even the aloof detached artist, even René Magritte ("I detest my past. And anyone else's") is touched, supremely & profoundly & to the very tips of his fingers, by history.

. . . . (While writing prose I disdain myself as a poet. But in rereading some of my poems & in writing these I feel somewhat differently. These poems *are* good. Aren't they?—at any rate I feel so good writing them, the patience of rewriting & restructuring—lovely to hold the "artwork" in one hand and contemplate it. So short. So tight. Airless, to prevent rust, decay. If not perfect they weigh perfect.)

. . . . Why the journal distresses me, but also fascinates: I'm required to use my own voice. And to record only the truth. (But not to record *all* the truth. There have been many things I've eliminated over the years . . . or hinted at so slantwise no one could guess . . . for reasons too obvious to note.) Still, what *is* recorded is always true. At least at the time it is recorded.

. . . . The journal as a work-in-progress; no structure, no plot, no theme, no characters really (I don't invent a character to be an intermediary here: which is why the journal distresses since I don't feel comfortable or assured with my own voice)—where, in my serious writing, I always compose a persona to observe what I myself ("myself") observe. That twist, spin to words, that sense of a queer filtering other—what I most love.

. . . . (My uneasiness about my poetry, then. That the poems are very close to the journal, though abbreviated; image-centered. But clearly idea-poems. Philosophical poems. My voice there is always my voice. And I feel exposed.)

. . . . (Yet, still: the formal restrictions of the poems lend distance. Yes and the abrupt yoking together of memories, images, thoughts. That deer we'd seen at the Watersheds some months ago, lying dead, incredibly, almost in our path. And the thought we'd had, shared, I think it was most profoundly while driving into San Francisco years ago—another poem, then—*So many human beings who don't know us*—you want to laugh at such a childish thought, sentiment, but there it is, why not claim it. The poems yoke so much together otherwise lost. So much that is me—otherwise lost.)

. . . . (Writing prose, then, while intimate & surely draining, is, oddly, to be distanced, perhaps even disdainful, of my personal life; my very self. I choose to write about Enid, Felix, Warren, Lyle Stevick, because I value them beyond my own life's experiences, or interests; in this I know myself absolutely correct. To write of one's self thinly disguised—like my friend X, for instance—seems to me dull, uninspired, not only egocentric but imaginatively sterile. Unless it can be totally revolutionized by language and experimentation (Joyce, Proust, to a more modest degree Bellow) it must fail as serious literature. And then, convalescing from prose, I discover not only the world again but myself. But only through poetry.)

. . . . Thinking, still, about boxing. In the abstract. So many odd disjointed ideas!—the perfect image/emblem, evidently, for my interior state. Shadow-boxing; sparring; the perfectly matched opponent; the Opponent. (The other evening, Dan & Jeannie Halpern came over. & we talked of boxing—three of us (not Ray)—for Jeannie too knows a good deal of the sport. The astonishing Leonard/Hearns fight of some years ago—110° heat the men fought in—"the passion of Hearns" one might say: like that *King Lear* of fights, the first Ali/Frazier match; then the bout in Manila.) Plans to assemble an anthology of boxing essays by writers & poets, serious essays, perhaps with photographs. As the sport is downgraded, diminished, so much less popular than football & baseball, etc., I feel a greater kinship—like poetry, serious prose & literature: a minority fascination.

July 30, 1985
. . . . Waiting today for a friend to join me for lunch & thinking idly how it has been years, years! since I have eaten alone.

. . . . (How "food" is associated in my mind sheerly with "talk"— "companionship"—the ritual of love/friendship. And what would food taste like, otherwise. Bitter? Satirical? Delicious? Or like nothing at all?)

. . . . These past few weeks, the utter pleasure of writing poetry. Some strain it's true, some small short-lived tension, but in all it has been a total change. The anxieties of the novel are far behind, that sense of never having done enough, never having gotten it quite right. Impossible to think that I might ever transfer that anxiety to the writing of poetry but I suppose I might.

. . . . Note from an old, old friend, a former friend I should say, which I took pleasure in discarding in the wastebasket.

. . . . (Still, I think so often of Enid, Felix, Port Oriskany. The canal & the stone walls; the railroad trestle; Enid's room, wallpaper, etc.; Felix in the men's lavatory, or outside the Flanders Hotel beating the hell out of a pimp, then his euphoric ride downtown—that sense of exhilaration I've felt in Buffalo, Milwaukee recently—impossible to explain why. The very grittiness, melancholy, a kind of sorrow in the smudged air, the broken sidewalks & weedy vacant lots & razed buildings; but their beauty too. Without Enid and Felix I've stopped seeing these things, so I must move on to fiction again. Boyd & his ex-wife Debra & their "black" friend Gary. A story that ends w/ a telephone call. Or w/ a cigarette butt smouldering in a trash can.)

. . . . Less lonely now, though, for the novel. By degrees I understand I am moving from it; can go for hours without thinking of either Enid or Felix. The poetry is a fragile brave defense but a defense nonetheless. And isn't it, actually, so much more my "self."

September 1, 1985
. . . . Just back from a five-day visit with my parents: a lovely visit, & my emotions are with them, still: & caught in that odd hypnotic trance of (what can I call it? the spell—surely inexplicable to anyone else—of Lockport, NY) the past not quite remembered.

. . . . (My conviction that there's a secret there—somewhere. The second night, I drove by myself around the city. At dusk. Very slowly. Those streets: Grand St., Transit St., Green St., Hawley St. (the old ruin—it *is* a ruin—of the Hawley St. school where, sixty years ago, my father was a student), Outwater Park, Ontario St., Pine, Chestnut, Gooding, Mill, Prospect, Waterman, Harvey, Cottage, Locust, Washburn, Willow. The old Niagara Hotel, seedy, run-down. Walking along streets I'd walked thirty-five years before looking for —. Lost emotions. Lost feeling. That elusive lost self. Three times I drove along Grand St., past the house my grandmother had rented, the upstairs I should say, a house now much changed, perhaps even less distinctive than it had been. Yet to think of approaching it as it was in, say, 1953, or earlier, is to feel a clutch of emotion almost too powerful to contain. And to ascend those stairs! And to enter that small living room! the kitchen! my grandmother's bedroom & sewing room! And even the view from the front windows, slantwise to the factory (what sort of factory was it—I've forgotten, if I ever knew: it becomes the box factory in *The Green Island*).

. . . . We went to the canal, the railroad trestle & footbridge off Gooding St. God, how vertiginous! what a steep drop! The old footbridge is rotted away, merely skeletal (though to look at it—steadily—was to feel its eerie power), the new footbridge, steel, mesh, is of course safe enough but I hadn't gone out on it a few feet before I felt rather odd. Looking down, seeing the water so far below. & the risk of a train coming. I took several photographs, for what else can one do! Thinking so obsessively of Enid, who stands here, so many years ago. We inhabit ourselves without valuing ourselves, unable to see that here, now, this very moment, is sacred; but once it's gone—its value is incontestable.

. . . . (Seeking what revelation. Why. *I don't know.* Emotion is there, but memory has faded. Emotion devoid of content. "This passion for writing has dried up your heart," Flaubert's mother told him. But I seem to be afflicted with the reverse: the more I write, the more powerful the emotion, stimulated, stirred, mounting (almost?) to obsession. If I had a story to tell w/ a recognizable plot, characters, etc., I'd write & write all day—but there is no *story* that emerges from this past visit to Lockport/ Millersport. There is simply no story. There is simply no distance between the writer & her subject (but what *is* her subject, other than the familiar one of the loss of the past, the inaccessibility of the heart's most profound desire!)

. . . . Passion & no content, no story to tell. Out of this mood, yesterday, I rewrote (mainly cutting, abridging) "Black" & did a revision of "The Boy Friend" & mailed them to Blanche: now the desk is clear. Now I must think of —. I went to the Lockport Public Library, that surprisingly grand building, a temple of sorts, as I've done so many times—a pilgrimage—how sentimental I am!—yet drawn to these places. So

familiar. So distant. It's there—all of it, *there*—yet inaccessible. My love
for my parents & for my grandmother. Blanche Woodside, 1894–1970,
Glenview Cemetery. Those gorgeous white "snowball" bushes in the
cemetery—a beautiful cemetery, in fact. & the shock of seeing her name.
the grave marker. the damp green grass.

September 16, 1985
. . . . Now life moves so rapidly I can barely record its outline. It's the
torrent, the tidal wave, the avalanche I'd feared last month. . . .

. . . . Last week, Sept. 10, we went to NYC to see a special screening
of *Death of a Salesman*, and to the party afterward at lavish Lincoln
Center. Spoke with Dustin Hoffman for some time about the film (which
was magnificent—*he* was magnificent), and boxing, and Angelo Dundee
(he'd like to make a film based on Dundee's life and he'd like me to
collaborate in some way—but I doubt that I will). The next day, an
intense two-hour lunch with Michael Shapiro, the sportswriter for the
N.Y. Times and elsewhere, his primary interest (do I mean interest?—
obsession!) being boxing; Michael (the elder brother of Jim Shapiro
whom I'd met and liked so much at Goucher) and Ron Levao. We were
the last ones to leave Prospect's upstairs dining room and even then we
had a great deal more to say to one another. . . . And now I am going
to do a book on boxing, I'm fairly sure, with the photographer John
Ranard, who has numerous photographs of boxers, their milieu, etc.,
which seem to me awfully good. The difficulty with doing a book of this
nature is: how to put everything in it! how to leave anything out!

December 27, 1985
. . . . Looking with mingled curiosity & impatience through some pages
of this journal (which I rarely do: the head-on plunge of my life seems
not to allow it), the year 1978 in particular, & feeling that I hardly know
that person who takes herself so very seriously, speaking of writing
projects, dinner engagements, wayward ephemeral thoughts streaking
by the window; listing friends; recording epigrams, lines of poetry. It's
not that I dislike that person (do I?) but that I don't know her. I have
a mild interest in her, but not an overwhelming interest. (I would in fact
be far more interested in reading a stranger's journal.) Does this mean,
then, that the activity of journal-keeping is really pointless? to no sane
purpose? Is this why I virtually never make any entries now, except,
obliquely, by way of letters—in which I address other people and not
(presumably) my future self.

. . . . In which I don't altogether believe. Or, rather, I *believe* in it/her, but know that she, leafing back through her past, coming upon this page & this very passage, won't be interested in it, impressed by it; won't feel much identification.

. . . . A melancholy of some inexplicable sort often wafts through this journal. As through so many. Most? Yet in my personal life, particularly in my social life, that isn't my mode at all—*particularly* in my social life. (This has been a season of wonderful exuberant parties. And not without a good deal of literary/intellectual content—as at last night's dinner with the Bienens & the Falks; yesterday's Boxing Day gathering, at noon, at the Litzs', with any number of colleagues, & visiting Irishman/scholar/professor George Watson, from Aberdeen. And the night before, which is to say Christmas Day, we were at Ed's & George's for dinner, with, among others, the Weisses—Ted in top form, wonderfully funny, warm, conversational/informative, sheerly gold in any setting.) I halfway think that "melancholy" has to do primarily with language, & the recording of one's thoughts. "What I did yesterday"—so entrancing yesterday, but merely historical today. That already casts a sort of pall over the activity. We don't think of ourselves in the past tense; we are always present tense; to consciously record the past is therefore to invent a self to perform in it, consciously or unconsciously—that's where artifice comes in. I try not to lie in this journal—I really don't think I have ever (often?) lied—yet merely by not recording everything, by selecting from everything, I have misrepresented my life. And my impressions of that life—they're a cascade, a tumult, they really can't be recorded with any degree of honesty.

. . . . But all this is to say, feebly, why I rarely write in the journal any longer. It might also be to suggest that I don't "identify" even with my present-tense self.

February 10, 1986
. . . . A (temporary) equinox of the soul. For reasons too complex (and surely too temporary) to consider.

. . . . (Why don't you write in your journal any longer, X is asked. I don't know, X says uneasily. Don't you like yourself any longer, X is asked. I don't believe I have ever particularly "liked" myself, X says. And there is a certain morbid self-consciousness in recording . . . the things that one, being *one*, is likely to record. Such as? What we did last night, yesterday, the day before. For instance? —In fact a lovely evening yesterday, a Sunday, at the Bienens' and I gave them their copy of *Marya*, dedicated to them, and—and it was a memorable evening but what more is there to say? And what of the evening before? Again, a lovely evening, this time with Ted and Renée, we had dinner out and went to a performance of Schubert's *Winterreise* which I thought was uncannily beautiful—Fadlou Shehadi the baritone, Ed Cone the accompanist—and I haven't been so at ease in a sense (the equinox) for some weeks—but feel absolutely incapable of recording it; absolutely —. Now why *is* that? Why? I don't know why. Because you're convinced that this is —? Yes, I am convinced. . . . Self-consciousness ruins the journal; interferes with the sense that one is talking freely and in a way innocently. Consider the very messiness of this entry: surely it's deliberate? (It is. I could as easily, more easily, use the word processor.) How to break the web of such reluctance? Do I want to break it? —Recalling recent evenings looking through the journal for 1978 and truly disliking, not even recognizing, the voice. How earnest! how self-absorbed! But isn't that the very premise of the journal, if the journal is honest and not arty? —X for instance saying in midparagraph, Oh come on: you're writing this from two hundred note cards, pretending it's spontaneous and it isn't; and I suppose I simply want the real thing—the "spontaneity"; but also a certain degree of form, which means artifice, artiness. (You can't have it both ways.) (I detest these clichés . . . even an unintentional and intolerable rhyme.) (Surely this is comic? self-loathing in concert with self-consciousness?) (What I want is *honesty*. Otherwise I can't bear it.) Why not record facts?—though of course facts too can be made to lie.

May 20, 1986
. . . . Surpassingly lovely, precious days. What is there to say except: here they are. Sifting through my fingers like sand.

. . . . Last week, my parents' visit. And it was splendid. And it went by with painful swiftness. They arrived on Wednesday, left on Saturday afternoon, immediately the house seems too large, empty, quiet, unused. Lunch at Prospect, with Elaine (whom my parents like immensely); that evening, Isaac Bashevis Singer gave an excellent, if somewhat whimsical reading at the University (I introduced him, then fielded questions for him and repeated them to him since he's hard of hearing); next day a leisurely drive along the Delaware to Trenton, to the art museum; that evening, dinner here w/ the Bienens, and Ed and George—a marvelous evening with much good feeling and hilarity. My mother brought me a dress she'd sewed for me, blue print, quite feminine one might say; long-sleeved, full-skirted. "Demure"—to suit my image.

. . . . (Another family secret revealed, with a disarming casualness. Perhaps because of their age my parents don't want to keep secrets? Not that they are *old* at seventy or seventy-one. My father told of how his grandfather Morgenstern tried to kill his grandmother in a fit of rage, failed, then killed himself—gun barrel placed beneath his chin, trigger pulled, with my grandmother Blanche, a young woman in her twenties, close by. My father was about five at the time. They were all living in one household, evidently, since my grandmother's husband, Oates, had left her. [Or had she left him?] A sordid tale. Yet grimly comical: I asked what occupation my great-grandfather had, was told he was a gravedigger.)

(Family secrets! So many! Or, no, not really very many, I suppose; but unnerving. And I think of my sweet grandmother Blanche Woodside who nearly witnessed her own father's violent suicide. . . . She had come home to find the house locked. Her father was beating her mother upstairs in their bedroom. Hearing her at the door, he came downstairs with his gun, for some reason—frustration, drunkenness, madness—he killed himself just inside the locked door. I said several times, dazed, But you never told me any of this! and my father said several times, with that air of utter placidity, Didn't I?—I'm sure I did. [This is a countertheme of sorts. The secret is at last revealed, after decades; but it's revealed with the accompanying claim that it had been revealed a long time ago and isn't therefore a secret.] What am I to make of these nuggets of lead! What that, intuitively, with a dreamer's vague sense of dread and certainty, I have not already made of them in my fiction!)

July 2, 1987
. . . . My next project should be an essay, on pseudonymns; maybe a short "suspense" novel (by Rosamond Smith? or someone new?); an article for *Art & Antiques*. Perhaps a very short story . . . but no sequence of stories. And no poems. I don't want my soul dredged yet, everything is too raw, abraded.

. . . . "American Appetites" could not have been written anywhere else but Princeton, of course. Though fiction, it is also a story unique to this world; to the middle-aged (consequently "in power") personalities of this world. The Institute for Advanced Study, & the University itself. X. . . . irradiates through the text, here and there; yet is not *in* it; not at all. If anyone, Ian McC. is myself. A masculine version. (As only bits and shreds of Felix were "myself." And so very transmogrified, of course, as to be virtually indecipherable.)

. . . . The imposition of the mechanical upon the organic: Henri Bergson's definition of the comic. Thus to force form upon "living" matter is to make of the matter something less than living. (How wise, then, of me, to abandon the more formal structure I'd imagined for AA.)

. . . . One of the less agreeable consequences of finishing AA is the inevitability of being, here, rather too alertly; which is to say, being conscious of *You Must Remember This* approaching ever so rapidly. I am in love with writing, that's clear; but not so much in love with being published. If only one could slip through a time warp, and come out the other side . . . the book read by whoever will read it; on whichever library shelves it is destined to wind up on; and that's it. "Good" reviews, "bad" reviews, how they grate the soul . . . the former a happier occasion than the latter, of course, but, still, grating. I've felt, this past year or so, w/ the success of various literary ventures, and, even, "Smooth Talk," so unnervingly lucky . . . I know such luck cannot last. Also, *On Boxing* resulted in an almost alarming "celebrity" of a minor sort . . . quite different from anything I've known previously. So I begin to get restless with "attention" . . . yet, in the matter of something so large as a novel (Dutton is printing 50,000 copies) it would be a sad thing not to have this attention. . . . If only we could create public selves, autonomous beings, to deal with such things. . . .

. . . . How like a crowded jammed storage room it is, the "notes-for-a-novel"; a closed-off room out of which, piece by piece, objects are brought, into a public room, and arranged with painstaking care. This "public" room is all that the reader will ever know of the so-called creative process while the storage room is what the writer has known . . . has anguished in. . . . So it's a shock one day to come home, and see the public room perfectly furnished; everything in its place; *with its false look of inevitability*. Ah, ecstasy! Art's sole trickery.

. . . . I want to record, while the wonder (the almost visceral wonder: taking the breath away!) is still with me, before another sort of mood (and I don't doubt but that I can already make out the lineaments of this "other" mood) intervenes . . . how happy, how ecstatic, how pleased, how grateful, how, simply, surprised I am . . . that "American Appetites" turned out as it did; after so much uphill straining, more than the usual (except for *You Must Remember This*) perplexity, anguish. . . . Yes I am *very* amazed by it; and have only to glance through my early notes, now so groping, wrongheaded, blind, pathetic . . . to see what a problem I'd had; and to see how far (no matter what others may think) I managed to come. This is the sort of dazed beatific mood I want to record instead of the other; because it's so fleeting; but also because it really does explain why people write. Or why, at least, I write.

EDNA O'BRIEN

◆ ──────────────────────────── ◆

Diary

> Virginia called them "holdalls" to reflect the light of our lives. The dark, I fear, creeps in rather more, in my case.

January 10

A long dreary wait at London airport in which fret frenzy and dismay reigned. The human race in bulk leaves one in grave doubt as to the possibility of a creator. What I remember most is the image of an emaciated Indian woman dragging a pink mop along the floor endlessly. In contrast, most other people pollaps, their girth combined with their luggage giving them the look of tubs. Snow falling outside. Then after nine hours hunched in the plane beside the grossest man I have ever set eyes on, who said "I should be in Club Class by rights, I need the space because I'm so *tall*."

Paris

A small room with purple velveteen walls and old furniture. Breakfast on a little folding table. Several jams. Bread and rolls body temperature. Across the narrow garden a window with a shirt over it. Ye Olde faithful squalor. The play was good, at least it worked in French and Catherine Sellers was very good, also the direction. Liked the image of windows on the back screen and once a dual reflection on screen and on the floor giving or complimenting the topsy-turvyness of Virginia's mind. A hell of a liberty was taken by cutting the end so that Virginia dies but does not speak the lines that were the motif of her resurrection though her words.

Very impressed by Jean Louis Barrault. His face can do anything it wants, his muscles like wires, obedient to him. Saw Françoise Sagan at Brasserie Lipp. Off now to buy fine aids to Beauty. For what I may ask.

Norfolk

A weekend in which I was rereminded of the sad fact that pretentiousness is more widespread than I feared. A small woman with dimples stands in her manor house doorway and says to one of the men—"How do you like my new car, it was the best numberplate in London." It says CEX. Later she comes to dinner and spouts opinions about writers, actors, furniture, and food. It seems a friend of hers who had a cat left the first course for a dinner party in her larder and the cat got in—"ten people for dinner and no starters" she kept saying.

The White Hotel is the literary bonbon of all these ladies. One who took it to hospital with her said, "I had to take a sleeping pill after it . . . too like my own experience," and we are supposed to infer madness, debauch, and God knows what. I am amazed that people read anything as their minds like their souls are buried in duvets of dudness.

The marshes very beautiful with icy water like lace, their surface dappled and the air moist because of the thaw. Brent geese occupying a whole corner of the heavens and making a unified sound as they veer upward, then some flying underneath making zigzag patterns and depending on their positions they looked either gray-black or as moving points of white. The grass a wiry yellow and underneath the frozen water a green weed like magic fetuses.

N. does not listen—it comes from living alone. I may be guilty of the same sin, hope not. Dull lunch. Walking home I had to help an old woman who had fallen and cut her temple. She didn't really talk, she muttered as she kept dabbing a Kleenex on the blood while I searched in my handbag for some more. Handkerchieves are a thing of the past. Shakespeare would have to rewrite a whole chunk of Othello. Another woman offered to take her into the public library and I was relieved because I did not know what to do with her. Then I went to the chapel to light a candle to Saint Anthony and the chapel proper being locked I had to write a note and clip £5 to it and ask whoever found it to light the candles for me. In the porch a man stopped me and said, "Can I have two pounds for a meal." He was Irish. His accent triggered off a whole retinue of thoughts.

"Art can bring us consolation against individuals but it is powerless against reality." (Roman Rolaind) Reading that sent me back on the road to literature which I have been neglecting in the interests of more ephemeral pursuits—men for instance. Does ephemeral apply only to women? Shouldn't.

Kurt Schwitters
Got the jitters
Did collages
In garages

February 2
James Joyce's birthday and in the paper a joke of his. A man upon
wishing to shake the hand of the man who wrote *Finnegans Wake* was
warned "It did a lot of other things as well."

The sea is marvelous at night. All night it pounds, lover, thief, army
marching in. In the day it can be so many colors, a blue of infinite
delicacy, a gray, a black, a mist color. If only people were like that.

Amazing dream. I am shedding the past. It comes off like scales. Bags
packed and so forth. I have to go in to a church to say goodbye. I dread
seeing my mother there. Instead as I open the door I see a band of bright
light. In a saner person this might mean illumination.

Mexico
Before a cock fight, those holding the destined birds pull the feathers out
to rouse their anger. Merciless. It all seemed to happen so quickly before
one could gather one's senses—the skirmish, one cock lying down and
the other the victor pecking at its head and eyes, finishing it off. A jet
of blood on the feathers. The men who held the cocks had a curious
bruised vacant damaged look. A fat man with blood spattered all over
his T-shirt registering nothing. The place swarming with people. Between each fight, bingo cards were passed around and incongruously and
almost daintily waitresses were endeavoring to serve drinks. I thought I
was in Babel. I thought too that people crave stimulus, the stimulus of
either winning or losing. A swell of people outside trying to get in. The
doors are closed while the fight is on, so that no one can escape, as the
money is taken after, then when they are opened a gush of hot air bursts
in. A big sign saying that the judges' decision is irrevocable. I think the
cocks would agree. I wonder what they do with the dead cocks—eat
them I suppose.

The hummingbirds here. So small you could squeeze them to death.
Their needley beaks immersed in flowers for the nectar. The place is
teeming with sand crabs. If only it would rain. Everything, myself in-

cluded, is screaming out for rain and to think that in Ireland one longed for sunshine. The tropics are not for me, I rather hold with what Pythagoras said—"when the wind blows worship its echo."

Flaubert says that the heart is like a palm tree—"it grows again as soon as it is stripped"—I disagree. The heart is constantly gouged until in the end it is a ghost of a heart.

A builder who failed to show up for three days arrived this morning at cock crow—"sorry to let you down but basically I can't walk so what I done is to try and rest myself."
ME: "Oh what happened?"
HIM: "I seem to have injured myself. I can't think how I done it."
    They come at 7:30 like Macbeth porters and are gone by 8:00 for their first break. Then back from breakfast they are happy to have a series of refreshments, one tea with two sugars, one weak tea with three sugars, and I'll have a coffee, not instant if you don't mind. They'll never leave. I am resigned to that now. My horoscope says, "You will have many bright days soon." No sign of them. I am having a floor handpainted—camelias and birds. Costs more than three Persian carpets, also useless for stiletto heels. No doubt, as soon as this house is finished I will be on the move as at heart I am a gypsy but not as carefree as a gypsy. One sees them outside Harrods with the bits of heather—I give them a lot of money, out of fear. I like them, though. I like their pluck.

Oh the zest of champagne, the way each bubble touches the tongue and as it were sends a little headiness to the brain. Eugene O'Neill thought it was the most insidiously dangerous drink. He looks so like my uncle—enraged eyes, hurt, and moustache.

In the country. Why the hell don't I live here, what am I doing in the city, dizzy, addled, demented from people. A magic walk at sunset. First through woods and then on to a path with a golf course beyond that seemed unreal, such was its perfection. At the bottom of the hill a large Tudor house with wood stacked to one side, trees, shrubs, flowers. I heard the cuckoo, then met a little dog Judy and its owner. It was such a joy to meet a country person who actually knew about trees, grass, birds, knew when each blade of grass was put down on the tee, told me that the cuckoo was wicked this year and that blackbirds everywhere were nursing large greedy young cuckoos. The cuckoo is the color of the pigeon and not brown as I thought. The midges made a meal of us. If one lived in the country one might write deeper things. Novels rarely tell deep stories nowadays, it's either calisthenics or garbage.

"My conviction is that the goal of man's existence is not happiness but spiritual growth." A. Solzhenitzyn. My conviction is that I have not become resigned to that statement. I dream in Russian nevertheless.

Went to S.'s eightieth birthday at Claridge's. I never saw such an assembly of old but well preserved people. I spoke to a Greek Orthodox priest who told me that they did not have a harsh confessional system like the Catholics, theirs being more humane. D.—one of my women friends—put her arms around me and told the room at large "there was a time when *she* was as fat as me" and then looking at me with false concern said "soon you'll be too thin." Parties are killing. The thing I hate most in women is their picking curiosity, dying to know who one's lover is and even more dying to dump on one highlights of their sexual romps.

The ceremony was in the Thomas More chapel in Chelsea. A lady usher held a black umbrella over one as one got out of the taxi. Inside I went in search of the embroidered Henry James kneeler which said that he was an interpreter of two continents. Was he? Plaques of stone and marble along the wall to commemorate the dead. Sad to read inscriptions. One by a husband to his young wife—he talked of trying to reach the sky to get nearer to her. Another concerning three people whose boat was slumped in a squall on the Thames. White lilies on the altar. Prayers and some hymns, including a beautiful hymn about enduring the steep and rugged.

Went to a hypnotist in order to learn to swim. She was so inaudible I couldn't hear her so that the "influences" that were supposed to work on me, did not. Cost £15. A dud.

Dreamt last night that I was cooking for droves of people, had not enough utensils or enough food or enough drink or enough anything. I also was doing a bit of mending and hoovering. As if that was not enough I was the ghost rewriter of someone else's play. To my great surprise I wakened from these numerous charges saying aloud—"I am a born-again slave"—I laughed. I also remembered a phrase, "in dreams begins responsibility."

Long time and no entries. Why? Must be a reason. No wish to describe nature again or to dredge up old love or old pain. There's that and what Rilke (my beloved) called "the dull quotidian." But there must be something else.

February 13
A beautiful day with bright warm sun and a sheen on the leaves. The birds are hopping along the grass, their tails held archly high. Two birds are cavorting; amazingly comic to see them separate, simulate huff and return. Joyce was superstitious about thirteen and did I think, die on January 13th. Think of him often and for some reason wonder what his skin was like, if he had irate skin. Cried in a café as I picked up tiny shreds of watercress and ate them and remarked to myself how flavorless, even textureless they were. If I had begun a story that day it would have to be called "Cress." People stare at one as if somehow one had the secret of existence. I asked a man if he loved his wife—"Got to, she's a Tooting Girl," he said. It spoke multitudes. Poetry always goes straight to the marrow. Shakespeare caught every branch of it; Shakespeare caught everything. Wonder what would happen if he and Joyce met in the after-world. Fisticuffs?

GORDON PARKS

◆ ———————————————————— ◆

Diary

Paris / 1951

O for the courage to age without fear, to salvage youth's gems and blend
them gracefully into one's lot. As the perimeter narrows, one strains
against the inevitable and is forced along, knowing full well that the force
is far greater than the resistance. Energy consumed in the struggle only
hastens the collapse. *S'effondrer sans dignité. S'effondrer sans honneur.*

Shouldn't have tried this run. It's dangerous, but how boundless the
space; how light and clean the snow. Hell, as a boy, I did this a million
times, and I feel capable right now. Perhaps youth is still in the harness.
Lovely girl whipping past; I'll stay in her tracks. It's steeper, more
winding than I remember—a bit treacherous, but a wonderful run. The
silent motion of those mountains shooting upward; the startled snowflakes rushing back to the riders close behind. Watch them. They're
young and reckless, Christ! This one must be insane, attempting to pass
me on such a sharp curve—and at such speed! Hold on. Don't give the
crazy bastard an inch. Damn! The young fool leapt right over my tips!
Let him go. He won't live long like that. Careful now. Jump coming
up. Steady. Flatten grooves. Poles in. Bend knees. Pull up—more—
more—more! Spring! Spring! . . .

   I was gaining consciousness when they wheeled me from the operating room into the ward. The walls weaved and the ceiling spiraled crazily.
Then came the laughter—unrestrained laughter echoing through space,
going and coming in lacy patterns. Suddenly, things came into focus, and
I saw this boy propped up in bed—shaking with laughter. I found out
later that he was reacting to a joke another patient had told. He was about
twenty, rather handsome, thick-bodied with bunchy black hair curling
wildly over his forehead. They lifted me into the bed next to his. The pain
was like a dozen knives stabbing, but he kept on laughing. Perhaps it was
my delirium, but he seemed to go on laughing forever. Louder. Louder
and louder. Just my luck to wind up next to him.

   This accident presented the final straw. There would be months
before I could work again. The debts would pile mountain high. I had

surrendered to pain and despair when he finally spoke to me. "My name's Mike, Mister. How're you feelin'?"

Before I could answer, another spasm of pain jolted me into unconsciousness and a mask came hurtling toward me—a youthful, robust laughing mask.

Delirium is versatile, even magical. Shapeless images lifted me into air thinner than air, and the mask and I drifted on to a puffy white cloud. I wore the mask now, but it kept falling off—laughing, always laughing at me. I tried tying it on, but the string cut through the mask and my head, scalping both of us. Then I did a very careless thing. I punctured the cloud with the jagged edge of my splintered leg bone. The cloud burst apart and I plummetted downward. Down! Down! "Help! Help!"

"Wake up, Mister. Ya hurtin'? Want me to call the nurse? Hey, wake up. It's Mike."

"I'm falling. Catch me. Catch your face."

The sun shone brightly the next morning when I awoke. Everyone was eating except Mike. He was tying a pair of GI boots together. He secured the knot, attached a white card and signed his name. "Ya had quite a time last night, Mister. Feel better?"

"A little better, Mike—a little better. Why aren't you eating like everyone else?"

"I won't be eatin' today. Surgery comin' up."

Ten minutes later they came for him, and there was a hush as they wheeled him out. "Good luck, Mike," someone said.

"So long, fellas. Good knowin' y'all. Take care of gramps over there in the corner." He was laughing again.

"So long, Mike." The entire ward had answered as one.

"Isn't he coming back?" I asked.

"Nope," someone said.

"But—they forgot to take his boots!"

"He won't be needing those boots. They're cutting off both his legs this morning."

LETTER TO A BROTHER

New York / 1952

Dear Sebastian,

The marketplace is dreadfully quiet this morning, cold and full of yellowish light. There's hardly a sound among the discarded crates and rotted garbage. There're only three of us here—a street cleaner, a monstrous cur of a dog, and me. The street cleaner will be gone soon, and only that cur and I will be left to forage for our grub. We're enemies, that cur and I, but there's little difference in us—both shelterless and hungry. His mangy coat is falling off his ribs in patches, but then, you might say the same of me. All I've had to eat for twelve hours is a link of sausage I picked from the gutter. I'm hungry, weary, lonely—and patient. As you know, I've the patience of a stupid ox. It's so intense it kills the pain of hunger sometimes. And recently I've gotten to be rather vain about my misery. I do hope all this has some meaning. Oh so much I hope to become a good writer someday.

Every morning, garbage cans. Anything will do—a crust of bread, meat skin, spoiled fruit—anything to deaden the hunger. I tell myself some good will come of this suffering, and for periods I actually believe it.

Serving this apprenticeship, as dad would call it, gets to be awful sometimes. (Poor dad, the only thing we have in common is our stubbornness.) During these motionless days, I go about searching for the sun, and when I get a chance to sleep, I have despairing dreams. I have to confess that, sometimes, I'm without hope, and I wait for stupid things to happen—death from some hoodlum, the sudden collapse of a building, an explosion, the strike of a blade into my neck. Then, sometimes, the touch of Carmelena's hand upon my cheek again. But, in this waiting, I neglect my desires, and this is silly. Without desire, you lose the power to attract. Probably none of those things will happen. The incredible thing is that I wait.

There's a reason for that cur and me to be enemies. The other morning, a pigeon flew head-on into a window next to where I was standing. Stunned, it fell to the sidewalk. I bent over to pick it up and set it to flight again (remember our love for pigeons?). But, as I stopped, that bastard let out a growl that sent shivers up my back. His fangs were bared and his jowls were distorted and dripping with saliva. I kicked at him, but he held his ground as the bird flopped between us. There was a stick about a foot away. I grabbed it just as he mouthed the bird. I swung with all my strength, smacking him square in the ribs. He yelped and fled. When I picked up the bird, I saw the damage was done; its neck was broken.

I had stuffed it in my pocket and was walking toward the waterfront when the realization struck. I had food. This will be hard for you to believe. I turned into an alley, gathered bits of paper and wood, defeathered that poor bird, roasted it and ate it. Oh, Sebastian, perhaps

I am as much animal as that dog; certainly my intentions were no more honorable. I'd fought for my hunger, not for the bird.

Oh well, all this is my own choice. How are things going at the bank? Is Bertie still at Harvard? None of this to mom or dad. They're only to hear that I'm doing fine. My fingers are freezing. I'll have to stop. Love, dear brother,

Roger

NYPD FORM LETTER

Dear sir:
Your *brother Roger's* effects, itemized below, are enclosed:
—letter to Sebastian.
The Department will continue to investigate his death.
Sincerely . . .

December 21, 1964
Strange dreams of late—exhausting in their complexity. One last night mixed of death and homosexuality. The reviews of Genet's *Thieves' Journal* and a reference of Sartre's words about an incident in his (Genet's) experience in the South of France probably stimulated this.

A tormenting dream about my mother—dead, but not dead—left me ill. I awoke with the taste of death in my mouth. Elizabeth brought me a ripe melon to bed and I ate it hurriedly to kill the morbid flavor the dream left. In this last dream I came upon two men who claimed to be embalming my mother's body. When I saw her move and sit up, I became angry, screaming that she was not dead. They kept claiming she was dead, that they had already cut sections of her insides away. Eventually, I proved them to be fakes and tried to expose them to the authorities—but to no avail. The dream ended with my mother lying in the nearby woods; and my running to get help from some nuns who were at a monastery a short distance away. Only twice before have I seen my mother so vividly in dreams. Once was in Philadelphia; the other time in White Plains. Both times, I remember, I was about to do something she didn't approve of.

After a year's work on *A Choice of Weapons*, it seems flat—almost one-dimensional. Perhaps my approach is wrong, but I don't think so. Try something new tomorrow. Break pace. Give more depth to certain areas in each chapter. Publication by fall seems hopeless now. I am tiring of something, not the book, but something. Maybe it's the style. I hate first person. In any case, I must close myself off more—too many people; too many interruptions. Beginning to feel I write only in between everything else, that the book is not the primary thing. This is bad.

December 23, 1964
For the first time in my life I am hating Christmas. It's cutting up my thoughts and time. All these traditional niceties seem so pointless when there are so many things undone.

January 3, 1965
Got a criticism from David Scherman today on the Harlem chapter. "I couldn't put it down—exciting, but my nine-year-old could have written it. Full of clichés, but goddamn powerful. I couldn't put it down." As I remember, his comments were exactly the same about *The Learning Tree*. "The critics will roast you," he said. Four months later, he was eating crow. He urges me on. Thank God. Bless him. He makes me work harder and harder to make him wrong.

February 6, 1965
More and more I feel the intense suffering of doing something wrong.

February 10, 1965
Why does love have to be so secretive, so involving and terrifying? Sometimes, it is so unimaginable to a harsh memory.

HARLEM: THE FONTENELLE FAMILY

November 26, 1968
No heat in the place at all today. Last night, all the kids slept huddled together on a mattress in the kitchen with the oven on. Norman, Sr., lay shivering on a cot in the front room when I arrived. "How's it going?" I asked.

"Bad."

"Any hope for work?"

"Nothing doing—nothing doing."

December 1, 1968
Ran into Norman, Jr., standing on a street corner tonight, warming over a garbage-can fire. The smell of snow was in the air. He had on beat-up tennis shoes and a light windbreaker.

"Why are you out here so late in the cold?"

"Poppa put me out. He's mad about not having work."

"Would you like to go home with me?"

"Naw, thanks. Mamma will get me in some way."

Upstairs, Bessie Fonetenelle was stirring a large cauldron of boiling water. Norman, Sr., was asleep in a corner—smelling of whiskey. I stayed around for about an hour. Bessie went with me to the door. "Things are rough around here tonight. A friend gave him a bottle."

December 2, 1968

Bessie lay groaning when I got there this afternoon. Her neck was bruised and swollen. Little Richard was beneath her arms. She managed a half-smile. "My ribs feel like they're broken. He gave me a good going over last night. I just can't take it anymore."

"Where is he?"

"In the hospital."

"Hospital?"

"Yes, I sent him there. When he got through beating me. I waited until he was asleep and poured that scalding water over him. I put in sugar and honey so it would stick."

Norman, Jr., and I went to the hospital. He couldn't recognize his father. Sugar and honey still coated what little skin was left on his face and shoulders. He sat on the side of the bed daubing at his eyes with kleenex. His hands were also horribly burned. "I don't know why your mother did it, boy," he said. "I just don't know why."

BROUGHT TO MY NOTICE BY A WELL-MEANING FRIEND

No. 42

JOURNAL

of the

HOUSE OF REPRESENTATIVES

74th Legislature

REGULAR SESSION OF 1968

2 o'clock P.M., Lansing, Michigan, Tuesday, March 12, 1968

Rep. Del Rio, having reserved the right to enter his protest against the passage of the bill to amend Act No. 269 of the Public Schools Acts of 1955 . . .

"Mr. Speaker and Members of the House:

". . . What I want, what I am, and what you force me to be is what you are. For I am you staring back from a mirror of poverty and despair, of revolt and freedom. Look at me and know that to destroy me is to destroy yourself. You are weary of the long hot summers. I am tired of the cold hungered winters. We are not so far apart as it might seem. There is something about both of us that goes deeper than blood or black and white. It is our common search for a better life, a better world. I march now over the same ground you once marched. I fight for the same things you still fight for. My children's needs are the same as your children's. I too am America. America is me. It gave me the only life I know—so I must share in its survival. Look at me. Listen to me. Try to understand my struggle against your racism. There is yet a chance for us to live in peace beneath these restless skies. . . ."

All good words, Representative Del Rio, but since they were *all* mine, I would appreciate being given *all* the credit for them.

TWO MOMENTS

Michael Trott was strapped into an electric chair at 5:57 Sunday morning. Wayne Olsen, the prison warden, placed his hand on the switch. A little over a minute was left when the storm struck the area—knocking out the power. The blackout lasted for two hours and thirty-one minutes. The governor, having had ample time to think things over, reduced Trott's death sentence to life.

Two mornings later, a flock of starlings, following their leader, suddenly wheeled westward. A big jet, banking northward, sucked them into its motor. The plane shuddered—and fifty-two people plummetted to a fiery death.

(Two unusual moments that leave me with a sense of something unexplainable. During one, a convicted murderer is given the right to life; during the other, fifty-two innocent human beings are granted their legacy to death. Both moments seem to have happened with no more meaning than the swish of a wave.) I don't know why I question such things. I've always been told they are decisions made by a higher power.

SOUTH AFRICA

New York / September 14, 1986
Visit today from a Mr. Leonard Brown. Calls himself "Rabbi." Wants me to accompany him to South Africa, especially to the Republic of Ciskei. It's one of the "homelands" set aside by the white Pretoria government. I'm curious about the "Rabbi," his invitation, and why it was extended in the first place. Never been to S.A., and I would like to go, but I doubt they will give me a visa. He assures me I'll have no trouble getting one. We are to leave in a couple of days—to London on the Concorde, then on to Johannesburg and Ciskei. I'm to apply for the visa tomorrow morning. Still have doubts. It's all so unexpected, and, as yet, unexplained.

September 15, 1986
Surprisingly, the visa office was only a couple of blocks from me, an obscure building with a gray façade. It looked deserted. A squad car sat out in front with a policeman in it. A surveillance camera perched on the roof. A receptionist behind a foot-thick glass asked me what I wanted. I told him and he directed me through two more doors. Neither door would open until the one I entered closed. Another thick glass, with two young women behind it. "Yes, can I help you?"
"I would like a visa to South Africa."
"Your name please."
"Gordon Parks."
"Your occupation?"
"Poet."
"Poet?"
"Yes, poet."
Silence.
"You're also a filmmaker, journalist, and photographer."
"You seem to know all about me."
"You may pick up your visa about this time tomorrow."
The Rabbi was obviously well connected.

South Africa / September 17, 1986
So far, all's well—except for a couple of lost bags. It was, indeed, the Concorde, and it lived up to expectations. From New York to London in about three hours. Felt a little apprehensive as we approached Nairobi about dawn. Far below was Kilimanjaro, the mountain Gordon, Jr.,

loved so much, then later the spot where his plane had crashed and burned. Seven years had passed, but I had a feeling that the spot still looked charred. We were aboard a 747 now, and I was a bit shocked to see a fully-robed figure in yalmuke standing up front, with arms raised as if in the act of worship, mumbling prayers. I nudged our traveling companion, Clinton Crocker. He wiped sleep from his eyes. "It's just the Rabbi," he said, and went back to sleep.

Would like to have walked around the airfield, but no one was allowed off the plane. Trouble was brewing. Soldiers with machine guns were all over the place. The Rabbi didn't seem to mind. He settled into his seat with a large dish of kosher food. I said a small prayer for Gordon, Jr., as we took off for Johannesburg, wondered what the last few seconds of his life were like, shuddered, and put it out of my mind.

Johannesburg looked so peaceful and civilized from the air. A sparkling industrial complex surrounded by a vast sea of black and white hatred.

"You're in luck," Crocker informed me as we took off for Ciskei. "The Rabbi's worth well over fifty million and interested in all your various projects. Thinks you're a genius."

"Why am I so important to Ciskei?"

"He's close to its President. Wants you to see the country."

Me? My curiosity heightened. It skyrocketed when two oversized Mercedes Benzes met us at the airport, whisking us through New London and into the African "homeland." I had steeled myself against grubby living conditions and droves of starving black people, but this hotel I'm in is as luxurious as most I've seen back in the States: saunas, tennis courts, golf course, lush green landscape with hauntingly beautiful mountains off in the distance. The place is run by blacks and I saw at least three black and white couples in the dining room tonight. There's even a gambling casino with black-tie croupier. The Rabbi just smiles and tells me to look toward tomorrow. He senses my state of shock.

September 18, 1986
Something's wrong here. In no way does Ciskei resemble the homelands I've heard about. A Mercedes Benz whisked me to nursing homes, schools with uniformed black students, a fine supermarket and new factories going up. Loaded down with magazines, brochures and pamphlets today—all praising the black president of this republic. His pictures project the looks of a well-dressed doctor or lawyer. Indeed, he is addressed as His Excellency, Dr. L. L. W. Sebe. I am to meet him soon.

September 19, 1986
A statement in a tribute to Sebe begins to shed a little light. It reads: "Our Republic of Ciskei may not have too many friends beyond our borders. But there is the one aspect that makes our friends unique, and that is, they are true friends. The Prime Minister of South Africa, Mr. P. W. Botha and the majority of his people are our friends. . . ." I hear now that he, with the help of Botha's government, turned black militants away from Ciskei's borders when they tried to enter the country. The Rabbi admits that this tends to bother him. Certainly, it bothers me! I read, too, that Yigal Griffel, Deputy Mayor of Tel Aviv, and its citizens are helping to develop Ciskei. I'm suddenly aware of the Rabbi's political connection. *He's also in the investment business.*

September 20, 1986
Sebe presided over the House of Parliament today. At least seventeen chieftains attended, their wives colorfully dressed in African headpieces and gowns. The building is newly built and an impressive bit of architecture. Later, I was ushered past four soldiers with machine guns and into the presence of the African chieftains who had made Sebe a permanent president of their republic. And there I at last found out why the Rabbi had flown me into their presence. Very frankly I was asked, "How do you intend to give visibility to our Republic?"

I answered, "It would be impossible for me even to mention your Republic without putting it in context with the whole of South Africa. I'm astounded at the progress you've made here, but most South Africans must loathe you."

"They do," one of the chiefs admitted.

An hour later, I was taken past even more soldiers with machine guns, and in to see His Excellency. For the first ten minutes, he seemed to suffer with his breathing; seemed not to realize I was in the room. Then, suddenly, he opened up and spent an hour justifying his country's position in this purgatory of apartheid. He is a big man, well over six feet, solidly built, and he spoke with sluggish intelligence. During our conversation, I asked him if Ciskei experienced any inner violence. None, he assured me. When, three years before, his brother, Charles Sebe, tried to overthrow his government, he had thrown him into prison—and he was still there. His last words to me were, "Go back to America, my friend, and let the rest of the world know about Ciskei."

"Is there any chance for reform here, Mr. President?"

"Sorry, but no."

"Then, it will eventually be slaughter. How will Ciskei fare?"
"In that case, we're in trouble, I'm afraid."

Johannesburg / September 21, 1986

Picked up a Johannesburg newspaper, *The Star*. There were two banner
headlines: HALF-EMPTY SCHOOLS SAY NO TO BLACKS; the other, MACHINE-GUN
GANG FREES CHARLES SEBE FROM PRISON. "And, in a second incident in
Ciskei yesterday, President Sebe's son, another Charles Sebe, Major-
General of Communications, was abducted by a group of unidentified
men." The paper failed to say that the gang consisted of white mercenar-
ies. Strange, most of this happened during my conversation with His
Excellency President Lennox Sebe. The Rabbi seemed mildly surprised
when I showed him the headlines. I had been delivered and he was in
a hurry to catch a plane for Israel. Crocker swore to me, "The Rabbi
had a check for fifty million dollars in his hands. I saw it with my own
eyes."

New York / March 8, 1988

I've never heard of, nor laid eyes on, the Rabbi since. He, not I, is the
genius—he damn near murdered my solitude.

RUSSIA (INVITATION TO GORBACHEV'S DISARMAMENT CONFERENCE)

February 15, 1987

New York to Frankfurt, via Pan Am—en route.
This small Aeroflot jet from Frankfurt is more like a corporate plane—
but not as plush. Had taken a seat in the rear, but my name was called
and I was moved up to first class, given presents, and lots of attention.
Didn't know that first class existed in the USSR! My visa had been so
long in coming after the initial invitation. Now, at last, two hours out
of Moscow. Not much to see. All fog, and we're bouncing all over the
sky. A long way from our dirt farm back in Kansas. Rain sweeping in.
No—snow, and sleet pelting the windows, and the sky is turning black.
Hope the pilot knows the way home. There's nothing in sight to give
him a bearing. Relax. Drink vodka. All I ask for is the justice of a safe
landing. Weary of worrying about safe landings. Had so many by now.
Can think of nothing now except the history I am flying into—the
Kremlin, the palaces of the Czars, the revolution, Pushkin's home, and,

of course, the Hermitage. They are all waiting. Somewhere out in the distance lies Siberia. Another vodka, then sleep. There's nothing to see, in any case.

Moscow / February 16, 1987
Morning: Russian breakfast—boiled eggs, cold pork, lettuce, radishes, and brown bread. A pitcher of liquid resembles urine and tastes like smoked grapefruit. The different caucuses have finished. We're to be bussed to the Kremlin to hear Gorbachev.

Evening: the great hall was packed. Ran into Gregory Peck, Peter Ustinov, Norman Mailer, Gloria Steinem, and Joseph Papp. We drifted through the great hall of chandeliers. What opulence. People there from all over the world, many in their native costumes. A group from Kansas recognized me and invited me to sit with them. I did. Read Gorbachev's speech a few minutes before we took our seats, but it was impressive hearing him, in this historic place, giving his voice to it. He was taking a big gamble. If applause counted, he'd won. Notables from several countries spoke first. The most applause was expected for Graham Greene; he got the least. The day, begun gray and cold, turned bright and warmer by the time the banquet—for thousands—commenced. The fare was exotic and good. KBG men moved like robots through the throngs.

February 17, 1987
Pravda issuing a piece I wrote for it to *Jintepatyphar*, a Soviet weekly, and to all the satellite countries. They asked me to add something about Gorbachev's speech, and gave me only a half-hour to do it. They seemed delighted. A radio interview with the Voice of the USSR this afternoon—beamed to all the African countries. Everyone is clearing out, but I've been asked to stay on. Interviews, and a trip to Leningrad. Red Square and Kremlin—pure magic, and me without a camera. Forgot it. Unbelievable! To me, and the Russians!

View from hotel window: Melancholy winter landscape. Cross-country skiers, skating rinks, hockey rinks. Trees—naked, spectral, and somber. Solitary, black-clothed figures trudging through the snow. On the horizon—rows of low-rent high rises/Nikita Kruschev's monument to the lower class.

Visited Alexander Pushkin's home where he and his bride Natalya spent three months. Rather sumptuous living quarters for a poet who lived on the brink of poverty. Paintings of the couple and their contemporaries, glimpses of their dress and times. Furniture was highly polished. Chandeliers sparkled. Everything seemed so precious. Had the feeling the couple might enter any moment. Asked to write a note to Pushkin. Honored, I did. Beneath my words, a translator wrote my sentiments in Russian. Meanwhile, I was to sit in a nearby chair until he finished. A delicate chair, I sat down gently, heard the cracking as the legs burst out in four directions. Then me, flat on the gleaming floor. Embarrassing! Most embarrassing! I was relieved to see smiles of apologies on the two caretakers' faces. Sorry, Pushkin.

As in every corner of the universe, black money marketeers are here. One emerged from a dark corner as I was entering my room tonight. "Dollars for rubles? Cheap."

"No, thanks."

Serge, my interpreter, is nearly six feet seven inches. I taught him the "Harlem Handshake," and he's killing everybody with it. Better to put your hand in a vise. He's like a big smiling bear, but with a small sense of humor. Spells his name four different ways—Sergio, Sergey, Serebga, and just Serge. The Russians know me as ГОРДОН ЛАРКС. Met with Elem Kimov, USSR Film Industry Chief. He had been to my apartment in New York. We discussed the possibility of my making films there. He felt encouraged. It's a long shot, but who knows. Hollywood wasn't exactly a pushover for me. Tomorrow night—Leningrad.

Leningrad / February 18, 1987
The train from Moscow, The Red Arrow, was comfortable, elegant, with only sleeping compartments. Tea served before bed. 500 kilometers through flying snow, but couldn't manage to sleep. Too excited, perhaps.

The Hotel Europeiyaska is miserably cold. Maids wearing layers of heavy sweaters. My room is spacious, but drably appointed with odds and ends of furniture. Radio is ancient and the television doesn't work. Bright red telephone seems out of character. There is a narrow foyer, then a bathroom. The tub is remarkably large, with small shower attachment. Must have been fashioned for the Czars. The lobby is big, noisy, and spotted with elegant remnants of the past. The food, except for breakfast, is terrible. I've always thought the Russians would be great cooks. A mistake. The steak for lunch was charred beyond recognition and tough as leather. Oh, for a Burger King!

Beautiful city! Terribly cold and gray, but beautiful! So many churches. They stand regimented, like soldiers of the white winter. The Russians seem to love moving about in this freezing dreariness—visiting historic sites. Aged painters stand numbly in the snow, their brushes stiff from cold, making a few rubles for the day.

Visited the Palaces of the Czars. En route, saw where the Germans were stopped, a few miles out of the city. A monument is being erected there to honor Russian heroism. Magical forests surround the palaces. Acres and acres of leafless, black trees standing above the snow. Waves of pale light. A blood-red moon appeared for a few moments; behind the grayness, the spindly branches. For the first time, I longed for a camera.

The Czars lived well—incredibly well. Halls, halls, halls—for thrones, for banqueting. Rooms, rooms, all elegantly appointed. The blue drawing room, the Chesme, divan, portrait, partridge, crown, and presence rooms. The study of Peter the Great, State rooms, and the Empress's Study. Avenues of fountains spraying high in the air. Overwhelming to the eye!

Aging, beefy women sit like sentinels at every door, seeing that nothing is touched or disturbed. Their drab clothes add irony to the splendor they are there to protect.

Both Moscow and Leningrad are paradoxical. The peasant classes loathed the Czarists, yet show enormous pride in preserving their past. At the Hermitage, they are reconstructing the opulence they hated so much. The chandeliers in "Catherine's Cottage" now outnumber those she had installed. The walls are weighted with great art treasures from all over the world. The luxurious past emerges as the most important to pull in tourist trade.

Invited to Bolshoi Ballet tonight, but too tired. Off to bed. Would like to stay a couple of days more, but the cold is too much. No amount of clothing seems to help. The cold seeps right into the bones. Back to

Moscow tomorrow night. Thinking about my New York apartment, the comfort and warmth. There is a difference—a great difference.

Serge writes screenplays. "No success yet, too young to be noticed." Acted in one film. "A bad one." The phone rang at two-hour intervals all night. You pick up—and always a busy signal.

Moscow / February 19, 1987

Almost missed the Red Arrow back here. It left around midnight. At 11:30, Serge hadn't showed. Five minutes later, he stumbled into my room—tanked to the gills with vodka. We reached the station with eight minutes to spare, only to find we were six tracks away. After a lot of shepherding, I managed to get him to our car. Then, trouble. The conductor, a runt of a man, informed us that we had come to the wrong car. Serge exploded. The conductor trembled and dropped our tickets beneath the train. "Get them! Crawl down and get them!" Serge bellowed. The Red Arrow was about to move off, but the frightened man endangered his life and retrieved our tickets, then ushered us aboard. We found strange bags in our compartment. No problem. Serge hurled them into the passageway. A woman ran up, protesting—until Serge threatened to throw her off the train. He pulled out a fifth of vodka. "Now, my friend, we celebrate your trip to Russia. My friend Upakiun Kenenkagza is to join us. He, too, is a director."

"But, Serge, I'm dead tired."

"No problem. Call him Paki, for short."

Paki asked a thousand questions, but Serge's translation was shaky. Half the time he spoke Russian to me—English to Paki. They drank until I fell asleep. At dawn, I was trying to arouse Serge. We were nearing Moscow. Might as well try to arouse a stone. I got him off just before the Red Arrow started for the train shed. I admired his fox-fur hat. "You look good in it, my friend. It's yours," he said.

"How much?"

"Nothing, my friend. It's yours."

"Two hundred and fifty?"

"Ah, but it cost three hundred."

"Okay—three hundred. Dollars or rubles?"

"I can't take either." He sighed. "Ah, my friend, I love those portable jukeboxes. I do love them."

"Where can I buy one?"

"Across town. Come on. We go there."

For two hundred and seventy-five dollars, I bought the jukebox. He had been good to me. I smiled and gave it to him. Since I had been good to him, he smiled and gave me his hat. "No problem, no problem," he said. "It was not for me, that hat. On you, it looks good."

En route to New York / February 22, 1987
Thinking back to Gorbachev's policy of reconstruction: his is a hard row to hoe. Distrust for America is so deeply rooted throughout the Soviet Union—in all aspects of the culture. I'm afraid it will take another century to overcome the past. Gorbachev's openness seems to be a sincere gesture toward peaceful co-existence. So far, it's been like trying to open a door that doesn't exist. Both sides are too single-minded about their particular slice of the universe. It would be a high moment if, in the pursuit of understanding, we could, for once, speak one language, stop threatening ourselves with death. But, first, the leaders have to change clothes, set aside the past, then let the roots of peace get to work. We should be weary of wiping out cities and mourning fallen heroes. Do away with hostile citadels and have no more talk of death.

We're high above the clouds. I've already had vodka and caviar. Now, for the first time in days—the sun. Home in seven hours and thirty minutes. It's nice to be headed that way again.

Much to Reagan's dismay, Gorbachev will be Man of the Year.

Florida / March 14, 1988
Willie Darden, a black man, goes to the electric chair tomorrow morning. It's one thing to know you will die someday; another thing to know that death will arrive for you at daybreak. Every life comes to an end—but, how cruel of the hour to tell you its name. That always leaves the world a bit dirtier.

STEPHEN J. PYNE

◆ ─────────────────────── ◆

Monsoon Lightning

For fifteen summers I worked on a forest fire crew at the North Rim of Grand Canyon, and from time to time I kept a journal of daily life. What follows is a distillation of that experience. Some terms will be unfamiliar: "The Area" refers to the Park Service–developed "area" at Bright Angel Point; "fire cache" is what forest firefighters call their fire station; "fedco" is the tradename for a five-gallon backpack pump; "Affirms" is the acronym for a computer-based information system which also calculates fire-danger ratings; "SWFF" stands for Southwest Forest Firefighters—in this instance, a squad of Navajos. "Rim" of course refers to the North Rim.

The Area / June 26

Another day in the cache. SWFFS sent with Stieg to repair fence. *T'oo bah'ih,* they call it; "no good." Dry, hot, windy. Fire weather great: fires lousy.

Fires everywhere but on the Rim. Took coffee break at the Lodge and watched the smokes on the Hualapai Reservation. Joe says they burn to clear off the chained juniper and the hotter the fire the better. Everything smoked in to the southwest. Kent sighted what looked like a smoke to the south of Kendricks Peak, on the Coconino; Forest Service action. When he took the situation report on Affirms this morning, Joe says, half the national forests in Arizona have a project fire. Kent and The Kid drove to North Rim Tower for lunch and a look and found nothing.

Ran heliport—routine shuttle flights between rims. Mostly just moved in and out of the fire cache, painting and sharpening tools and wrestling with the saws; the Big Mac is the only one that works, which Joe says is about normal. Later The Kid attacked Joe with a fedco and we nearly had an all-out water brawl. If Kent hadn't sabotaged the pumper, Joe would have retaliated by flooding The Kid out of the cache.

Listened to Uncle Jimmy reminisce about the Old Days—lots of fires, no jerry jobs, no idiot bosses. B.S., no doubt. Says we have to wait for the monsoon. Says that all the fires we see around the Rim have been set by people, but almost all our fires are set by lightning. Says we have to wait for the monsoon lightning.

After everyone had left for Lodge, I walked to the helispot and watched stars over the Canyon. Strong, crazy winds along Rim. There are always winds along the Rim. You can hear it from the cabin. The Rim is a strange, violent place: it simply, directly joins Plateau and Canyon, and there is nothing to grade between them; a kind of geographic rite of passage. I guess that is why the winds are so busy there. But the Rim is where we live and work. Our cabin is right along Rim. Joe says most of our fires occur along the Rim, which figures. Uncle Jimmy says the Rim is a time as much as a place. Whatever that means.

Read, and wrote in journal. Lots of time to write, not much to write about. Have entered nothing for several days. Glad I didn't join the rest of crew at the Lodge. Things got pretty rowdy in the saloon and the rangers had to shut it down. Uncle Jimmy says that's what happens when there aren't enough fires.

The Area / June 29
It seems crazy to live on the North Rim and not see the Grand Canyon the tourists see, so yesterday—my lieu day—I left the Area for the scenic drive. When I got back Stieg told me about the fire at Ribbons Falls, along the Kaibab Trail.

Everyone went save him and me. Had I been here, he says, I would have gone too. I may be happy I missed it. Joe says that it was a typical Canyon fire—most of it burned out before anyone arrived (a bitch of a hike, too: everyone had to jog down with packs in noon heat). Joe and The Kid followed the flames up some talus slopes and chased them into pack-rat middens. Winds were too squirrely to fly in or out so they had to hike back up. Waited for the shadows. Too bad they didn't have any fishing tackle. I watched some of the fire from Bright Angel Point. Joe says I can go by myself next time.

This afternoon the Forest Service had a big fire break out in Moquitch Canyon. We hung around the cache, sort of waiting for a call as backup. But nothing came through. The Kid climbed the tree-tower by the office and watched the smoke billow skyward. He says he could see clouds building up on the Peaks, too. Uncle Jimmy said, yes, he thinks the monsoon is coming. Then tonight we all went to the Lodge (I was more or less told I was going) and sat on the veranda and watched the storms plaster the San Francisco Peaks with lightning. Everything was pitch-black—cloudy overhead, no moon, just lightning silhouetting the Peaks in orange and yellow. Joe said it's converging on us, it'll be our turn soon. As we left I thought I could hear thunder rumble through Bright Angel Canyon.

Walked home; the others drove.

Cape Final / June 30
Fire at Cape Final. Everyone went—SWFFS too. Fire was along Rim: Joe and The Kid had to go into the Canyon to catch part of the fire that slopped over into Canyon brush; the rest of us stayed on Rim, hotspotting; still don't have a complete line around fire. Got the blue pumper in. McLaren (Park fire officer) called for slurry and a plane (B-17?) from South Rim airport made two passes. Hard time finding fire until it flared up. Lots of confusion. Uncle Jimmy disgusted. Joe says it's about time; says we ought to name it the Finally fire.

Cape Final: furtherest point east on Rim. Sticks out like a sore thumb. Near nothing else. Kent says we may might as well be in Chuar Amphitheater. No source tree, and may not be lightning-caused. Fire-road E-7 not far from here, so a tourist might have walked out this far. No one knows.

Using pocket notebook. Will transfer notes to journal later. Rations at 21:00 hrs. Mopped up until midnight. Kent and The Kid sent back to the Area for sleeping bags and headlamps and more rations.

Cape Final / July 1
Mopped up all day. Worked in early dawn, then had breakfast. Kent found a swath of white ash and thinks fire started there. Two crews working pumpers, and we have lots of water, though Uncle Jimmy and a SWFF (Henry John) stayed with shovels and fedcos; says too much water is bad for your technique. Says we still don't know how to fight fire. We had some snag fires early in the season, but not everyone had arrived and the rookies like me hadn't even gone through fire school and we haven't really worked together since then. Joe told me to put down my pulaski and take care of the real mopup. He meant my times.

Keep track of every hour, he said. Nothing fancy, just the fires and times. Don't trust them to do it for you. They never make mistakes in your favor. Better yet, he said, fill out the report yourself. No report, no pay. Yes, I told him. I have my pocket notebook in my firepack.

Broke for dinner around sunset and sat on Rim. Not a great view—the Kaibab puts the Canyon into shadow, but sky colors wonderful.

Took half-hour dinner so we could claim another hour of O.T. Left some handtools and a couple of canteens and a fedco in case more smokes show up after we leave. The Kid says he'll return tomorrow to check and pull up the flagging. We should make it back to the Area by 23:00.

The Area / July 2

Spent day in cache. The Kid and Uncle Jimmy checked the Finally fire and declared it out. Fixing tools and re-outfitting pumpers. Hot, cloudless.

Filled out a time report for the first time. This would normally be done by the fire boss, but I figured it would be good practice and that way Uncle Jimmy could make sure my times agreed with his. He spent day in Fire Pit completing the report. Every so often he would emerge and shout obscenities about the idiotic codes that you have to use to record everything and how he couldn't find the right code and what the hell difference did it make if the fire burned in fuel model C or U because it burned on the Rim which meant it burned in every kind of fuel. Then he would get a cup of coffee or fuss with the saws or pumpers before going back to the Pit.

Heard an incredible rumor. The rangers have coveted some Pivetta boots for their uniforms but haven't had any way to pay for them, so Kent says they told Uncle Jimmy to give them some overtime—charge it to the fire—enough to cover the costs. They say the fire was so disorganized, so many folks came and went, that no one would know. Uncle Jimmy refused. He says if they had any sense they would connive to get to the fires rather than to the money. But Kent thinks the reports were doctored after Uncle Jimmy sent them on.

A couple of the SWFFS came by looking for rides to the Lodge. Everyone else had gone, so I said I would drive them. Stayed for a couple of hours.

Copied jottings from notebook into log pretty much as is. I had thought that I could make it into a story. Now I find that there isn't much else to say. Can't write and fight both.

Swamp Ridge / July 4

Monsoon lightning. Fantastic storm throughout afternoon—bolts every few seconds, lights in cache and Pit blinking with each flash, rain and hail piling up on asphalt. Dispatched in pairs, one fire crew regular and one SWFF. Five fires so far. Sent out with Tommie Begaye to fire on Swamp Ridge.

Long drive, through national forest, then back into Park. Recon 1 gave us a bearing of 172°, corrected; snag fire; about half mile from Swamp Point road. Flagged our route in. Tommie spotted smoke, about forty yards from compass line. Gigantic ponderosa, base half-rotten. Cleared out swath along lean, then dropped tree. Put in a line. Bucked up and split open bole and scraped embers out and cooled with dirt and water. Little surface spread: needles and duff still wet from rains. Both of us made an extra trip back to pumper for fedcos and rations (only brought in one pack initially: took saw and fedco and handtools instead); dark when we left fire for vehicle. Mopped until now, around 23:00. Tommie has gone back for sleeping bags. Should finish in morning. Decided to name it the Independence fire. Listening to radio.

Half of crew on the Grail fire at Lancelot Point. Drier there and a patch of bug-killed snags, and fire got caught in strong winds along Rim and downdrafts from thunderheads. Uncle Jimmy says it's probably an acre, with maybe a dozen snags that need to be dropped. Lots of mopup. Reinforcements came in by helicopter—found old helispot not far from fire. Other fires about like ours. No one can raise Joe, somewhere in Kanabownits Canyon, and Chuck may send out a search party. Plan to go to Grail fire and help mop tomorrow. Uncle Jimmy says more fires will probably show up in morning. Got Joe on radio: says his fire was too easy and there won't be enough overtime and he wants another.

Twilight Zone, north of Point Sublime Road / July 5
Six fires this morning. Everyone dispatched from their fire to another except for the Grail fire, where two were left to drop snags and baby-sit. Recon 1 discovered smoke not far from us along Swamp Ridge, and we not only arrived there early but got pumper in (only couple hundred yards from W-4B fireroad). Green ponderosa, little spread by ground fire, fire mostly confined to lightning scar. Dropped and hosed down tree, then scratched a line. Over by noon. Sent to make initial attack on larger smoke in Twilight Zone—that's what Joe calls it. No fireroads here. Long hike on compass bearing (22°, corrected) from pumper. Joe and Henry John followed our flagging in. Tommie and I already had one small snag down and were ready to fell another. Joe said to finish it off. He said he and Henry would help clear a drop site, then dig line while Tommie and I bucked up the trunk. Took all afternoon. The Kid and two SWFFS joined us after dinner; brought in some fedcos and rations and canteens. All other fires out except Grail fire. Everyone else will go there tomorrow, and looks like they will call for Forest Service assistance—

we're spread too thin. Uncle Jimmy wants to sling in some cubitainers of water and fedcos by helo to speed along the mopup at Grail. No storms today, but Uncle Jimmy thinks there may be more fires—sleepers, he calls them. Monsoon only starting.

Need to get new pocket notebook. This one nearly filled. Joe was right: if I hadn't kept score, I wouldn't remember which times went with which fire.

The Area / July 6

Grail fire still being mopped up, but everyone else back in Area; one FS tanker crew at Grail. Cache in uproar. Spent morning putting everything back in order—saws, pumpers, firepacks, times. Have to be ready for next bust. In afternoon, after Recon 1 gave us an all-clear, we returned to check old fires. Found a few smokes on Independence fire and dumped rest of canteens on them and worked the duff with shovels. Mopup—it's like proofing, it never ends. Waited twenty minutes; no smokes, so left and pulled flags. The tough fires are on the Rim.

The Area / July 7

Rechecked Twilight fire—one small smoke in duff. Spent afternoon extracting a fire report from my notebook. As fire boss I have to submit reports (times) for both Independence and Twilight fires. Much more fun to fight fires than report them. The Kid says it's indecent to make fires continue by having to write them up. Joe says it's like double mopup. Affirms calls for drying spell over next few days, then new surge of monsoon moisture. Everyone back tonight, and I joined them at Lodge, but too tired for more than a couple of beers.

The Dragon / July 10

Big smoke reported on The Dragon around 16:00 two days ago. Chuck called for a helo, and Uncle Jimmy and I and Henry Goldtooth flew for initial attack. Winds too strong and squirrely to land; backed off on full power. Returned to Harvey Meadow and dropped Henry off and went back to Dragon and landed this time. Kent told to round up some reserves and drive them to the Dragon trailhead and hike in. Rest of regular crew and SWFFs to be flown in until dark. Uncle Jimmy and I flagged route from helspot to fire. Fire on Rim, a few acres in size.

Winds blustery. We jogged around fire with shovels and canteens. Lots of surface fire, whipped into red whitecaps by winds. Some fire apparently spilled over Rim into Canyon. Rim fire burning in a shallow basin, so we began lining it along the flanking ridges. Joe and Henry arrived. Sounds of helo overhead, the scrape and thunk of handtools on rock and duff and root, the whoosh and snap of flame. Work slow but heart fast: adrenalin flashed like lightning. More arrivals. Kent reached trailhead, but still had a couple-hour hike ahead of him; would arrive after dark. Sunset painted sky on fire.

Uncle Jimmy organized us into two squads—regular fire crew and swffs. Almost lost line at one point (flame advancing like a surf), but Henry John rallied swffs and they cut a scratch line and burned out and held. Joe found a good fire burning over Rim; but Uncle Jimmy wanted nothing to do with it at night. Kent and his mob arrived, and one fee collector crashed beneath a pine, and a thirsty ranger from the inner Canyon grabbed a quart canteen filled with chain oil, thinking it was water, and took a big swallow of thirty-weight; pretty well lubed for the night. Last helo flight brought in hot meal from Lodge. The Kid and Tommie Begaye sent back to the helispot to get it. Very dark: only light comes from fire, boiling like lava. Cold. Sweat congealed. Joints stiff. Hungry. Can hear winds over and around Rim.

Ate late and by headlamp. Quiet; everyone tired. Joe and I sent on patrol. Kent told to take his mob and find a place to bed down; they'll begin mopping up in morning. Uncle Jimmy sat down on a small rise, with his back to the Rim—probably trying to take notes, get our times straight. Joe says we'll have to write a narrative for the fire because it is big and will cost more. We hiked around the perimeter, knocked fire out of the base of one snag, then lined it, and located a large flat rock that overlooked most of fire. Stars thick as embers.

The Dragon is a curious place, a peninsula that thrusts south into Canyon, nearly segregated from the Kaibab by erosion. It is all Rim: Canyon and Plateau nearly perfectly balanced, so that you are never far from either. Lots of fires. Fire signs everywhere. Lightning scars on many trees. Charred bark, scabs of brush where ponderosa burned out, bare limestone paves ground. Eerie, yet compelling. Joe says The Dragon has the highest fire load on North Rim. He says no one can be on the crew long and not experience a fire on Dragon, and no one can claim to have fought fire without coming here. No one else comes here; no rangers, no tourists, no one except the fire crew. Uncle Jimmy said in fire school that The Dragon was located at the apex of the Rim's fire triangle. Cute phrase, I thought. But The Dragon isn't cute: it's all fire and all Rim.

Listened to radio. Stieg didn't come. Suddenly refused to get into helo, and Kent had already departed, so he was left behind. Another fire was located just before sunset, however—small snag fire on Crystal Ridge. Stieg took Bundy (garbage collector), and our helo, on a return flight, helped guide him into smoke. Now his radio was stuck on broadcast, and we listened as he explained to a skeptical Bundy how they would drop the tree. Bundy didn't want to spot for Stieg under the tree, wanted to stand back with a fedco and squirt water on him if any branches fell; hilarious. Joe said that Stieg told him he planned to transfer to the rangers soon. Said it was too bad he froze up about flying because he had never been to a Dragon fire before. I guess he had had enough without The Dragon. Joe said Stieg deserved what was happening to him. Finally whatever jammed Stieg's radio open broke free. Joe called him and kidded him about not coming to a real fire. Then I saw it.

It was just a glow at first, an orange specter over the Rim. I saw tongues of flame and then Joe and I both heard it and we stared as the whole Canyon flank seemed to erupt into fire and Joe grabbed his radio and warned Uncle Jimmy who ran to the Rim in time to watch a thin stream of flame rush up to the Rim, then Uncle Jimmy shouted for the rest of the crew to get their asses out of their sleeping bags and get some tools because the whole fucking Canyon was on fire and if we didn't hold it at the Rim we would lose everything. Then it got really interesting.

A wild, true Rim fire. For half an hour everything was a frenzy of men and noise; saws whined and coughed, trees fell in crashes, handtools scraped and chipped in atonal splendor, radios and voices shouted over the roar of flames. Not once but several times long strips of flame rushed out of the Canyon. We stood on the Rim, our faces flushed with firelight, our backs in darkness. Uncle Jimmy was everywhere, shouting and cutting. But the line held. By the time we crawled back into our bags, a false dawn edged into view.

The fire went on for two more days. We dropped retardant from a PB4Y2 for several hours in that first morning to prevent another blowup. Uncle Jimmy reasoned that the fire had slopped over the Rim then crept along the surface downslope, drying out the brush above it, then caught some updrafts and swept up through the dessicated crowns. He didn't want that to happen again. Then mopup. All day. Sent Kent and the irregulars home; fire was lost on them. Joe and I donned fedcos and plunged down the slope into the scene of the night burn, the rocks slippery with slurry, careful to stay in the burned-out zones. Mopped up along slopes. Hot. Crummy night, slept only from exhaustion. Then another day of the same. Joe and I again had to go over the Rim and mop up. But that evening we were all flown home. Uncle Jimmy declared the fire out. He told me that Stieg would transfer soon and I could take over the blue pumper if I wanted.

Nothing left but the paperwork. Glad I took notes. Things were so confused that no one could agree on exactly what happened or to whom or when. Uncle Jimmy looked at my notes and gave me his and told me to write up a narrative. For a fire like this, he explained, you have to have a narrative as well as the coded report. You can't leave it in your pocket, he said. It has to be a public document. I hardly knew where to begin. First there is nothing to write about, then there is too much. It was as though a whole season had to be distilled into one bust, one fire. No report, no pay, Uncle Jimmy reminded me. All flame and no fortune. Write it.

Everyone planned to meet at the saloon and talk about The Dragon and fire and what a great time we had. The Kid suggested someone ought to write it up, and Joe said I was, and everyone laughed because they knew no one would read the narrative, only the times, and a real smokechaser would only want to go to another fire, not write up an old one. Sitting in the Pits, Joe calls it. Uncle Jimmy told everyone to go home and get ready for some serious drinking. Then he asked if I felt any different. Yeah, I said. I feel richer.

Walking to the Lodge tonight I saw Tommie Begaye on the other side of the road, mad that he had missed a ride and that I had chosen to walk rather than drive. This road *t'oo bah'ih*, he yelled. He ran over and then ahead of me. I ran past him. The pavement glistened like black scales. Then we both ran, shoulder-to-shoulder along the Rim, all the rest of the way.

MORDECAI RICHLER

◆ ——————————————— ◆

Journals

*M*onday, *April 4*

The mail. Today's batch yielded the usual requests for funds to stop acid rain, fight apartheid, support abortion-on-demand, and to send a personal item, however modest, for auction at the hard-pressed public library in Regina. More to my taste was the following letter from the Nigerian Society for the Advancement of Management & Business Studies (N.S.A.M.B.S.), P.O. BOX 426, Owerri—Nigeria, W/A.

Dear Professor Richler,

REQUEST FOR YOUR ACADEMIC TREASURES/PUBLICATIONS

We are very happy to write you for the first time today and perhaps not the last, this humble and friendly letter which we sincerely believe would receive your gracious blessings.

First and foremost, we wish to express through this medium our appreciation, immeasurable gratitude and great admiration for your remarkable, highly examplary and fruitfully inspiring contributions towards the rapid advancement of higher learning in the world today.

Unfortunately, we only read about your wonderfully motivating and practically rewarding academic works from some Overseas Academic and Book-review journals, as we have not been lucky to find your nice publications in any of our local bookshops and libraries. As a result therefore, we have decided to approach you as a world great writer and publisher for immediate assistance. We therefore, strongly request you to help us by sending to us some of your brilliantly authoritative academic treasures/publications such as:

"JOSHUA THEN AND NOW" "IMAGES OF SPAIN" "THE STREET" "SHOVELLING TROUBLE" AND "CANADIAN WRITING NOW"

We should in addition to above, graciously welcome any other book(s), journals, posters or even reprints you may wish to send to us in any field.

As we optimistically and anxiously look forward to hearing

favourably from you soon, we pray God to guide and bless you in
your wonderful academic works. We wish you the best!

Yours sincerely,

P. ABANGWEL OSUAGWU

Secretary (NSAMBS).

Tuesday / April 5

For the past year my wife and I have been rooted in our country cottage,
where I continue to struggle with a long and convoluted novel. Given
the opportunity I could shaft it right now with a more scathing review
than any I am likely to see when I finish it. I've always suspected that
every novelist writes one too many, and now that I'm fifty-seven all those
luminous brain cells I once counted on seem extinguished by Rémy
Martin or Glenlivet. I wonder if my turn has come.

Our cottage is on Lake Memphremagog, some seventy-five miles
southeast of Montreal, hard by the Vermont border. Originally we only
came out here for two months of summer and weekends in winter, but
now that we are no longer tied to the school year (our five children grown
up) we are about to give up our Montreal apartment and make this our
home. It's a wrench. It means finally giving away books (bought maybe
thirty years ago, crated and carted from continent to continent) that I
now have to admit I'll never get round to reading. Florence is being
difficult. She won't let me discard novels she has read years ago and will
probably never turn to again. "I am what I have read," she says, settling
matters. And me, I won't part with my three volume *History of Ferdinand
and Isabella*, by W. H. Prescott, not that I'm ever going to read it but
because it reminds me of the sunny afternoon I bought the set at a stall
alongside the Seine. From there I went on to meet Mason Hoffenberg
at The Old Navy on Boulevard St.-Germain. We were joined briefly by
Terry Southern. Then Mason and I strolled down to the Ile St.-Louis,
talking about Céline and Duke Snider's season and the merits of hashish
vs. booze and the incomparable view from the hilltop overlooking
Toledo. Mason died a couple of years back. I ran into Terry quite by
accident three years ago in Elaine's. We embraced, exchanged addresses
and phone numbers, and haven't been in touch since.

Florence and I have come to terms. We agree to begin simplifying
our lives, as they say, by disposing of two shelves full of old *National
Geographics*, possibly the first move in any housecleaning since the children have gone.

We like it in the country. As I write, the winter ice has finally begun to rot in the bay, I can see more open water each morning, but the earth is still hard, the trees bare. However we have survived another seemingly endless Quebec winter. Florence now spends her evenings contemplating garden catalogues and I, lying without shame again, promise once more to help establish the vegetable garden. Then I stretch out on the sofa before the TV set, a prisoner to the Stanley Cup playoffs that will last a month. Tonight Montreal takes Hartford 4–3 in the opener. Good.

Wednesday, April 6
Certain of my soul foods are unavailable out here. Pickled herring. Rye bread. Smoked meat. The nearby town of Magog also lacks a decent butcher or fishmonger. So once a week we drive into town to shop and to see our youngest son, Jake, who still lives in Montreal.

Five o'clock I pop into Winnie's for a drink. Julian is the only one of my friends standing at the bar. He has just returned from a trip to Toronto, where he found what appeared to be a decent French restaurant, sat down, and looked at the menu. "What's the soup du jour?" he asked the waiter.

"One moment please, sir," the waiter said.

He drifted off to the kitchen and came right back. "It's the soup of the day," he said.

I laugh and make a mental note to remember that. I can use it somewhere. I should keep a notebook, but I'm far too lazy. Besides, I don't trust writers who keep notebooks, suspecting they also make copies of their personal letters and keep scrapbooks and write smarmy thank-you notes to reviewers.

Got back to the country in time to catch the last two periods of the hockey game. Montreal 7, Hartford 3.

Thursday, April 7
No matter where we've lived (London, Rome, Amagansett, Lisbon, Montreal, etcetera) I've always worked at home and come five o'clock repaired to a favored pub or bar to drink and mull over the day's events with real men, men who actually went to offices and then home to dinner with dazzling tales to charm their wives. Me, descending from my second-floor work room, I've usually got nothing to say.

"Work hard today, darling?"

"Yeah," I reply cautiously, because I know when I'm being teased.

"Did it go well?"

"Ah, come on."

Strangers married to dentists or real estate developers say to my wife, "Oh, your husband's a writer. You must lead such an interesting life."

Florence, bless her, is loyal. She doesn't break up laughing, neither does she punch anybody out. Instead she smiles graciously and says, "Oh yes, yes of course."

Mind you, I put up with my share of guff too. Real men with offices who tell me, "Of course I haven't got time to read, but my wife enjoyed your last book." Or take, for instance, the twinkly morning TV interviewer who once asked me, "Do you base your stories on real people or do you just make them up out of your own head?"

Still, being married to a writer must be hell. I count on Florence's judgment. She's not only my wife, but also my editor-in-residence, a most unenviable chore. If she doesn't like something I've done, I won't submit it to my publisher, but neither will I take her out to dinner, come home with flowers, or even water the vegetable garden. And if she does approve of what I've done, I'm inclined to doubt her honesty. What if it's just compassion for an aging, often disagreeable novelist?

Out here my bar is The Owl's Nest, a nondescript box slapped together on the 243 roadside. My good companions at the Nest include Jigsaw, Sweet Pea, Dipstick, Buzz, Coz, and Buff, all of whom were raised on scratch farms (invariably rocky, the soil shallow) that were lost to the banks years ago. The first thing their struggling fathers sold off, because it was no damn good for anything, was the steeply inclined lake frontage land, now worth a fortune. In winter the regulars at the Nest plough snow, serve as caretakers to the affluent Montrealers with cottages on the lake, stitch together pickup carpentry jobs, work at one of the local bobbin mills or hibernate, sitting out the season on welfare. Jigsaw's wife, who puts in long hours as a cleaning lady, is understandably unimpressed with what I do for a living. "I could write a book too," she once told me, "but I just wouldn't know how to put it into words."

"That never stopped him," Sweet Pea said.

Today Robert George, one of the owners of the Nest, has banged a new notice into the cork board on the wall over the Double-Up Joker Poker machine.*

FOR THE "BENEFIT" OF THE GEORGE CEMITARY
ON VALE PERKINS ROAD
"AUX PROFITS" DU CIMETIERE GEORGE SUR LE
CHEMIN VALE PERKINS

WRAFFLE: ¼ Beef	TIRAGE: ¼ Boeuf
1 Ticket $1.00	1 Billet
6 Tickets $5.00	6 Billets
10 Tickets $10.00	10 Billets (1 souper gratis
including one free meal ticket	inclus)

I buy six tickets and Robert, appreciative, immediately sends me a double scotch.

Bad news. A couple of days ago Spiderman, a notorious drunk, fell and cracked his head on the pavement outside the Legion Hall just over the border in North Troy, and now he can't even recognize his wife. All the same he leaped at her this morning, fists flying, and they had to tie him up and take him away in an ambulance. Mind you, Spiderman, an ugly drunk, never did know any Saturday night satisfaction until he found a fight. His nose has been broken more than once and most of his teeth have been knocked out. His kids are terrified of him. "Yeah," Sweet Pea says, "but if you caught him early enough in the morning, when he was still sober, you could never find a nicer guy."

Hello, hello. Jigsaw is with us today. Jigsaw reads the Montreal *Gazette*, not only the sports section but even the editorials, and he watches The National on CBC-TV every night. He votes. He writes letters to his MP. And this afternoon Jigsaw is extremely upset about the free-trade deal soon to be signed by Canada and the United States. Sipping on a Bud, he turns to me, the only other intellectual in the bar, and says, "If we sign that fucken deal we're gonna lose our fucken national identity. The fucken Yanks will wipe the floor with us. We're gonna become the fifty-first state."

"About time too," Sweet Pea says, going on to point out that gas is much cheaper in Vermont, and so is beer and vodka and tires for a grader. All of life's necessities.

Fortunately there's no hockey game tonight, the teams are traveling. I make another attempt to thin out my books. But I can't let go of my torn Tauchnitz Edition paperback of *Daisy Miller*, which I picked up for sixpence at David's bookstall on the Market Square in Cambridge on a Saturday morning in 1951. A printed note on the first page reads: "I desire it to be understood that the present is the only edition of 'Daisy Miller,' 'An International Episode' and 'Four Meetings' published on the Continent of Europe with my assent." It is signed Henry James, Jr., and dated April 1870. And then a previous owner of the volume has scribbled a note in pencil on the title page: "a weakness—Giovanelli's dismissal from the plot is contrived by his not having attended Daisy on her illness—most unlikely."

And what's this? A signed copy of *Edward Gordon Craig, Designs for the Theatre*, by Janet Leeper. Craig presented it to me on the village square in Tourettes-sur-Loup in 1952. In his eighties at the time, he was living in a pension in Vence. Craig said, "A young man came to see me yesterday and told me that he was my son, but I think he was just trying to make an impression."

Florence and I watch The National together at 10:00 P.M., sick at heart over the events in Israel. I try to lighten matters with a lame joke. "On the other hand, there is a certain symmetry in the sons of Isaac and Ishmael stoning each other again after 5,000 years."

Friday, April 8

Happy days ahead. According to today's *Gazette*, Mayor André Auger of St. Lin (pop. 6,000) is pushing through a new bylaw to properly reward French-Canadian fertility. Under his innovative scheme, which will do zilch for TV ratings but keep a lot of couples busy elsewhere, a family will now receive $500 for having a third child, $600 for a fourth, $700 for a fifth, and so on. "I am a Quebec nationalist," Auger said. "I believe Quebec should repopulate itself *itself*."

Quebec's birthrate, once legendary, is now among the lowest in the western world, and this has also got jolly Jacques Parizeau, the new leader of the separatist Parti Québecois, thinking deep and dirty. He is concerned lest French-Canadians, failing in their conjugal obligations, wake up one morning to find themselves a minority in their own home-land. And so, if elected, Parizeau will stand up for more fruitful fucking, sponsoring a baby-bonus program. Well, okay. Very nice. But like most proposed PQ measures this one does not go nearly far enough. Obviously something will also have to be done about randy Jews (I speak as an unapologetic father of five), horny Wasps, and what the PQ charmingly calls neo-Quebecers, that is to say, Greeks, Italians, and Portugese, all notoriously sex-crazed. In order for the bonus to do its work I think it should apply only to bona fide Québecois and that the rest of us should be fined rather than rewarded for not being more careful between the sheets.

Look to South Africa or Israel for tragedy. In this room of the North American attic we are living through a farce. Ours is an Alice-Through-the-Looking-Glass province, the only North American territory where so-called anglophones are a threatened minority. Under the terms of Bill 101, the French Language Charter, tradesmen are not allowed to post bilingual signs outside their stores. If, however, they employ four workers or less they are allowed bilingual signs inside their stores by the inspectors of the Commission de Protection de la Langue Française or what we, the oppressed, irreverently refer to as the tongue-troopers.

The issue has now gone to the Supreme Court of Canada, which is expected to rule that Quebec's French-only sign law violates freedom-of-expression guarantees under the Canadian Charter of Rights. But hold the phone, this won't be the end of it, not in our delightfully loopy country. In Canada, if a province disagrees with a freedom *guaranteed* under the charter it can simply opt out, invoking something called "a notwithstanding clause." And this is precisely what Bobby Bourassa, our slippery Liberal premier, is expected to do. He is being counted on to disallow outside bilingual signs to—as he puts it—keep the social peace, but as a sop to the linguistically deprived it is expected that he will continue to wink at inside bilingual signs. Yes, yes, awfully good of him I'm sure. King Solomon would approve. But, speaking as an old hand at Talmudic distinctions, I fear that even such a compromise begs further questions. I assume that some of those inside signs will hang in dark corridors and will therefore require lighting from above. A tricky business, one that requires more legislative guidance. What wattage, for instance, would be considered defiant, a menace to the French face of Quebec, and what would be considered respectful? Would an inspector from the Commission de Protection de la Langue Française take 200 watts to be subversive, a call to arms? 150 watts pushy? 50 watts sufficiently humble?

Florence is in Montreal today, dealing with our income tax papers which I, being such an artistic fellow, am too pure of heart to cope with. So I'm alone here, which I don't like very much. Alone and guilt-ridden, having laid such a nasty boring job on my wife. I decide to impress Florence by doing another cleanup before she returns tomorrow night, making some room for all the useless stuff that will be coming here from our apartment. Sifting through old letters, pausing to reread just about every one of them, I figure I'm clearing an inch of space an hour, not quite good enough. But at least I do find something I feared was lost. An item sent to me by a bright student in the Maritimes. It is an advertisement he found posted on his university notice board, and I quote it in full.

quote it in full.

A

GATHERING OF

JEWISH LESBIAN DAUGHTERS

OF HOLOCAUST SURVIVORS

(and Partners—

Lovers and Lesbian

Friends)

NOVEMBER

13–15 1987

If you are a Jewish Lesbian with one or more parents who survived
the holocaust, or a partner, join us for a weekend in New Hampshire.
Workshops, discussion, and support around the issues we share.
For more information contact:

JLDHS, Box 6194
Boston, MA 02114

Satire is becoming a very difficult business. Possibly there is no
longer any need to invent.

OLIVER SACKS

◆ ─────────────── ◆

Travel Happy
(1961)

In October of 1960—I had just arrived in the States, after hiking and brooding in Canada, through the summer—I set out to explore my new country, on a motorcycle. I covered ten thousand miles in my erratic, zigzag travels, and kept a Journal constantly as I traveled—"Travel Happy" is a fragment of that vast Journal.

In 1962 I "settled down" to the clinical work and writing which was to occupy me for the next twenty-five years—I wrote *Migraine, Awakenings, Leg,* and *Hat,* and a dozen more books, which I kept to myself. I seemed to be living my life, like my patients, in the bowels of Institutions.

In the past few months I have revolted, felt a passionate need to travel again, to be on the Road, to see other people and places, to see, once again, the real, uninstitutionalized World. But this impulse is now *combined* with the scientific one—it is a desire, now, for exploration, a sort of scientific travel: I want to see how it is for the Deaf, for those with Tourette's Syndrome, in remote parts of the world. I have again taken to the Road, and have been zigzagging here and there, but now in search of some fresh (perhaps anthropological) vision and reality, with a sense of fresh air, the outdoors, the real world, blowing through it. I want to write a book which is at once a travel narrative, a series of portraits, and a new Tourettology, an inseparable mixture of landscape, human life, and science.

Finding myself in Alabama this Spring—I had heard interesting reports of the Touretters of Tuscaloosa—I had an impulse to look up "Travel Happy," to find Mac and Howard and Carol and Sue, to find them (and, of course, my own youthful self)—and perhaps, most of all, my own youthful self—miraculously vivid and unchanged, in a changeless, timeless 1960. I didn't go, I would have felt like a revenant—but on my return I dug up this piece, blew the dust of twenty-seven years off it, and found it as fresh as the day it was written.

Rereading it, reliving it, *was* a return to "Travel Happy," a magical re-entry to that little piece of the past. I keep photos and souvenirs, like everyone else, I keep letters, but, above all, I am glad I keep Journals—as I have done, on and off, for the past forty years—for they are the best way of bringing to life what it was really like, *once*, recapturing and recovering the otherwise irrecoverable past.

Something was wrong, no doubt of it.

It was an April morning, a few miles north of New Orleans, and I was tinkering with the engine of my bike, in some forsaken lay-by. As I lay there on my back I detected, with some sixth seismic sense, a distant tremor, like a far-off earthquake. It advanced toward me, becoming a rattle, then a rumble, and finally a roar, culminating in the screech of air brakes and a terrific cheerful honking. I looked up, paralyzed, and saw the vastest truck I had ever seen, a very Leviathan of the road. An impudent Jonah stuck his head out from the window, and hollered at me, from the great altitude of his cab:

"Anything I can do?"

"She's shot!" I answered, "busted rod or something."

"Shit!" he remarked pleasantly, "if that breaks loose, it'll cut your leg off! Be seeing you."

He grimaced, ambiguously, and maneuvered his huge truck onto the road once more.

I rode on and on, and soon left the swampy lowlands of the Delta. Soon I was in Mississippi. The road meandered here and there, capricious and unhurried, winding through thick forests and open pastures, through orchards and meadows, over a score of intersecting rivers, and in and out of farms and villages, all tranquil and motionless in the morning sun. I sang wordlessly as I rode; the bike was holding up and I had no worries.

But after I crossed into Alabama the bike grew rapidly worse. I hung on every variation of its sound, pondering on noises which were sinister, but unintelligible. It was disintegrating fast, this much was certain: but ignorant, and fatalistic, I felt I could do nothing to arrest its fate.

Five miles beyond Tuscaloosa the engine faltered and seized. I grabbed the clutch, but one of the cylinders was already smoking by my foot. I drew to a halt, shouting in the desolation: THIS IS THE END, THIS IS THE END!! I dismounted and laid the bike out flat upon the ground, covering its poor dead headlamp with my leather jacket, reverently. Then I advanced toward the roadside, holding in my left hand a clean white handkerchief.

An hour passed, and another, and yet a third. A hundred cars passed by, and none pitied my frantic waving. It was not that the drivers failed to see me, for I was a conspicuous, perhaps fantastic, figure in the empty plain. Indeed, they would gaze at me, with a close and fearful attention; and then they seemed to shudder, and accelerated hastily.

The sun was dropping in the heavens, and an icy wind sprang up. The traffic was diminishing, and soon I would be abandoned, helpless, in the winter night, alongside my wrecked machine. I yelled with fury and frustration, cursing America for her ruthlessness.

Had I had a pocketful of caltrops I would have hurled them on the road, giggling sadistically as the punctured cars lined up. But I had no caltrops. I could only rant and rave.

I had almost given up hope, and was waving quite mechanically, when abruptly, incredulously, I realized that a truck was stopping. It looked familiar. Narrowing my eyes I spelled out its registration: 26539, Miami, FLA. Yes, it was it: the vast truck which had stopped for me this morning.

As I ran up to it, the driver descended from his cab, nodded toward the bike, and grinned:

"So you finally fucked it up, huh?"

A boy followed him down from the truck, and together we scrutinized the wreck.

"Any chance of a tow to Birmingham?"

"Naah, law says no!" He scratched the stubble on his chin, then winked: "Let's heave the motorcycle inside!"

We struggled and panted as we hoisted the heavy machine into the belly of the truck, moving wordlessly like performers in some grotesque charade. Finally it was secured among the furniture, tethered with ropes, and hidden from prying eyes by a tumbled mass of sacking.

He climbed back into the cab, followed by the boy, and then myself, and we esconced ourselves—in this order—along its broad seat. He gave a little bow, and performed formal introductions:

"This's my trucking partner, Howard. What's your name?"

"Wolf."

"Mind if I call you Wolfie?"

"No, you go right ahead. And yours?"

"Mac. We're all Mac, you know, but I'm the genuine original Mac! You can see it on my arm."

For a few minutes we drove in silence, "taking stock" of one another, surreptitiously.

Mac looked about thirty, though he could have been five years either side of this. He had a vigorous, alert, and handsome face, with a straight nose, firm lips, and a clipped moustache. He could have been a British cavalry officer; he could have played small "romantic" parts on screen or stage. He was, no doubt, a gallant lover, as one day he would be an admirable father. These were my first impressions.

He wore the peaked and crested cap all truckers wear, and a shirt emblazoned with the name of his company: ACE TRUCKERS, INC. Upon his arm was a red badge with the legend: PLEDGED TO COURTESY AND SAFETY, and half-concealed under the rolled-up sleeve, his name: MAC, entwined with a struggling python.

Howard could have passed for sixteen, but for the set lines which arched above his mouth. His lips were always slightly parted, revealing large yellow teeth, irregular but powerful, and an astonishing expanse of gum. His eyes were of the palest blue, like the eyes of some albino animal. He was tall and well-built, but graceless.

After a while he turned his head and gazed at me with his pale animal eyes. First he stared straight into my own eyes for a minute; then his gaze widened to embrace the rest of my face, my visible body, the cab of the truck, and the monotonously moving road outside the window. As his attention widened, so it faded, until his face resumed once more its vacant dreaminess. The effect was first disquieting and then uncanny. With a sudden horror and pity, I realized that Howard was feeble-minded.

Mac gave a short laugh in the darkness.

"Well, think we make a good pair?"

"I'll soon see," I answered.

"How far do you reckon you'll be taking me?"

"To the ends of the earth. New York anyhow. We'll make it Tuesday, maybe Wednesday."

He lapsed into silence again.

A few miles later he asked me suddenly:

"Ever hear of the Bessemer process?"

"Yes. We 'did' it in chemistry at school."

"Ever hear of John Henry, the steel-driving nigger?"

"No, I never heard of him."

"Well he lived right here. When they made a machine to drive a steel pick into a riverbed, they said that human labor could never compete. The niggers made a wager, and brought up their strongest man:

John Henry. They say his arms was bigger'n twenty inches. He held a mallet in each hand, and he drove in a hundred picks quicker than their machine. Then he lay down and died. Yessir! This is steel country."

We were surrounded by scrapyards, autowreckers, railway sidings, and smelting works. The air resounded with the clangor of steel, as if the whole of Bessemer was some gigantic forge or armory. Torches of flame topped the high chimneys, roaring as they swept up from the furnaces below.

I had only once before seen a city illuminated by flames, and that was as a child of seven, when I saw London in the great blitzes of nineteen forty.

After we had negotiated Bessemer and Birmingham, Mac started to speak freely of himself.

He had bought his truck for $500 down, and the balance—$20,000—over a year. He could take up to 30,000 lbs. of cargo, and traveled anywhere and everywhere: Canada, the States, Mexico, so long as there were decent roads and money to be made. He averaged four hundred miles in a ten-hour working day; it was illegal to work longer at a stretch, though frequently done. He had trucked, on and off, for twelve years now, and had been "riding double" with Howard for just six months. He was thirty-two, and lived in Florida; he had a wife and two children; and he made $35,000 a year, he said.

Education? Not too much of that. He ran away from school when he was twelve years old, and, looking older, got himself a traveling salesman's job. At seventeen he joined the police force, and at twenty was a considerable firearms expert. That year he'd been involved in a gunfight, and narrowly escaped being shot in the face at point-blank range. He lost his nerve after that, and changed to trucking, though he was still an honorary member of the Florida police force, and received one dollar a year in token of this.

Had I ever been in a gun fight? he enquired. No. Well, he'd been in more than he could remember, both as a policeman and a trucker. I'd find his "trucker's friend" right under the seat, if I cared to look; they all carried guns on the road. Though the best weapon in an unarmed fight was a piece of piano wire. Once you had it round your opponent's neck there was nothing he could do. You gave a little tug—and the head fell off: easy—like cutting cheese! There was no mistaking the relish in his voice.

He had carried everything in trucks, from dynamite to prickly pears, but had now settled down to trucking furniture, although this included anything which a man might keep in his house. He had the contents of seventeen homes on board, including seven hundred pounds of weights (the property of a muscleman, moving out to Florida); a grand piano made in Germany, said to be the best there was; ten television sets (they had one out at the truckstop last night, and plugged it in); and an antique four-poster (for sex in the grand old style), on its way to Philadelphia. If I wished to, I might sleep in this at any time.

The four-poster brought a nostalgic smile to his face, and he started talking of his sexual exploits. He seemed to have had an incredible success at all times and places, though four women held pre-eminence in his affections: a girl in L.A., who once eloped with him as a stowaway in his truck; two maiden ladies in Virginia he slept double with, who had showered him for years with clothes and money; and a hot-bellied Mexican nymph in Mexico City, who could take twenty men in a night and still cry for more.

As he warmed up, the last traces of diffidence disappeared, and he emerged as the full-blown Sexual Athlete and Storyteller, passionately involved, yet remembering all details with a lucid accuracy. He was profoundly funny, without knowing it, and occasionally tragic. He was God's gift to lonely women.

It was during this recital that Howard, who had been lying in a sort of stupor, pricked up his ears and showed his first signs of animation. Mac, seeing this, first humored him, then started to goad him with a teasing banter: tonight, he said, he was going to get a girl in the cab and lock Howard in the trailer, though one night, if the boy looked sharp, he might procure a real whore (he pronounced it "hooorrh") for him. Howard grew hot and wild, and started panting with excitement; finally he lunged angrily at Mac.

As they struggled in the cab, half in fury, half in play, the steering wheel was jolted violently, and the huge truck rocked dangerously along the road.

But between his taunts Mac was also educating Howard, informally:

"What's the capital of Alabama, Howard?"

"Montgomery, you filthy sonofabitch!"

"Yeah, that's right. 'Tain't always the biggest cities that's the State Capital. And those are pecan trees, look—over there!"

"Fuck you, I don't care!" grumbled Howard, but craned his head to see them, nonetheless.

We grew hungry around nine o'clock, and Mac suggested a roadside barbecue.

"We'll get spareribs and frankies and steaks, man, and have ourselves a ball. I got a heap of charcoal at the back there."

But all the groceries we passed were closed. A thin damp mist arose, checking our ardor for a roadside barbecue, blunting the edge of our euphoria. We had slowed down to a crawl in the thickening fog, when finally Mac spied a wan yellow light flickering ahead of us. It was an ancient general store, lit by a single gas flame.

We bought three French loaves, a mound of sliced Bologna, and a quart of buttermilk, their standard food for cross-country journeys, and designed to "settle the stomach," as Mac explained, old-maidishly. He ransacked the little place for something else, a "treat" in honor of their guest. Not finding what he wanted, he bawled at the wizened shop man:

"How about some banana peppers?"

The old man's face puckered, then burst into a pleased smile as he drew from behind the counter an enormous dust-covered jar, with dim shapes floating in it. I eyed the jar with fear, but Mac swooped on it exultantly.

An hour later we pulled in at a truck stop: Travel Happy, somewhere in the wilds of Alabama, for Mac had decided we should stay here overnight.

We unwrapped our food, and started to eat it in the cab. Howard refused the buttermilk, with a childish gesture. I tasted and then declined the banana peppers, after searing my tongue on the first morsel. But Mac ate the whole jar with insistent pride, exclaiming constantly how much he relished them. Yessir! He could eat them all day—why, he almost lived on them: And he had never had a cold since the day he started eating them. Nowadays, he gloated, there weren't too many men around who could "take" a good old-fashioned banana-pepper.

I hung my head in shame. I wasn't man enough to eat one quarter of a pepper, let alone a whole huge jar of them.

Finally the ritual of the peppers was over and done with, and we went inside for coffee. Mac settled down, with polite determination, to entertain me with "funny stories," of which he had an endless, execrable store, much inferior to his own first-hand experiences. Having discharged this friendly duty, he wandered off to join the crowd around the jukebox.

Truckers always gather round a jukebox on Saturday evenings, and try desperately to make the truck stop on this one night. The jukebox at Travel Happy, in particular, enjoys a certain fame, for it has a magnificent collection of trucking songs and ballads, epics of the road: savage, bawdy, melancholy, or wistful, but all with an insistent energy and rhythm, a special excitement which spells the very poetry of motion and endless roads.

Truckers are generally solitary men, with the conceits and consolations of solitary men: often morose, arrogant, and antisocial. Yet occasionally—as in a hot and crowded truckers' café, listening to some infinitely familiar record blaring on the jukebox—they are stirred, transfigured suddenly, without words or actions, from an inert crowd to a proud community: each man still anonymous and transient, yet knowing his identity with those around him, all those who came before him, and all who are figured in the songs and ballads.

Mac and Howard had become tonight, like all the others, rapt and proud, in unwitting transcendence of themselves. They were sinking into a timeless reverie.

Around midnight Mac gave a violent start and then tugged Howard by the collar, as if jerking the two of them abruptly from some viscous and enervating spell. He rubbed the smoke from his bleary eyes, and yawned prodigiously:

"Okydoke, Kiddo, let's find ourselves a place to sleep. Wanna say the trucker's prayer before you turn in?"

He took a creased card from his pocket-book, and handed it to me. I flattened it out and read aloud:

> Oh Lord give me strength to make this run
> For U.S. currency and not for fun.
> Please help me not to have a flat
> No engine trouble or likes of that.
> Help me pass the scale and the ICC
> Or make the JP make me go free.
> Keep the Sunday drivers out of my way
> And the woman drivers too, I pray.
> And when I wake in the stinking cab
> Let me wake where there's ham and eggs to grab.
> Make the coffee strong and the women weak

And the waitress cute, and not some freak.
Make the highway better and the gasoline cheaper
And on my return, Lord, get me a sleeper.
If you'll do this, Lord, with a little luck
I'll keep right on driving a darned old truck.

Mac took his blanket and pillow into the cab; Howard crept into a nook among the furniture; and I bedded down in a heap of sacks beside the bike (the promised four-poster was at the front, inaccessible).

I closed my eyes and sharpened my ears. Mac and Howard were whispering to one another, using the truck's solid walls as a conductor. Putting my ear to part of the latticed framework I now heard other noises too—the sounds of joking and drinking and making love—coming from the other trucks all around us, impinging on the antenna of my ear.

I lay, contented, in the darkness, feeling myself in a very aquarium of sound; and very soon I fell asleep.

Sunday

A pane of lighted glass above me; smell of straw and sacking; smell of the leather jacket which serves me as a pillow. For a moment of confusion I fancied myself in a great barn somewhere, and then I instantly remembered.

I heard a gentle sound of running water, which started suddenly and ended gradually, lingeringly, with two small afterspurts. Someone was pissing against the side of the truck; of *our* truck, I thought, with a new possessiveness. I scrambled out from under the sacks and tiptoed to the door. A steaming trail from wheel to ground bore testament to the crime, but the offender had crept away.

It was seven o'clock. I seated myself on the high step of the cab and started to scribble in my journal. A shadow fell across the page; I looked up and recognized a trucker seen dimly in the smoke-filled café the night before. It was John, the blond Lothario from the "Mayflower Transit Co," perhaps the very man who had pissed against our wheel. We chatted for a while, and he told me he had left Indianapolis—our immediate destination—the night before: it had been snowing there.

A few minutes later, another trucker shambled up, a short fat man wearing the floral shirt of the "Tropicana Orange Juice Co. Fla.," half-unbuttoned to expose a hairy pudding belly.

"Christ, it's cold here," he muttered—"it was ninety in Miami yesterday!"

Others gathered round me, talking indifferently of their routes and journeys: of mountains, oceans, plains; of forest and desert; of snow and hail and thunder and cyclone—all encountered within the span of a single day. A world of traveling and strange experience was gathered at Travel Happy on this, and every, night.

I walked round to the back of the truck and saw through its half-open doors Howard asleep in his niche. His mouth hung open, and his eyes too—I noticed with a qualm—were not fully closed. I thought for a moment he had died in the night, until I saw him breathe and twist a little in his sleep.

An hour later Mac awoke, tousled and disheveled, and staggered from the cab; he vanished in the direction of the truck-stop "bunkhouse," carrying with him a massive gladstone bag. When he came back a few minutes later I gasped in wonder: for now he was perfectly groomed and shaven, coolly and cleanly dressed for the Lord's day. Once more he was the spruce suave major.

I joined him and we walked toward the cafeteria.

"What about Howard?" I asked "Shall I wake him now?"

"No. The kid'll wake up later."

Mac obviously felt the need to talk to me without his being around.

"He'd sleep all day if I let him," he grumbled over breakfast. "He's a good kid, you know, but not too bright."

He had met Howard six months before—a bum of twenty-three—and taken pity on him. The boy had run away from home ten years before, and his father—a well-known banker in Detroit—made little effort to retrieve him. He had taken to the roads and wandered round at large, doing a little casual work from time to time; occasionally begging, occasionally stealing, and managing to avoid churches and prisons. He was briefly in the army, but soon discharged as feeble-minded.

Mac picked him up in the truck one day and "adopted" him: he took him along now on every trip, showing him the country, teaching him how to pack and crate (and also how to talk and act), and paying him a regular salary. When they returned to Florida, after a journey's end, Howard would stay with Mac's wife and family, where he had the status of a younger brother.

But it was an uphill business, probably an impossible one. The kid seemed unable to learn the simplest things; he instinctively did everything wrong; he swore incurably (here Mac smiled with a father's pride), and he always managed to put people's backs up.

As we drank our second cup of coffee, Mac's handsome face grew clouded:

"He won't be with me much longer, I imagine. Maybe I won't even be driving myself for too much longer."

He explained that he had had a curious "accident" some weeks ago, when he blacked out without warning, or being tired, and his truck had run into a field. The insurance paid, but insisted that he would have to have a medical examination; they further objected to his having a trucking partner, whatever the outcome of the examination.

Clearly Mac fears, as his insurance company must suspect, that his "blackout" was due to epilepsy, and that the medical will see the end of his driving days. He has had the foresight to line up a good job, in insurance, in New Orleans. Mac is nobody's fool.

Howard walked in at this point, and Mac rapidly changed the subject. As they started talking together, I got up, suddenly restless, and loped about the little café, noting its contents with a sharp, documentary curiosity.

Opposite the counter and the tables stood a solid trio—jukebox, air conditioner, and cigarette machine—balanced, in an adjacent corner, by a weighing machine and a sickly rubber plant. There were two revolving stands of wire, one containing the local (Birmingham) newspapers and a selection of cheap socks, face cloths, and rolls of film, and the other a variety of "funny" postcards (mostly the breasts-and-buttocks type, with a few "sick" ones thrown in), ranged about a single serious one, of the Ave Maria grotto in Alabama: the first for mates and girls, scattered here and there, the second for the wife, back home.

One wall bore innumerable Polaroid prints of Travel Happy's waitresses (Sue, Nell, and Carol), photographed with a hundred different trucking escorts.

The last remaining wall was covered with funny notices and stickers, daubed in scarlet fluorescent paint:

HIT ME EASY—I'M FULL O' GAS
CAUTION—ROADHOG!
I'M IN THE MOOD—FOR LOVE
LOVE THY NEIGHBOR AS THYSELF—BUT LEAVE HIS WIFE ALONE!!!

I saw nobody buy the funny stickers, nor even waste a glance on them. They had, I believe, a purely formal or talismanic significance, like a mezzuzah upon a door.

After breakfast Mac and Howard sat on a discarded tire, shying stones at a wooden post. We talked vaguely and incoherently of many things, spelling away the gentle Sunday indolence of a truckers' lot. After a couple of hours they got bored, and climbed back into the truck to sleep again.

I grabbed a couple of burlaps from the trailer and settled down to sunbathe, surrounded by broken bottles, sausage skins, food, and beer cans, decaying contraceptives and an incredible litter of torn and screwed-up paper: here and there a stalk of wild onion or lucerne was poking through the rubble.

As I lay and dozed, or wrote, my thoughts turned often to food. Behind me were a score of beggarly chickens scrabbling in the dust, which I gazed at, from time to time, with a wistful sigh, for Mac had waved his "trucker's friend" (an efficient-looking automatic) at them earlier, saying:

"Poultry for dinner tonight!" with a pleasant chuckle.

Every hour or so I would get to stretch my legs, and consume four coffees and a black-walnut ice cream in the café, leading to my present total of twenty-eight and seven, respectively.

I have also paid many visits to the bunkhouse washroom, having had an incandescent diarrhea since tasting Mac's peppers last night.

There are five contraceptive machines in the little room, an interesting example of how commercial pressures will follow a man into his most intimate activities. The cost of these beautiful articles ("electronically rolled, cellophane-sealed, supple, sensitive, and transparent," as they were rapturously described) was three for half a dollar, though this had been modified, clumsily, to read: THREE FOR A DOLL. There was also a machine called Prolong, which dispensed a local anaesthetic ointment designed—it was stated—"to aid in the prevention of premature climax." But John, the blond Lothario, who is turning out to be a veritable compendium of sexual information, says that piles ointment is much better. Prolong is too strong—you never know whether you've come or not.

Several carloads of high-school kids have come and gone, for their Sunday afternoon sparring with the famous Travel Happy waitresses.

The kids rarely make out, despite their braggadocio: John tells me that Sue, Nell, and Carol reserve their delicious favors for truck drivers, who are more "mature."

In the middle of the afternoon Mac suddenly announced that we would be staying at Travel Happy for another night. He wore a pleased, deliberately "mysterious" smile—no doubt he has lined up Sue or Nell for an assignation in the cab tonight. Howard has been behaving like an excited dog in this atmosphere of intrigue. Despite his brave show I suspect (and Mac has confirmed) that he has never yet made out with a girl. Indeed, Mac has procured him girls from time to time, but Howard—so vociferous in imaginary achievement—becomes timid and boorish when confronted with the reality, and things always "fall through" at the very last moment.

Mac vanished, leaving John and Howard behind. Both of them are fascinated by my incessant activity, and keep on asking to see what I am writing. I demurred for a while, and then read them some carefully edited fractions, praying they would not become resentful or self-conscious. But they seem delighted at having become "characters" in my journal. John has given me his address and made me promise to send him a copy, and even Howard wants one too. *He* sits opposite me as I write, and is uncommonly clever at deciphering his own inverted name. I will probably have to disguise it, in order to protect us both.

Eight o'clock, and I am still sitting in the café with John and Howard. No sign of Mac, yet all around us a sense of covert and clandestine excitement. Howard is tremendously restless: he says he'll "beat the shit out of Mac" tomorrow, for running off and leaving him in the lurch.

He has just left us, sulkily, and is walking toward the truck.

Alone with me now, John has become confidential. He tells me that I should particularly look over the D and D club in Elko—as I pass through it on my journey back—and ask for Kim, mentioning that I have been sent by a Mayflower man. They lay out the red carpet for Mayflower men. He tells me too that I must be sure to visit Deadwood, where he was born. It has five top-quality cathouses, as well as the ghosts of Wild Bill Hickok and Calamity Jane.

At ten o'clock he said he would have to take off to sleep. He used to prefer night driving, like all truckers, but now finds it difficult to keep awake on the road at night. Although he has only been a trucker for two years now, he says that he has had the wanderlust since childhood. He has, like Mac, a wife and two kids, whom he constantly uproots and moves from place to place—Wyoming, Chicago, Texas, California—whenever the itch overwhelms him. He is often away from them for nine or ten weeks at a time. His wife gibs at this, and is always threatening to leave him; but in her heart she knows that no other life is possible for him, psychologically, and would not have him any other way.

He had been on the road for a week now. He is often on long cross-country trips, driving all day and sleeping in the cab at night, and may hardly see another soul for two weeks or more: his only social contact is waving to other truckers by day, and signaling to them with his lights after nightfall. After a spell of this he feels half-crazy, and starts talking to himself. Once in a while, on Saturday nights if possible, he will pull into a truck stop, and there he loves to yarn and bullshit with the others.

He knows all the truck-stop girls in America, and has the reputation of being a tremendous lover.

"But you wanta know something," he concluded, with a proud yet apologetic air: "I've never once been unfaithful to my wife!"

He yawned and nodded asleep in the chair where he sat; a few minutes later he woke up with a violent start, gave me an embarrassed smile, and then lurched off to his truck.

I returned to my writing and my cups of coffee. Occasionally I walked outside to stretch my legs, and to peer curiously at all the truckers round me, snoring in their cabs, comparing their faces and their postures in repose.

At 4:20 the dawn appeared, dim and indecisive in the East. One trucker woke up and walked toward the bunkhouse to take a leak. Returning to his truck he checked over his cargo, pulled himself into the cab, and slammed the door. He started his engine with a roar, and slowly lumbered out. The other trucks remained silent and sleeping.

By five o'clock the stillborn dawn had been replaced by a fine and drizzling rain. One of the ragged cockerels was kicking up a din, and the twitter of insects had started in the grass.

Six o'clock, the café is filled with the smell of hotcakes and butter, bacon and eggs. The night waitresses take their leave, wishing me good luck in my travels around America. The day staff troop in, and smile to see me seated at the table I occupied all yesterday.

I can come and go now as I please in the little café. They no longer charge me for anything. I have drunk more than seventy cups of coffee in the past thirty hours, and this achievement deserves some small concession.

Eight o'clock, and Mac and Howard have just hurried off to downtown Coleman, to help the Mayflower men unpack their cargo. The pace is suddenly different, for today they have said nothing, they have skipped breakfast, and they haven't washed. Mac's gladstone bag has been put away for another week.

I crawled into the cab which Mac had just vacated—it was still warm from his humid sleep—covered myself with his old worn blanket, and in a moment fell asleep myself. I was awoken briefly, at ten, by a heavy fusillade of rain upon the roof, but there was no sign yet of Mac or Howard.

They finally turned up at half past twelve, heavy-footed and bedraggled from shifting the heavy cargo in a rainstorm.

"Christ!" said Mac. "I'm shot. Let's eat—and we'll be on our way in an hour."

This was three hours ago, and still we have not moved! The three of them have been smoking and boasting and fiddling and flirting, as if an unhurried thousand years lay before them. Mad with impatience I withdrew to the cab with my notebooks. Lothario John tried to mollify me:

"Take it easy, kiddo! If Mac says he'll make New York by Wednesday, he'll do it, even if he stays at Travel Happy till Tuesday evening!"

After forty hours here this truckstop has become infinitely familiar. I know a score of men—their likes and dislikes, their jokes and idiosyncrasies. And they know mine, or think they do, and call me "Doc" or "Prof" indulgently.

I know all the trucks—their tonnages and cargoes, their performances and quirks, and their insignia.

I know all the waitresses in Travel Happy—Carol, the boss, has taken a Polaroid snap of me, standing between Sue and Nell, my face unshaven and dazzled in the flashlight. She has stuck it up along with her other photos, so that now I have my place in her thousand-brothered family, her "boyfriends" who come and go on the long cross country trucking routes.

"Yeah!" she will say to some future, puzzled customer who scrutinizes the print. "That's 'Doc.' Great guy he was, bit strange maybe. He rode with Mac and Howard, those two over there. I often wonder what became of him."

Mac, Oliver, Howard—at "Travel Happy," Alabama. May, 1961.

CHARLES SIMIC

◆ ———————————————————— ◆

From Notebooks: 1963–1969

"Time, where are we, you and I, since I live in you and you do not exist." —Alphonso Cortes.

O beau pays!
   The monkey at the typewriter.

The art of making gods with earwax. Venus, for example, in full splendor of her naked beauty.
   Went to see Mrs. Murphy and ask her if she could make a teeny black dress for my goddess? Her ears turned cherry red. When she calmed down, she let me measure her waist with a piece of red thread bit off at the end.

In my childhood women mended stockings in the evening. To have a "run" in one's stocking was catastrophic. Stockings were expensive, and so was electricity. We would all sit around the table with a lamp in its middle, the father reading the papers, the children pretending to do their homework, while secretely watching the mother spreading her red-painted fingernails inside the transparent stocking.

I went to see Ionesco's *Bald Soprano* with B. It was being shown at the small theater on the Lower East Side. There were only six people in the audience, and that included the two of us. They gave the performance, anyway. When it came to the love scene with the woman who has three noses, the actors got carried away on the couch. Their voices went down to a whisper. All of a sudden, they began taking their clothes off. I could feel B. trembling. I was afraid to touch her . . . I don't remember where we went afterward, what we said, or what came after that scene in the play. Nothing, except that the streets were covered with newly fallen snow.

A scene from the fifties French movie which still delights me:

A fly gets shut in a room with three armed thugs and a woman gagged and bound who watches them with eyes popping.

In front of each man on the table there's a sugar cube and a pile of large bills. No one stirs. A naked bulb hangs from the ceiling by a long wire so they can see the fly count its legs. It counts them on the table, it counts them on the wall, then it just sits at the end of someone's nose.

Of course, that wasn't exactly the way it was in the movie. I worked on it over the years, making delicious little adjustments, as one does with a poem being written in rigorous meter and rhyme.

"This thing came from a maximum-security penitentiary," she told me.

I could not say what kind of metal it was made of. I could see it had been bent and straightened badly. It had been a part of something, but I had no idea what that could be. I put my tongue against it, and was surprised by how cold it felt.

"One writes the dates of one's imprisonment with such an object," I said.

"One must keep it concealed at all times," she added.

The man who left it with her was her lover for a week. That was many years ago.

"He used to scratch my back with it," she told me.

She wore a flowered silk robe and red Turkish slippers on her bare feet. They kept falling off when she crossed her legs. I wanted the thing. I kept wondering if she would give it to me, if I asked her for it, if I pretended to plead.

Her robe was slightly open. The thing lay on the table between us. Outside it was beginning to rain. She got up to close the windows, and I put the thing in my pocket. It was raining so hard, the room had darkened. Now we could not see the look in our eyes.

I leave the dentist after what seems an eternity in his chair. It's an evening in June. I'm walking on a tree-lined street full of dark, whispering trees. The streets are badly lit, but there are people everywhere strolling close to each other as if they were all lovers. The thought crosses my mind that I'm immensely happy.

"I have the impression," she said to me one day, "that in my life there have been more nights than days. It was like night came, and then, just as the new day was about to break, another night would follow immediately in its wake.

"I forgot the face of my great and only love because it was always so dark. I would sit looking at his face which the shadows had already obscured. Only his naked shoulders kept their ghostly whiteness. I wanted to touch them, but I no longer had the right.

"It was much too dark now. My memory is a store specializing in the fashions of the eclipse. My love and I are trying on all the suits and dresses, but the mirrors work only dimly. They hold only vague outlines of somber clothing of another era."

"My history is at the mercy of my poetry. (Marx revised.)

I thought "nosology" had to do with noses. Something like a science of noses. Many noses coming to be examined. The pretty nosologist is measuring them and making entries on a sheet of paper.

Is the perfect nose a Platonist's dream, or is such a nose to be encountered in nature? The perfect nose, for example, crossing the street in our neighborhood. Or the perfect nose in a lobby of a grand hotel lighting a gold-tipped cigarette behind some potted palm tree?

Nosology, unfortunately, has nothing to do with noses.

A tower of clichés fell upon the two lovers. You could only see a solitary arm or a leg sticking out of the rubble. The foot that was in her mouth was not mine. The ace was not up my sleeve, but over my eyes, etc.

"He seeks the secret and meaning of Time," we are told upon entering. If we weren't told, we'd say he's just staring out of the window at the rain. His mother wants us to walk on tiptoes. "Make yourselves at home," she tells us using improvised deaf-mute signs.

"*Povera e nuda vai, Filosofia*," wrote the Italian poet Petrarca.

Steady rain, then the sound of distant thunder over Manhattan.

There was a maid in our house who let me put my hand under her skirt. I was five or six years old. I can still remember the dampness of her crotch and my surprise that there was all that hair there. I couldn't get enough of it. She would crawl under the table where I had my military fort and kept all my weapons. I don't remember what we said, if anything. Just her hand, firmly guiding mine.

In a park, dangerous to the public after dark, the soapbox speaker shouting: "Everything I say has been misunderstood!" Something to do with justice in the world, with forces of evil . . .

O century of bad dreams! They all want us to bite their morgue attendants' nails for them, and we refuse to!

When my grandfather was dying from diabetes, when he had already one leg cut off at the knee and they were threatening to do the same to the other, his old buddy, Savo Lozanic, used to visit him every morning to keep him company. They would play chess and talk.

One morning my grandmother had to leave him alone in the house as she had to attend a funeral of a distant relative. That's what gave him the idea. He hopped out of bed and into the kitchen where he found candles and matches. He got back into his bed, placed one candle above his head and the other one at his feet. Then he lit them. Finally, he pulled the sheet over his face and began to wait.

When his friend knocked, there was no answer. The door being unlocked, he went in, calling from time to time. The kitchen was empty. A gray cat slept by the cold woodstove in the living room. When he entered the bedroom and saw the bed, the lit candles, the sheet—he let out a wail, and then broke into sobs as he groped for a chair to sit down.

"Shut up, Savo," said my grandfather from under his sheet. "Can't you see I'm only practicing?"

The exiled general's only grandson was playing war under the table, cheeks puffed to imitate bombs exploding. The grim daughter wrote the old man's memoirs. There was a smell of bad cooking, the view of a busy highway through the window.

The general was in a wheelchair. He wore a bib and smoked a cigar. The daughter was smiling in welcome in a way that made her small teeth show.

I liked the general better. He remembered a distinguished East European prime minister pretending to wipe his ass with a peace treaty, the captured enemy officers drinking heavily and toasting some cabaret singer from their youth.

In Chicago, in the 1950s, there was still an old woman with a street organ and a monkey. She turned the crank with both hands while the monkey went around with a tin cup. Some tune that made our grandmothers in their youth sigh.

If the woman was a hundred years old, she must have known the cow that started the Great Fire. Later she married the Sicilian with the street organ. He kissed her every night with the monkey still on his shoulder.

The animal I saw looked young and full of mischief. He wore a coat with brass buttons which must have come down to him from his great grandfather, or thereabouts. That day, they had for an audience a small boy who looked fearful, but also curious. His beautiful mother kept pulling his arm. The old woman had her eyes raised heavenward in a manner favored by saints at the time of their martyrdom.

The night of my farewell dinner in Chicago, I got very drunk. At some point, I went to the bathroom and could not find my way back. The restaurant was large and full of mirrors. I would see my friends in the distance, seated at the table, but when I went toward them, I came face-to-face with myself in the mirror. With my new beard I did not recognize myself immediately. I even apologized before realizing who it was. I finally sat down at an old man's table. He said nothing, and I lit a cigarette. Time passed. The place was emptying. The old man, who could have been an undertaker, pushed his wine glass toward me. I would have remained with him indefinitely if one of the women from our table hadn't found me and led me outside.

They sit on the table, the tailors do. At least, they used to. A street of dim shops in Beograd where we went to have my father's coat narrowed and shortened so it would fit me. The tailor got off the table and stuck pins into my shoulder. "Don't squirm," my mother said. Outside it was getting dark. Large snowflakes fell.

Years later in New York, on the same kind of winter afternoon, a dry-cleaning store window with an ugly, thick-legged woman standing on the chair. She's having the hems of her skirt pinned by the gray-headed Jewish tailor who kneels before her like a beseeching tutor.

"Truth brushes me with its wing!"
"It's not a wing but a dog comb," we tell him.

Young black woman in pink haircurlers, arms crossed on her chest, as she leans out of the first-floor window to speak to a boy on a bicycle. A beer bottle raised to his lips, he's taking a long swig before offering her what's left. He has to reach up, and she has to stretch down a little, just a little more, and still they can't connect! Her bathrobe opening, one big naked breast slipping out for all to see—before she gets hold of the beer.

I got the idea of sleeping on the roof on hot nights from my mother and father. That's what they did during the War, except it wasn't a roof but a big terrace on the top floor of a building in downtown Beograd. There was a blackout, of course. I remember immense starry skies, and how silent the city was. I would begin to say something, but someone—I could not tell for a moment who it was—would put a hand over my mouth.

Like a dark ocean liner adrift on the dark sea—that's how it felt when clouds were racing over our heads. We were sailing full speed ahead. "Nearer to the infinite," I remember my father whispering.

Ideas to make your hair stand up, just as if you were to stick your finger in a socket.

"The external world," she assures me, "is the work of our sense organs."

"Sweet Jesus! Does that mean our sweaty, naked bodies, being a part of the external world, are merely the work of our sense organs?"

"Not so loud, you fool," she says as she pulls the covers up to her chin. "Our sense organs themselves are the products of our sense organs."

"In that case," I say pulling off her covers, "if I understand you correctly, we might not even be here!" But, she just glares at me and calls me stupid.

In that huge city there's a woman he has met the night before. She has left his bed in the morning, telling him only that she works as a secretary in an office just off Grand Central Station. That afternoon, he gets the bright idea to go and find her as she leaves the office at five. Against infinite odds, knowing neither the building nor the street she works on, he decides to look for her.

And that's what he does. He stands on the corner of 42nd Street and 5th for more than two hours searching the faces in the crowd for a fleeting glimpse of her. At times, he thinks he sees her. His heart jumps! He rushes, pushing people aside, only to overtake a complete stranger, someone equally beautiful, equally ethereal.

When the streets begin to empty, he walks around the neighborhood still full of hope. "I'm practicing magic," he thinks. The night has now fallen and the more he walks the fewer people there are on the street. He's certain, however, that when he rounds the next corner, she'll be there.

He's astonished that she is not. And yet, with each disappointment, he feels closer to her. She's working late, it occurs to him. There are still a few lights on the upper floors of these dark buildings. Her accounts won't balance to the last penny. Any minute now she will step out of a dark doorway. He can already hear the rustle of her dress, the sound of her heels as she rushes off in the opposite direction, never to be overtaken.

Chance is . . . "the humorous master."—Ernst.

"You look like Franz Schubert," a crazy-looking woman told me as we were introduced.

At that same party, I spoke to a a lawyer who insisted we had met in London two years ago. I explained my accent to a doctor by telling him that I was born in Gary, Indiana, and grew up among people who didn't speak English.

There was a girl there, too, who was blind. She kept smiling sweetly. Her mother told me that I reminded her of her brother who was hung by the Germans in Norway. She had witnessed the atrocity, and was going to give me the details, but I excused myself telling everyone that I had this sudden and terrible toothache that required immediate attention.

I became more and more lucid the later it got. Everybody was already asleep. I tried to wake J., but she drew me down on her breasts sleepily. We made love, and then I talked to her about philosophy, to my heart's content, while she slept.

STEPHEN SPENDER

◆ ──────────────────────────────── ◆

Last Autumn of the War:
September–October 1944

September 13, 1944

Julian wrote to me some weeks ago from Wales that he was very depressed. A love affair had gone wrong, he had been disappointed in his hopes that he would have a position at the Peace Conference after the war. Evidently he has reached a crisis in his life. He is fifty-five. He has been living for several years on easy successes, journalism, committees, broadcasting, journeys to places about which he has written books. Planning and so on. All these are generalized activities, in which he has been able to live off his general intelligence, good will, and progressive opinions.

He has not done the scientific work in which he might have specialized. He has not thrown everything else up in order to lead a political crusade. He is not a teacher. He has the gifts to have done any of these, and he might also have become a distinguished writer. What is more important, he has never revised his assumption that one can be good merely by supporting progressive causes, and that the basis of morality is the evolution of the society in which one lives. The natural goodness in himself—which is considerable—remains childlike, charming, and unself-knowing, because he thinks of goodness as a kind of contribution made to a public cause, not the development of a potentiality within himself.

Now he has had, at the age of fifty-five, a real crisis. He has an illness, contracted in Africa, combined with a nervous breakdown. He was sent to the London Hospital. There he was given injections which put him to sleep for several days on end. His first night there, a bomb fell on a wing of the hospital. Julian was badly shaken and woken from his sleep. He was then moved to Harrow Hospital.

Juliette, his wife, went to see him after the move. He complained that the nurses were very unintelligent and could not even read to him correctly, confusing words such as "peasant" and "pheasant." He asked

Juliette whether she could not come to the hospital and read to him every day. She explained matters to the doctor, who flew into a temper and said that she had called his nurses illiterate. He added that she must certainly not come and read to Julian as it was most important to keep him from his family. Julian, he added, had been sent to the hospital to be cured, not to be made worse.

After this several specialists were consulted as to the nature of J.'s illness. It was decided to give up the sleeping cure, and try electric-shock treatment. Juliette was sent for, to get her consent. The doctor came in while she was with Julian and asked whether she agreed to the treatment. She hesitated a moment, and said: "Well, it's rather a difficult thing to decide." The doctor said to Julian: "You see, your wife is trying to obstruct the treatment. I am confident that I can cure you, but she is trying to prevent me." Juliette protested: "I only wanted to think things over." The doctor left the room, and returning a few minutes later, said to Julian, "I have decided not to treat you. I cannot be responsible for you, in view of your wife's attitude."

September 15

Dunstan Thompson, the young American poet and a GI in London, came to spend the night with us. We talked much of Catholicism. He said that he believed in the supreme authority of the Church but that he could no longer be a Catholic. He was homosexual. He could not think that to be homosexual was a sin; therefore he convicted himself of the still worse sin of pride. He found it impossible for him to go to confession every week and confess always the same sin, of which he could not sincerely repent.

He shares a room in the Catholic college where he lives with a friend. They are lovers. Every week they confess, and after confession try for a few days to keep apart. Dunstan said he could not resolve this dilemma for himself by finding a pansy priest as confessor. So he left the Church.

I thought much of religion later because Adam von Trott had been sentenced to death by the Nazis, and I prayed for him all day. Passionate conviction that by concentrating my mind on Adam I could comfort him in his cell where he was waiting to be hanged.

During the night, I dreamt of God, or of light. I seemed to realize in my dream that the essential requirement of religious belief is belief in a spiritual force beyond the human. The idea of humanity is only the projection on an immense screen of the individual self, oneself magnified.

The human race dies with each self that dies. The sense of God beyond humanity is the sine qua non of religion.

September 20

Saw Julian at his home. He looked white and tired, but less physically ill than I had expected. When we were alone he explained to me that his disease of the liver caused him the most frightful depression. He said: "What I can't explain to you is that I am obsessed by the most terrible longing to kill myself. I suppose that you, as a person outside my situation, think that suicide is an inexcusable crime?" I said I did not think this was necessarily so; but I was convinced that if he could overcome this impulse, he would probably do his best work in the coming years, work enriched by what he is experiencing now. Just as I was saying this, Juliette came in and suggested that we all three go for a walk on Hampstead Heath. We went for a short walk past the place where the flying bomb ("doodle bug") had fallen only a few days ago, just when we were all, having breakfast at their house. (Sometimes during air raids, Natasha and I would sleep in the Huxley's air raid shelter as we had none in our apartment.) I reminded Julian of this, but he did not seem to remember about it. Juliette asked: "Shall we walk a bit further on?" Julian said he didn't mind. Juliette: "But do you want to?" He said: "I do exactly what I'm told."

At lunch he seemed to have a return to his old self, and discussed this morning's leading article in the *Times*. He said, "Even they admit that International Control is necessary."

Over coffee, when Juliette was out of the room, I said to Julian: "In six months' time the war will be over, and you will be better, and everything will be quite different, if only you have the patience to endure these six months." He said in an almost surprised tone of voice: "Oh, but do you think everything will be better? I am sure it will all be much worse."

HARRY ROYALL. Royall is the boy aged nineteen whom I met at Sidcup Hospital for patients suffering from pleural diffusion. He is so thin as to seem almost two-dimensional, but in his face like cardboard are brilliantly shining eyes. I have been trying to get him a place at Oxford University. He seems divided between wanting to be a schoolmaster and wilder ambitions—being an actor, going into politics. The London County Council have provided him with scholarships amounting to £150 a year. Recently Oxford University sent him a kind of preliminary bill for £15 to be paid before he goes up.

Two days ago he asked me if I would lend him £25, I said that I could not do so unless he would pay it back within six months. I also discussed with him the problem of going to Oxford with only £150 a year. I recommended him not to go unless he could raise another £100.

We dined at the Hamish Hamiltons. Sam Behrmann was there. Very friendly. An American, Captain Kennedy, badly burnt, with a beard to hide his scars, came in after dinner. He described the German P.O.W. camp where he is stationed. He said: "The Germans are gullible. They can be fooled. The thing is, always to shout at them."

September 27
Lunched with Cyril Connolly. E. M. Forster was there. Forster always gives me the impression that, in his extremely diffident way, he is making moral judgments on everyone in any room where he happens to be. The very reticence of his personality shows up everyone else, like a color besides which almost any other color seems tawdry and vulgar.

The effect of his presence on me was that I talked a great deal about myself. All the time I was thinking, while he looked at me—his head slightly on one side—how abominably vulgar I am. How often the word 'I' comes into my conversation.

After Forster had gone, I told Cyril this. Cyril said: "I quite agree. When I served the steak I wondered whether Morgan would notice that I had taken the largest piece, and I prayed that if he did he would also realize that his piece, though smaller, was juicier and more tender and had less fat on it. Then I also hoped that at dessert, he would realize that although I took the largest apple, it was a green one, whereas the one I gave him was the ripest."

October 3
Two days home with a cold.

On Sunday I got up to go to the Savile Club, as I could not get hold of Rudi——, my guest, to put him off. He was heavy and Germanic and dull, and I'm afraid I did little to encourage him. We joined the Australian poet and music critic W. J. Turner for coffee, and Turner and I, ignoring Rudi, discussed Alex Comfort's novel, or, rather, Alex Comfort, for neither of us had read his novel. Turner said he had no sympathy with Comfort's brand of pacifism. He did not see why Comfort was so squeamish and why, on humanitarian grounds, he objected to killing Germans.

Turner went on to argue that there was nothing essentially more terrible in killing or being killed than in many other of the evils of the world. He also said that modern life had no more violence in proportion to the number of people living than life had always in the past. He quoted a story by James Stephens to illustrate that if one had three wishes which would change the world, one would end by wishing it to remain the same. The special case of the modern world and the cause of our present distress lay in our having acquired such an immense quantity of unmanageable knowledge, that we had lost faith in the idea that we could attain any universal final source of truth, which had comforted our ancestors.

Dunstan Thompson rang and said he had persuaded Harry Royall to accept money to help him get to Oxford. Dunstan added: "I also gave him two of your books, though I mentioned that two books by Auden might be a better investment." Although I think this myself, the remark annoyed and depressed me. Why? Because I was feeling ill and frustrated perhaps and it reminded me of my frustration? Because, although I do not consider myself better than Auden, I do feel that in my work I am unique; and the comparison suggests that I am trying to do the same thing as Auden, which he does better? Because the remark, coming from Dunstan, is depressingly familiar in a way that slightly jars me? It does not matter.

Another autumn of war. The longer blackout, the darkness beginning at seven or eight, the cold canopy of night packed and bristling with malice, the city exhausted and weary beneath. The sense of all the will and energy that has now gone into destruction, unable to stop until everything is destroyed. Fear. Exhaustion. All the people I know who are ill.

The world may not be any more miserable than it always has been, but the modern disorder outrages our intelligence and moral sense to a degree that oppresses the spirit perhaps more than ever before.

Yet all we pray in our hearts for is happiness. Stop the bombs. Give us security and the power to organize our material and human resources. Give us strength to make a deal with Russia and America. If this can be done, after all we may be happy. But happiness is piecemeal: goodness is the view of the whole good applied to all the separate particulars of life. The aim of happiness cannot make each one of us sacrifice enough for all to be happy or good.

Dunstan Thompson rang last night at about eleven, to ask whether he could stay the night, bringing a friend. I was unwilling, as N. has a bad cold. However I changed my mind when I learned that the friend was Harry Royall. The latest about Royall is that Oxford refused him a grant on the grounds of his health. Dunstan is anxious to raise him the money to go there from rich friends. Dunstan now seems very involved with Royall. However I have seen neither of them today, having to leave for the office* this morning before they got up.

October 4
Dined with Juliette, Anthony and Francis Huxley (her sons). Julian being back in hospital. The architect Jane Drew was there. She has just been appointed head of planning in Nigeria. Very excited about West African negroes whom she describes as spontaneous, creative, happy, polygamous, incapable of making anything ugly, etc., etc. She said that the English have the defects opposite to all these good qualities. At dinner she pronounced that married people should always be perfectly honest with each other about their love affairs. I said that honesty usually meant the guilty party putting responsibility for his/her infidelity on the shoulders of the innocent party. After dinner she criticized our civilization for its lack of "natural flowering"! She said that machinery was a mistake, etc., etc. People were without faith in any religion. Nevertheless most people were, by nature, good, and so on. We argued a bit about how many people were good and how many cared about having values of any kind. Juliette, Francis, Anthony and I agreed with her criticism of western civilization. Our difficulty, we said, was to know what to do about it. We could not transform ourselves into West African negroes.

I walked home with Anthony afterward. He said that the war had made him skeptical of people like Jane Drew with her simplicist primitivist view of life. He was convinced that the Germans had some very good ideas: given ten to twenty years in which to perfect rockets and flying bombs, they would be able to destroy England completely with robot weapons.

October 12
At the theater (*Pier Gynt*!) we saw Royall and Dunstan, whom we scarcely spoke to.

I felt convinced that they are having an affair. I was annoyed that Royall should not have written or talked to me about several changes in his plans. Thinking about this kept me awake several nights. At this

*At this stage of the war I was transferred from the National Fire Service to the Foreign Office.

stage of the war small worries tend to exaggerate themselves in one's mind. Knowing this, I decided to do nothing about Royall. However later in the week I decided that I really ought to concern myself about him, and risk quarreling with Dunstan. Accordingly I wrote Dunstan a letter saying that I did not think Royall's problems could be solved by taking him to night clubs. I pointed out that though the stage might seem a suitable career for him at the present moment, it might not seem so as soon as the war was over and that unless Royall was a genius at acting, it might be desirable for him to acquire a general education. Teaching might still be the best profession for him.

Dunstan rang and said he was not at all offended by my letter. We had tea to discuss Royall's future. We agreed that the best thing was to find out what Royall really wanted, putting all the advantages and disadvantages of teaching, acting, and Oxford before him; and then to raise the money to help him.

This morning Dunstan rang and said it was quite clear that what R. really wanted was to go to Oxford. Natasha rang Nevill Coghill at Exeter College, who said that if we could find the money, Exeter would take him. Two hours later, however, he rang to say that the Rector of Exeter told him that Royall had been rejected on grounds of health.

I want to be happy more than I want to be good. Or, rather, I think I do. Every time a buzz bomb flies over, every time I read the newspaper, I pray that the catastrophe will not strike *me* down, that somehow *we* will reach through these dark days to the bright sky months or years beyond, to where we can enjoy happiness in peace. My will is obsessed with happiness.

At the same time, though, I feel that I shall never escape from the unhappiness of *the others*. The trouble about happiness is that it is a purely selfish sensation. The innocent, the simple, and the selfish can be happy even amid general unhappiness. But those who are fully conscious will always be aware of the misery of *the others*, and of the too great price paid for their own good fortune. Sometimes I even wish for a universal catastrophe to occur, so as to involve me in the total sum of the surrounding unhappiness. This is because I feel that to escape from the unhappiness of *the others* is weakness, since one's mind is flooded all the time with the reality of their suffering. One should imagine in one's own life the unhappiness which is today's world.

This brings me back to the idea of goodness. But for me goodness seems *ausgeschlossen*. To begin with, I have to earn too much money. My whole way of life is too compromised, too much dissipated by a hundred concessions. Beside this, goodness repels me. Goodness is anti-social, to be good would be to be disloyal to my friends, my fellow conspirators—*mes semblables, mes frères.*

October 23

Two days ago I met Dunstan Thompson. He began by telling me how offended so-and-so would be by my having, in a review, compared Frederic Prokosch's poems to a good wine or a beautifully fried Red Mullet. Next he told me how offended already so-and-so-and-so-and-so were by my having referred somewhere to Eliot's *Four Quartets* as "sententious." Having heard that the Sitwells are in town, he seems suddenly to have altered his opinion of Edith Sitwell's poems. In fact, rather to my surprise, he said he would like to meet Edith. I said I would arrange this. He also said that he liked Herbert Read's poems extremely, and mentioned that he had met Read with Sir William Beveridge and E. M. Forster, only yesterday, when Herbert Read had been very cordial. He expressed the wish *not* to meet MacNeice, adding that MacNeice's poetry was tinsel. He wanted to meet Day Lewis again, observing that Day Lewis' poems were good "except that they were soft in the middle." He went on: "Of course, Stephen, only you and Auden are any good, of your generation, as, in their generation, only Dylan Thomas and George Barker were any good."

This mixture of malice, flattery, and opinionatedness had the effect of shutting me up. It is insulting of him to talk as though we both take it for granted that I write reviews only as part of a game of literary politics—not even literary—social.

After this we drank a lot of Oozoo(?) and the rest of the afternoon was pleasant. A touch of warmth pleased me in Dunstan when he spoke of Harry Royall. Later, he showed me a letter from an American friend—the poet Harry Brown—which was in the same amazingly brittle, glassy style as his own conversation.

One evening I went to a party at Cyril Connolly's, to meet a French editor—Bedel(?) of *Lettres Françaises.* The French intellectual's style is curiously like that of these young American writers—aphoristic, witty, merciless, intelligent. Yet with the French it seems very tired—a pale imitation of itself, where theirs is brash.

At this party the French of us English seemed very rusty. Suddenly, during a gap in the conversation, Cyril, looking embarrassed, exclaimed: "*Montherlant? Est-ce-que il sera fusillé ou non? Question académique, qui interesse Bloomsbury beaucoup.*" I'm sure he asked this just because he thought of it as words he could say within the present limitations of his French.

October 24

Lunch with Osbert and Edith Sitwell and E. M. Forster. Forster seemed both genuinely amused and genuinely shocked when the Sitwells referred to the literary critic Desmond McCarthy as "Dingy Desmond." I told the story of Harry Royall, knowing, as I did so, that I was telling it to impress Forster with my generosity and moral correctitude according to what I took to be Forsterian standards, in dealing with Harry's situation.

October 30

Several days of the Sitwells. Edith stays at the Sesame Club, which consists of genteel ladies, most of them old. One of these stopped her on the stairs a few days ago and said: "I quite like what you've been writing recently, Miss Sitwell." Edith raised her hand with an episcopal gesture of blessing, and said: "You mustn't spoil me. Take care, I'm not used to being spoken to in such a flattering manner."

Edith looked round the dining room of gaunt, haggard, nodding female faces—some of them bearded—and sighed audibly: "Now if only I had been asked to find the cast for the witches in *Macbeth!* What an opportunity lost!"

Edith's tea parties are held in the upstairs reception rooms of the Sesame Club. They are fantastic assemblies, consisting of her oldest friends, her newest friends, and numerous other people who, for obscure reasons, she feels "have to be asked." One of these is "Wiggy," a tall man who wears a wig. He is secretary of the Sesame Club. His wig is obvious. One of Edith's guests commented. "Since it is impossible to disguise a wig, I wonder why people don't wear stylized ones." "But Wiggy's *is* stylized," said Osbert.

Edith's appearance is fantastic. How to describe it? She is like a medieval ivory carving of herself, robed, and ornamented with enormous pieces of jewelry. Her skin has the cold texture of ivory. Like a statue carved from ivory, her body seems to consist either of round almost tubular surfaces, or else sharp, beaky ones. She wears clothes of the stiffest brocades, heavy chains, immense aquamarine rings and brooches, some pinchbeck. Her manner recalls that of Queen Elizabeth, gracious and feline, warm and icy, in great need of giving and receiving affection and attention, and, at the same time, filled with a kind of suppressed fury. One is either dangerously popular or dangerously unpopular with her. Her conversation is extremely malicious but amusingly so, for the sake of the amusement, not for delight in causing pain, like Dunstan Thompson's and Harry Brown's. We saw her fury after a party given by the pianist Franz Osborn. Edith sat all evening on a sofa where a lady from Wolverhampton had planted herself next to her. This lady told Edith all about the troubles of the deputy town clerk of Wolverhampton. This went on for two hours, Edith said. After the party, Edith was in a terrifying rage, which shows no sound of abating twenty-four hours later. She will never invite Franz Osborn either to her tea parties or to Renishaw again. She is thinking out her revenge. Natasha was so taken aback by this outburst that she had to leave Edith, as she was frightened.

October 31

CONVERSATION OVERHEARD ON A BUS

SHE: I didn't have a single dream last night,
          That means a healthy sleep.

HE: You didn't dream of me?

SHE: What do you think? I never dream of you.

HE: At least you must have woken for the bomb
          That fell at six this morning?

SHE: You mean the rocket
          That woke me at 5:30? It shook the house
          But made no sound before it fell. The rockets
          Make houses tremble because they penetrate
          To the foundations.

HE: They say they weigh ten tons.

SHE: They only weigh two tons when they arrive.
          The remaining eight tons is the fuel
          Which lifts them up into the stratosphere.

HE: I say, you read the newspapers!

SHE: Of course, I do.
          I like to know the reason for everything
          And then I am not frightened.

HE: These bombs are only sent to frighten us.
          They have no military use whatever.
          They prove the Germans fight against civilians;
          Unlike our saturation bombing.

SHE: The only thing that's ever frightened me
       Was the noise of our own guns in earlier raids.
HE: Oh, the more guns I hear, the merrier!
       But probably a bomb never fell near you?
SHE: Indeed it did! There was that one a stone's throw
       Away, in Hampstead Garden Suburb,
       And that one at Mill Hill!
HE: A pretty stone's throw
       I'd like to see you throw a stone, my darling,
       Two miles at the least.
SHE: Still, I'm not afraid
       Of dying. Of course, the thought of being dead
       Is not nice. I wouldn't like to be dead,
       But—still, I don't mind dying.
HE: If someone asked me
       Whether I'd sooner be alive or dead,
       I'd say, "alive, old chap." But still
       There's not all that amount of difference.

C. K. WILLIAMS

Journal

Soon after I began to write poetry, I began to keep a sort of notebook-journal, in which I recorded, for whatever lost reasons—loneliness, perhaps, or shyness; the not wanting to expose my innocence and ignorance to anyone else—my observations, thoughts, frustrations, and—mostly—false-alarm intuitions about what I was trying to do at the time. The frequency of the entries seems to be in inverse proportion to the amount of actual poetry writing I was doing at a given time. I've made a selection here from the years 1971–74, because these were years of great change in my work and in my life, and I suppose because all of it is far enough behind me that I can forgive myself the more obvious obtusenesses and immodesties.

1971–1972

To use pity as a mode of inspiration rather than as suffering to be overcome is the worst offense.

The question of image: the feeling that I've used up all the readily available images: that I'm repeating myself, that my associative store is diminished so much that all I can do is to re-elaborate, by metaphor, the same consciousness again and again. So then to the books. Which is what they're for, but not what I've used them for. Strangely enough, the most imageless books have always been the most inspiring for me: Nietzsche, Brown . . .

Rimbaud, "The Infernal Bridegroom": "Does he have perhaps secrets for *changing life?*" This is what I don't believe about myself now, or if I do, very dimly. It's what makes writing poetry seem a vain, preposterous occupation. Since the war started, it's as though all the effort made could only bring us back to scratch. Paradise itself would be neutral, a beginning: everything is just to let us start.

Before, I was trying to mediate politics with sexuality, and the reverse happened along with it: sex became politicized. Now, sex faced plainly, by itself, becomes frankly boring to write about, although I haven't admitted it until now. When it is interesting it's always mixed in with something else: religion, absolute loneliness—not horniness—etc.

Don't ever forget: the task is to be as sane as possible, to find the permutations of sanity, never of insanity!!!

Kinnell: why he's so compelling—even in his bleakest moments he's celebrating and what he celebrates is *language*. The language always brings him back from the abyss. He joys in his consciousness of it, even with playfulness.

Kinnell again: how much his tone is perfected. By the end of the book there's a slight falling off, as though the tone, though even more purified, is carrying more weight than the wisdom that's being attempted. (I remember I never used to believe in wisdom: I think probably this would be a good attitude to go back to.)

To be able to use what I've been finding in those two long-lined poems, not toward a metaphoric structure, but toward a vision! Although I think I might have to get back sometime to the metaphoric business as a basis of consciousness. Or, it might be that there would have to be a change from metaphoric to *mythic*. Beware storytelling: what sounds like myth—probably the worst lie. Probably the most important thing about myths is that they are *structures*. Unlike metaphor, which is epiphany within a structure, or even without it. Duino Elegies: see again.

Torn between imagination and reality: it's very simple. In approaching the notion of the poem, whether to put the materials for the poem in a structure which is answerable to the poem itself, or whether to make the poem directly responsible to reality. The second is the most compelling but the most dangerous because it so easily falls off into the banal, the meaningless, and also because it seems limited, boring. . . . The other always has the thrill of discovery about it, the second more of allowing things to find their proper places: precision, exactness, which has never of itself interested me.

A poetry where statements, images, etc., seemingly unrelated, make an emotional structure: this has been done, in surrealism for instance, but

I think I have a new notion of it: maybe just through the commitment to each statement.

To make a passion, not a poetic structure.

The other poems have tried to string it together into a particularly designated meaning structure: this would drive *away* from that, but not into willful capriciousness, rather into an emotional whole that would be greater than any coherent structure would be.

THIS IS THE KEY! The dissatisfaction I've felt with having to omit so much, but at the same time wanting lyric, not narrative structures. This way I possibly could touch everything without having longer poems. . . .

To begin to face life not as pain to be resolved, but as joy to be discovered: it would have to be a whole new kind of poetry, of life, and I don't know how yet, or if I ever will. . . .

This is a critical time in my life and the trouble with critical times is that they seem so much like any other time. You live, you act, you think in the same rhythms, the same images, and the inner being is in a terrific turmoil with no images and rhythms to objectify itself . . . so it objectifies in the old terms, which affect the consciousness' ability to cope with the turmoil, and gives it false clues, false solutions, and the turmoil becomes unfruitful, a sham.

The dream of destroying evil is only a reflection of the sense of despair which comes from loss of faith. In reality one can only achieve an aesthetic enjoyment of life as a result of the "most humble ethical experience." (Kafka)

Kafka again, "Humble ethical experience," the most important phrase in the book, it's all there is. . . .

For most people, the only grand ethical experience is in deciding whether or not to kill themselves—this is Kierkegaard, too. . . . Maybe it's the real ground of suicide, and that suicide isn't an ethical gesture at all, but an aesthetic one! Refusing to live with humble suffering, humble choices, humble selfhood . . . always the notion that somehow with death one could become beautiful, significant, morally effective. How about murder? Reading about the Manson family, it was as though they were involved in the same sort of quest, to try to find the larger experience, but reading about the actual murders, there's the feeling of small tasks, small decisions. . . . Arendt on Eichmann . . . Rashkolnikov:

his tragedy, the moment the murder happens, is that he realizes it was still the most normal, untransfiguring experience. He's doomed then to the everyday, to the investigator, and he knows it: he's only playing out his life then, aesthetically, but tragically.

Where is any grand ethical experience then?

Start from the other end: what's the humblest ethical experience? (It very well might be, again, suicide, because you can't be less ethical than by never leaving the self at all, which suicide, qualified as it might be, is.)

And would the next smallest be in deciding whether to murder someone or not? Because that decision refuses to face the reality of the other, and without the reality of the other, there is really nothing at all: the murderer then is an aesthetician, no matter how unconscious of it. Whether to have a child: to face mortality, profound ethical risk, because the other becomes all. To commit one's self to time, process, species. This might be the grandest then.

To love another: the riskiest, most profound choice: again, that it happens so unconsciously and without apparent choice makes it harder to realize, but this is obviously the ground of all real ethics, the most terrifying, the one that demands the most commitment and energy, the most potentially annihilating, the most demanding of both identity and non-identity.

To love god: I think I'm not ready to face this yet. I've been so long without god that I can't really get a feeling for what the decision involves. I don't feel any risk, any possibility of choice; god is just the most profound other, the way I am now he has actually less reality than those I must love or not love now.

How could I begin a poem with this?

Having to decide to be a *great* poet, to *will* it, but at the same time somehow to keep a sense of play, because without that there's just dullness, the seriousness of mediocrity. This is the real difficulty, it's why the romance of loneliness doesn't hold, because one becomes too self-important, self-involved. There has to be laughter behind the absurdity of confronting mysteries. A *gaiety*. There are no possible answers: here are my answers.

The problem with political poems: there seems to be so much certainty that all you want to do is tell it. Kafka: about not getting down to the depths where the contradictions are . . .

Never poetry as an escape, a solution, a resolution. The tension of the poem is always in its refusal to allow a resolution until the last possible moment. . . . But on the other hand, there's nothing more dangerous than false irresolution—it's what makes immoral poetry and art. The trouble with most painting and most poetry now is that this is apparent. What's happened in the last few years in poetry is that the poetics themselves, because they were once viable, become resolutions. The growth within the poem is crippled, but it's terribly hard to see it. This is why I respect Bill Knott so much, because he won't allow it, no matter what mad lengths he has to go to. The poem has to present the contradictions fully until they inherently resolve each other, or don't. . . .

Hearing someone speaking last night about insistent, recurrent images at certain times of life. Now it occurs to me: if images are of things at *rest*, this can happen. If images are actions, of the self or others, it can't or is less likely to.

In Rimbaud's poems, always the feeling of the masses, of the people standing somewhere in the poem, in the way, observing, doing mad things. Even the escape to nature is obviously an escape from the press of the democratized mass. Always trying to exult them, come to terms with them, not despise them: to find their mystic, atavistic power. . . .

There's no such thing as the unconscious; it's just a mathematic to allow us to look at the emotional processes which are right there. In one language.

The possibility of a more conceptual poetry. . . . Reading Vallejo's *Trilce*, the totally embodied life, how completely exciting it is, though mystifying: I think I would be bored by the conceptual, abstract commitment. Problem: at no time in recent years have I been less concerned with the conceptual and isn't it strange that now I want to write it? I think I don't mean conceptual anyway: what I mean is a wider use of language, being able to use intellectual language on the same scope as "poetic"—of course I can't not do it.

You can't write a good poem without an intact set of values: they can be values in flux, but for the instant of the poem, there has to be a certainty about *everything!*

If you use the word "I" in a poem, then clearly you're talking to someone else.

Using "you" directed toward the self is one way of talking to one's self.

Using no subject is another.

So, strangely, a pure narrative, without a subject, I or you, can end up being the most personal of poems! Astonishing. (My logic might lack a little, but it's an interesting notion.)

If you make up a fictional character, then what? Is that another way of saying "you" or "I"? So what I need is a narrative poem without characters. Using "you" is ugly: the game's given away. "The man": just as ugly. Another way is to completely break down the rational notion of ego: to make subject completely fluid; you, I, he, the man, she . . . I think I've done this occasionally without knowing what I was doing. To flow into things and people and the self, then the self becomes superpersonal, because it's so humbled . . . no identity . . . Keats' "negative capability." (Although he never did it in this way.)

The simple reason Greek Tragedy is so profound: because the solution, the resolution of every problem is absolute; death, blindness—*irrevocability*. There's no hedging, no compromise, no attempt at redemption through the accumulation of small merits.

Whitman: such a pure vision that the completion was always of the vision itself, never merely technical.

It might very well be that the problem of limited vision, of having been trapped by so many negative assumptions . . . it must be that one can truly write only in celebration of one's assumptions: you can't write against life, you just omit those parts of life which are in contradiction to those assumptions. (Is this what Whitman means by the great poem of death which must be written: a poem that would leave out nothing, even death?) The problem then is to find a more encompassing, more courageous vision, which doesn't run away, in the deepest self from what is horrid and terrifying, but includes them, in the most intimate way, as equal to all the joyful elements, and celebrates all.

A key: how much is written about the *possible* self, (Merwin), instead of the *actual* self (Stafford).

The possible self: is it grounded in fear of the actual self? Perhaps its song is always of what I will become instead of what I am. Whitman: I do not ask for good fortune, I am good fortune.

Then you come around again to the old problem of experience, fantasy, imagination: the wish to *create* experience. . . . There's a hairline between the possible and actual self that it might be impossible not to cross. In Rilke's early poems: the real struggle in them is of someone looking into the world, wandering through the world, trying to find in the world events, visions, that matched the enormity of his solitude: this is the last thing you think when you read his poems, though. What you think is of how the world is suddenly transfigured, burning. His self isn't apparent at all until the poems become so much a part of you that they become your own solitude.

Question: which poets *don't* have that sense of solitude about them? Homer, Shakespeare . . . maybe some of the ceremonial primitive poems, maybe Sophocles. I think it isn't that the solitude wasn't there, but that there was so much else that it wasn't an issue worth considering. I think *every* contemporary poem is in one way or another about solitude, about its limits, its horrors, where the self begins and ends, where the other is not.

In love poems, how many actually include the other? Reading Wyatt lately, certainly his don't? How much more love is in Shakespeare's plays than in his sonnets?

Abstraction, generalization as the basis of evil. . . . As soon as you generalize, there's something which remains to be done, there is imperfection, which offends, and disorder, which disheartens. Therefore you must force the world, other people, to your will, to your ideal: it's intolerable that the world isn't as your ideal of it is, you are personally offended, threatened, the future becomes a dire series of chances for degradation.

1973–1974

I don't want to renounce, to lose, the unconscious in the poems. That's where I've been heading with all the dissatisfactions with what I've done, and with the desire to open out into the world. . . . It isn't a question of opening out, because there was that before; rather it's that I've been dissatisfied with the substance of the questioning I have about the turning outward.

Because my view of the unconscious, therefore the conscious, has been so particular—analytic, analytic-religious, sexual—I've actually used up the language I was employing for it. Recognizing that the unconscious can't be touched without one kind of language or another, what could my language be for investigating it now? Jung comes to mind, but somehow that seems merely a reaction against Freud's emphasis on pathology. Brown's new book: new eclectic, but he knows what I know. Somehow the feeling again of facing an abyss of having to re-invent man all over again for myself, in terms that haven't been used yet. But where to begin?

Go back: the Greeks, the epics, the Bible; what were the rudiments of consciousness which were being touched by these, what was their vital, unconscious efficacy?

That kind of short intense lyric poem on a specific subject . . . what's implied by them is somehow the notion of facing an experience, transfiguring it so that it can be discarded, overcome, never dealt with again. You can name a poem "Death" or "My Life" and that's still generally what the tone will imply.

I want a way of doing it that opens out into experience, that evokes more and more experience, that has implied in it a greater willingness to face life at the end of the poetical experience, not to solve it, to philosophically surmount it.

Shadows: to try to remember how magical my shadow was when I was a child.

A novel in verse?

Who's the hero? What's his travail, what the setting?

An inner struggle, inner journey, inner novel? (*Love's Body* as an associative direction?)

The struggle between fantasy and reality? Philosophy and psychology? Truth and fiction? Solitude and community? Rimbaud's "Season": it's that, in so many ways . . . to rewrite that? To use it as a form, but only a form . . . there's been no second use of it. His terminology and structure are essentially Christian: what would mine be? That's the real problem, and why it hasn't been done again, because there hasn't been a coherent enough system to really hold a simultaneous narrative-lyric structure.

Conversation with H. Boatwright about myths: he says that they explain something which can't be explained in any other way. . . . And I suddenly realized that isn't what they are at all. Rather that a successful myth *opens* a *new* mystery. . . . Because mystery to us is the source of our most profound emotions . . . awe, reverence, ecstacy. . . . Then, reading this morning Eliade: "Every time man becomes aware of his true, existential situation, that is to say of his specific manner of existence in the Cosmos, and accepts this way of existence, he expresses these decisive experiences by images and myths which will afterwards enjoy a privileged position in the spiritual tradition of humanity."

Problem: if I go too deeply, extensively into the banal, it begins to have such compelling power that I can't go back to the labor of meaning.

Dante: the divine cosmology. Blake: a variation on it, but still it. Rimbaud: an attempt to defile it, then into, not the banal, but everything against it, its myths and destructiveness.

What's our myth? The war? Marquez: an eclecticism, using whatever fits from whatever myth-system. This has to be the way I go, but he had as a notion a national, continental consciousness, which he loved. What have I? Surely not that.

Love? Love and sex have been the predominating myths in my life: maybe this should just be an attempt to discover where I am now and how I got there?

The move into specific moral commitments, direct, articulate, is to open the self to the charge of being "wrong." But given my mind, my particular epistomology, I have, *have* to take those risks. . . . The unconscious is not just to be elicited, enacted, acted out: it has to be made part of the ego, and my ego works by articulating as absolutely far as it can go. The problem is how to maintain the passion, the deepest feelings which are the real root, the real material, while at the same time being utterly specific. Maybe this is a contradiction, I'm not sure.

There's no such thing as "compression" in poetry. There's only omission. And accepted conventions of indication, so that the omissions don't matter. Part of the thrill of "tight" poetry is the thrill of being in a community which shares these conventions. Part of it is in the reverberations through the self, through the whole emotional-intellectual structure, which the recognition of a sign triggers.

What I'm trying to do now is to re-establish, on a more extensive level, the conventions—by not omitting so much—so that I can allow more people to share the celebration of the poetry.

Brotherhood, community: there is a community of poetry readers, and, as a rule, they are gentled and transfigured by their experiences with poetry: to be able to extend this, without losing the intensity of compression.

The whole notion of making the poetry banal, flat enough, common enough so that what's crucial isn't the style, but the experience which is being considered itself. I've thought about this before, but it's absolutely critical. The difficulty, again, is that experiences have to be so carefully chosen: there isn't room for the joy of simple observation, of the "It," to use Buber. There must be experiences in which the "Thou" is present in full force.

Structure: looking at Dante, longing for the structure he found, that I could pour everything into. Then I thought that our times might be defined by their structurelessness, and that it's futile perhaps to try to find one. Then, that the whole point of a poet's work is to find one where there apparently is none.

I have a pretty good sense, I think, of what the issues are. I have discarded so many theories now though, that there isn't any certain ground to work on. Or, on the other hand, I think what may really have happened is that the grounds are so much given to me now, that they are so much a part of my own mental construct, that I have to search inside me where they're commingled with every moment of my past, and to use them from there. This would be enormous. Everything is.

Always starting from the non-theoretical experiences: why do I distrust them so?

Something I've been doing with the longer poems: letting the narrative part of them go slack and get out of hand instead of finding the same concision I would with an image. Finding the core of gestures. (I did it without knowing what I was doing in "Spit.") The struggle with the poems about Jessie and the supermarket have been with this. On the other hand, mustn't find too quickly what appears to be a right move because there's a good chance it would be very unresonant, like a flat Bly-like image, and in this instance there'd be an instant tedium evoked. . . .

Diane Arbus: when she said she meant to photograph "evil" she was taken to mean human evil. What she meant was the evil of the cosmos, of nature as it is inflicted on man's consciousness. That's what makes the feeling of terrific congruity one feels with the freaks and misfits in her pictures: the recognition that we are all victims or potential victims of that evil, the evil whereby God refuses to recognize man's conception of what should be given to him, but rather imposes His own vision upon us. We are "created," all of us; that's the common denominator which can't, no matter what, be denied. Her figures in Halloween masks: where that "evil" is remanifesting itself: the jokees becoming jokers. The eyes of the retarded figures that show through are completely "normal," merely frightened, terrified; and pathetically, they are saying, "Fuck you, God."

The long line: trying to increase the natural measure toward what the mind really deals with in its apprehension of sound and the sound of language. How poetry actually has done it, only working off the lines as a literary tradition rather than off the much longer unit of "natural speech." (Shakespeare for instance; his musical units are actually terribly long: that he worked in blank verse means little in this regard.) Once rime falls away, the line becomes variable: what determines it is the measure of the sense fusing with the structure of the music.

A style is always driving to perfect itself. As it is perfected, it becomes self-sustaining: that is, it has no need of any particular content. What it does with its content is always enough to satisfy the aesthetic needs of its perpetrator and audience. A religion becomes a style and a rhetoric: a philosophy does, a politic. . . .

There is a fusion in the consciousness of poetry, metaphysics, politics, religion . . . whatever. Real poetry—poetry—has the particular function in modern times of being the first element in the rhetoric to break down, to lose meaning, to bore, because the meaning of poetry must always exist on the forefront of consciousness, otherwise it's self-defeating.

If I conceive of a book as a whole structure, I can begin to move out of the very definite first person into a more abstract, indirect mode of speech.

Every poem or artwork can be reduced to one single emotional decision. Brooks calls it "kernel": the image of an emotional perplexity. If this kernel, core, whatever you call it, hasn't intrinsic profundity, crucial importance, the rest of the work will be a hollow shell.

The problem is finding that core by going down through all the modes of apprehension, thought, and aesthetic form. Because if you attempt to begin with this kernel, then the information, the complexity of the lived elaboration of the emotion, will only surround it and not organically adhere with it.

It is such effort to work down to knowing what that kernel is; there is despair, after all of it, at finding it worthless. Right now, I haven't the strength to start upward again from the perceived ground, or grounds, because I don't trust any emotion except despair. Everything else is momentary, dissolved in the same crucible of self-distrust and uncertainty.

Jessie (age three): "Don't read me a story, tell me one with your mouth."

What about those parents who send their sons off to die for their country right or wrong? It can't be as simple as it seems: that they're deluded, that they're involved in some awful system of repression and sublimation so that they don't even know what death is anymore. "Your son is extinct." No, what if they have a truer grasp of the human soul than I do? What a terribly despairing thought: but mightn't they have a deeper acceptance of God, even in His basest guises? My project always seems to have been to fight death and all its manifestations, but what if I'm really fighting God?

The opposite of death is originality: the original moment over and over. But originality must also kill God, because God can't live one moment at a time, and maybe to kill God is to kill the human soul, and what arrogance to consider that the soul might be the curse of humanity rather than its salvation. Ordinary people, whose soul happens to them only in moments of bitter or glorious crisis: they *are* humanity, we, we seekers of the soul—mightn't *we* be the real murderers?

Reading Faulkner, *Absalom:* when his characters speak in that incredible rhetoric, he still keeps them grounded, facing each other, all the tiny acts within the speech . . . that what evolves is the language that we *should* speak: the astounding complex, complicated, evocative, attempting language which the relating of anything between two people really entails.

Isn't this what is always the definition of literature?

Tragedy: that the things which happen to the characters in tragedy aren't things which happen to anyone else, but they're the things that *should* happen, to fit what we feel in living in the world. This is the basis of Freud's use of Oedipus. What isn't spoken or enacted but should be, because the soul is so overgrown, so gigantic that it can't comprehend or grasp those day-to-day events which happen to it and that it answers with its puny vocabulary and musicless music.

The world of myth is always just behind us . . . we keep groping back with our foot for it like first basemen.

The sense sometimes when I think of a poem not begun, not conceived, but with a reality, of it having no words to it, no time . . . almost the pure image of the object the poem is, and any attempt to materialize it seems a loss, and that there's no poem ever written which can satisfy this.

The original impulse for the book was to deal in actions instead of meditations. What's happened is that what I've called actions are instead the smallest kind of encounter, the same kind of absurd poet's encounter, where something is happening, and he goes by and watches it, someone's life, someone's non-life. . . .

Talking with Paul yesterday about "Hog Heaven," his casual remark that you should have to puzzle out a poem after you finish it, and now I realize that this is exactly what this whole series was trying to overcome, that special kind of taste which desires to be puzzled, and to think its way out of its perplexity. . . . When I started them, I was after the kind of transparency which prose has, putting the intensity—the equivalent of perplexity—into the human situation that had evolved poetically, instead of in the figures, the associate elements, etc. . . .

A sign of ultimate immaturity: the belief that suffering entitles you to something.

The task: to try to examine experience in the terms of complexity it actually has: to overcome the arbitrary, intellectual divisions we set up in our minds and allow to become images there, of realms, areas, so that a political idea is conceived of as actually a political idea instead of what happens simply to have risen to the top and been named as the mode of experience of a moment; whatever the name of the experience attempts to be, love, sex, etc. To fuse those so that the lyric moment begins to approximate any moment in life and to somehow liberate *within* those moments. . . .

If violence is perhaps the real resolution of every act: if every act, closely examined, ends in violence, then perhaps the problem I have isn't that there's too much, but not enough. How to find the violence in morally acceptable acts? Without violence, there's only lassitude—Nietzsche would perhaps change "power" for "violence," but I think violence is the less horatory word: in the most tranquil moments of love, there's an amazing violence of emotion. Non-violence is sleep, exhaustion, passivity. Sexuality as the obvious violence of love, but that's only in the body. . . . In the soul, the sexuality not only isn't essential, but sex itself can sometimes be less spiritually violent than the still, unspoken moments between lovers or friends. . . .

Reading Spengler: that a sense of astronomical space and the notion of "will" are one and the same . . . those visionary moments I used to have which were concerned solely with space. . . .

Once you consider your qualities, you stop being a poet and become a critic. B., who in too many moments is a critic . . . and it shows in his work. The goal isn't success, but deep activity, not "great poetry" but fulfillment: one set kills another. Somehow my interest shifted from the self to poetry. One kind of selfishness perhaps to another, but at least the first had a genuine humility—meaning a search for completion—about it, while the second is something which exists halfway into the past, in the satisfaction of created needs . . . and those needs and their nourishment are so satisfying. This is the real temptation: that the needs in a sense create a person—the poet—who didn't exist before the public perception of him, and then they nourish that false image. . . . The poet again, as truly a false image, something for the professors and philosophers to use. To find a *positive* way toward all this.

Modesty is the illusion of privacy in situations where there is none. It moves the self's boundaries to within the actual body instead of leaving it at the edges of the perceptual field, where it's too vulnerable.
 (Neurosis: moving the boundaries into the mind.)